Palgrave Studies in Cultural Heritage and Conflict

Series Editors
Ihab Saloul
University of Amsterdam
Amsterdam, Noord-Holland, The Netherlands

Rob van der Laarse
University of Amsterdam
Amsterdam, The Netherlands

Britt Baillie
Centre for Urban Conflicts Research
University of Cambridge
Cambridge, UK

This book series explores the relationship between cultural heritage and conflict. The key themes of the series are the heritage and memory of war and conflict, contested heritage, and competing memories. The series editors seek books that analyze the dynamics of the past from the perspective of tangible and intangible remnants, spaces, and traces as well as heritage appropriations and restitutions, significations, musealizations, and mediatizations in the present. Books in the series should address topics such as the politics of heritage and conflict, identity and trauma, mourning and reconciliation, nationalism and ethnicity, diaspora and intergenerational memories, painful heritage and terrorscapes, as well as the mediated reenactments of conflicted pasts. Dr. Ihab Saloul is associate professor of cultural studies, founder and research vice-director of the Amsterdam School for Heritage, Memory and Material Culture (AHM) at University of Amsterdam. Saloul's interests include cultural memory and identity politics, narrative theory and visual analysis, conflict and trauma, Diaspora and migration as well as contemporary cultural thought in the Middle East. Professor Rob van der Laarse is research director of the Amsterdam School for Heritage, Memory and Material Culture (AHM), and Westerbork Professor of Heritage of Conflict and War at VU University Amsterdam. Van der Laarse's research focuses on (early) modern European elite and intellectual cultures, cultural landscape, heritage and identity politics, and the cultural roots and postwar memory of the Holocaust and other forms of mass violence. Dr. Britt Baillie is an Honorary Research Fellow at the Wits City Institute, University of the Witwatersrand and a founding member of the Centre for Urban Conflict Studies at the University of Cambridge. Baillie's interests include the politics of cultural heritage, urban heritage, religious heritage, living heritage, heritage as commons, and contested heritage.

More information about this series at
http://www.palgrave.com/gp/series/14638

Tuuli Lähdesmäki · Luisa Passerini ·
Sigrid Kaasik-Krogerus · Iris van Huis
Editors

Dissonant Heritages and Memories in Contemporary Europe

palgrave
macmillan

Editors
Tuuli Lähdesmäki
Department of Music, Art
and Culture Studies
University of Jyväskylä
Jyväskylä, Finland

Luisa Passerini
Department of History
and Civilization
European University Institute
Florence, Italy

Sigrid Kaasik-Krogerus
Department of Music, Art
and Culture Studies
University of Jyväskylä
Jyväskylä, Finland

Iris van Huis
Department of Political Science
Radboud University Nijmegen
Nijmegen, Gelderland
The Netherlands

Palgrave Studies in Cultural Heritage and Conflict
ISBN 978-3-030-11463-3   ISBN 978-3-030-11464-0   (eBook)
https://doi.org/10.1007/978-3-030-11464-0

© The Editor(s) (if applicable) and The Author(s) 2019. This book is an open access publication.

Open Access This book is licensed under the terms of the Creative Commons Attribution 4.0 International License (http://creativecommons.org/licenses/by/4.0/), which permits use, sharing, adaptation, distribution and reproduction in any medium or format, as long as you give appropriate credit to the original author(s) and the source, provide a link to the Creative Commons license and indicate if changes were made.

The images or other third party material in this book are included in the book's Creative Commons license, unless indicated otherwise in a credit line to the material. If material is not included in the book's Creative Commons license and your intended use is not permitted by statutory regulation or exceeds the permitted use, you will need to obtain permission directly from the copyright holder.

The use of general descriptive names, registered names, trademarks, service marks, etc. in this publication does not imply, even in the absence of a specific statement, that such names are exempt from the relevant protective laws and regulations and therefore free for general use.

The publisher, the authors, and the editors are safe to assume that the advice and information in this book are believed to be true and accurate at the date of publication. Neither the publisher nor the authors or the editors give a warranty, express or implied, with respect to the material contained herein or for any errors or omissions that may have been made. The publisher remains neutral with regard to jurisdictional claims in published maps and institutional affiliations.

Cover illustration: Wishing tree in front of the Peace Palace in The Hague, Netherlands. Yuliya Mykolaïvna Heikens/Alamy Stock Photo; all rights reserved, used with permission.

This Palgrave Macmillan imprint is published by the registered company Springer Nature Switzerland AG
The registered company address is: Gewerbestrasse 11, 6330 Cham, Switzerland

Preface

Stemming from the encounter between two research projects, this edited volume was born from the dialogue between their core results and the cross-fertilization of their methodological and theoretical approaches. These two projects, BABE and EUROHERIT, were both funded by the European Research Council, which finances innovative research projects that seek to open novel horizons for future research. The exchange between the two projects was started to provide a broader perspective on their shared topics and themes, thus transcending the thematic scopes of the individual projects and placing them in a bigger framework. We hope that this collaboration will serve further scholarship and feed a much-needed critical discussion on the topics this volume covers, such as heritage, identity, memory, mobility, and Europe.

While BABE and EUROHERIT projects have several differences, they share a common area of interest that deals with contestation of meanings and uses of memories and heritages in today's Europe. While EUROHERIT focuses on institutional and political discourses in the construction of heritages in contemporary Europe, BABE explores various forms of embodiment of memories and experiences at the level of individual and collective subjectivities. The exchange between the two projects has aimed to advance the entanglement between these two research approaches. Both projects perceive the entanglement of politics and culture as an instrument for responding and reacting to the dissonance of heritages and memories and as a tool to enhance consonance between people in Europe and beyond.

BABE (Bodies Across Borders: Oral and Visual Memory in Europe and Beyond, 2013–2018), led by Professor Luisa Passerini, was based at the Department of History and Civilization at the European University Institute in Florence, Italy.[1] BABE particularly focuses on two nations, Italy and The Netherlands, chosen for their similarities and differences in relation to the past and present movements of people. The project's central conceptual focus is the connection between memory, mobility, and visuality. It aims to enlarge the theory and practice of oral memory, extending the methodology of the interview—understood as intersubjective communication—to the field of visual memory. At its centre is the mobility of embodied subjects within the global diaspora who cross frontiers, both geographical and cultural ones, in and around Europe. The project's visual dimension tackles the ongoing construction of new forms of memory which challenge the traditional concepts of a European sense of belonging and identity, and thus reveal new ways of envisaging Europe and Europeanness.

BABE's research stretches out into three different fields: visual art concerned with mobility, including artists' use of autobiographical memory, and art activism in particular; fieldwork comprising collective and individual interviews with protagonists of mobility towards and across Europe, with whom works of visual art are discussed before asking interviewees to produce images themselves; and a critique of the role of archives, in both a literal and cultural sense, including the notion of the body as a living archive. The results of the BABE project not only take the form of publications, but also multimedia products, documentaries, maps, photographs, and videos. All these products will be accessible at the Historical Archives of the European Union at the European University Institute, Florence.

EUROHERIT (Legitimation of European cultural heritage and the dynamics of identity politics in the EU, 2015–2020), led by Adjunct Professor Tuuli Lähdesmäki, is based at the Department of Music, Art and Culture Studies at the University of Jyväskylä, Finland.[2] It examines EU heritage initiatives, EU heritage and identity policies and politics,

---

[1]Under the European Union's Seventh Framework Programme (FP7/2007–2013)/ ERC Grant Agreement no. Project 295854 (2013–2018).

[2]Under the European Union's Horizon 2020 Research and Innovation Programme/ ERC Grant Agreement no. Project 636177 (2015–2020).

and the notions of European cultural heritage constructed in them. This scope is motivated by the EU's increased interest in heritage, which has the potential to impact various social, societal, political, and economic challenges in Europe. Heritage initiatives and policies are EU "technologies of power", in the Foucauldian sense, which on the one hand construct certain kinds of notions of European cultural heritage and on the other hand seek to legitimate certain political ideas and ideologies, such as European identity-building and cultural integration in Europe. Hence, EUROHERIT focuses its analysis on the EU, examining it as an active heritage actor and its heritage politics as an attempt to create a heritage regime in Europe. The most recent EU heritage action, the European Heritage Label, is the project's core object of critical research.

EUROHERIT combines both desktop analysis and ethnographic field research. The project's contributions in this volume particularly emphasize the analysis of policy documents and a qualitative reading of promotional material and exhibition narratives of selected heritage sites recently awarded the European Heritage Label.

In addition to heritage and memory, both BABE and EUROHERIT explore borders and the bordering in and of Europe, transforming identities, belonging, access, and contemporary European realities influenced by various forms of human mobility in Europe and its border zones. These cross-cutting themes formed fruitful ground for the encounter between the projects. This dialogue first took shape in "Dissonant Heritages. Contestation of Meanings and Uses of Memory in Today's Europe.", a workshop organized at the European University Institute in Florence, Italy, on 27–28 April 2017. The workshop's aim was to show that instead of one heritage, Europe contains a plurality of traditions, which have seen social, cultural, and political contradictions and ruptures in different times and places. The workshop sought to help break down the notion of Europe's cultural heritage from within, studying the pluriform developments of Europe's fractured past from the point of view of heritage and memory studies.

The workshop included eight papers from both projects, accompanied by opening and closing speeches. To enrich the discussions on heritages and memories, and to increase dialogue and cooperation between European research projects, an external keynote speaker was invited, Professor Rob van der Laarse from the University of Amsterdam, The Netherlands, who in 2016 was awarded a HERA Joint Research Program grant under its "Uses of the Past" call, funded jointly by the

European Commission and national academies in Europe. Van der Laarse's broad interdisciplinary project is called Accessing Campscapes: Inclusive Strategies for Using European Conflicted Heritage.

Inspired by the fruitful discussions during the workshop, both research teams decided to continue the dialogue between the projects in an edited volume. The book at hand is the result, revealing the complexity and richness of its core topic, heritage, and memory in today's Europe. As this includes a rich variety of thematic areas and enables various theoretical and conceptual approaches, we hope to participate in the ongoing scholarly debate on heritage and memory as well as their dissonances and power regimes in Europe.

We want to thank all the contributors of this book for their thorough work in developing their papers into volume chapters. We thank Liliana Ellena, Associate Researcher of the BABE Project, for her contribution to writing the Introduction and her suggestions on the structure of the book. We are also grateful to all other participants in the "Dissonant Heritages" workshop for the fruitful, critical and interdisciplinary discussions, particularly the workshop's keynote speaker Rob van der Laarse, as well as its discussant, Professor Anna Triandafyllidou from the Schuman Centre, European University Institute. In addition, we thank BABE Project Assistant Laura Borgese for the workshop's practical arrangements. This book has been proofread by Florian Duijsens, who deserves thanks for his detailed work in language editing. We also wish to thank Assistant Editor Glenn Ramirez from Palgrave Macmillan for their smooth cooperation in the publishing process, as well as Palgrave's anonymous reviewers for their fruitful comments, which helped us develop the volume and sharpen our conceptual approach. Finally, both project leaders want to thank our core financer, the European Research Council, for our project funding and thereby enabling the editing of this book.

Jyväskylä, Finland	Tuuli Lähdesmäki
Florence, Italy	Luisa Passerini
Jyväskylä, Finland	Sigrid Kaasik-Krogerus
Nijmegen, The Netherlands	Iris van Huis

Contents

1 Introduction: Europe, Heritage and Memory—
Dissonant Encounters and Explorations   1
Iris van Huis, Sigrid Kaasik-Krogerus, Tuuli Lähdesmäki
and Liliana Ellena

Part I Conflict and Reconciliation

2 Conflicts and Reconciliation in the Postmillennial
Heritage-Policy Discourses of the Council of Europe
and the European Union   25
Tuuli Lähdesmäki

3 Interconceptualizing Europe and Peace: Identity
Building Under the European Heritage Label   51
Katja Mäkinen

4 Europe's Peat Fire: Intangible Heritage
and the Crusades for Identity   79
Rob van der Laarse

Part II Borders and Mobility

5 Bodies Making Spaces: Understanding the Airport as a Site of Dissonance   137
Milica Trakilović

6 Politics of Mobility and Stability in Authorizing European Heritage: Estonia's Great Guild Hall   157
Sigrid Kaasik-Krogerus

Part III Colonial Pasts in the Present

7 A Geography of Coloniality: Re-narrating European Integration   185
Johanna Turunen

8 Contesting Cultural Heritage: Decolonizing the Tropenmuseum as an Intervention in the Dutch/European Memory Complex   215
Iris van Huis

9 Geography of Emotions Across the Black Mediterranean: Oral Memories and Dissonant Heritages of Slavery and the Colonial Past   249
Gabriele Proglio

10 Epilogue   273
Luisa Passerini

Index   281

Notes on Contributors

Liliana Ellena is a Research Associate in the ERC project "Bodies across Borders: Oral and Visual Memory in Europe and Beyond" (BABE-European University Institute, Italy). Her research has revolved around the cultural history of visuality with a focus on formations of colonial and postcolonial memory in fascist and postwar Italy. She has edited the Italian translation of Frantz Fanon's *I dannati della terra* (2001) and written a contribution to the edited volume *Il colore della nazione* (2015). Currently, she explores methodological approaches to the performativity of archival practices addressing the legacy of decolonization, exile, and migration in decentering contemporary normative and exclusionary assumptions of European memory.

Sigrid Kaasik-Krogerus is a Postdoctoral Researcher at the Department of Music, Art and Culture Studies, University of Jyväskylä, Finland. She currently works in the Legitimation of European Cultural Heritage and the Dynamics of Identity Politics in the EU (EUROHERIT) research project funded by the European Research Council. From 2015 to 2018, she was a member of the Jean Monnet Module "East within Europe" funded by the Erasmus+ at the Aleksanteri Institute, University of Helsinki, Finland. Kaasik-Krogerus specializes in media and communication, identity and belonging, heritage, and European studies in the context of the EU and Central and East European countries.

Tuuli Lähdesmäki is an Academy of Finland Research Fellow and Adjunct Professor working in the Department of Music, Art and Culture

Studies, University of Jyväskylä (JYU), Finland. Lähdesmäki currently leads an ERC Starting Grant project, "Legitimation of European Cultural Heritage and the Dynamics of Identity Politics in the EU" (EUROHERIT). She is also leading JYU's consortium partnership in the "Dialogue and Argumentation for cultural Literacy Learning in Schools" (DIALLS) project, funded by the EU's H2020 Programme. In addition, she is one of the PIs in JYU's "Crises Redefined: Historical Continuity and Societal Change" (CRISES) research profiling area.

Katja Mäkinen is a Postdoctoral Researcher at the Department of Music, Art and Culture Studies, University Jyväskylä, Finland. She works in the "Legitimation of European Cultural heritage and the Dynamics of Identity Politics in the EU" project. Mäkinen specializes in citizenship, participation, identities, cultural heritage, participatory governance, EU programmes, and conceptual and ethnographic research. She was convener of the Citizenship Standing Group in the European Political Consortium for Political research in 2016–2017 and a Visiting Fellow at the European University Institute in Florence, Italy in 2018. She is co-editor of *Shaping Citizenship: A Political Concept in Theory, Debate and Practice* (2018).

Luisa Passerini is Professor Emerita at the European University Institute in Florence, Italy, former Professor of Cultural History at Turin University, Italy, recipient of the All European Academies 2014 Madame de Staël Prize for Cultural Values. She was the Principal Investigator of the European Research Council Project "Bodies Across Borders: Oral and Visual Memory in Europe and Beyond" from 2013 to 2018. She has studied the subjects of social and cultural change, ranging from African liberation movements, twentieth-century workers', students' and women's movements, to migrants to and through Europe, using memory in its oral, written and visual forms.

Gabriele Proglio is an FCT researcher at the Social Studies Centre, University of Coimbra, Portugal. His research specializations include the history of the Mediterranean. He was a Research Associate in the ERC-funded research project "Bodies Across Borders: Oral and Visual Memories in Europe and Beyond" which was based at the European University Institute in Florence, Italy. During the five-year project, he conducted a study on oral and visual memory, collecting interviews with people coming from or culturally connected to Ethiopia, Eritrea, and Somalia—all former Italian colonies—on various topics such as the idea of Europe and Europeanness and the memory of different types of colonialism.

Milica Trakilović is a Ph.D. student in The Institute for Cultural Inquiry (ICON) at Utrecht University, The Netherlands. She has also been teaching in the Graduate Gender Programme at Utrecht University since 2013, mainly in the Postcolonial Studies and Gender Studies minors. From 2015 to 2018, she was Research Assistant in the ERC project "Bodies Across Borders: Oral and Visual Memory in Europe and Beyond" at the European University Institute in Florence, Italy. Her research interests focus on visual culture, feminist art practice, post-socialist/postcolonial frameworks, and reconceptualizing notions of (European) belonging.

Johanna Turunen is a Doctoral candidate at the Department of Music, Art and Culture Studies, at the University of Jyväskylä, Finland. As part of the EUROHERIT-project, she analyses the EU's cultural-heritage policies and initiatives through insights from postcolonial/decolonial theory. In her research, Turunen especially focuses on the inclusive and exclusive practices entangled in the narrative practices of defining Europeanness in the European Heritage Label.

Rob van der Laarse is Professor and Research Director at the Amsterdam School for Heritage, Memory and Material Culture at the University of Amsterdam, The Netherlands. He also holds the Westerbork chair of War Heritage at Vrije Universiteit Amsterdam, The Netherlands. Van der Laarse's research interests focuses on European conflicted heritage, identities, and memories. In 2016, he was awarded a HERA Joint Research Program grant in the "Uses of the Past" call. This broad interdisciplinary project is titled "Accessing Campscapes: Inclusive Strategies for Using European Conflicted Heritage".

Iris van Huis received her Ph.D. at the Department of Political Science of Radboud University Nijmegen, The Netherlands, and is currently a lecturer at the University of Amsterdam, The Netherlands, teaching about "Cities and Change". In her Ph.D. research, she studied how social interventions that try to engage men in gender-equality issues impact on inequalities and intersections of gender, ethnicity, and class, while also studying normalizing and enabling angles. In the BABE research project, van Huis studied refugee migrants' visual and oral resistances against anti-immigrant discourse. She also studied how recent changes in the Amsterdam Tropenmuseum were initiated by a protest group called Decolonize the Museum, placing these efforts into a wider national and European perspective.

List of Figures

Fig. 6.1 This document of the sale of an Estonian peasant from the eighteenth century is an example of both oppressive stability and oppressive mobility from one owner to the next   177

Fig. 7.1 Spatial dispersion of different narrative dynamics among the 39 sites that have either received the EHL (29) or were evaluated as meeting the criterion of European significance (10) between 2011 and 2016 (At the moment, the EHL is not open to countries who are not EU members. Additionally, some member states are currently not involved in the initiative, which explains the apparent "emptiness" in, for example, Northern Europe)   204

CHAPTER 1

Introduction: Europe, Heritage and Memory—Dissonant Encounters and Explorations

Iris van Huis, Sigrid Kaasik-Krogerus, Tuuli Lähdesmäki and Liliana Ellena

Heritage and memory, as closely related concepts, have great relevance to our world and European society today. Contemporary Europe faces political, economic, social, and humanitarian challenges that influence both how people deal with their past and how they build their identities

---

I. van Huis
Faculty of Social and Behavioural Sciences, University of Amsterdam, Amsterdam, The Netherlands
e-mail: iris@vanhuis.com; i.vanhuis@uva.nl

S. Kaasik-Krogerus · T. Lähdesmäki (✉)
Department of Music, Art and Culture Studies, University of Jyväskylä, Jyväskylä, Finland
e-mail: tuuli.lahdesmaki@jyu.fi

L. Ellena
BABE Research Associate, European University Institute, Florence, Italy
e-mail: liliana.ellena@eui.eu

© The Author(s) 2019
T. Lähdesmäki et al. (eds.),
Dissonant Heritages and Memories in Contemporary Europe,
Palgrave Studies in Cultural Heritage and Conflict,
https://doi.org/10.1007/978-3-030-11464-0_1

and ideas of the future as they remember and reshape the past within, and related to, larger power structures.

With, on the one side, the ongoing debates on migration proving a divisive issue with regards to understandings of European integration and identity, and, on the other side, the EU investing more and more in projects related to European heritage, museums, and cultural-memory networks, the dynamics between transnational and transcultural memory-making in Europe make for a significant and compelling case study. To pull together the concepts of "Europe" and "transnational memory" reveals a complex puzzle that poses challenging questions for anyone involved in academic research, heritage practices, and policy debates. Contemporary Europe includes both old and new nation states' borders and those of the European Union, a sui generis supranational political formation. These intersect with the endless ways in which individuals and groups forge their relations to the world in manners that diverge from the geopolitical borders imposed upon it.

With this puzzle at its core, this volume explicitly focuses on slippery and transforming notions of Europe and critically discusses the above-mentioned challenges' impact on power structures of heritage and memory in today's Europe. These challenges and the multifaceted transformations of European societies they brought about impact the practices, processes, and discourses of heritage and memory, including collective and individual struggles over them. To consider the relationship between mobility and European memory requires acknowledging the role of multiple and conflicting combinations of time and space in "shifting patterns of spatio-temporal overlap and disjunction" (Donnan et al. 2017, 2). Accordingly, we approach contemporary European heritage and memory regimes through a critical analysis of both institutions and the embodied experiences of individuals, including those born in Europe and those who have migrated to Europe from across its current borders. The volume explores the intersections of heritages, memories, and identities by approaching them as constituted by the politics and actions of both institutions and individuals.

The volume thus seeks to scrutinize contemporary European heritage and memory regimes from "above" and "below" simultaneously, agreeing with Chiara De Cesari and Ann Rigney (2014, 4) that studying transnational memory opens up "an analytic space to consider the interplay between social formations and cultural practices", as well as "between state-operated institutions of memory and the flow of mediated narratives within and across state borders". Cross-border dynamics, human movements, and cultural circulation all shape the ways in which individuals and groups accommodate and reinvent the relationship between past and present within historically and socially specific languages, ideologies, and power relations. At the same time, supranational and intergovernmental institutions and actors play an increasingly important role in addressing audiences and policies, allocating funding, and transforming the cultural values attached to specific heritages.

In this light, this volume combines theoretical and methodological contributions to the debates on European heritage and memory studies and in-depth analyses of empirical case studies. Its main aim is to bring these two research fields into a closer dialogue and thus explore the cultural and political dynamics of contemporary Europe.

Encounters at the Crossroads of Research Agendas

The book is the result of an encounter and dialogue between two different research projects that were both stirred by an interest in the transnational and transcultural dimensions of memory across contemporary Europe, EUROHERIT and BABE. The first focuses on the European Union's (EU) heritage policies and politics in order to explore and critically assess the assumptions on which the idea of a European Heritage is framed and implemented in different EU heritage initiatives. The research builds on the potential and limitations of various connections between cultural heritage, European identity, and memory. The empirical material on which EUROHERIT's research in this volume is built consists of policy documents, cultural sites' promotional and information material, and exhibitions that explicitly address the European dimension of heritage. The BABE research project, meanwhile, centers on the mobility of human bodies that cross frontiers, both geographical and cultural, in and around Europe within the global diaspora. It aims to explore the changes this global mobility has on visual memories of Europe, focusing on memory's artefacts and narrations produced by mobile people and on contemporary art.

BABE approaches cultural memory as reflected in various cultural products and material cultures produced by movements across borders, foregrounding subjectivity and transcultural practices as rooted in everyday life.

The tensions generated by the two projects' different premises have accompanied the design and writing of the book. The first set of tensions revolve around the ways in which the two projects thematize "Europe". In this volume, EUROHERIT's researchers approach Europe from the point of view of institutional actors and discourses shaped by institutional practices, specifically the guidance, control, and regulation of heritage policies and management, whether on the supranational, national, or local levels. BABE, on the other hand, explores Europe from the perspective of subjective narrations. The ways in which Europe is thus imagined, experienced, and resisted are considered part and articulations of the lived experience of movement itself.

The second set of tensions concerns the discrepancy between conceptualization of memory as produced and negotiated by institutional and political discourses, and one of memory as an intersubjective and embodied practice. The first emphasizes the power structures included in heritage policy discourses and heritage management practices and how they seek to create subject positions, top-down identities, and a feeling of belonging among citizenry in Europe (Lähdesmäki 2014, 2017). The second emphasizes how the narrations people use to sustain their own identity and their identifications with others and the world at large are shaped by intercultural contact and exchange. If memory is a constitutive dimension of the subjects' ongoing self-creation and adaptation within the world around them (Passerini 2007, 2016), the cultural processes of negotiation, appropriation, and reinvention increasingly occur within transnational and transcultural contexts.

Despite these differences, the dialogue developed in this book is built on three key interfaces between the two projects. Firstly, both projects involve the changes and challenges that have marked post-Cold War Europe in political and cultural terms. The fall of the Berlin Wall and the disintegration of the Soviet bloc have inspired plans and hopes for a new European order that is able to fulfil the ideal of a Europe of peace founded on human rights and democracy which was put forward in the immediate post-World War II period. The reunification of Europe and the enlargement of the EU are the two most evident processes that have influenced the development of new cultural practices and policies at the EU level. These have emerged along with, and also in response to, recurrent upheaval in Eastern Europe, the enduring economic unbalance between East and West, and the global war on terror after 9/11. The 2008 financial crisis and the politics of austerity, meanwhile, have reproduced a North/South dichotomy and have intersected with responses to the increasing migration stemming from wars, growing economic exploitation, political instability, and the effects of the structural adjustment programmes imposed by the International Monetary Fund and the World Bank on the so-called Third World.

The 1990s saw the third wave of the European integration, as the process of cultural Europeanization intensified in relation to the collapse of the communist regimes and the end of the Cold War. In this context, memory and commemorative practices have become a cornerstone for cultural integration, the attempt to enhance the spread of common values among the citizens of the EU's new and old member states (Karlsson 2010). While freedom of movement has been celebrated as one of the key achievements of the EU's 2004 and 2007 enlargements, the Schengen Agreement on free movement in the signatory countries and the Dublin Convention addressing the responsibilities for examining asylum seekers' applications reveal a strict relationship between European integration and the development of a restrictive migration policy. And not only that, but the securitization of Europe's external borders associated with Fortress Europe has been legitimized and implemented through racialized notions of Europe rooted in hierarchal ideas of identity and civilization forged during colonial modernity (Goldberg 2006; Van Houtum 2013; De Genova 2016).

This volume's main timeframe is between now and 2004 (the largest expansion of the EU), as this is an ideal period to explore the potentialities and paradoxes underlying the relationship between memory's changing configurations under the contemporary global intensification of human mobility on the hand and the use of cultural heritage to enhance forms of identification with Europe on the other. In this regard, the politics of memory play a crucial role within the volume, which explores how acts of remembrance and representations of the past relate to power, identity formations, and political actions and struggles from different perspectives. Its various contributions all articulate the double role played by memory: though memory is key to claims of recognition and empowerment on the part of subjects and groups in marginalized positions within Europe, it is also part of power/knowledge regimes that define forms of selective inclusion and exclusion. The politics of memory that emerge from discussions on heritage policies call attention to the fact that memory practices "from below" need to be accompanied by concomitant radical changes "from above" in the political conditions of migrants' and refugees' lives for these practices to achieve their full potential. This reveals the tension between transcultural ethics and praxis of memory on the one side, and its material and political preconditions on the other (Rotheberg and Moses 2014).

A second, related interface between this volume's two research projects is represented by the relationship between borders and belonging, which constitutes a central focus when investigating both memory practices and heritage uses. The link between durable, tangible heritage and the idea of continuity of people across generations is widespread, implicit—and often also explicit—in the Western world, especially Europe. Sharon Macdonald's study on remembrance practices in Europe (2013) emphasizes how ambitions of materializing remembrance always involve materializing identity. This relation between political space and culture based has also been sustained by assuming that territory, social formation, mentalities, and memories are isomorphic, as argued by Astrid Erll (2011, 7). As much as the idea of "container cultures" has been contested, not only as ideologically but also epistemologically untenable, over the last decades a rich literature has investigated how borders constantly recompose themselves both outside and inside the European space in connection with the crisis of the nation state, the European constitutional process, the interplay between local and global dynamics, and the ongoing transformations enacted by migrants and their movements from and to Europe (Mezzadra and Neilson 2013; De Genova 2017).

Drawing on these debates, this volume considers memory and heritage as battlefields of border-making and border-crossing, constituted first and foremost by regimes of practices. From this point of view, migration and heritage policies interact and mutually shape the practice of bordering. As suggested by multiple authors working at the intersection between critical border studies and memory studies, the verb "border" is a better fit than the noun to address the processes, activities, and procedures through which the individual and collective past is called into question and reframed in order to make sense of individual trajectories and imagine and organize cultural and political life (Oates-Indruchová and Mueller 2017; Donnan et al. 2017, 2). In this volume, bordering involves the interplay between social ordering and memory-making, and is understood as a practice that disseminates borders in physical and socio-political space that is strictly related to politics of belonging (Yuval-Davis 2011). Several contributions deal with border zones between nation states and continents, or borders within city spaces, where technologies of everyday belonging intersect with larger legal and policy contexts. The different geographical frameworks in each chapter show how the values and meanings that are attached to Europe in connection to memory and heritage are not just defined at the EU level, but emerge within and across a multiplicity of contexts, which include world-heritage policies and protocols, national and regional settings, and even single sites. In addition, focusing on the tensions between various "scales" of memory—subjective, local, regional, trans-European, diasporic—we aim to contribute to the debate in the field of memory studies on the "scalarity" of memory by inscribing it within the specificities of the EU frame (De Cesari and Rigney 2014; Kennedy and Nugent 2016).

The third and last main interface between the two research projects is presented by the relationship between memory and heritage. For a long time, the heritage-memory dyad has been sustained by a series of dichotomies like individual/collective, material/immaterial, and subjective/official. Yet these oppositions have been transformed by the shifting meanings of "memory" and "heritage" across the humanities and social sciences.

Scholars in memory studies have long approached memory as a process in which individual and collective dimensions mingle. Simultaneously, memory itself has become an elastic concept which is frequently applied in studies dealing with interpretations of the past, human experiences and self-understanding, and meaning-making of various cultural and social phenomena. It has been localized within a broader framework of social and cultural practices and artefacts (Brockmeier 2010; Pakier and Stråth 2010), and perceived as produced within sociocultural settings defined by specific resources and asymmetric access to them. For Jens Brockmeier (2010), memories are "trans-individual" cultural creations which are made sense of through stories and are often materialized and objectified, for example in monuments, museums, libraries, anniversaries, and landscapes. The materiality of memories is embedded in explanatory and interpretive discourses, in which narratives play a crucial role (Brockmeier 2010). Memory thus is an act intermingled with language in its manifold oral, written, and performative forms. This cultural aspect of memory emphasizes the intertwined nature of past and present, "truth" and stories (Lähdesmäki 2017). And, as several chapters in this volume indicate, understanding it like this makes it possible to understand how memories are created, transformed, and cemented through the narration and materialization of stories.

Sociocultural setting and narration are also crucial parts of heritage. Scholars in heritage studies have emphasized how heritage is not a material thing, but rather an act of communication (Dicks 2000), a cultural process, and a performance dealing with the assertion and mediation of historical narratives and collective memories, and the cultural social values that underpin these (Waterton and Smith 2009, 15). Heritage only emerges when something is narrated, defined, and/or treated as heritage in the "right" sociocultural context.

Uncovering the key role that "dissonance" plays in discussions of different uses of memory and heritage in Europe is one of the most productive outcomes of the dialogue that shaped this book. We acknowledge how dissonance opened up new perspectives in the field of heritage studies, where it was originally introduced to discuss heritages that involve discordant stories and public uses of memories and representations of pasts that are contentious (Tunbridge and Ashworth 1996). Further conceptualizations of the dissonance of heritage have foregrounded how dissonance should not only be understood as a culmination of divergent views or as an open conflict over the meanings of heritage, but conceived in relation to the ever-changing values attached to heritage both in time and within and across communities. Instead of emphasizing dissonant heritage as a heritage type distinct from "normal" heritage, Višnja Kisić (2017, 31) has conceptualized "heritage dissonance" as an intrinsic quality of all heritage that does not pose a problem in itself but includes "a tension and quality which testifies to the play among different discourses, and opens the space for a number of diverse actions".

Rather than dissolving the tension between memory and cultural heritage, the perspective put forward by the volume builds on their multiple interrelations in order to shed light on implicit or overlooked dimensions. The volume's contributions articulate different engagements with the concept of migrating heritage (Innocenti 2014), both in implicit ways, embedded in migrants' oral self-narrations, and in more explicit forms dealing with struggles over the decolonization of Eurocentric museum and heritage practices. In a parallel move, studying the transcultural dimensions of memory-making discloses the relevance of critically considering European heritage policies from the points of view of individual and groups not fully recognized as European. The interaction between the two research projects on these issues thus is particularly evident in the book's discussions of exhibitions, museums, and artistic practices.

In this volume, belonging, memory, and heritage are approached and discussed as entangled concepts that get their power from their narrative and performative nature, that is, their ability to produce reality, action, and affect. Since the linguistic, narrative, and cultural turns in the social and human sciences, identities have been explained and theorized as processes constantly produced, varied, and altered through representations and narration. People tell stories about themselves in order to give continuity to their existence, but narratives also produce and express the shared and public aspects of identities (Delanty and Rumford 2005, 51). Narratives thus are a means to connect the "self" and the world, as well as past and present. However, stories are always created within a certain cultural context and narrative order that "delimit what can be said, what stories can be told, what will count as meaningful, and what will seem to be nonsensical", as Steph Lawler (2002, 242–243) points out. For her, narratives are powerful in the way they structure and renew certain cultural meanings and, conversely, foreclose others (Lawler 2002, 252). In this volume, identities are examined by emphasizing their cultural and narrative qualities, and their processual and ongoing nature. Moreover, narration is considered as a form of social action in which various "mute" cultural phenomena, such as those defined as heritage, are operationalized by language and turned into symbolic markers of identities.

Dissonant Heritages in Europe

This volume's contributors draw on "dissonant heritage" to analyze, interpret, and rethink contemporary challenges, all the while adding new angles to the concept in the process. Though their combined perspectives are not free from dissonances themselves, together these different viewpoints provide dialogues and insights that can be helpful for future scholarly debate and research in various fields.

As explained above, the concept of "heritage dissonance" helps examine how the past is used in present situations, thereby indicating a lack of agreement and consistency in the meaning and content of heritage (Tunbridge and Ashworth 1996, 20; Kisić 2017). In this volume, that insight has been key to shed light on heritage sites, objects, and practices that have recently gone through changes or received formal recognition, more specifically, sites that have acquired the European Heritage Label: a label awarded by the EU to monuments, cultural landscapes, places of remembrance, or cultural goods that are seen as landmarks in the creation of Europe and/or the EU. The processes towards this recognition and the changing narratives involved not only evince struggles over heritage in micro and institutional settings, but they also illuminate broader contemporary heritage challenges: attempted constructions of European and national identities, for instance, and how these can create dissonances, or how the colonial past is remembered or fails to be a part of these constructions. The contributors to this book examine how current debates are materialized, showing how physical and symbolic places help understand broader heritage dissonances. This includes reflections on the "domestication" of what the EU proposed as European heritage and on the Europeanization of national heritage that reveal the flows between, and struggles over belonging by, nation states, the EU, and Europe (Kaasik-Krogerus in this volume).

This volume extends such reflections to places that are not commonly seen as heritage sites, such as ethnography museums, airports, refugee camps, and other borders or sites of transit, including the Mediterranean basin. Dissonant heritage is a useful concept for examining such places, and the objects and bodies in them, because it reveals how they are part of more than just institutional heritage struggles, also showing how subjects shape and understand heritage struggles through their bodily experiences at these sites, which of course depend on a subject's positioning. Examining these "sites of dissonance" (Trakilović in this volume) and how different subjects experience them reveals how certain subjects' bodily experiences and practices influence how particular places and their past can form a dissonant heritage for marginalized subjects. By analyzing the dissonant heritage of such places, this book extends the scope of the concept, exploring new ways of applying and conceptualizing it while building on the work of others (e.g. Tunbridge and Ashworth 1996; Kisić 2017).

This extension of the concept's scope also accounts for this volume's contributions' use of dissonant heritage in relation to intangible heritage. Although it is not the first to do so (Deacon 2004; Smith 2006; Smith and Akagawa 2009), this volume includes an elaborate discussion of how intangible heritage is especially used in nationalist identity politics (van der Laarse in this volume). This usage risks fixating cultural activities that are assumed to be "authentic" characteristics of national identity into static (and thus "inauthentic") forms and are therefore in need of critical evaluation. This is also relevant in any analysis of (the creation of) "authorized heritage discourses" (Smith 2006, 29–34). This concept refers to the way agents in power control and regulate practices and discourses, which commonly leads to the formal fixation of heritage through policy, administrative, and legislative documents. UNESCO and the EU are examples of such agents listing heritage sites that they consider as important to be transmitted for future generations. Several contributors to this volume particularly investigate how the EU's practice of awarding sites with the European Heritage Label produces their European content, for example by emphasizing certain "European values" (Mäkinen in this volume; Turunen in this volume). This EU label seeks to spread a unifying EU discourse, bypassing dissonances included in the concepts of Europe, heritage, and values in Europe.

Appearing in contributions from both research projects, perspectives from postcolonial and decolonial theory help critically examine dissonant heritages in the European context. As has been rightly argued by postcolonial theorists, this theory is useful beyond research on former colonies and postcolonial migrants in Europe, as it offers perspectives on Europe that challenge the "insularity of historical narratives", which is desperately needed (Bhambra 2014, 117; also discussed by Turunen in this volume). In relation to heritage, such perspectives help challenge European heritage narratives that are presented as universal and objective, thereby "marginalizing and silencing other experiences and voices" (Bhambra 2014, 117). Besides engaging with these problematic static and objectivist discourses critically, contributors in this book have looked beyond the physical space of Europe and the EU, examining diasporic relations and (dissonant) memories beyond Europe. The way memories and heritage are "used, misused and exploited" (Said 2000, 177–179) in the creation of national and cross-national identities, as well as in the way divergences between "we" and "they" are constructed (and possibly broken down), is discussed from several theoretical perspectives as well as through the lens of interviewees who migrated to Europe. These interviewees reflect both on their individual identity and on colonial history, discussing their thoughts and emotions when moving between memories of their journey and of colonial heritage, and thus offering dissonant "emotional geographies" (Davidson et al. 2012; Proglio in this volume). Activists who protest the way the European colonial past is (not) represented in heritage sites, including the way dichotomies between Western art and non-Western artefacts are reproduced in ethnographic museums (van Huis in this volume), have further incited critical reflections, resulting in a conversation between academic production and artistic and activist practices.

Our chosen theoretical and methodological approaches have led to insights that help examine in greater detail how dissonance is publicly expressed in heritage and memory. Such approaches helped analyze how heritage dissonance can be less or more strongly felt, as well as more or less publicly voiced, depending on moments in time and different actions. During times of protest, heritage dissonances, as embodied experiences that might be omnipresent in individual subjects' lives, are transformed into representations visible in public (van Huis in this volume). These expressions of dissonance can be used as powerful political instruments that make those being protested uncomfortable (though they can affect protesters themselves as well), making it possible to further scrutinize and speak back to majority populations and institutions. These moments of dissonance can furthermore be understood as forms of disrupting "white innocence" (Wekker 2016), an internalized self-image of the majority population—constructed over centuries of colonialism as part of a collective cultural archive (but paradoxically ignoring large parts of this history)—that ignores racism and white privilege exists (as well as sexism, ableism, homophobia, classism, etc.). Such bottom-up moments of disruption, of overt heritage dissonance, show that there can be more equitable processes than the top-down integration interventions common to the cultural policies of nation states and the EU.

Together, these perspectives—the critical analysis of institutionalized formal discourses and struggles over formalization, the extended scope to include intangible heritage and sites that are not commonly associated with heritage, and the bottom-up approach to analyze individually experienced dissonance as used in political and artistic practice—form crucial contributions to dissonant-heritage theory and can be further used in scholarly debate and research, not only in the fields of history, and heritage and memory studies, but also political science, anthropology, sociology, cultural studies, geography, and beyond. At the same time, we are aware that traces of Eurocentrism remain in this book. Although we aimed to critically study European heritage, memory, and identity, the focus on Europe in itself sometimes directed the book towards reproducing a cohesive idea of European identity and heritage, and more divergences can be seen when these issues are examined more closely or broadly. Between the chapters and between the two research groups there were also divergences in the way dissonant heritage and memory are examined. The most important differences are found in the way contributors view heritage, either from the institutionalized perspective or from the bottom up, and in the extent to which the idea of a unified European identity and the idea of a shared European heritage is criticized. Furthermore, extending the concept of heritage to places and practices that are not commonly viewed as such is mostly done by the BABE's research group, whereas the institutionalization is mostly studied by the EUROHERIT team, although there are also overlaps. These overlaps are also thematic, and therefore all three sections of this volume have contributors from both research groups, offering institutional and bottom-up perspectives to each theme. The failure to thoroughly discuss gender and class is another issue that leaves us feeling uneasy. Gender is discussed in the intersectional perspective used by an activist group protesting representations of the colonial past in an ethnographic museum (van Huis in this volume), but gender and class deserve more attention when discussing heritage, memory, and identity because they are crucial dimensions to how these are formed and how they impact our lives.

Altogether, dissonance—this uncomfortable sense of disharmony, confusion, or conflict—has been a central sensitizing concept in the writing and composition of this volume's chapters. It revealed itself able to lead us to new ideas and sometimes to new harmonies. It helped bring researchers from different backgrounds and research interests together, while also constructively acknowledging the continuing dissonance between and within our work, and the need to be even more critical in the future. In the course of the book's development, dissonance has not only been explored with reference to our fields of research, but it also increasingly became a part of our encounter's development into a fruitful and creative conversation. Dissonance was extended to include discrepancies not just between different directions of research or theoretical frameworks, but also to different uses and understandings of the very concepts that had originally fostered our encounter: "Europe" and "transnational memory". By moving back and forth between the points of convergence and divergence between different scales of analyses, conceptual tools, and objects of research, dissonance has increasingly become more of a method of thinking and of asking each other questions. After all, the metaphor of dissonance, borrowed from music theory, reminds us that what is considered stable or unstable, pleasant or unpleasant, in the interaction between different sounds does change over time. Sounds thus not only produce friction, but also interpenetration and exchange. What Joan Scott (2011, 78–79) has noted for reverberations can be applied also to dissonances: they characterize the non-linear ways in which circuits of influences work in our globalized present.

These elements also inform the experimental mode of the book in which the mobility of borders applies just as much to research practices and disciplinary languages. This volume thus does not aim to recompose different perspectives into a coherent frame, but to highlight the productive and creative effect of frictions and connections emerging from the different contributions.

Explorations of Heritage and Memory Dissonances in Contemporary Europe

This volume examines the web of dissonances emerging from the triangulation of heritage, memory, and contemporary Europe. At the core of its structure are two phenomena: on one side the contradictions raised by attempts to establish a direct link between cultural and political identity, and on the other the challenges that contemporary responses to the transformations of European societies by global forms of governance, transnational interactions, and movements of people within and across borders pose to understandings of memory and heritage. The main tension between heritage policies and memory practices is not only refracted and complicated by the specificity of this volume's case studies, but also by the variety of methods authors deploy in their analyses. They include participant observation, close reading of images, discourse analysis of speeches and official documents, interviews, auto-ethnography, and social network analysis. The chapters of the volume are divided into three sections that identify the main convergences of our conversations and exchanges.

The first section opens the volume with a discussion of the role that uses of Europe's conflicted and martial past play in contemporary heritage discourses. These chapters discuss both conflicts and the attempts to solve and reconcile them in recent heritagization processes and transnational heritage policies of the Council of Europe, the EU, and UNESCO. The section thus explores European heritage and memory regimes "from above", focusing on "authorized heritage discourses" that construct and maintain these regimes through linguistic and discursive practices and performative processes. The section starts with Tuuli Lähdesmäki's analysis of the heritage policy discourses of two core European-level political actors, the EU and the Council of Europe, exploring how these actors deal with the challenges the idea of heritage faces in postmillennial Europe, and the opportunities to respond to these challenges. The analysis reveals how, on the one hand, the EU and the Council of Europe recognize and seek to reconcile heritage-related conflicts in contemporary Europe. These attempts see heritage as a space for civil participation, interaction, intercultural dialogue, and conversation about divergent values and narrations of the past. On the other hand, the policy discourses and their conceptions often rely on a static and materialist notion of heritage, which sustains geographical, cultural, political, socio-economic, and religious power hierarchies, not to mention an exclusive notion of a common European cultural heritage.

Katja Mäkinen continues the discussion of the EU's problematic relation to Europe's past in her analysis of the inter-conceptualization of Europe and the idea of peace. She particularly examines the meanings that the remembrance of World War II take on in the European integration process and in the imagination of the EU as a peace project. Her empirical analysis focuses on the European Heritage Label, the European Commission's recent flagship initiative, more particularly nine sites that have received this label on the basis of their aims to build peace in Europe. The chapter discusses how these sites' informational and promotional material presents the physical, practical, and imagined aspects of peace, how cultural heritage is entangled with political heritage, and how heritage's tangible and intangible dimensions of are intertwined in the EU's attempts to tell a European grand narrative of peace.

The section ends with the chapter by Rob van der Laarse, who explores conflicts of the "ownness" of intangible cultural heritage through examples from the recent (political) rediscovery of folklore in contemporary Europe. The promotion of, and identification with, national and regional folklore have recently been hijacked by European populist parties and movements. In their discourses, real and imaged folklore phenomena have been transformed into political means to foster territorial cultural identities and their "authenticity". Using examples from the Netherlands, the chapter critically discusses the UNESCO Convention for the Safeguarding of Intangible Cultural Heritage (2003) and its role in stimulating contestation of heritage's ownership by enabling (political) actors to utilize the concept of intangible cultural heritage for cultural identity-building projects. Moreover, van der Laarse explores how emotionality is intertwined with intangible cultural heritage, and how this entanglement can easily cause emotionally charged conflicts and even exclusion over heritage. The question of "ownness" is explored through the example of folk songs and fairy tales that are recognized as particular to several different European countries.

In the relationship between bordering practices and mobility, the second section identifies the contested ground where dissonances between and across politics from "below" and from "above" emerge. The authors in this section scrutinize the reactions and responses to national and European institutions' "authorized heritage discourses" by exploring exhibitions and urban spaces. By emphasizing the individual, the body, and experience in memory and heritage politics, their analysis offers different perspectives on these aspects' roles and effects on memorialization and heritagization processes in today's Europe.

In the first chapter, Milica Trakilović examines Europe's internal borders as building blocks of European cultural heritage and identity. The chapter uses a phenomenological approach to explore the connections between spaces, bodies, and European identity and the figure of the migrant and the refugee in the creation of a European space. Using Schiphol airport in the Netherlands as a case study of the airport as a bordered cultural space and building on interviews with asylum seekers, the chapter explores how the borders of the Dutch cultural archive affect the experience of "unwelcome" others. As this symbolic archive is built on the country's colonial legacy, the chapter draws parallels to the larger European cultural archive to showcase how the European identity is protected by erecting "a myriad of invisible new borders that are ideological, radicalized, and politicized" (Ponzanesi and Blaagaard 2011, 3).

Sigrid Kaasik-Krogerus' chapter confronts the notion of mobility in Europe with stabilization and domestication processes. She explores the dissonance between forced or voluntary mobility and stability through exhibitions in the Great Guild Hall, a medieval guild building in Tallinn that functions as the venue for the Estonian History Museum, awarded with the European Heritage Label in 2014. The chapter indicates how two of these exhibitions seek to "Europeanize" heritage while simultaneously domesticating the "European" as well, that is, incorporating it within the national and local context and making it familiar on the national and local level. The European thus becomes part of a national and local narration as the exhibitions construct Europe as a multi-scalar process.

The volume's final section discusses present-day Europe's relationship with its colonial heritage and memory, and the postcolonial interpretations and critical cultural interventions that seek to respond to this legacy to recognize and dismantle the power hierarchies affecting present-day heritage and memory regimes and their identity-building processes. The section focuses on spatiality and geography and explores the colonial legacy from both macro-level national and European narratives and individual experiences, emotions, and actions. Similarly to Lähdesmäki, Mäkinen, and Kaasik-Krogerus, this section's first chapter, written by Johanna Turunen, focuses on European authorized heritage discourse. By analyzing EU policy documents related to the European Heritage Label, Turunen explores the relationship between "European values" and the construction of "Europeanness", re-evaluating and reconstructing these values' meanings in the broader frame of European history. Using postcolonial theory, the chapter seeks to show how "European values" (like the ones related to the EU as a 'peace project', see Mäkinen's chapter) take on ambivalent and dissonant meanings, especially when analyzed from the vantage point of the often silenced and hidden heritage of European imperialism. These reflections foreground how the emphasis on "European values" forges exclusionary narratives of Europeanness, an analysis that resonates with the argument developed in Kaasik-Krogerus' chapter.

Iris van Huis continues the analysis of Europe's colonial heritage by focusing on the Dutch colonial past and the contestation of its present-day meanings and uses. This chapter further elaborates on "politics", which van Huis deals with as interventions by change agents and activist critical groups, including impacts of these interventions, thus emphasizing politics as an active and activist act "from below". The chapter returns to the discussion of the contesting ethno-nationalist and postcolonial discourses that characterize the current public debates on heritage in many European countries. Like van der Laarse and Trakilović, van Huis also focuses on issues related to the Netherlands' colonial past. Scrutinizing Amsterdam's Tropenmuseum, she asks how it has portrayed the past and how activist individuals and groups now contest and seek to change the prevailing racist and discriminatory dimensions of the Dutch cultural archive—of which the Tropenmuseum functions as an example.

The section ends with a chapter by Gabriele Proglio, who discusses the idea of dissonant memories in the Mediterranean basin. He develops the notion of "emotional geography" in relation to Europe's official and canonized geography, and explores dissonant memories of recent refugee crises and immigration from Africa that not just migrants from Ethiopia, Eritrea, and Somalia in Italy have, but also the second-generation people who were born in Italy but are still culturally connected to the Horn of Africa. Proglio's analysis of the interview data shows how the memory of crossing the Mediterranean—also when this experience and memory is not direct but intersubjectively shared in the diasporic community—can elaborate new forms of cultural identities through emotions. Similarly to van Huis and Turunen's approaches, Proglio's conceptualization of the Black Mediterranean helps foreground forms of resistance to the coloniality of power that informs mainstream representations of contemporary Europe.

The volume ends with Luisa Passerini's Epilogue, which discusses the theoretical and conceptual implications of the volume in decentering heritage and memory. Looking at the terminological and conceptual history of terms such as "heritage" and "dissonance", Passerini's reflections point to possible directions for future research and debates in heritage and memory studies and beyond.

Acknowledgements This work received funding from the European Research Council under the European Union's Seventh Framework Programme (FP/2007–2013), ERC Grant Agreement number 29585 (BABE), as well as under the EU's Horizon 2020 Research and Innovation Programme under Grant Agreement number 636177 (EUROHERIT).

References

Bhambra, G.K. 2014. *Connected Sociologies*. London: Bloomsbury Academic.
Brockmeier, J. 2010. After the Archive: Remapping Memory. *Culture and Psychology* 16 (1): 5–35.
Davidson, J., M.M. Smith, and L. Bondi (eds.). 2012. *Emotional Geographies*. New York: Routledge.
Deacon, H. 2004. Intangible Heritage in Conservation Management Planning: The Case of Robben Island. *International Journal of Heritage Studies* 10 (3): 309–319.

De Cesari, C., and A. Rigney. 2014. Introduction. In *Transnational Memory: Circulation, Articulation, Scales*, ed. C. De Cesari and A. Rigney, 1–15. Berlin: De Gruyter.

De Genova, N. 2016. The European Question: Migration, Race and Postcoloniality in Europe. *Social Text* 34 (3): 75–102.

De Genova, N. 2017. *The Borders of "Europe": Autonomy of Migration, Tactics of Bordering*. Durham: Duke University Press.

Delanty, G., and C. Rumford. 2005. *Rethinking Europe. Social Theory and the Implications of Europeanization*. London: Routledge.

Dicks, B. 2000. *Heritage, Place and Community*. Cardiff: University of Wales Press.

Donnan, H., M. Hurd, and C. Leutloff-Grandits. 2017. *Migrating Borders and Moving Times. Temporality and the Crossing of Borders in Europe*. Manchester: Manchester University Press.

Erll, A. 2011. Travelling Memory. *Parallax* 17 (4): 4–18.

Goldberg, D.T. 2006. Racial Europeanization. *Ethnic and Racial Studies* 29 (2): 331–364.

Innocenti, P. (ed.). 2014. *Migrating Heritage: Experiences of Cultural Networks and Cultural Dialogue in Europe*. Furhnam, Surrey: Ashgate.

Karlsson, K. 2010. The Uses of History and the Third Wave of Europeanization. In *A European Memory? Contested Histories and Politics of Remembrance*, ed. M. Pakier and B. Stråth, 38–55. New York and Oxford: Berghahn Books.

Kennedy, R., and M. Nugent. 2016. Scales of Memory: Reflections on an Emergent Concept. *Australian Humanities Review* 59 (April–May): 61–76.

Kisić, V. 2017. *Governing Heritage Dissonance: Promises and Realities of Selected Cultural Policies*. Amsterdam: European Cultural Foundation.

Lawler, S. 2002. Narrative in Social Research. In *Qualitative Research in Action*, ed. T. May, 242–258. London: Sage.

Lähdesmäki, T. 2014. The EU's Explicit and Implicit Heritage Politics. *European Societies* 16 (3): 401–421.

Lähdesmäki, T. 2017. Narrativity and Intertextuality in the Making of a Shared European Memory. *Journal of Contemporary European Studies* 25 (1): 57–72.

Macdonald, S. 2013. *Memorylands: Heritage and Identity in Europe Today*. London: Routledge.

Mezzadra, S., and B. Neilson. 2013. *Borders as Method, or, the Multiplication of Labor*. Durham: Duke University Press.

Oates-Indruchová, L., and W. Mueller. 2017. From the Iron Curtain to the Schengen Area: Memory Cultures of Bordering Communist and Postcommunist Europe. *East European Politics and Societies and Cultures* 31 (2): 227–233.

Pakier, M., and B. Stråth (eds.). 2010. *A European Memory? Contested Histories and Politics of Remembrance*. New York and Oxford: Berghahn Books.

Passerini, L. 2007. *Memory and Utopia: The Primacy of Inter-subjectivity.* London: Routledge.

Passerini, L., D. Gabaccia, and F. Iacovetta. 2016. 'Bodies Across Borders. Oral and Visual Memory in Europe and Beyond' (BABE): A Conversation with Luisa Passerini, Donna Gabaccia, and Franca Iacovetta. *Women's History Review* 25 (3): 458–469.

Ponzanesi, S., and B.B. Blaagaard. 2011. In the Name of Europe. *Social Identities* 17 (1): 1–10.

Rotheberg, M., and D. Moses. 2014. A Dialogue on the Ethics and Politics of Memory. In *The Transcultural Turn: Interrogating Memory Between and Beyond Borders*, ed. L. Bond and J. Rapson, 29–38. Berlin and Boston: De Gruyter.

Said, E. 2000. Invention, Memory, and Place. *Critical Inquiry* 26 (2): 175–192.

Scott, J.W. 2011. *The Fantasy of Feminist History.* Durham and London: Duke University Press.

Smith, L. 2006. *Uses of Heritage.* London: Routledge.

Smith, L., and N. Akagawa (eds.). 2009. *Intangible Heritage.* London: Routledge.

Tunbridge, J.E., and G.J. Ashworth. 1996. *Dissonant Heritage: The Management of the Past as a Resource in Conflict.* Chichester: Wiley.

Van Houtum, H. 2013. Human Blacklisting: The Global Apartheid of the EU's External Border Regime. In *Geographies of Privilege*, ed. F. Winddance Twine and B. Gardener, 957–976. London: Routledge.

Waterton, E., and L. Smith. 2009. There Is No Such Thing as Heritage. In *Taking Archaeology out of Heritage*, ed. E. Waterton and L. Smith, 10–27. Cambridge: Cambridge Scholars Publishing.

Wekker, G. 2016. *White Innocence: Paradoxes of Colonialism and Race.* Durham, NC: Duke University Press.

Yuval-Davis, N. 2011. *The Politics of Belonging: Intersectional Contestations.* London: Sage.

Open Access This chapter is licensed under the terms of the Creative Commons Attribution 4.0 International License (http://creativecommons.org/licenses/by/4.0/), which permits use, sharing, adaptation, distribution and reproduction in any medium or format, as long as you give appropriate credit to the original author(s) and the source, provide a link to the Creative Commons license and indicate if changes were made.

The images or other third party material in this chapter are included in the chapter's Creative Commons license, unless indicated otherwise in a credit line to the material. If material is not included in the chapter's Creative Commons license and your intended use is not permitted by statutory regulation or exceeds the permitted use, you will need to obtain permission directly from the copyright holder.

PART I

Conflict and Reconciliation

CHAPTER 2

Conflicts and Reconciliation in the Postmillennial Heritage-Policy Discourses of the Council of Europe and the European Union

Tuuli Lähdesmäki

INTRODUCTION

Europe is currently facing challenges that affect the contestation of the meaning of heritage. These challenges for example include: different forms of extremism in Europe, such as radical right and Islamist movements; Eurosceptic attitudes combined with new nationalist agendas; ethnic and religious confrontations; exclusion of minority, immigrant, and refugee groups; and various groups' sense that they do not belong to European societies. These challenges manifest in national, regional, and local discourses on heritage, and in their complex and dissonant relationship to the past, as the chapters by Rob van Laarse and Iris van Huis

T. Lähdesmäki (✉)
Department of Music, Art and Culture Studies,
University of Jyväskylä, Jyväskylä, Finland
e-mail: tuuli.lahdesmaki@jyu.fi

© The Author(s) 2019
T. Lähdesmäki et al. (eds.),
Dissonant Heritages and Memories in Contemporary Europe,
Palgrave Studies in Cultural Heritage and Conflict,
https://doi.org/10.1007/978-3-030-11464-0_2

in this volume indicate. These challenges also manifest at the most intimate level and are thus also embodied in the interaction between people, as Milica Trakilović and Gabriele Proglio show in this volume. As these challenges (and their causes and consequences) are not only local, regional, or national, but cross various territorial, social, and cultural borders, they also need to be responded to at the transnational level. But how do transnational policy actors respond to and tackle these challenges in their heritage policies?

The European Union (EU) and the Council of Europe influence in various ways heritage-policy discourses, not only at the European level, but also at the national and sub-national levels, as their heritage initiatives and programs are implemented by national, regional, and local actors. The heritage-policy discourses of the EU and the Council of Europe are commonly adapted to the policy goals of the actors at these levels. In general, the heritage policy discourses of the EU and the Council of Europe are closely connected; the recent heritage policy documents by both actors often refer to each others' policies, agendas, and cultural programs and initiatives. These discourses thus have a broad impact on the notions and conceptions of heritage in Europe.

While recent heritage research has devoted extensive attention to conflicts in processes and practices of heritage, the notion of dissonance is not tackled as much, and analyses of the role of dissonant heritages in cultural policy are few (Kisić 2017, 31). An analysis of heritage dissonances in and contradictions of transnational cultural policy is needed in particular, as the core European political actors (the EU and the Council of Europe) have recently emphasized the potential of heritage to solve conflicts and tackle contradictions and tensions between people. To that end, these actors have used heritage to actively promote intercultural dialogue, people's interest not only in themselves but also in others, and mutual understanding and respect between different groups of people.

In this chapter, I discuss heritage dissonance (Kisić 2017; see also Mäkinen and the introduction in this volume) in today's Europe, particularly focusing on the current challenges that the idea of heritage faces in postmillennial European reality and on the opportunities that heritage may have to respond to these challenges. I will discuss this by analyzing the current heritage-policy discourses of the EU and the Council of Europe, and explore how their policy discourse reflects and reacts to these challenges. My analysis focuses in particular on the means by which these actors seek to construct a feeling of belonging, communality, and identity (such as the notion of "European identity") through heritage in order to tackle exclusion and increase inclusion.

The idea of belonging has a central role in the different policy discourses of the EU and the Council of Europe. The concept itself explicitly recurs in EU policy discourse, as Katja Mäkinen and Johanna Turunen also note in this volume. The policy discourse's emphasis on belonging more generally reflects the recent scholarly interest in, and discussions on, the concept, especially when the notion of "identity" is considered less useful. Despite various efforts to conceptualize identity as a multilayered, fluid, and negotiated process, several scholars have argued that the concept of identity has lost its analytical power (on this discussion, see e.g. Lähdesmäki et al. 2016). Unlike identity, the concept of belonging has been perceived as capturing "more accurately the desire for some sort of attachment, be it to other people, places, or modes of being, and the ways in which individuals and groups are caught within wanting to belong, wanting to become, a process that is fuelled by yearning rather than the positing of identity as a stable state", as Probyn (1996, 19) has noted. Indeed, the concept of belonging has been perceived as flexibly combining various modes and degrees of "yearning". For analytical purposes, Yuval-Davis (2006) and Antonsich (2010) have made a distinction between psychological and political modes of belonging, respectively meaning "a personal, intimate feeling of being 'at home' in a place" and "a discursive resource which constructs, claims, justifies, or resists forms of socio-spatial inclusion/exclusion" (Antonsich 2010, 645). This latter mode constitutes what Yuval-Davis and Antonsich call a "politics of belonging". In this chapter, the EU's and the Council of Europe's policy discourses, and their explicit and implicit emphasis on people's belonging are understood as constituting a "politics of belonging"—an attempt to create discursive, performative, and emotional attachments to Europe and fellow people in Europe.

My empirical material consists of policy documents that explicitly address heritage and that have been produced by the EU and the Council of Europe since the Council's Framework Convention on the Value of Cultural Heritage for Society (commonly referred to as the Faro Convention, launched in 2005). This convention turned the emphasis of the Council of Europe's heritage-policy discourse from the conservation and preservation of heritage to its communal, social, and societal effects (cf. Kisić 2017, 28, 33–34, 65). The heritage-related documents produced by the Council of Europe that I analyzed include conventions and their explanatory texts, resolutions, declarations, and recommendations available on the Council's website. The documents produced by the EU were collected from the EUR-Lex, a database of EU legal texts, and include recommendations, resolutions, notices, communications, decisions, conclusions, and directives. Covering years 2005–2016 and including 30 Council of Europe documents and 15 EU documents, the data was examined by "close reading" (Brummet 2010) the policy rhetoric of the documents in order to identify the variety of roles and functions they gave to heritage and to perceive how the heritage dissonance was dealt with in the documents. I paid particular attention to the linguistic means, such as figures of speech and specific concepts, used when addressing issues of belonging, communality, and identity.

The EU and the Council of Europe are not monolithic or unanimous actors. Their policymaking is based on interactions and negotiations between several acting bodies, such the European Parliament, the Council of the European Union, the European Commission, and the European Committee of the Regions in the case of the EU, and the Committee of Ministers, the Parliamentary Assembly, the Congress of Local and Regional Authorities, and the Steering Committee for Culture, Heritage and Landscape in the case of the Council. Both the EU and the Council of Europe involve a number of European and national politicians, administrative officers, national and subnational authorities, advising and lobbying experts, and professionals commissioned for implementing specific tasks in their policy processes. Thus, all the documents included in my data have been produced as a result of a chain of negotiations and compromises seeking to reach consensus between the involved bodies. The texts in these documents usually undergo several amendments and revisions before their final publication. The analysis also acknowledged the genre of these documents; they commonly simplify the complexity of the issues addressed in the policy, avoid problematizing and raising explicit dissonance, and seek to consensually bring forth "one voice".

Instead of exploring the authors of these policy documents, this chapter focuses on the policies themselves as "actants"—as productive and performative processes in which actors, concepts, and policies interact as technologies of power. It is through policies that problems and subjects are constructed and governed (Shore et al. 2011; Lähdesmäki et al. 2019). In practice, the contents of policies are created through linguistic, conceptual, and semantic choices that seek to determinate and specify the object of policies, and bring about action. An in-depth analysis of policy discourses is crucial to critically understanding their performativity.

This chapter starts by contextualizing the EU's and the Council of Europe's heritage-policy discourses and policymaking. This section is followed by an analysis of these heritage-policy discourses and an examination of their attempts to solve various contemporary challenges through the notion of heritage and the notion of Europe's common cultural heritage in particular. The chapter ends with a discussion of the threats and possibilities that European heritage-policy discourses present to these current challenges.

The EU and the Council of Europe as Heritage-Policy Actors

The EU and the Council of Europe share an explicit aim to promote culture, identity, and values described and defined as European in their policy discourses. Both also act in the field of heritage management in various ways. Due to their different institutional natures, however the premises of their action differ. The Council mainly works through conventions developed by its member states. These member states maintain their sovereignty but commit themselves to conventions that function as common legal standards to be followed at the national level. The member states of the EU, in contrast, transfer part of their national legislative and executive power to the EU's administrative bodies. Although EU directives deal with culture in a rather generic manner, the EU has a broad impact to cultural issues in its member states through a diverse array of decisions and recommendations on specific cultural matters and various funding instruments and cultural programs. The EU-level policies are then implemented—and, in the case of the abstract concepts used in these policies, also interpreted—at the sub-European level.

Founded in 1949 in the aftermath of World War II, the main aim of the Council of Europe is to "achieve a greater unity between its members for the purpose of safeguarding and realising the ideals and principles which are their common heritage and facilitating their economic and social progress", as its founding statute declares (CofE 1949). Besides these abstract ideals and principles, the Council has also explicitly sought to safeguard "the common cultural heritage of Europe", as the first article in the European Cultural Convention states (CofE 1954). Since that Convention, the Council has created several conventions that focus on safeguarding specific areas of heritage, such archaeological heritage (1969 and 1992), architectural heritage (1985), and audiovisual heritage (2001). This safeguarding function has determined the Council's interest in cultural heritage until the Faro Convention. More recently, the social and societal shift in the Council's heritage policy has extended it to an entirely new political sector. For example, the Council now also fights against terrorism and organized crime through the Convention on Offences Relating to Cultural Property (2017) that seeks to prevent and combat the illicit trafficking and intentional destruction of cultural heritage. Through this convention, the Council's heritage politics explicitly address current armed conflicts and their effects on heritage.

The Council of Europe has had a major influence on the development and conceptualization of EU policy discourse. The Council's rhetorical formulations and interest areas have often been absorbed into the EU's policy discourse and their goals with only a short delay, particularly in questions related to culture (Sassatelli 2009, 43; Patel 2013, 6).

The foundation of the EU lies in the economic and political unification of Europe, developing from the European Economic Community, established by the Treaties of Rome signed in 1957, to the European Community, created by merging the European Economic Community, the European Coal and Steel Community, and the European Atomic Energy Community into a single institutional structure in 1967. In spite of this explicit emphasis on economic and political matters, culture has played an important role in the discursive formation of the Community since its early years. The concept of heritage first appeared in the Community's policy discourse in the 1970s (Lähdesmäki et al. 2019). Sassatelli (2009, 39) has located the emergence of the Community's identity discourse in that same decade, as the Declaration on European Identity was signed by nine European Community's member states in Copenhagen in 1973, forming the starting point for the EU's policy discourse on European identity.

The Maastricht Treaty—the founding agreement of the EU and deeper European integration, adopted in 1992—is considered as the start of the EU's cultural policy, as the treaty includes a specific article on culture. Since then, Europeans' cultural connections and identities have attained increasing attention in the EU's integration discourse and policies. In them, the idea and concept of cultural heritage is emphasized. Since the end of the 1990s, the EU has launched (or jointly organized with the Council of Europe) several initiatives that explicitly focus on promoting Europe's cultural heritage. These initiatives for instance include the European Heritage Days, the European Union Prize for Cultural Heritage, and the European Heritage Label. During the past ten years, the EU's emphasis on cultural heritage has increased as new heritage initiatives and policies have been launched to bind heritage management more closely to the other EU policy sectors and to enhance cultural dialogue and relations between people in Europe and beyond. These attempts were particularly important to the EU in 2018, when it celebrated the European Year of Cultural Heritage.

As a response to the recent turbulence in the grand narrative of nationalism (that is, its simultaneous "rupture" and reappearance), the EU has actively sought to construct and establish a new European narrative based on the supposed common heritage, values, and selected core events from the European past upon which Europeans could build their European identity. Initiatives that seek to identify and eventually find this kind of European shared past function as powerful tools in the EU's identity politics, or its "politics of belonging" (cf. Littoz-Monnet 2012). Indeed, the fundamental aim of EU cultural policy in general, and EU heritage and memory initiatives in particular, is to invoke in Europeans a feeling of belonging to Europe and the EU, a sense of communality among Europeans, and a European identity.

Identity politics and the "politics of belonging" are an important part of the EU's more general integration politics. In EU integration politics and policy discourse, cultural integration is noted as an important correlative of economic, judicial, and political integration (Bugge 2003, 70–71). European integration thus is a recurring topic in EU policy discourse on European heritage, history, and memory. As the European Parliament and the Council of the European Union's position document claims: "appropriate preservation of historical memory, a comprehensive reassessment of European history and Europe-wide recognition of all historical aspects of modern Europe will strengthen European integration" (EP 2010, 27). Similarly, the Council of the European Union has stated that "cultural heritage is a major asset for Europe and an important component of the European project" (CofEU 2014, 1).

In terms of membership and geographical scope, the EU and the Council of Europe represent two different ideas of Europe. While after Brexit the EU includes 27 member states that are bound together through diverse administrative bonds and forms of integration, the Council has 47 member states whose societal, economic, political, cultural, and religious contexts differ greatly. Geographically, the Council represents a much broader idea of Europe, spreading further to the east than the EU and also including transcontinental states. Both actors, however, share an interest in enhancing European identity, culture, and heritage that their members are assumed to represent.

Together, the heritage-policy discourses of the Council of Europe and the EU can be said to represent a European-level "Authorized Heritage Discourse" (AHD). This concept, introduced by Smith (2006) and developed by her and her colleagues, refers to heritage as "part of a wider social practice that has been specifically developed to regulate the management of heritage, often with reference to strict laws and prescriptive procedures" (Waterton and Smith 2006, 13). In AHD, heritage is not only managed and regulated by formal legislation, "but also by a discursive pressure to conform to what appears to be the normalcy" as Waterton and Smith suggest (2006, 13). Indeed, the administrative authorities' heritage discourse and legislation do not commonly question or problematize the idea of heritage. Transforming such an AHD's substantial emphasis is a slow process, as it involves many administrative actors and develops through multistage administrative procedures. Through its administrative—and thus also its symbolic—power, this AHD produces and maintains what is considered to be heritage in society. The AHD also naturalizes the AHD's representation and understanding of the past. Smith (2006) describes how this discourse often promotes a consensus approach to history, smoothing over the possible conflicts and social differences between people. The AHD of the Council of Europe and the EU seeks to find common views on Europe's history and culture, advocate a particular European narrative, promote the idea of a common cultural heritage, and foster an identity based upon them all. This AHD enables the very notion of a European cultural heritage and determines what is the right or normal way to narrate its contents and values, as the chapters by Katja Mäkinen and Johanna Turunen in this volume indicate.

European Heritage-Policy Discourses as Tools to Tackle Contemporary Challenges

For the AHD of the Council of Europe and the EU, the notion of heritage functions as a form of governance that seeks to structure and master space, people, material worlds, and time (cf. Winter 2015, 998). This governance is implemented through linguistic and conceptual choices, such as referring to the idea of a common cultural heritage in Europe without any discussion on the dissonances and conceptual, ideological, and political limitations that this idea entails. A common point of departure in this AHD is to bind together the idea of European history, heritage, identity, and values, and represent their connection as unquestioned and unproblematic. This connection is for example emphasized in the Council of Europe's resolution on the Cultural Routes Programme. In this programme, already launched in 1987, the Council of Europe awards the title of Cultural Routes to concrete routes or less concrete networks that the Council interprets as promoting shared culture, history, memory, and European integration. The resolution lists the basis of the programme as follows:

> Considering that highlighting the influences, exchanges and developments which have formed the European identity can facilitate awareness of a European citizenship based on the sharing of common values;
> Considering that it is essential for younger generations to acquire this awareness of a European identity and citizenship and the common values on which they are based;
> Considering that in order to uphold these common values and make them more tangible, it is necessary to promote an understanding of Europe's history on the basis of its physical, intangible and natural heritage, so as to bring out the links which unite its various cultures and regions. (CofE 2007, 1)

The rhetoric in the above extract clearly naturalizes the existence of a unity based on Europe's common history, heritage, identity, and values, and presents as natural the need and necessity to promote this unity. It also introduces the notion of "awareness", which presupposes that certain types of identity and citizenship exist, and that people, particularly young ones, should become aware of them. In general, the AHD of the Council of Europe and the EU commonly brings up and appeals to particular shared European values. In the extract, these "values"—or rather a group of societal ideals and political principles of liberal democratic societies—are perceived as being manifested in Europe's cultural heritage, but also as being a kind of heritage themselves. For example, in the Faro Convention the Council of Europe defines the "common heritage of Europe" as consisting of:

a. all forms of cultural heritage in Europe which together constitute a shared source of remembrance, understanding, identity, cohesion and creativity, and
b. the ideals, principles and values, derived from the experience gained through progress and past conflicts, which foster the development of a peaceful and stable society, founded on respect for human rights, democracy and the rule of law. (CofE 2005a, Article 3)

In the AHD of the Council of Europe and the EU, the promotion of Europe's cultural heritage turns into a promotion of values—and eventually into a promotion of liberal democratic social and political order. The emphasis on these values also brings up their counterpart. As the rhetoric in the Faro Convention exemplifies, the fostering of these values derives from past conflicts that ought to be avoided.

Europe's twentieth-century history of war and conflict, particularly World War II, the Holocaust, and totalitarian regimes in general have gained a lot attention in the heritage and memory politics of the Council of Europe and the EU. The Council of Europe introduced of a "Day of Holocaust Remembrance and Prevention of Crimes against Humanity", launched in 2002, and has supported the development of various educational programs dedicated to Holocaust remembrance and teaching the conflict history of Europe. Similarly, the EU has emphasized the need to increase the awareness of the Holocaust, and with the EU's Eastern expansion also the awareness of the crimes of communist regimes. Since 2006, both the European Commission and the Parliament have launched several programs, initiatives, and resolutions that seek to promote the remembrance of the victims of totalitarian and authoritarian regimes in Europe (Prutsch 2013). In 2008, the European Parliament declared a "European Day of Remembrance for Victims of Stalinism and Nazism" to jointly mourn all victims of the past totalitarian and authoritarian regimes in Europe.

In recent years, both actors have also promoted the reconciliation of more recent conflicts through heritage initiatives that seek to reconstruct and conserve damaged or demolished tangible heritage, and to create cooperation and respectful interaction between conflicting cultural, ethnic, and religious communities. For example, in the project "Ljubljana Process: Rehabilitating our Common Heritage", jointly funded by the Council of Europe and the EU, numerous monuments and heritage sites were restored in Albania and the countries of former Yugoslavia in order to create relationships between diverse local stakeholders and to enhance stability, development, and economic growth in the region (RCC, TFCS Secretariat 2014). The Ljubljana Process, just like several other recent heritage projects by the EU and the Council of Europe, has its basis in the policy goals of respecting cultural diversity and promoting intercultural dialogue.

Tackling Challenges: The Council of Europe

The recent policy discourse of the Council of Europe includes both implicit and explicit attempts to recognize, react to, and tackle exclusion, tensions, and conflicts in contemporary societies through heritage. The Faro Convention includes a conceptual innovation that seeks to deconstruct the previously territorially defined notion of heritage and detach it from so-called "thick" identities, which are based on the idea of traditionally, territorially, and historically rooted shared features and cultural elements (on the concept, see e.g. Delanty 2003; Davidson 2008; Terlouw 2012). As much as they build identities up, these elements also simultaneously divide people by excluding others. Instead of using vocabulary that might deepen or create divisions between different groups of people, the Council of Europe's Faro Convention introduces the concept of a "heritage community" that "consists of people who value specific aspects of cultural heritage which they wish, within the framework of public action, to sustain and transmit to future generations" (CofE 2005a, Article 2). As Dolff-Bonekämper (2009, 71) has noted, the Convention's rhetoric does not evoke the traditional relationship of heritage to specific local, regional, or national territorial units, nor does it refer to any social or societal parameters such as national, ethnic, religious, cultural, linguistic, or class-based groups. The only social and territorial unit to which heritage is connected in the Convention is Europe.

The Explanatory Report of the Faro Convention explains that belonging to a heritage community is due to a "thin" tie: "One can be a member of a heritage community simply by valuing a cultural heritage or wishing to pass it on. Individual incapacity may prevent action or even physical contact with the cultural heritage in question without invalidating an individual's right to identify with that community" (CofE 2005b, 6). This easy and voluntary nature of belonging to a heritage community has been welcomed by various heritage professionals and scholars. Dolff-Bonekämper (2009, 71), for example, has emphasized how the notion of a heritage community enables individuals to

> opt to belong to several communities, sequentially or at the same time, as they move through topographical and social space, for these communities are not exclusive and involve no obligation in terms of identity. Individuals (alone) may feel an attachment to a heritage in a place where they are, where they are not, or where they are no longer, depending on their geographical mobility or immobility.

The concept of a heritage community can also be explored from a more critical point of view. The conceptual innovation of the Council of Europe's policy discourse in itself does not provide individuals automatic access to any community. Indeed, this type of belonging presupposes that access (cf. Anthias 2009), and access is not only a matter of choice. Minorities and marginalized and oppressed people are often confronted with explicit and implicit inequalities, discrimination, and exclusion caused by limited or blocked access to belonging to a community (Lähdesmäki et al. 2016). Individuals may want to belong to a certain heritage community, but others do not allow them to. According to nativist, xenophobic, and racists views, for example, belonging to a (national) heritage community may require having the "right" ethnic, religious, or cultural roots. The idea of a heritage community has various positive connotations, such as "giving a voice" to individuals in heritage matters and enabling the expression and promotion of alternative, suppressed, silenced, or marginalized memories and heritages. However, the concept does not solve the problem of "representing" a particular community. It does not explicitly define who can serve as a spokesperson of a community.

In general, the Faro Convention's idea of a heritage community imagines these communities and their heritages as coexisting happily. Its Article four reminds the reader that "everyone, alone or collectively, has the responsibility to respect the cultural heritage of others as much as their own heritage, and consequently the common heritage of Europe"

(CofE 2005a, Article 4). Although this kind of policy discourse rhetorically seeks to dissolve the dissonance between heritage communities, the discourse does not take a critical stand against traditional notions of heritage as such, nor does it try to resolve tensions and contradictions within any heritage. Indeed, the discourse also does not take into account that the notion of common heritage in Europe also includes exclusive, oppressive, and discriminative content, for example deriving from colonialist, imperialist, Eurocentric, and elitist narratives. Not all heritage is worthy of respect. The Council of Europe's Namur Declaration—which introduced the European Cultural Heritage Strategy for the twenty-first century—emphasizes "cultural heritage as an ideal means of transmitting values through the generations" (CofE 2015a, 3), but not all values embedded in cultural heritage are worth maintaining and transmitting into the future. Ferracuti (2017) claims that several European countries have not ratified the Faro Convention due to this very ambiguity and vagueness of the concept of the heritage community.

Since the beginning of the 2000s, the Council of Europe's policy discourse has promoted "intercultural dialogue" as a tool to tackle tensions and conflicts between individuals and groups, resulting in policy initiatives such as the White Paper on Intercultural Dialogue (2008). The concept is also used in the Council's heritage-policy discourse that seeks to "promote intercultural and interfaith dialogue and mutual understanding of differences, with a view to prevention of conflicts" (CofE 2005b, 2). Critical analyses of the uses of the concept of intercultural dialogue in the Council's policy discourse have, however, indicated that the concept itself embraces power hierarchies. The meaning of the concept is produced from a hegemonic point of view, which generates power positions of a *dialoguer* and *dialoguee* to the "intercultural dialogue". As Lähdesmäki's and Wagener's (2015) analysis of this white paper indicates, immigrants and minority communities commonly represent the *dialoguees* in the policy discourse, the people to whom Europe's culture has to be delivered and introduced in order to make them the other part of the dialogue. As a policy, intercultural dialogue aims at the more effective integration in European societies that is, according to the white paper, "needed to allow immigrants to participate fully in the life of the host country. Immigrants should, as everybody else, abide by the laws and respect the basic values of European societies and their cultural heritage" (CofE 2008, 11). The white paper acknowledges museums and heritage sites as actors and spaces that have the potential to enhance intercultural dialogue. Yet, on closer inspection, the white paper seems too one-sided and uncritical in its view on cultural heritage for this potential to be tapped:

> Exploring Europe's cultural heritage can provide the backdrop to the plural European citizenship required in contemporary times. Europe's historical transborder and continental routes, today rediscovered with the help of the Council of Europe as the network of "cultural routes", influenced the history of cultural relations and for centuries supported intercultural exchange; they provide access to Europe's multicultural heritage and illustrate the ability to live together peacefully in diversity. (CofE 2008, 33)

Instead of a critical discussion of past hierarchical inequalities and forms of dominance that still influence social relations between the various groups in today's European societies, the policy discourse in the white paper emphasizes promoting a consensual and conciliatory interpretation of Europe's cultural heritage.

In practice, the white paper seeks to promote intercultural dialogue by introducing five policy approaches on how European societies and their various actors could "offer opportunities for dialogue" with "newcomers". These approaches discursively distinguish between an us and a them, *dialoguers* and *dialogues*. Their encounter can also turn into conflict if the latter refuse the dialogue, as the following lines from the white paper indicate:

> Intercultural dialogue is not a cure for all evils and an answer to all questions, and one has to recognise that its scope can be limited. It is often pointed out, rightly, that dialogue with those who refuse dialogue is impossible, although this does not relieve open and democratic societies of their obligation to constantly offer opportunities for dialogue. On the other hand, dialogue with those who are ready to take part in dialogue but do not – or do not fully – share "our" values may be the starting point of a longer process of interaction, at the end of which an agreement on the significance and practical implementation of the values of human rights, democracy and the rule of law may very well be reached. (CofE 2008, 17)

During the 2010s, the Council of Europe has also paid attention to the role of heritage in tackling diverse ethnic conflicts. In the resolution on "Cultural Heritage in Crisis and Post-Crisis Situations", the Council's Parliamentary Assembly expresses a concern for "the deliberate eradication of culture, identity and existence of the 'other' through a systematic destruction of cultural heritage" that "has become a central component of modern conflicts that are ethnically driven" (CofE 2015b, 1). The text notes the potential of heritage in "conflict resolution" and "reconciliation and creating social cohesion", and how "it can also be misused to reignite division and hatred" (CofE 2015b, 1). The Council's general policy discourse on crises and post-crises does not single out or focus on any particular crises or territories, but the reports on the Council of Europe's website indicate that the preparation of the policy particularly stems from experiences from former Yugoslavia, Cyprus, Georgia, and Azerbaijan.

In recent years, crises have gotten emphasized more and more in the heritage-policy discourse of the Council of Europe. The Namur Declaration specifically notes that: "Climate change, demographic changes, migration, political, economic, financial and social crises are having a significant impact on our societies and heritage" (CofE 2015a, 1). These changes and crises are perceived to carry the risk of rupturing and imploding "our societies", as the Namur Declaration states:

1. [...] We need to be aware of these challenges and work together to prevent a development where our societies are weakened and lack points of reference, are tempted to adopt inward-looking attitudes, are experiencing an erosion of traditional bonds and sometimes risk rupturing or imploding.
2. Cultural heritage is a key component of the European identity; it is of general public interest and its transmission to future generations is a shared responsibility; it is a unique resource, fragile, non-renewable and non-relocatable, contributing to the attractiveness and the development of Europe and, crucially, to the creation of a more peaceful, just and cohesive society.
3. A Strategy for redefining the place and role of cultural heritage in Europe is therefore a necessary response to the current challenges in the light of the changing European socio-economic and cultural context. (CofE 2015a, 1)

As a response to the threats posed by various recent crises, the Namur Declaration proposes a European-level heritage strategy that seeks to transmit cultural heritage—and at the same time European identity, which is supposedly based on that heritage—to future generations in order to create a more cohesive society. Overall, its policy discourse suggests a static and invariant conception of cultural heritage: it cannot be renewed, nor can its location be changed. Thus, cultural heritage is considered to be fragile; instead of heritage being conceived as itself constantly changing, plural, and dissonant, its uniqueness is perceived to be threatened by the dissonance caused by recent crises.

Tackling Challenges: The EU

The EU's heritage-policy discourse reflects and follows the core emphases of the Council of Europe's discourse. Like the Namur Declaration, the EU's heritage-policy discourse defines heritage as a static phenomenon confronted with various challenges in today's Europe. The Council Conclusions on Participatory Governance of Cultural Heritage indicates this by claiming that: "cultural heritage as a non-renewable resource that is unique, non-replaceable or non-interchangeable is currently confronted with important challenges related to cultural, environmental, social, economic and technological transformations that affect all aspects of contemporary life" (CofEU 2014, 1). If cultural heritage is understood as a static, unique, and non-renewable phenomenon, transculturation, cultural hybridity, and reinterpretations of heritage may indeed pose a threat to it. This kind of conception of cultural heritage thus rather creates challenges than that it makes it possible to respond to such challenges. The EU's heritage-policy discourse emphasizes the challenging momentum in Europe, where "the heritage sector is at a crossroads" and is "facing challenges" ranging from the decrease of public budgets to climate change (EC 2014, 4). The policy discourses does not, however, recognize the challenges embedded in the very idea of common cultural heritage and European identity as such, nor does it seem to be aware of exclusive power structures that these ideas and their use may entail.

The EU's heritage-policy discourse utilizes many of the same conceptual choices that were introduced by the Council of Europe, emphasizing heritage as a vehicle for "democratic participation", "intercultural dialogue", and "social cohesion". In the EU's heritage-policy rhetoric, these aims are intertwined with more general goals of promoting European integration (Lähdesmäki 2014). While the Council emphasized the communal dimension of cultural heritage using the concept of a heritage community, the EU's heritage-policy discourse utilizes the concept of belonging in its identity-political aims. Through its heritage initiatives, such as the European Heritage Label, the EU seeks to strengthen

"European citizens' sense of belonging to the Union, in particular that of young people, based on shared values and elements of European history and cultural heritage, as well as an appreciation of national and regional diversity" (EP and CofEU 2011, 3). According to the EU's heritage-policy rhetoric, the ideas of strengthening people's belonging to "a wider community" and promoting intercultural dialogue are closely connected, as—according to the EU's Council Conclusions on Participatory Governance of Cultural Heritage—heritage "has the capacity to [...] promote diversity and intercultural dialogue by contributing to a stronger sense of 'belonging' to a wider community and a better understanding and respect between peoples" (CofEU 2014, 2). That quotation evinces a desire for more understanding and respect between "peoples", not between individuals or groups within a people. The vocabulary thus treats and construct a people as a coherent entity.

Recently, the EU has emphasized the role of heritage in its external relations and embraced it as a form of public or cultural diplomacy (as EU policy documents call it). The European Commission's communication "Towards an EU Strategy for International Cultural Relations" lists three main strands of these relations, the last of which focuses on "reinforcing cooperation on cultural heritage" (EC 2016, 3). The aim of this is to "stimulate inter-cultural dialogue and peace-building, support cultural production and tourism as drivers of development and economic growth, and use education, research and science as agents for dialogue and exchanges" (EC 2016, 15–16). The strategy also has more self-serving political goals, as the actions suggested in its main strands are expected to "contribute to making the European Union a stronger global actor, a better international partner and a stronger contributor to sustainable growth, peace and mutual understanding" (EC 2016, 16).

The EU is increasingly making an effort to strengthen its heritage-related cooperation with others, to use heritage in conflict resolution, and to reconcile conflicts and dissonances among different groups outside the borders of the EU (Lähdesmäki et al. 2019). These actions can be said to rely on two different approaches to diplomacy, which Winter (2015) has described as "heritage in diplomacy" and "heritage as diplomacy". Under the first approach, the EU is coordinating various heritage-related initiatives and projects as a part of other diplomatic actions with its partner countries. In addition, the EU finances conservation work and conservation- and preservation-related capacity building in these countries. In these cases, diplomatic actions do not depend on the notion of mutual or shared heritage as a mediator of relations (Winter 2015, 1010). The second approach, heritage as diplomacy, draws on the idea that we should foster shared heritage and build of bridges by identifying shared pasts. Winter (2015, 1011) has noted how states around the world are using a rhetoric of "shared heritage" to semantically shift material culture from a category that is considered dissonant to one that that is perceived to be more productive. Various contemporary powers and former colonial powers are discursively framing certain material culture as "shared heritage" in order to create forms of historical and cultural unity, and to give more diplomatic weight to their contemporary international relations (Winter 2015, 1011). The EU's emphasis on common values, cultural ties, and shared heritage seeks to articulate the historical and present-day connections with its external partner countries, thus also justifying the EU's cultural diplomatic actions with these countries.

Threats and Possibilities of European Heritage-Policy Discourses

What kinds of threats and possibilities do the EU's and the Council of Europe's heritage-policy discourses present for heritage management in today's Europe? In general, the cultural emphasis on "European identity" and the notions of a common past and shared cultural roots as markers of "Europeanness" can all be used to justify discriminative discourses and actions, as the rhetoric of the European extreme-right, populist, and new nationalist movements and parties already indicates. A cultural emphasis on "European identity" thus promotes social exclusion and a sense of not belonging among those who feel that they do not share or have access to the correct European cultural roots or cultural markers.

The concept and idea of cultural heritage is never neutral in any discourse, as it is always represented and defined from some perspective. One of the threats of strengthening the European-level AHD is its power to represent certain ideas, values, ideals, and political principles as natural and thus to legitimize action promoting them. This understanding of cultural heritage raises various questions about the EU's and the Council of Europe's interests in heritage diplomacy and cooperative projects with non-European countries. A threat is that these projects and diplomatic actions also narrowly promote Eurocentric values and notions of cultural heritage.

Several scholars have pointed out how the notion of heritage and its relation to materiality differs between Western and non-Western cultures (e.g. Wei and Aass 1989; Byrne 1991; Stille 2002; Akagawa 2015). In Europe, the emphasis on the materiality of heritage stems from the intellectual and scholarly movements of the Enlightenment and their desire to preserve material cultural relics (Byrne 1991). During the age of Enlightenment in particular, collecting cultural objects turned into a means to measure, order, and grasp the world (Gillman 2006). The emphasis on the materiality of heritage only strengthened during the nineteenth century, fueled by a fear of losing the material traces of the past caused by the Industrial Revolution (Wei and Aass 1989). Western notions of authenticity and originality are more closely connected to materiality and historical continuity of material traces than the way those concepts are used in non-Western traditions (Stille 2002; Akagawa 2015). Moreover, the idea of the materiality of heritage is intertwined with the Western conception of identity. The widespread linkage between a durable tangible heritage and the continuity of people across generations is implicit—and often also explicit—in the Western world, especially in Europe, as Macdonald (2006) notes. In this conception, material culture as heritage is understood not simply as representing and transmitting an identity but also as materializing and objectifying it (Macdonald 2006, 11). According to this conception, the idea of an identity extends from an abstract mindset of people to also include cultural representations; material objects thus function as manifestations of identities and as a means to construct them. Future analysis of the effects of European heritage diplomacy will have to indicate whether it also transmits and disseminates these materialist and preservationist values of heritage to its non-European partner countries, and whether it thus continues or even recreates European cultural hegemony in this sense.

Besides these threats, the heritage-policy discourses of the EU and the Council of Europe also offer numerous possibilities to positively influence and respond to the present challenges in Europe. These possibilities concretize in the implementation of the EU's and the Council of Europe's initiatives at the local level. Although the notion of a common cultural heritage in Europe is problematic, it may also enable bypassing the tensions and controversies that are attached to heritage at the national and regional levels, and offer a more broad, abstract, and flexible framework to perceive heritage and its meanings in today's

Europe. It may thus enable a feeling of belonging and inclusion for a transnational and culturally plural community, the boundaries of which are less strict than those of a nation or an ethnic, religious, or linguistic community, thus activating new European identities that are agile and flexible enough to react to the transformation and pluralization of Europe. The Council of Europe's concept of a heritage community particularly suggests that the idea of belonging can be approached from an agile point of view. Besides its limitations and practical weaknesses, discussed above, the concept does also present possibilities in that it stresses the power of civil agents to create communities and define the values of heritage. This kind of approach to the ideas of communality and belonging reflects the nature of the Council of Europe as a bigger, more heterogeneous, and institutionally looser organization compared to the EU.

The European-level heritage policies are a good—if rather underdeveloped in its current state—arena to respond to various transnational challenges and to address meanings and values of cultural heritage that are "more than national" or post-national. This arena presents the possibility to deconstruct the hegemonic grand narratives that include a discriminative ethos towards various "others". To utilize this opportunity, European-level heritage-policy discourse could for example benefit from a notion of European cultural heritage that Delanty (2010, 2017) has described as "cosmopolitan". For him (2010, 16–17), the idea of a cosmopolitan heritage stems from a plural notion of the European civilizational constellation—that is, from the idea of transcontinental and inter-civilizational encounters and from a notion of the internal pluralization of not only the European civilization(s) but also those of non-European civilizations.

The EU's and the Council of Europe's heritage-policy discourses reflect the participatory turn in heritage management. The emphasis on civil participation and engagement with heritage practices and processes presents the opportunity to promote a new kind of perception of heritage: heritage as communication. This kind of approach to heritage turns it into a space for conversation and a resource for reflection, interaction, and recognition (Bodo 2016). Kisić (2017, 31) has referred to this communicative dimension of heritage by emphasizing the need for an "inclusive heritage discourse" in which "dissonance is acknowledged, and the possibility for different voicing is recognized". For her,

[t]his discourse allows that heritage can be talked about and worked with in ways that give space for articulating diverse meanings. As such, dissonance can empower de-naturalization of heritage, foster critical thinking and create opportunities for intense intercultural mediation. (Kisić 2017, 31)

The dissonant meanings, values, and narratives of cultural heritage can thus be seen as enabling both a deeper understanding of that heritage and a critical understanding of how heritage emerges and is actively created and redefined.

The EU and the Council of Europe's emphasis on the concept of intercultural dialogue seeks to frame cultural heritage as a space for conversation. This understanding of cultural heritage also forms the basis for the EU's heritage diplomatic efforts. In the EU's heritage-policy discourse, cultural/public diplomacy refers to cooperation with the EU's external relations and thus focuses on territories outside the EU, while the concept of intercultural dialogue particularly refers to interaction and relations within EU societies and in the EU community. In today's world characterized by the movement of people, global communication, and multidimensional cultural interactions, however, that distinction between external and internal relationships is difficult to draw. Indeed, these two kinds of relationships should be perceived and treated as closely intertwined. The EU's internal relations would in fact also benefit from enhancing heritage diplomacy *within* the EU.

Conclusions

As we have seen, the EU and the Council of Europe have both sought to react to the transforming European reality in their heritage-policy discourses. One of the core focuses of these policy discourses is the "politics of belonging" through which the EU and the Council of Europe seek to enhance social cohesion, people's feeling of belonging and inclusion, as well as—in the case of the EU—integration in Europe. The heritage-policy discourses of both actors particularly focus on encouraging civil participation in, and engagement with, the preservation and valorization of heritage and on enhancing access to heritage—a goal that is, however, often only superficially addressed in the policy texts by treating access narrowly, as a matter of digitization, licensing, intellectual property rights, and dissemination of digitized material. The aim of enhancing people's feeling of belonging and inclusion in Europe furthermore contradicts with the policy rhetoric that creates, maintains, or enhances a distinction between "us" and "them".

The policy discourses of the EU and the Council of Europe seek to promote Europe's cultural heritage and common values as its basis. Although both actors actively seek to tackle dissonances between different groups in Europe through heritage-related actions, their policy discourses do not problematize the notions of shared European culture, history, memory, heritage, or values, nor do they tackle the dissonances that these notions may entail. The discourses do not seek to deconstruct or critically rethink the geographical, cultural, political, socio-economic, or religious power hierarchies that these notions involve, nor do they problematize *whose* culture, history, memory, heritage, and values are explicitly and implicitly perceived as European.

Since 2000, the EU's and the Council of Europe's heritage-policy discourses have increasingly turned their interest from preservation and conservation to the effects that cultural heritage has on societies, communities, and individuals. Recent policy discourses treat cultural heritage as an instrument of multi- and inter-sectoral politics whose political feasibility is based on an epistemological change in understanding heritage. Instead of treating heritage as a mere cultural category or as a question of preserving material traces of the past, the recent European heritage-policy discourses have turned heritage into a resource impacting various sectors of governance, ranging from economics to sustainable development, and from integration of migrants to European external relations. As a result of this epistemological change, European heritage-policy discourses increasingly perceive heritage as being about communication—both communication within a community and between communities. It is framed as a dialogical space to increase knowledge about others—but also to rethink oneself. European heritage-policy discourses thus also function as a signpost or a roadmap that presents a possibility to bring about action. This possibility concretizes through actors below the European level whose task is to turn policy into practice. The challenges in the implementation of the European heritage policies are further discussed in the chapters by Katja Mäkinen, Sigrid Kaasik-Krogerus, and Johanna Turunen in this volume.

Acknowledgements This work was supported by the Academy of Finland under Grant SA274295 (EUCHE) and by the European Research Council (ERC) under the EU's Horizon 2020 Research and Innovation Programme under Grant 636177 (EUROHERIT). The work is also related to the University of Jyväskylä's profiling area supported by the Academy of Finland under Grant SA311877 (CRISES). The content of this chapter does not reflect the official opinion of the European Union. Responsibility for the information and views expressed in the chapter lies entirely with the author.

REFERENCES

Akagawa, N. 2015. *Heritage Conservation in Japan's Cultural Diplomacy: Heritage, National Identity and National Interest*. London: Routledge.

Anthias, F. 2009. Thinking Through the Lens of Translocational Positionality: An Intersectionality Frame for Understanding Identity and Belonging. *Translocations: Migration and Social Change* 1 (4): 5–20.

Antonsich, M. 2010. Searching for Belonging—An Analytical Framework. *Geography Compass* 4 (6): 644–659.

Bodo, S. 2016. Rethinking Research and Policy Agendas on Cultural Heritage and European Identities. Presentation in the Cultural Base Policy Workshop, December 1, the EUI, Florence, Italy.

Brummet, B. 2010. *Techniques of Close Reading*. London: Sage.

Bugge, P. 2003. A European Cultural Heritage? Reflections on a Concept and a Program. In *Rethinking Heritage: Cultures and Politics in Europe*, ed. R.S. Peckham, 61–73. London: I.B. Tauris.

Byrne, D. 1991. Western Hegemony in Archaeological Heritage Management. *History and Anthropology* 5 (2): 269–276.

CofE (Council of Europe). 1949. *Statute of the Council of Europe. London, 5 May 1949*. Strasbourg: Council of Europe.

CofE (Council of Europe). 1954. *European Cultural Convention. Paris, 19 December 1954*. Strasbourg: Council of Europe.

CofE (Council of Europe). 2005a. *Framework Convention on the Value of Cultural Heritage for Society, Faro, 27 October 2005*. Strasbourg: Council of Europe.

CofE (Council of Europe). 2005b. *Explanatory Report to the Council of Europe Framework Convention on the Value of Cultural Heritage for Society. Faro, 27 October 2005*. Council of Europe Treaty Series No. 199. Strasbourg: Council of Europe.

CofE (Council of Europe). 2007. *Resolution CM/Res (2007)12 on the Cultural Routes of the Council of Europe* (Adopted by the Committee of Ministers on 10 October 2007 at the 1006th Meeting of the Ministers' Deputies). Strasbourg: Council of Europe.

CofE (Council of Europe). 2008. *White Paper on Intercultural Dialogue*. Strasbourg: Council of Europe.
CofE (Council of Europe). 2015a. *The Namur Declaration. The Ministers of the States Parties to the European Cultural Convention Meeting in Namur on 23–24 April 2015*. Strasbourg: Council of Europe.
CofE (Council of Europe). 2015b. *Resolution 2057. Cultural Heritage in Crisis and Post-Crisis Situations. The Parliamentary Assembly of the Council of Europe, 22 May 2015*. Strasbourg: Council of Europe.
CofEU (The Council of the European Union). 2014. Council Conclusions on Participatory Governance of Cultural Heritage. *Official Journal of the European Union*, C 463, 1–3.
Davidson, A.C. 2008. Through Thick and Thin: "European Identification" for a Justified and Legitimate European Union. *Journal of Contemporary European Research* 4 (1): 32–47.
Delanty, G. 2003. Is There a European Identity? *Global Dialogue* 5: 3–4. http://www.worlddialogue.org/content.php?id=269. Accessed 28 June 2017.
Delanty, G. 2010. The European Heritage from a Critical Cosmopolitan Perspective. *LSE 'Europe in Question' Discussion Paper Series* 19: 1–20.
Delanty, G. 2017. Entangled Memories: How to Study Europe's Cultural Heritage. *The European Legacy* 22 (2): 129–145.
Dolff-Bonekämper, G. 2009. The Social and Spatial Frameworks of Heritage—What Is New in the Faro Convention? In *Heritage and Beyond*, ed. D. Thérond and A. Trigona, 69–74. Strasbourg: Council of Europe Publishing.
EC (The European Commission). 2014. *Towards an Integrated Approach to Cultural Heritage for Europe. Communication from the Commission to the European Parliament, the Council, the European Economic and Social Committee and the Committee of the Regions*. COM(2014) 477 Final, 22 July 2014. Brussels: European Commission.
EC (The European Commission). 2016. *Joint Communication to the European Parliament and the Council. Towards an EU Strategy for International Cultural Relations*. JOIN(2016) 29 Final, 8 June 2016. Brussels: European Commission.
EP (The European Parliament). 2010. European Parliament Resolution of 2 April 2009 on European Conscience and Totalitarianism (P6_TA(2009)0213). *Official Journal of the European Union*, C 137 E: 25–27.
EP and CofEU (The European Parliament and the Council of the European Union). 2011. Decision No 1194/2011/EU of the European Parliament and of the Council of 16 November 2011 Establishing a European Union Action for the European Heritage Label. *Official Journal of the European Union*, L 303: 1–9.

Ferracuti, S. 2017. European Museums of Ethnography in the Global Sphere: New Complicities in the Age of Heritage Communities? Paper Presented at the SIEF Conference Ways of Dwelling: Crises, Craft, Creativity, 26–30 March 2017, Göttingen, Germany.
Gillman, D. 2006. *The Idea of Culture Heritage*. Cambridge: Cambridge University Press.
Kisić, V. 2017. *Governing Heritage Dissonance: Promises and Realities of Selected Cultural Policies*. Amsterdam: European Cultural Foundation.
Lähdesmäki, T. 2014. The EU's Explicit and Implicit Heritage Politics. *European Societies* 16 (3): 401–421.
Lähdesmäki, T., and A. Wagener. 2015. Discourses on Governing Diversity in Europe: Critical Analysis of the White Paper on Intercultural Dialogue. *International Journal of Intercultural Relations* 44: 13–28.
Lähdesmäki, T., T. Saresma, K. Hiltunen, S. Jäntti, N. Sääskilahti, A. Vallius, and K. Ahvenjärvi. 2016. Fluidity and Flexibility of 'Belonging'. Uses of the Concept in Contemporary Research. *Acta Sociologica* 59 (3): 233–247.
Lähdesmäki, T., S. Kaasik-Krogerus, and K. Mäkinen. 2019. Genealogy of the Concept of Heritage in the European Commission's Policy Discourse. *Contributions in the History of Concepts* 14 (1): 115–139.
Littoz-Monnet, A. 2012. The EU Politics of Remembrance: Can Europeans Remember Together? *West European Politics* 35 (5): 1182–1202.
Macdonald, S. 2006. Undesirable Heritage: Fascist Material Culture and Historical Consciousness in Nuremberg. *International Journal of Heritage Studies* 12 (1): 9–28.
Patel, K.K. 2013. Introduction. In *The Cultural Politics of Europe. European Capitals of Culture and European Union Since the 1980s*, ed. K.K. Patel, 1–15. London: Routledge.
Probyn, E. 1996. *Outside Belongings*. London: Routledge.
Prutsch, M.J. 2013. *European Historical Memory: Policies, Challenges and Perspectives*. Directorate-General for Internal Policies. Brussels: European Parliament.
RCC, TFCS Secretariat (Regional Cooperation Council, Task Force on Culture and Society Secretariat). 2014. *Comprehensive Report of the Ljubljana Process II—Rehabilitating Our Common Heritage 2011–2014*. Sarajevo: Regional Cooperation Council.
Sassatelli, M. 2009. *Becoming Europeans. Cultural Identity and Cultural Policies*. New York: Palgrave Macmillan.
Shore, C., S. Wright, and D. Però (eds.). 2011. *Policy Worlds: Anthropology and the Analysis of Contemporary Power*. New York: Berghahn Books.
Smith, L. 2006. *Uses of Heritage*. London: Routledge.
Stille, A. 2002. *The Future of the Past*. New York: Picador.

Terlouw, K. 2012. From Thick to Thin Regional Identities? *GeoJournal* 77 (5): 707–721.
Waterton, E., and L. Smith. 2006. There Is No Such *Thing* as Heritage. In *Taking Archeology out of Heritage*, ed. E. Waterton and L. Smith, 10–27. Cambridge: Cambridge Scholars Publishing.
Wei, C., and A. Aass. 1989. Heritage Conservation: East and West. *ICOMOS Information* 3: 3–8.
Winter, T. 2015. Heritage Diplomacy. *International Journal of Heritage Studies* 21 (10): 997–1015.
Yuval-Davis, N. 2006. Belonging and the Politics of Belonging. *Patterns of Prejudice* 40 (3): 197–214.

Open Access This chapter is licensed under the terms of the Creative Commons Attribution 4.0 International License (http://creativecommons.org/licenses/by/4.0/), which permits use, sharing, adaptation, distribution and reproduction in any medium or format, as long as you give appropriate credit to the original author(s) and the source, provide a link to the Creative Commons license and indicate if changes were made.

The images or other third party material in this chapter are included in the chapter's Creative Commons license, unless indicated otherwise in a credit line to the material. If material is not included in the chapter's Creative Commons license and your intended use is not permitted by statutory regulation or exceeds the permitted use, you will need to obtain permission directly from the copyright holder.

CHAPTER 3

Interconceptualizing Europe and Peace: Identity Building Under the European Heritage Label

Katja Mäkinen

Peace was a key aim in the European integration process after World War II. The present situation in Europe, I argue, also requires us to pay more attention to peace. Near the EU's borders, there is war in Ukraine and Syria, causing fear of war in some of the closest member states. In many member states, new nationalism and right-wing populism are gaining support and creating hostility, particularly against immigrants and in the context of immigration policy. At the EU's borders, refugees die on their dangerous journeys. Member and other states as well as people heading to the EU countries and those already staying in them have certain expectations about "opening" or "closing" the EU borders. Finally, among other "founding ideas" of the EU, peace has become topical in a new way as a Euro-sceptic and anti-EU atmosphere has been growing at least since the financial crisis in 2008, as Britain has decided to exit the

K. Mäkinen (✉)
Department of Music, Art and Culture Studies,
University of Jyväskylä, Jyväskylä, Finland
e-mail: katja.a.p.makinen@jyu.fi

© The Author(s) 2019
T. Lähdesmäki et al. (eds.),
Dissonant Heritages and Memories in Contemporary Europe,
Palgrave Studies in Cultural Heritage and Conflict,
https://doi.org/10.1007/978-3-030-11464-0_3

Union, and as the legitimacy of EU is strongly questioned. All this provides more than sufficient motivation to reflect on the meanings given to peace today in light of the history of Europe and its integration.

Cultural heritage, its definition now including elements like values, political ideas and systems, linguistic diversity, and remembering past events, is often mentioned as a building block of "European identity" in key documents from different EU institutions (Declaration on European Identity 1973; Treaty on European Union 1992; Treaty of Lisbon 2007). These documents use it to construct European identity through an invented common past. One way of doing this is through "founding stories"—or constitutive stories (Ringmar 1996) or founding myths (Lähdesmäki 2018). The narrative of EU integration as a peace process can be seen as the founding story of the EU. It started during integration's intensification phase after WWII, when the key aim was to prevent new wars by binding European countries—notably France and Germany—together. The idea that peace and reconciliation are at the core of European integration, and thus a fundamental element of the EU community, is repeated still today. With this "European peace narrative", the EU is represented as an actor willing and able to safeguard peace. Focusing on the European Heritage Label (EHL), a central instrument in the EU's cultural-heritage policy (see also Kaasik-Krogerus and Turunen, in this volume), this chapter investigates how the European peace narrative is told through the EHL sites, and how peace is used in attempts to build a collective identity for the EU and Europe (i.e. the EU and its member states). Simultaneously, it also pays attention to war in the EHL context, since peace heritage includes war heritage.

By appealing to the idea of cultural heritage and by framing it as European—through the EHL discussed in this chapter, as well as through other cultural-heritage initiatives, such as the European Heritage Days, Europeana, and the Europa Nostra Awards—the EU adopts a strategy typically used in nation-building processes (about nation building, see Hobsbawm and Ranger 1983; Smith 1991; Harrison 2013, 96–97) and represents itself as a state-like actor, thus aiming to strengthen its legitimacy. As an EU action, the EHL can contribute to the idea of a common past that implies that there has "always" been cooperation across state borders and that the "roots" of EU integration are located deep in the past. A teleological narrative of history is thus constructed, and the history of Europe and the EU is represented as a unified continuum. This is problematic, both in the national and

European contexts, as the assumption of continuity essentializes memory (Passerini 2011, 49). Instead of presenting history as a unilinear process and the EU as a "natural" outcome of this history, any discussions about the past should pay attention to its discontinuities and ruptures. Such an approach would enable dissonant interpretations to emerge without excluding those who do not identify with the "dominant" story.

The EHL was launched as an intergovernmental scheme in 2006 and turned into an official EU action in 2011. It is not a funding scheme, but being awarded the EHL is expected to improve the image of the sites and create cooperation among them. Since 2013, the EC has awarded 38 sites with the EHL. The action has been given two general aims: "(a) strengthening European citizens' sense of belonging to the Union, in particular that of young people, based on shared values and elements of European history and cultural heritage, as well as an appreciation of national and regional diversity; (b) strengthening intercultural dialogue" (European Parliament 2011, 3, Article 3). The aims given for the EHL sites follow these general objectives and include "highlighting their European significance [and] raising European citizens' awareness of their common cultural heritage" (European Parliament 2011, 3, Article 3). As such, the EHL, like many other EU actions, is also used as an instrument in the identity-building attempts of the EU. The assumption of citizens' "common cultural heritage" is an explicit attempt to construct a common identity for the EU through the notion of cultural heritage. Phrases such as "European citizens' sense of belonging to the Union", "shared values and elements of European history and cultural heritage" and "European significance", highlighted throughout the official EHL documents, contribute to this too.

Since the "European significance" of heritage is strongly emphasized and explicitly discussed as the justification for the EHL selections (European Parliament 2011), this chapter discusses how "peace" and "Europe" are conceptualized together and how these interconceptualizations are used to produce "European identity" in the empirical material I collected about the EHL. I analyse official EHL documents as well as websites of the EHL sites using a conceptual approach that focuses on the uses, meanings, and articulations of the concept of peace, particularly investigating the links made between peace and Europe.

I first introduce the research material and my conceptual approach to analysing it. Then, to introduce my theoretical framework, I discuss how notions of past, memory, and heritage can be seen as political.

After that I briefly sketch out the roles "peace" has played in the history of European integration. The analysis section then explores how peace is discussed in the empirical material related to the EHL. I divide the ways of peace is discussed in four thematic categories: peace treaties, institutions, practices, and symbols. Finally, I sum up how peace and Europe are conceptualized together and what conclusions can be drawn from those interconceptualizations regarding the EU's identity building.

Material and Methodological Approach

The selection of the EHL sites is based on applications by local heritage actors, first preselected by national panels and finally selected by a European panel of heritage experts appointed at the EU level. The research material for this chapter firstly includes panel reports produced during the EHL selection process during the first three selection rounds, in 2013, 2014, and 2015. The panel reports explicate the panel's justifications for its selections, and the European Commission then awards the label. Each site is described on one page in the reports. Among these site descriptions, there are nine in which peace is explicitly mentioned. I chose to perform a closer analysis of those descriptions. They discuss the following sites: Abbey of Cluny (France), Camp Westerbork (Hooghalen, Netherlands), Peace Palace (The Hague, Netherlands), European District of Strasbourg (France), The 3 May 1791 Constitution in Warsaw (Poland), Mundaneum (Mons, Belgium), The Pan-European Picnic Park in Sopron (Hungary), Robert Schuman House (Scy-Chazelles, France), and the Sites of the Peace of Westphalia in Germany (Münster and Osnabrück). In addition, I included two sites in the description of which peace is not mentioned but which are thematically linked to war: Franja Partisan Hospital (Cerkno, Slovenia) and WWI Eastern Front Cemetery No. 123 (Luzna-Putski, Poland). This chapter's analysis focuses on these EHL sites where peace and war play a role.

The EHL was monitored in 2016, and the report written by the monitoring panel is also included in the research material. Finally, in addition to the four panel and monitoring reports, the material also includes the websites of the eleven selected sites.

As a part of the EU's cultural-heritage policy, the EHL documents are here understood as part of an "authorized heritage discourse" (AHD; see also Kaasik-Krogerus, Lähdesmäki, and Turunen in this volume): linguistic practices that work "to construct a sense of what heritage is – and is not" and "structure and frame different heritage experiences and acts of remembering and commemoration" (Smith 2006, 6, 11). They construct "not only the idea of heritage but also its practices" (ibid., 12), and may be used for various purposes and for both maintaining and changing states of affairs. The producers of AHD include professionals and experts in heritage conservation, preservation, and management. AHD also includes power relations in terms of "who have the ability or authority to 'speak' about or 'for' heritage… and […] who do not" (ibid.). Crucially, within the AHD, ideas of cultural heritage can be used in identity making (ibid., 10–13). The AHD related to the EHL thus provides interesting empirical material to analyse how "European identity" is constructed.

Both identity and cultural heritage are produced through language and concepts that are used to make interpretations about the past, "us" and "others" (Burke 1962; Connolly 1989, 1992; Anderson 1999; Smith 2006). At different times, the idea of a European identity has been linguistically constructed in different ways through various elements such as traditions, histories, and myths (Serfaty 1992; Ahrweiler 1993; García 1993; Delanty 1995). If "Europe does not have an essence beyond one which is shaped by language", as Bo Stråth (2010a, 14) argues, the idea of the European identity needs to be investigated through textual materials and linguistic approaches. The identity constructions related to Europe are in this chapter thus explored by paying attention to key concepts used in the selected EHL materials, particularly that of peace.

This conceptual approach understands concepts as constructed in debates, constantly changing and contested, and therefore political. According to this perspective, concepts are always contingent and controversial in their use, meaning, content, range of reference, and normative colour (Wiesner et al. 2018). Through this approach, the chapter seeks to study the politics of the concept of peace by investigating how peace is used and constructed in the context of producing the idea of a European identity. It explores the complexities and controversies related to the conceptual relations between Europe, peace, identity, and cultural heritage in the EHL context.

This theoretical and methodological perspective is inspired by the conceptual-historical approach, familiar from political science and history. It offers heuristic tools for understanding the interrelations of political, institutional, and social changes, and for grasping changes to the meaning of concepts (Ball and Pocock 1988; Koselleck 1996, 65; Palonen 1997, 64; Skinner 1999, 60). As concepts not only describe reality but also produce it, changing interpretations of concepts both influence and indicate institutional, political, and social changes. The related controversies are hence situated at the intersections of empirical changes and changes in meaning (Koselleck 1996, 61, 65). For instance, the changing interpretation of the concept of peace had a significant influence on the empirical process of integration after WWII (Stråth 2010b, 391–396), which I will discuss after sketching my theoretical framework.

Theoretical Framework: Politics of Past, Memory, and Heritage

Memory, heritage, and identity are often discussed together, as a cluster (Waterton and Smith 2009; Kisić 2016; Delanty 2017). The term "memory complex" (Macdonald 2013), for example, refers to the close entanglement of memory, heritage, and identity. This cluster and the understanding that it is constructed through discursive practices forms the heuristic framework for the analysis in this chapter (see the Introduction to this volume). The perspectives of the politics of the past and the politics of memory provide inspiration for investigating the uses of peace in identity building within the EHL context. These perspectives share the idea that the past is contested (e.g. Stråth 2000; Hodgin and Radstone 2003). These contestations concern the interpretations and meanings attached to the past and questions around who is entitled to produce these interpretations and meanings, and which of them will gain the dominant position. The practices of history and memory are not only about the past but also about the present, and the relations between past and present are complex (ibid.). The relation between memory and its representations is mutually constitutive (Hodgin and Radstone 2003, 14). Heritage materials and practices are not merely channels through which memories are represented, but the representations themselves, such as the EHL sites discussed here, form memories too.

Which aspects of the past are chosen to be remembered and retold, and which are left in silence and oblivion, is determined through a complex political process: the field of memory can be a battlefield (Stråth 2000, 22; Passerini 2003). Official EU discourse frequently appeals to the past, and WWII and Europe's past totalitarian regimes both have a permanent place in it, but other aspects of Europe's difficult past, such as colonialism, are usually not discussed (Pakier and Stråth 2010; see Turunen, in this volume). Yet "dark" (Clarke et al. 2017) or "difficult" heritage (Macdonald 2016) is also used in collective identity-building processes in various ways.

Different modes of remembering imply different ways of perceiving and using the past. Anna Cento Bull and Hans Lauge Hansen (2016) suggest an "agonistic" remembering as an alternative to "antagonistic" and "cosmopolitan" modes of remembering. Agonistic remembering, according to them, is reflexive and dialogic, taking into consideration the past's contexts, agencies, and emotions. Unlike antagonistic remembering, which makes clear oppositions between "us" and "others", agonistic remembering is multiperspectivist. Unlike cosmopolitan remembering, which emphasizes reconciliation and may depoliticize history, it acknowledges struggles and controversies. As such, it allows for exposing the constructive and dissonant nature of both heritage and identities (Cento Bull and Hansen 2016).

The heritage associated with peace is necessarily contested, as peace always has war or conflict on its flipside. Similarly, the narrative of the EU as a peace project takes as its point of departure a highly controversial and serious conflict, WWII, yet according to this narrative, it was European integration that delivered peace. However, it is not only the heritage that is related to controversial topics that should be considered dissonant: any heritage is thoroughly dissonant, because it is a social construct constantly created and shaped by various actors according to their different political, economic, and social interests. It is dissonant because it is about utilizing selected aspects of the past to design scenarios for the future based the concerns of the present (e.g. Turnbridge and Ashworth 1996; Graham et al. 2000; Smith 2006; Graham and Howarth 2008; Harrison 2013). As such, cultural heritage inherently includes "political process of negotiation, mediation and regulation of identities, conflicts and power relations" (Kisić 2016, 57). The term "heritage dissonance" (Kisić 2016) highlights this intrinsic contestedness. Using cultural heritage in identity building is hence a conflictual process inclined to produce various borders and exclusions that are always already embedded in identity-construction processes themselves.

Governing heritage dissonance is entwined with preventing, mediating, and resolving conflicts, Kisić (2016, 271) claims in her study about heritage, conflict, and peacebuilding. Inclusive heritage discourse, suggested by Kisić (2016), would allow for a dynamic and pluralist understanding of the past. It provides space for heritage dissonance: different memories, interpretations of the past, and meanings given to heritage.

Such a heritage discourse relates heritage "to understandings and memories as practiced by diverse social groups, recognizing their active agency choices and responsibility in making and using heritage" (ibid., 281). In the context of (post-)conflict or difficult heritage, inclusive heritage discourse enables using dissonance for dialogue and intercultural mediation. Such a discourse actually has the potential to promote intercultural dialogue, a key aim of the EHL.

THE CONCEPT OF PEACE IN EUROPEAN INTEGRATION

The idea of a European confederation was already conceptually linked with peace in the eighteenth century (Stråth 2010a, 29). Earlier, too, "Europe" as an entity was connected with attempts to create peace through political, economic, and cultural cooperation (Heffernan 1998, 95). Yet as an element of the integration and of the European identity under construction, peace has been given contradictory meanings (e.g. Heffernan 1998; Orluc 2010; Stråth 2010b). After both world wars, there was a brief "dream of a pacifist Europe" but soon afterwards a conceptual change occurred: the idea of a pacifist peace was absorbed by the rhetoric of armed peace (Stråth 2010a, 19). After WWII, this conceptual change took place in the context of the Cold War (Stråth 2010b, 391). The Western camp was looking for a way to make West Germany economically strong and rearmed without posing a threat to the rest of Western Europe, and the idea of the European Coal and Steel Community was developed as a solution (ibid., 393). The purpose was to pool the production of the raw materials significant for warfare so that "any war between France and Germany becomes not merely unthinkable, but materially impossible" (Schuman Declaration 1950). The conceptual shift regarding peace thus had remarkable implications for the process of European integration.

The concept of peace also played a role in the conceptual struggle of what to call the emerging "unidentified political object" (Delors 2001, 7). In the post-war years, the "European project" was called "cooperation", "unification", and "integration". In this conceptual struggle, peace was conceptually linked to the latter. The eventual winner of the struggle, "integration" connoted a promise of preventing war and promoting peace through the intensification of communication, trade, and other economic and political networks (Stråth 2010b, 395).

Peace is mentioned at the very beginning of the Schuman Declaration (1950), a prominent post-war statement in the process of integration: "World peace cannot be safeguarded without the making of creative efforts proportionate to the dangers which threaten it. [...] this proposal will lead to the realization of the first concrete foundation of a European federation indispensable to the preservation of peace". The same goes for the treaties of Paris (1951) and Rome (1957) respectively establishing the European Coal and Steel Community and the European Economic Community. Indeed, peace, reconciliation, and solidarity were central values in the starting phase of integration (e.g. Laffan 2004). Claudia Wiesner (2008, 114–117) includes peace in the legitimating ideas, together with a constitutional tradition, peaceful foreign and security policy, borders, and a social model related to welfare-state traditions, that can be derived from the history of the European integration and might be used to make up the EU's identity.

Peace is seen as important for the EU in the more recent treaties too, though these no longer discuss it as a fundamental issue. In the Treaty of Maastricht establishing the EU, peace is mentioned at the beginning—and attached to identity—but only in the context of a common foreign, security, and defence policy. These policies are seen to strengthen "the European identity and its independence in order to promote peace, security and progress in Europe and in the world" (Treaty on European Union 1992, 1). In the Treaty of Lisbon (2007, 11), peace is mentioned as one of the aims of the Union, together with promoting the values of the Union and the well being of its peoples. It is listed among other aims such as security, sustainable development, solidarity, mutual respect among peoples, free and fair trade, elimination of poverty, human rights and the rights of the child, and observing and developing international law, including the United Nations Charter. In 2012, the EU was awarded the Nobel Peace Prize. It can be seen as a recognition of the European peace narrative but, in light of the relative decrease in significance of the concept of peace in the treaties, one wonders whether it refers more to the earlier phases of the narrative than to the EU's current peace efforts.

The narrative of European integration as a peace process can be interpreted as an attempt to create a "political heritage" for the integrating collective. According to Delanty (2010, 9), "the constitutional and democratic state, human rights and the integrity of human person, social solidarities, civil society and the critical reason associated with modern thought" are "products of the European political and cultural heritage". Peace is often mentioned in this kind of list enumerating the perceived social/political/civilizational characteristics of Europe. Here, I do not make a sharp distinction between political and cultural heritage: issues related to political systems and ideas are part of cultural heritage, and cultural heritage, in turn, is always political due to its constructed, plural, changing, and contested essence. Peace is a great example of the entanglements of the political and cultural dimensions of heritage.

Interconceptualizations of Europe and Peace in the EHL Sites

While peace is often discussed as a general and abstract value, in the EHL context it is pinpointed to concrete places. This is manifested in the monitoring panel's report that connects the Nobel Peace Prize and the EHL sites.

> In 2012, the Nobel Peace Prize was awarded to the EU. Some European Heritage Label sites remind us of battlefields and destructive periods, and of our struggles for peace. Examples are: the sites of the Peace of Westphalia and the Peace Palace, World War I East Front Cemetery No 123, Camp Westerbork and Franja Partisan hospital. (Panel Report on Monitoring 2016, 40)

After referring to the Nobel Peace Prize, some of the EHL sites are linked both to battles and destruction and to "our" efforts related to peace. The first-person plural pronoun is frequently used in EU documents. It refers to the EU, with the assumption that both the speakers and the audiences of the texts belong to it. It is a way to construct the EU as "our" community, but this type of top-down "we-speak" may also exclude some people. Hence, mentioning "our struggles for peace" is an attempt to construct the EU as "our" peacebuilding community, as well as to convince the readers that the EU is doing something for peace and that these efforts are supported by the speakers and the audiences. The quality or sufficiency of these efforts is not problematized.

The meanings attached to peace in the EHL discourses analysed here can be divided in four thematic categories: peace treaties, institutions, practices, and symbols. These meanings can be understood as different aspects of peace-related heritage that constitute a "memory complex" (Macdonald 2013). Memory complex as a concept draws attention to how heritage is always constructed through various practices, effects, and materializations, as well as human and non-human and conceptual and physical elements, and how different elements attached to heritage can constitute complex assemblages. As such, it combines the tangible and intangible aspects of heritage. It can be conceived as "the memory-heritage-identity complex" (ibid., 5), and an analysis of the various meanings given to peace in the EHL discourse can hence shed light on the ways of peace is used in identity construction.

Peace Treaties and Conventions

Some of the EHL sites focus on peace treaties. The sites of the Peace of Westphalia in Germany include the towns Münster and Osnabrück. The cores of the site are the town halls of both cities, where the Peace of Westphalia (1648) was negotiated. The treaty marked both the end of the Thirty-Year War, which involved several European countries, and that of the Eighty-Year War between the Netherlands and Spain. The central ideas attached to the treaty in the panel report are agreeing to peace through diplomatic negotiations instead of force, accepting religious tolerance as the basis of international relations, and securing sovereign rights for peripheral states. According to the panel report, the effects of the treaties are still present in international law and relations today (Panel Report 2014, 9).

The site itself is given a European frame. On the city of Münster's website (Peace of Westphalia 2018), the cities of Münster and Osnabrück are associated with "the new European order" and its "principle of tolerance through dialogue". According to Osnabrück's website (Friedenstadt 2018), the peace of Westphalia developed something entirely new: the European idea, which included seeking a general peace order to promote trade and cultural exchange in Europe. The hope for peace as formulated in the peace treaty became, according to the website, a model for subsequent conferences on peace, security, and cooperation in Europe. The idea of Europe has indeed been connected to the desire to avoid war through international cooperation. Yet the ways of trying to avoid war—and organize Europe—have largely been based on the balance of power, which was a core objective of the Treaty of Westphalia (Heffernan 1998, 92–94). In the doctrine of the balance of power, the idea of peace remains vague, as the balance between competing states is more central, resulting in dissonant interpretations of peace and its heritagization.

On the Osnabrück website, the European, local, and regional is intertwined, and the local is represented *as* European. The introductory text about the reception of the EHL starts with a question bringing together Osnabrück and Europe: "What has the Townhall of Osnabrück to do with the united Europe of the 21st century?" (Kulturerbe Siegel 2018). As an answer, it is emphasized that Osnabrück is "a European community" in which "the European idea still plays a specific role today and the awareness of young people of the European identity becomes stronger", echoing the official EHL objectives. Osnabrück's cultural activities and its participation in transborder associations such as the Euregio are also presented as fostering the process of European unification. The heritage related to the peace treaty is used for identity building at the local level, and critical reflection on the national-socialist past is seen as a building block in Osnabrück's profile as a peace town as well (Erinnerungskultur 2018). On the Website of Münster, the Münster town hall is depicted as a central place for residents and visitors (Peace of Westphalia 2018). Nevertheless, though both of them associate it with the Peace of Westphalia, their interpretations may differ between and among the two groups.

The Peace Palace in The Hague in the Netherlands commemorates the conventions signed during the peace conferences of 1899 and 1907. These conventions were multilateral treaties that include the Convention for the Pacific Settlement of International Disputes, as well as laws and regulations for the conduct of warfare and for war crimes. Even though these peace conferences and conventions included countries outside Europe, the European dimension of the Peace Palace is clearly emphasized in the panel report (2013, 5) and in the monitoring report (2016, 22): the Peace Palace highlights "the significance of Europe's efforts in the complex and long-term process of building and strengthening peace and justice". In the monitoring report (ibid.), the site is given the task "to further strengthen the important message of peace as a core value of the European Union", and to emphasize "peace as a result of the common willingness for cooperation and as a shared European value". The wish to settle international conflicts with the help of law and justice is also given long and "European" roots on the website of the Peace Palace itself (Vredespaleis 2018): it "can be traced back to European history and traditions". This exemplifies the European peace narrative as going beyond the EU. According to this narrative, solving conflicts peacefully is deeply embedded in "European history and tradition", and the Peace Palace continues this narrative. (It is of course equally possible to claim that it was wars that were central to "European history and tradition".) The EU does not have anything to do with the Peace Palace, but by awarding the EHL, the EU seeks to join in this narrative, thereby supporting the idea of European integration as a peace process.

Peace Institutions

On their websites, some of the sites present themselves as homes to present-day peace institutions. The Peace Palace houses the International Court of Justice and the Permanent Court of Arbitration. Regarding the sites of the Peace of Westphalia, many trans-regional peace organizations have their offices in Osnabrück (Friedenstadt 2018). In Münster, a peace prize is given every other year. In the prize's documentation, peace is explicitly linked to European integration, as it is given to individuals in the realm of politics or economy who have specifically been involved in the European integration, yet it does not explain why the winner of the prize needs to act in the field of European integration, rather than in any other field. The goals of the prize are also defined in relation to Europe: the prize aims to contribute to the discussion about the internal structure of Europe and the coexistence of people in Europe (Preis des westphälischen Friedens 2018). The site is thereby attached to the European peace narrative even though the site itself refers to times in which the narrative had not yet been invented. Conceptualizations like this link peace to European integration and represent that integration as a peace process.

Two EHL sites that focus directly on EU integration, the European District of Strasbourg and the Robert Schuman house, are also linked with peace. The institutions located in the European district of Strasbourg include the Council of Europe, the European Court of Human Rights, and the European Parliament. They were all, according to the panel report, established to maintain peace. A list of values including human rights, democracy, and the rule of law is attached to the institutions too.

> Bilingual Strasbourg has a symbolic location in the centre of Europe. After the Second World War, European institutions created for maintaining peace were housed in an area which became the European district of Strasbourg. These institutions are the drivers of European consolidation; they are central to the strengthening of human rights and to the defence of democratic values and the rule of law. (Panel Report 2015, 12)

Strasbourg admittedly has a "symbolic location" on the border between France and Germany as one of the key battlefields in World Wars I and II. Hence it is at the core of the European peace narrative about the EU integration, tying together France and Germany to prevent wars. The Robert Schuman house, the home of one of the founding figures of European integration, is also located close to the French–German border. It is said to contribute to the promotion of "the values of peace and international cooperation" (Panel Report 2014, 17). Through these kinds of sites, and particularly by conceptualizing them as places of peace, the panel reports seek to illustrate that peace has been a central value of the integration process since its inception. However, the conceptions of the EU as an institution of peace and integration as a peace process have also been questioned (see Turunen, in this volume).

Peace Practices

On the websites of several EHL sites, peace is also understood in terms of practical activities. In Münster, an event series called "Münster 1648: Dialogues for Peace" takes place yearly. According to the city's website, "Münster uses its history to take responsibility for the present and the future in issues related to the crisis areas of the present day and to develop new methods for conflict mediation, conflict resolution, and securing peace" (Dialoge zum Frieden 2018). The past related to peace is thus used to find ways of dealing with present-day crises and building peace. Osnabrück organizes peace talks too (Friedensgespräche 2018).

As a form of "peace work", Osnabrück has established an exchange of young "town ambassadors" with its partner towns in other countries. It has also adopted a "scheme of fostering the peace culture" as a result of an "active peace-political work". "Peace culture" includes a wide range of events and activities related to topics from tolerance and interculturality to ecological responsibility and equality between rich and poor countries (Friedenstadt 2018). It is also committed to a "culture of remembrance" commemorating the victims of national socialism (Erinnerungskultur 2018). Through these practices, the cities' peace heritage is connected to the conflicts and controversies of today.

The idea of peace represented by the Mundaneum, an archive and documentation centre in Mons, Belgium, is practical: peace should be sought through culture, dialogue, and sharing knowledge at the European and international level by the means of bibliographic enquiry (Panel Report 2015, 12). The peace practices of the Mundaneum include exhibitions and peace classes. Ongoing peace practices are highlighted in the report's description of the Peace Palace in The Hague as well: "every single day, people are working to establish peace here, in Europe and the rest of the world" (Panel Report 2013, 5). The Palace also serves as a venue for events in international law and politics.

These practices can be seen as ways to use the past in the present and make it feel more concrete and "alive". It remains unclear, however, whether they provide space for different interpretations of the heritage itself. Based on Kisić's (2016) analysis of heritage interventions in a post-conflict situation, we know that heritage practices can provide an arena to tackle a difficult past if they acknowledge heritage dissonance and enable an inclusive heritage discourse. There are but few hints to such heritage practices in the EHL documents. Camp Westerbork plans "to adapt the discourse to a larger variety of cultural and historic backgrounds" (Panel Report 2013, 8), which can be seen as a reference to heritage dissonance. The plan of the European District to "make a participatory documentary about Europe in Strasbourg" (Panel Report 2015, 14) implies the notion of an inclusive heritage discourse and a participatory approach to cultural heritage. Such practices may bring together authorized and inclusive heritage discourses, but not necessarily overcome the power imbalance between the two.

Peace Symbols

In the process of constructing identities, values are often utilized. It is common for official EU documents to list values and depict these as characteristic of the EU and Europe (terms often used synonymously) (see also Lähdesmäki, in this volume). Such lists typically include peace.

The EHL documents make a close link between peace—and other values—and the EHL sites: "The sites tell stories about Europe but with a focus on values, peace, democracy, human rights…" (Panel Report on Monitoring 2016, 36). According to the report (ibid., 5), "Even outside of Europe, the sites are strong symbols of peace, the rule of law, welfare and democracy". The material sites are here tightly interlinked with abstract values and principles. However, the sites not only "tell stories" about values, peace, and other principles, but also ones explicitly "about Europe" (ibid., 36; see Turunen, in this volume). These examples show how the official EU discourse can simultaneously represent the EHL sites as symbols of peace and of the idea of Europe. Both peace and Europe are abstract and complex ideas, and while material sites admittedly can narrativize some aspects of them, they also inevitably simplify them. No site can symbolize all the interpretations different actors have of Europe and of peace. This indicates the key struggle, inherent to heritage, about whose stories are told and whose are not.

The category of peace symbols in the EHL material overlaps with the other three categories. Thus, the panel report highlights the symbolic dimension of the Peace Palace in addition to the peace practices, conventions, and institutions it hosts (2013, 5). And the monitoring report states: "The Peace Palace is thus an icon and a symbol of Peace and Justice in Europe and in the world, a 'Peace Shrine'" (2016, 22). Similarly, the 3 May 1791 Constitution in Warsaw, Poland, the first democratically adopted constitution in Europe, by the Polish-Lithuanian Commonwealth, is described as "a symbol of democratic and peaceful transformation of a political system", which is explicitly defined as "part of the European ideals" (Panel Report on Monitoring 2016, 19; Panel Report 2014, 11).

The sites of the Peace of Westphalia are also seen as "a symbol of peace achieved through international negotiations" (Panel Report on Monitoring 2016, 18). The Pan-European Picnic Park in Sopron, Hungary, commemorates a peaceful freedom protest in 1989 when the border between Hungary and Austria was symbolically opened for a few hours. This event—which in a very concrete and practical way started as a mass picnic—"has become a symbol of breaking down the fence system between countries", according to the Panel Report (2015, 5). The site is described as "a strong symbol of the end of the Cold War and of a borderless Europe" (Panel Report 2014, 20) and thereby linked to the freedom of mobility, a core idea of European integration.

Mobility is here—like in many other EU documents—celebrated as a great achievement of integration, without taking into account its controversiality and exclusive nature (see the chapters by Kaasik-Krogerus, Proglio, and Trakilović, in this volume). The Pan-European Picnic Park exemplifies how the panel reports conceptualize the "European significance" of several sites through cross-border mobility, cooperation, and the cross-border context of the site.

The Mundaneum is described as "a landmark in the intellectual and social fabric of Europe", the holdings of which "trace the evolution of values now fundamental to Europe, in particular peace through culture" (Panel Report 2015, 12). At the Mundaneum's website (Expositions 2018), peace and Europe are interconceptualized: "the project of European integration […] and the project of the founders of Mundaneum [are] born from the same ideal: peace through culture". The Mundaneum is located in the context of the European integration, and both are said to share the idea of peace.

Sites referring to war are also used as symbols of peace in the EHL context. Camp Westerbork in Hooghalen, the Netherlands, is a site with a multilayered history. Before, during, and after WWII, it was used as a camp for Jewish refugees from Central Europe, as a deportation camp for Jews and Sinti and Roma gypsies, as a prison for Nazis awaiting trial after the war, as temporary accommodation for the Dutch coming back from the West Indies at the end of the colonization period, and as a refugee camp for South Moluccans until the end of 1960s. This site demonstrates that mobility, a core idea of European integration unproblematically highlighted in the EU documents, is anything but unequivocal, and thus that any heritage related to it is deeply dissonant.

The discussions about Camp Westerbork indicate that "dark" (Clarke et al. 2017) or "difficult" heritage (Macdonald 2016), which explicitly refer to troubling pasts, can also be utilized to construct the idea of the European identity. In the official EHL documents, the site with its supposedly "shared European memories" is represented as a nexus of peace, memory, and the EU.

> The site supports the "Culture of Peace and Reconciliation" through shared European memories. Its layered history and relevance is an invitation to reflect on the values on which the European Union is built. The European significance is clearly articulated in the site's narrative. (Panel Report on Monitoring 2016, 25; Panel Report 2013, 8)

Inviting the readers to reflect on the values can be interpreted as an attempt for an inclusive heritage discourse (Kisić 2016) in which the process of European integration could be contemplated from the perspective of its core values. However, it is not specified who can be involved, what those values are, or whether they can be questioned. In another panel report (2015, 5), Camp Westerbork is connected to the current migration situation, saying that sites like this "can help contextualise recent events from the perspective of European history and may help European citizens to deepen their understanding". The EU's external border policies and migration discussions currently do raise questions about the values of the EU, and these questions could indeed be contemplated in light of the contested histories related to sites such as Camp Westerbork. Such sites have the potential to increase understanding about various types of mobility as a historical phenomenon and stimulate empathy towards refugees, but this potential is hardly explicitly discussed in the EHL materials analysed here. Nor are the stories of migrants themselves referred to in the official EHL documents, which shows how demarcations and exclusions are always embedded in identity-building processes.

Two other EHL sites that focus specifically on war are also used as symbols of peace. Franja Partisan Hospital in Cerkno, Slovenia, was built by the Yugoslav underground army in the territories occupied by the Nazi Germany. Operating in secrecy during WWII, it is described as "an outstanding symbol of human fortitude and medical care, of solidarity and companionship in hardship, between staff and wounded, from various nationalities and from the enemy" (Panel Report 2014, 16). The WWI Eastern Front Cemetery No. 123 in Luzna—Putski, Poland, was established near the Eastern Front battlefields between the Austro-Hungarian and German armies and the Russian army. The cemetery is described as "a tangible reminder of World War I [and] the heritage of the Eastern Front" (Panel Report 2015, 13). Both sites are introduced with emphasis on the coexistence of national, linguistic, religious, and military diversity. Emphasizing the diversity of population groups related to the sites is a way to construct their "European significance" (Lähdesmäki and Mäkinen 2019). Both of them are represented as symbols of peace through concepts like solidarity, companionship, equal respect, and reconciliation. The dissonant heritage of the camp, the hospital, and the cemetery is thus used for telling the European peace narrative.

European Peace Narrative: Harmonious and Dissonant

Heritage related to peace is inherently "dark" (Clarke et al. 2017) and "difficult" (Macdonald 2016), as it includes war heritage. This "dissonant heritage" (Turnbridge and Ashworth 1996; Graham et al. 2000) of peace is inevitably present in the EHL sites. For instance, the sites of the Peace of Westphalia represent the end of war, and the Pan-European Picnic Park symbolizes the end of the Cold War. The Peace Palace and European District of Strasbourg focus on the preventing and regulating war, and the Mundaneum and Robert Schuman House refer to preventing war through practices. Moreover, war is the explicit topic of Camp Westerbork, Franja Partisan Hospital, and the WWI Eastern Front Cemetery No. 123. In the AHD of the EHL, they are also used to help construct the European peace narrative by describing them with concepts referring to reconciliation and solidarity. This demonstrates how the peace narrative mobilizes "dark heritage" and uses as a "soft power" to construct the identity of the EU as a promotor of peace (Clarke et al. 2017).

Following the clear goal defined for the EHL to foster belonging to Europe, the official EHL documents emphasize the European significance of the sites: the European spatial layer is given a dominant position, even though it would be equally meaningful to discuss both peace and heritage in other spatial frameworks or from more non-spatial perspectives. The websites of some of the sites themselves do mention the local, regional, national, global, and individual scales. In both the EHL and the sites' documentation, though, these other scales are often narrated as European. The intrinsic multiscalarity of the EHL sites refers to the dissonance of cultural heritage through the implicit controversies between the scales: actors at local, regional and national level may interpret the same past events in different or even contradictory ways. Explicitly, however, the European peace narrative constructed in the EHL documents primarily appears as a harmonious one. The more local stories and representations only appear as building blocks within the idea of European identity. When peace is conceptually framed as European and pinpointed to the EHL sites, both the individual EHL sites and the entirety of Europe—or at least the EU and its member states—are depicted as spaces of peace. In the EHL materials explored here, Europe is created as a discursive and imaginary space, but the concrete sites labelled European are also used to produce it as a material space that can be experienced and felt by visitors (see Lähdesmäki 2016; Passerini 2010, 60–61). Peace heritage is thereby constituted as a "memory complex" (Macdonald 2013) combining tangible and intangible aspects of heritage. The spatialities of the peace narrative are thus employed in the identity construction.

Through the lists of values and principles attached to the sites of "European significance", Europe is depicted as the cradle and protector of those values and principles. This demonstrates the use of values in producing the European identity (Laffan 2004, 75–76). And value as a concept is indeed used repeatedly in the EHL discourse, often prefaced with the adjectives "European" or "common". As such, the EHL discourse does not include "a critical and reflexive distance to value production, where the values are under constant negotiation and transformation", which, according to Stråth (2010a, 18) could alternatively be seen as an indication of "a European culture" rather than the idea of universal values.

Another common way of producing a European identity, the appropriation of the concept of Europe (Laffan 2004, 75–76), is also constantly employed in the EHL discourse analysed here. The concept of Europe is frequently used and equated with the EU and its member states. It is used as an attribute of the most variegated matters—such as memories, history, ideals, values, and peacebuilding efforts—in order to conceptually produce the "European significance" of the sites. "European" thus appears as a natural and fitting attribute of any sphere of life. A ritualistic repetition of this European dimension is typical for the EHL texts and for EU discourse in general, and can be interpreted as a banal way of producing identity (Billig 1995). It produces the image of Europe as something familiar and close, and as a relevant framework for citizens' activities and identifications. Simultaneously, it excludes those who do not share the same conceptualizations, for instance the same interpretations of history.

The multilayered histories of the EHL sites are controversial and contested, and so are the present activities of the EU, but in the AHD of the EU, the cultural heritage related to peace is depicted as harmonious and consensual. By referring to this peace-related heritage and discussing it in an uncontroversial manner with a strong European framing, the EU positions itself in a long chain of previous peace projects as a relevant agent in peacebuilding. This harmonious and Eurocentric narrative represents the EU as something very positive and easy to identify with.

At the same time, it does not leave room for the complexity and multivocality of heritage, and may hamper a nuanced discussion of the past and its significance for the present.

Few would be against peace, which makes it an especially viable tool for identity construction. However, despite all its positive meanings, there is no actual agreement about the concept of peace. For example, in Europe peace has primarily meant attempts to avoid and regulate wars within the doctrine of the balance of power (Heffernan 1998). Hence, even though "Europe" has been constructed out of the idea of peace, Europe's wars have just as much shaped the idea of what a "European identity" may be (ibid.). The EHL sites' dissonant and multilayered histories might enable discussion on the different interpretations of peace, the past, and the current conflicts, as well as their role in identity construction. In the official EHL documents, these questions are mostly not discussed, even though dialogue is stated as a key goal in the EHL Action and EU policies more broadly. Instead, some EHL sites, such as the Mundaneum, the Peace Palace, and the Sites of the Peace of Westphalia, do take up some of these questions on their websites and link the peace heritage to current contestations.

Hence, there are different types of AHD (Smith 2006) at play in the context of the EHL. The discourse in the official EHL documents frequently interconceptualizes peace and Europe, offers consensual interpretations of the past, smooths over conflicts, and constructs a harmonious narrative combining peace and Europe, thus narrowing the space for debate on the past and its relation to the present. This harmonious narrative resembles the cosmopolitan mode of remembering criticized by Cento Bull and Hansen (2016): it depoliticizes the past and does not acknowledge the contestedness and politicality of cultural heritage. Such a harmonious narrative deviates from the dissent and conflict that also underlies the European integration process (e.g. Stråth 2000, 2010a). On the other hand, the websites of the sites themselves sometimes do provide alternative or more complex narratives by mentioning several spatial frameworks, by linking peace with the current concerns, or by discussing both past and present conflicts. They thus make space for a more agonistic way of remembering, as supported by Cento Bull and Hansen (2016), and hence provide inspiration for thinking about the idea of European identity and heritage in terms of dissent.

However, neither the official documents nor the EHL sites' websites provide a discursive space that is "thought provoking, de-naturalizing, non-dogmatic and include multi-vocal narratives" (Kisić 2016, 281) or can articulate the idea of heritage dissonance in the European peace narrative. At different times in Europe, democracy was one of the key concepts within utopias of peace, but its relationship to peace has always been complex (Stråth 2016, 421). I argue that if the EHL seeks to use heritage sites to tell its narrative of peace, it be more sustainable if democracy was not only mentioned as a value but also concretely enabled in the discussions around heritage by opening space for inclusive and participatory meaning-making and decision-making concerning heritage in particular. For example, the websites of the EHL and the individual sites could be used as interactive platforms for participation and dialogue, allowing visitors and locals to upload their stories, both texts and images, about the heritage.

Conclusions: Building Identity Through a European Peace Heritage

In the EHL documents and on the websites of the EHL sites, peace is depicted as one of the indispensable, core elements of the EU. The frequent use of the concept of peace reproduces the European peace narrative related to European integration since its inception. All the meanings given to peace are located in a European framework. This supports the peace narrative and contributes to the idea of a European peace heritage. The peace narrative is used as a constitutive story (Ringmar 1996) to legitimize the EU, and shape its identity as a stable and justifiable actor.

Peace is given various meanings in the official EHL documents and on the websites of the EHL sites themselves: The Peace Palace, the Sites of the Peace of Westphalia, and the Abbey of Cluny focus on peace treaties and negotiations, and the 3 May 1791 Constitution on the peaceful transformation of a political system. The Peace Palace and the European District of Strasbourg represent institutions for promoting peace. The Mundaneum is about promoting peace through practices and institutions related to knowledge, and the Robert Schuman House refers to the idea of creating peace through practices and institutions of economic integration. The Pan-European Picnic Park commemorates a peaceful freedom protest for breaking down the fence system between the Western and Soviet blocks. Camp Westerbork, Franja Partisan Hospital, and the WWI Eastern Front Cemetery No. 123 reflect a history of war and conflict and are used as symbols of peace and reconciliation.

A range of different aspects of peace is attached to the EHL sites in various combinations. Material, concrete, physical, and practical aspects of cultural heritage are present in sites commemorating peace treaties, negotiations, and institutions, as well as practices related to peace or war. Abstract and imagined aspects of peace heritage are to some extent present in all the sites discussed here, as many of the sites are explicitly conceptualized as symbols of peace. For instance, the symbolic dimensions of the Peace Palace, the 3 May 1791 Constitution, the sites of the Peace of Westphalia, and the Pan-European Picnic Park are highlighted alongside their more concrete aspects. Tangible and intangible dimensions of heritage are thus intertwined in the EHL sites, and all the sites together form a "memory complex" (Macdonald 2013) related to peace. The coexistence of several elements—such as values, institutions, and concrete, practical activity—in one site can be seen as an indication of heritage dissonance, which, according to Kisić (2016, 57), refers not only to contradictions but also to unusual combinations embedded in heritage.

Despite this conceptual variation, the EHL discourse's dominant mode of presenting the past is as harmonious and consensual, omitting contradictions, which is typical for an AHD (Smith 2006; see also the chapter by Lähdesmäki, in this volume). Remembering war and discussing peace heritage could be used as an invitation to act towards building peace. In the EHL materials explored here, such an invitation is not clear, although peace to some extent is linked to present-day conflicts. Instead of providing space for dissonant interpretations, Europe and peace are interconceptualized in an unquestioned way.

Acknowledgements This work was supported by the European Research Council (ERC) under the EU's Horizon 2020 Research and Innovation Programme under Grant 636177 (EUROHERIT). The content of this chapter does not reflect the official opinion of the European Union. Responsibility for the information and views expressed in the chapter lies entirely with the author.

References

Research Material

EHL Documents
European Parliament. 2011. Decision No. 1194/2011/EU of the European Parliament and of the Council of 16 November 2011 Establishing a European Union Action for the European Heritage Label. *Official Journal of the European Union* 303: 1–9.

Panel Report. 2013. *European Heritage Label.* Brussels: European Commission.
Panel Report. 2014. *European Heritage Label.* Brussels: European Commission.
Panel Report. 2015. *European Heritage Label.* Brussels: European Commission.
Panel Report on Monitoring. 2016. *European Heritage Label.* Brussels: European Commission.

Other EU Documents
Declaration on European Identity. 1973. *Bulletin of the European Communities*, December, No. 12: 118–122. Luxembourg: Office for Official Publications of the European Communities.
Delors, Jacques. 2001. Where Is the European Union Heading? http://www.notre-europe.eu/uploads/tx_publication/DiscoursIV01-en.pdf. Accessed 22 November 2017.
Schuman Declaration. 1950. https://europa.eu/european-union/about-eu/symbols/europe-day/schuman-declaration_en. Accessed 18 June 2018.
The Treaty of Paris. 1951. Treaty Establishing the Coal and Steel Community. http://sixthformlaw.info/06_misc/europe/04_treay_of_paris_1951.htm. Accessed 18 June 2018.
Treaty of Rome. 1957. Traité instituant la Communauté Économique Européenne. http://eur-lex.europa.eu/legalcontent/EN/TXT/?qid=1490687157391anduri=CELEX:11957E/TXT. Accessed 28 March 2017.
Treaty on European Union. 1992. *Official Journal of the European Communities*, C191, Volume 35, 29 July.
Treaty of Lisbon. 2007. *Official Journal of the European Communities*, C306, Volume 50, 17 December.

Websites of the EHL Sites
Dialoge zum Frieden. 2018. http://www.stadt-muenster.de/tourismus/westfaelischer-frieden/dialoge-zum-frieden.html. Accessed 18 June 2018.
Erinnerungskultur. 2018. http://www.osnabrueck.de/friedenskultur/kultur-des-friedens/erinnerungskultur.html. Accessed 18 June 2018.
Expositions. 2018. http://expositions.mundaneum.org/en/european-heritage-label. Accessed 18 June 2018.
Friedensgespräche. 2018. http://www.osnabrueck.de/friedenskultur/kultur-des-friedens/osnabruecker-friedensgespraeche.html. Accessed 18 June 2018.
Friedenstadt. 2018. http://www.osnabrueck.de/tourismus/wissens-und-sehenswertes/friedensstadt.html. Accessed 18 June 2018.
Kulturerbe Siegel. 2018. http://www.osnabrueck.de/kulturerbe-siegel.html. Accessed 18 June 2018.
Peace of Westphalia. 2018. http://www.stadt-muenster.de/en/tourismus/peace-of-westphalia/the-european-heritage-label.html. Accessed 18 June 2018.

Preis des westphälischen Friedens. 2018. http://www.stadt-muenster.de/tourismus/westfaelischer-frieden/preis-des-westfaelischen-friedens.html. Accessed 18 June 2018.

Vredespaleis. 2018. https://www.vredespaleis.nl/building/european-heritage-label/?lang=en. Accessed 18 June 2018.

LITERATURE

Ahrweiler, H. 1993. Roots and Trends in European Culture. In *European Identity and the Search for Legitimacy*, ed. S. García, 30–45. London: Pinter.

Anderson, B. 1999 [1983]. *Imagined Communities: Reflections on the Origin and Spread of Nationalism*. London and New York: Verso.

Ball, T., and J.G.A. Pocock (eds.). 1988. *Conceptual Change and the Constitution*. Lawrence, KS: University Press of Kansas.

Billig, M. 1995. *Banal Nationalism*. London: Sage.

Burke, K. 1962. *A Grammar of Motives and a Rhetoric of Motives*. Cleveland: World Publishing Company.

Cento Bull, A., and H.L. Hansen. 2016. On Agonistic Memory. *Memory Studies* 9 (4): 390–404.

Clarke, D., A. Cento Bull, and M. Deganutti. 2017. Soft Power and Dark Heritage: Multiple Potentialities. *International Journal of Cultural Policy* 23 (6): 660–674.

Connolly, W. 1989. Identity and Difference in Global Politics. In *International/Intertextual Relations: Postmodern Readings for World Politics*, ed. J. Der Derian and M. Shapiro, 232–343. Lexington, MA: Lexington Books.

Connolly, W. 1992 [1991]. *Identity/Difference: Democratic Negotiations of Political Paradox*. Ithaca and London: Cornell University Press.

Delanty, G. 1995. *Inventing Europe: Idea, Identity, Reality*. Chatham, Kent: Macmillan Press.

Delanty, G. 2010. The European Heritage from a Critical Cosmopolitan Perspective. LSE 'Europe in Question' Discussion Paper Series No. 19/2010. London: London School of Economics and Political Science.

Delanty, G. 2017. *The European Heritage: A Critical Re-interpretation*. London: Routledge.

García, S. 1993. Europe's Fragmented Identities and the Frontiers of Citizenship. In *European Identity and the Search for Legitimacy*, ed. S. García, 1–29. London: Pinter.

Graham, B., and P. Howard. 2008. Heritage and Identity. In *The Ashgate Research Companion to Heritage and Identity*, 1–18. Burlington: Ashgate.

Graham, B., G.J. Ashworth, and J.E. Turnbridge. 2000. *A Geography of Heritage: Power, Culture and Economy*. Abingdon and New York: Routledge.

Harrison, R. 2013. *Heritage: Critical Approaches*. London and New York: Routledge.

Heffernan, M. 1998. War and the Shaping of Europe. In *Modern Europe: Place, Culture and Identity*, ed. B. Graham, 89–120. London: Arnold.

Hobsbawm, E., and T. Ranger. 1983. *The Invention of Tradition*. Cambridge: Cambridge University Press.

Hodgin, K., and S. Radstone (eds.). 2003. *Contested Pasts: The Politics of Memory*. New York: Routledge.

Kisić, V. 2016. *Governing Heritage Dissonance: Promises and Realities of Selected Cultural Policies*. Amsterdam: European Cultural Foundation.

Koselleck, R. 1996. A Response to a Comment on Geschichtliche Grundbegriffe. In *The Meaning of Historical Terms and Concepts: New Studies on Begriffsgeschichte*, ed. H. Lehmann and M. Richter, 59–70. Washington, DC: German Historical Institute.

Laffan, B. 2004. The European Union and Its Institutions as 'Identity Builders'. In *Transnational Identities: Becoming European in the EU*, ed. R.K. Herrmann, T. Risse, and M.B. Brewer, 75–96. Lanham: Rowman & Littlefield.

Lähdesmäki, T. 2016. Politics of Tangibility, Intangibility, and Place in the Making of a European Cultural Heritage in EU Heritage Policy. *International Journal of Heritage Studies* 22 (10): 766–780.

Lähdesmäki, T. 2018. Founding Myths of European Union Europe and the Workings of Power in the European Union Heritage and History Initiatives. *European Journal of Cultural Studies*, 1–18. https://doi.org/10.1177/1367549418755921.

Lähdesmäki, T., and K. Mäkinen. 2019. The 'European Significance' of Heritage: Politics of Scale in EU Heritage Policy Discourse. In *Politics of Scale: A New Approach to Heritage Studies*, ed. T. Lähdesmäki, S. Thomas, and Y. Zhu, 36–49. New York: Berghahn.

Macdonald, S. 2013. *Memorylands: Heritage and Identity in Europe Today*. London and New York: Routledge.

Macdonald, S. 2016. Is "Difficult Heritage" Still "Difficult"? Why Public Acknowledgement of Past Perpetration May No Longer Be so Unsettling to Collective Identities. *Museum International* 265–268: 6–22.

Orluc, K. 2010. Decline or Renaissance: The Transformation of European Consciousness After the First World War. In *Europe and the Other and Europe as the Other*, ed. B. Stråth, 123–155. Brussels: PIE-Peter Lang.

Pakier, M., and B. Stråth. 2010. Introduction: A European Memory. In *A European Memory? Contested Histories and Politics of Remembrance*, ed. M. Pakier and B. Stråth, 1–20. New York and Oxford: Berghahn.

Palonen, K. 1997. An Application of Conceptual History to Itself: From Method to Theory in Reinhart Koselleck's Begriffsgeschichte. *Redescriptions (Finnish Yearbook of Political Thought)* 1: 39–69.

Passerini, L. 2003. Memories Between Silence and Oblivion. In *Contested Pasts: The Politics of Memory*, ed. K. Hodgin and S. Radstone, 238–254. New York: Routledge.
Passerini, L. 2010. The Last Identification: Why Some of Us Like to Call Ourselves Europeans and What We Mean by This. In *Europe and the Other and Europe as the Other*, ed. B. Stråth, 45–65. Brussels: PIE-Peter Lang.
Passerini, L. 2011. The Ethics of European Memory: What Is to Be Done? *Moving Worlds* 11 (2): 48–56.
Ringmar, E. 1996. *Identity, Interest and Action: A Cultural Explanation of Sweden's Intervention in the Thirty Years War*. Cambridge: Cambridge University Press.
Serfaty, S. 1992. *Understanding Europe: The Politics of Unity*. London: Pinter.
Skinner, Q. 1999. Rhetoric and Conceptual Change. *Redescriptions (Finnish Yearbook of Political Thought)* 3 (1): 60–73.
Smith, A. 1991. *National Identity*. London: Penguin Books.
Smith, L. 2006. *Uses of Heritage*. London and New York: Routledge.
Stråth, B. (ed.). 2000. *Myth and Memory on the Construction of Community: Historical Patterns in Europe and Beyond*. Brussels: PIE-Peter Lang.
Stråth, B. 2010a [2000]. Introduction: Europe as a Discourse. In *Europe and the Other and Europe as the Other*, ed. B. Stråth, 13–44. Brussels: PIE-Peter Lang.
Stråth, B. 2010b [2000]. Multiple Europes: Integration, Identity and Demarcation to the Other. In *Europe and the Other and Europe as the Other*, ed. B. Stråth, 385–420. Brussels: PIE-Peter Lang.
Stråth, B. 2016. *Europe's Utopia's of Peace: 1815, 1919, 1951*. London and New York: Bloomsbury Academic.
Turnbridge, J.E., and G.J. Ashworth. 1996. *Dissonant Heritage: The Management of the Past as a Resource in Conflict*. Chichester: Wiley.
Waterton, E., and L. Smith. 2009. There Is No Such Thing as Heritage. In *Taking Archaeology out of Heritage*, ed. E. Waterton and L. Smith, 10–27. Cambridge: Cambridge Scholars Publishing.
Wiesner, C. 2008. Democratic Legitimacy, Democratisation and Democratic Identity of the European Union—Old Questions, New Challenges. *Redescriptions, Journal of the Finnish Centre of Excellence on Political Thought and Conceptual Change* 12 (1): 96–122.
Wiesner, C., A. Björk, H. Kivistö, and K. Mäkinen (eds.). 2018. *Shaping Citizenship: A Political Concept in Theory, Debate and Practice*. London: Routledge.

Open Access This chapter is licensed under the terms of the Creative Commons Attribution 4.0 International License (http://creativecommons.org/licenses/by/4.0/), which permits use, sharing, adaptation, distribution and reproduction in any medium or format, as long as you give appropriate credit to the original author(s) and the source, provide a link to the Creative Commons license and indicate if changes were made.

The images or other third party material in this chapter are included in the chapter's Creative Commons license, unless indicated otherwise in a credit line to the material. If material is not included in the chapter's Creative Commons license and your intended use is not permitted by statutory regulation or exceeds the permitted use, you will need to obtain permission directly from the copyright holder.

CHAPTER 4

Europe's Peat Fire: Intangible Heritage and the Crusades for Identity

Rob van der Laarse

What's in a Song?

Europe, Oh Europe is the title of a yet-to-be-released road movie by the successful Greek filmmaker Elina Psykou on the hopes and fears of five young Europeans travelling through their countries while discussing recent laws on gay rights, euthanasia, abortion, and the like. Although this is mostly what I found on her Creative Europe-funded project, it strikes me that her project actually addresses the currently much-debated European dream, as defined by its idealist, progressive agenda, in a wish of "shedding light on the competing forces which can hold the European Union together or push it towards division" (*Europe,*

Oh Europe; Elina Psykou). This is indeed what's at stake, and one may wonder if the transnational dream of Europeanization will ever be able to overcome the dividing persistence of the nation state as long as cultures will be perceived as fixed identities instead of dynamic configurations.

Thus my Dutch family members cherish the memory of a local brass band in a remote Austrian mountain village, where our friendship with the *Kapelmeister* turned the *gemütlichkeit* on a Sunday morning village square into a kind of backstage tourism experience (for an ethnographic description of the community and its brass band, see Steiner and Benedik 2005, and for backstage experiencing, MacCannell 1989, ch. 5 "Staged Authenticity", 91–108). At the end of the *Knappenkapelle*'s performance, we even joined in singing the regional anthem *in Dutch*, as to our surprise (and that of the locals) we knew the melody from a children's song in our own country about two musical hares and a hunter in a turnip field. This, of course, is less strange than it seems. Folk songs, dances, and marches have been circulating throughout Europe for ages, and, as noticed by Peter Burke (1978, 124–125) in the case of early modern folk music, the same tune might be different and different tunes the same because motifs "wandered" from one tune to another. Yet the fact that some residents wondered how we could actually sing "their" song, also reveals that parts of popular culture have been appropriated by communities as *heritage*.

This canonization of folk songs and tales goes back to the early nineteenth century. After the universalist Napoleonic era, a new generation began to unearth the pre-revolutionary past in search for "forgotten" national and regional identities waiting to be revived in the Romantic "rhetoric of awakening" (Crane 2000, 12–13). One such collector on the eve of the age of nationalism was August Heinrich Hoffmann von Fallersleben. He was the pan-German poet of the *Deutschlandlied*, which has functioned as Germany's national anthem since the Weimar Republic, although, remarkably, sung to the melody of Joseph Haydn's Habsburg anthem *Gott erhalte Franz den Kaiser* (1797), and today without the post-1945 too loaded stanza "Deutschland über alles" (Geisler 2005, 68–74). Hoffmann, whose imagined Germany stretched out from Austria to the Netherlands, also published *Horae Belgicae* in 1856. This corpus of *Niederländische Volkslieder* contained the aforementioned Middle Dutch song "The Musical Hares" collected on his *literarische Reise* from the city archive of Leiden. It seems Hoffmann's text was rewritten in modern Dutch by Jan Goeverneur and set to music by Johannes Worp in their traditional children's songbook *De zingende kinderwereld* (1866), which resulted in the song we knew from our childhood.[1]

At first glance such "travelling" songs only confirm the impression of the richness of Europe's shared cultural heritage, as in the much quoted words of Claude Lévi-Strauss in his 1952 UNESCO lecture *Race et histoire*, no culture is closed, every culture is multicultural, or as he framed it later "all cultures are the result of a mishmash, borrowings, mixtures [...]" (Lévi-Strauss 1994, 424, and see for his impact and critique of (and from) UNESCO narrative, Müller-Will 2010). But considering the patriotic values attributed to them, one may ask to whom do they actually belong? This question came up for the Bulgarian filmmaker Adele Peeva during an Istanbul banquet with some friends from different Balkan countries, who suddenly joined in singing a song played by a local band, which they each immediately claimed as their own (Elefterias-Kostakidis 2013–2014). How could this be? Expecting that mutual heritage might bring people together in her ethnically divided region, Peeva decided to make a documentary about the many faces of that same song. Yet *Whose Is This Song?* (2003) not only offers a hilarious account of the endless transformations of a popular song known as a lullaby or love song in one country and as a religious hymn, patriotic polka, or military march in another, but also robs us of the illusion that such a rich shared heritage will lead to mutual understanding. Travelling through Turkey, Greece, Albania, Bosnia, Macedonia, Serbia, and Bulgaria, she let local people everywhere hear the same song in a foreign version. Sometimes they were amazed, like us and our Austrian friends, but more often they were astonished, and their disbelief turning into hatred. In Serbia, the filmmaker even faced death threats after her subjects heard "their" song in a Bosnian version, and in her homeland, the same thing happened during the commemoration of a historic battle against the Ottomans when she suggested that its origin might have been Turkish. Completely disillusioned at the end of her road movie, Peeva compared her lovely Balkan folk music with the threatening image of a smoldering peat fire, which, as the longest, and less noticed burning fires on Earth, offers a

---

[1] Hoffmann's poem on the musical hares, collected at the Leiden archive, was re-edited as the Dutch children song "De musicerende hazen" by Jan Gouverneur and Johannes Worp, *De zingende kinderwereld* (1866). Hoffmann, as a pan-Germanist, also supported the Flemish cultural struggle against the French-speaking Walloons in Belgium with poems like *Gegen die Franskiljons* (Weemaels 1969–1970, 146–148).

gloomy metaphor for the disruptive impact of nationalism spreading beneath the romantic surface of Europe's mosaic of living cultures.

As to me, these very different experiences of cultural diversity and cultural identity—one seeking universality, the other focusing on particularity—seem two sides of the same Euro coin, two ways of dealing with cultural traditions that tend to travel across borders, and yet can also be experienced as exclusively one's own. When, shortly after the founding of the European Union (2002), I asked David Lowenthal to give a lecture on what would bind Europeans together, he observed that it would not be the EU's top-down, bureaucratic centralization, but that "the commodified and touristic past" would foster a bottom-up process of Europeanization. Cultural heritage would play a leading role in the continent's unification, in the sense "of an historic past embraced within the present—a past conserved, used, and exhibited on behalf of our collective selves" (Lowenthal 2005, 29–39). Thus it seems as if the post-1989 European project was driven by a growing access to an immense public archive of collected and nationalized heritage items, which by means of tourism and the internet fostered a process of unification. While this packaging of Europe's past may look far removed from the progressive rights and liberties discussed among the twenty-first-century travellers in Psykou's documentary, such human rights and democratic traditions are actually strongly linked to the kind of heritage Lowenthal had in mind. For what was quintessentially European in his view was embracing a past that people not only take pride in, but also feel ashamed of. Human rights policy is therefore for many Europeans related to the twentieth-century legacy of totalitarianism and mass violence from World War I to the Holocaust and the 1995 Srebrenica massacre, as a unique "politics of regret" (Olick 2007).[2] It was this "contribution to the advancement of peace and reconciliation, democracy and human rights", for which the EU was even awarded the 2012 Nobel Peace Prize in Oslo (The Nobel Peace Prize 2012).

Yet the "Oh Europe!" sigh might also be understood as a reflection on the contested nature of the repertoire of recollecting and showcasing heritage of what, despite its huge size and variety, might be named with Sharon Macdonald "the European memory complex" (Macdonald 2013, 1–26). For if the transnational heritage tourism explosion and

---

[2] According to Olick (2007), the EU's much-praised politics of regret have primarily followed the German post-1980s model of *Vergangenheitsbewältigung*.

collective memory boom since the 1990s could be embraced as a powerful driving force for Europeanization, what then could explain the opposing obsession with the past—the peat fire of competing identity claims, which Lowenthal (1997) had earlier coined a "heritage crusade"? To better understand such a dynamic interplay of bottom-up and stately interventions, we may stay in the same region for a while. According to Tony Judt, what inspired 1989s "return to Europe" of many Central-Eastern European countries was above all the wish for a homecoming in prewar "Habsburgia". This nostalgic image of cultural heritage and identity, which had already been promoted in literature, film, and the heritage tourism policies of fin-de-siècle cities like Vienna, Budapest, and Prague since the 1970s (Judt and Snyder 2013, 236), however, was also ever-present in Western Europe. Anthony D. Smith (1981) noticed such an "ethnic revival" then already among Bretons, Basques, Scots, Flemish, Catalans, Kurds, and a host of other "neo-nationalist" communities, which inspired by a nineteenth-century "historicist" romanticism, revitalized the ancient bonds which progressives expected to have died with the rise of the cosmopolitan, western type of "scientific state". Likewise after the 1989 Fall of the Wall, the EU's liberal grand narrative might have too naively presumed that such deeper, essentialist notions of heritage and identity still present across Europe, could finally be overcome by intercultural dialogue and transnational, mutual heritage politics after the definite ending of its extremist, nationalist, authoritarian, and communist pasts.

Such dissonances of ethnic nationalism were also long concealed by the universalist discourses of the international treaties on material heritage protection, as framed for decades by the expansive heritage conservation apparatuses of the European nation states. Originally inspired by the same, romantic spirit of re-awakening and conservation, they became in the twentieth century themselves part of the modern, state-apparatus. Yet parallel with the European enlargements and new kinds of memory debates on the Holocaust and postcolonialism, these "state-organized heritage regimes" (cf. de Cesari 2012, 399–413) have received more and more competition from a transnational counter-discourse on *intangible* cultural heritage. Like the earlier transformative, internationalist notion of "world heritage", this intangible perception of cultural heritage is embraced by the European Community and promoted on a global scale by the Paris headquarters of the 1946 founded United Nations Educational, Scientific and Cultural Organization (UNESCO). And yet, at the same time, it neglects much of the deep-rooted symbolic identifications with Europe's dissonant pasts (van der Laarse 2013, 121–132; 2016a, 213–232) and identity crusades, and fosters the assumption of an almost touristic kind of bottom-up heritagization as a more democratic road to Europeanization.

To demonstrate the background of this turn towards intangible heritage, this chapter takes the discursive genealogy and metacultural context of the UNESCO Convention for the Safeguarding of Intangible Cultural Heritage (2003) as its starting point (Kirshenblatt-Gimblett 2004, 52–64; Tauschek 2011, 49–64). Just like other international treaties such as UNESCO's first heritage treaty, the 1954 Convention for the Protection of Cultural Property in the Event of Armed Conflict, known as the Hague Convention, UNESCO's 1972 Convention Concerning the Protection of the World Cultural and Natural Heritage, known as the World Heritage Convention, and the 1995 UNIDROIT Convention on Stolen or Illegally Exported Cultural Objects, this 2003 Intangible Heritage Convention's transnational agenda of cultural safeguarding and dialogue was unmistakably inspired by the earlier experience with the material and cultural destructions of two world wars, the Holocaust, and the decolonization wars. Seconding, however, Lynn Meskell's observation of the 1972 World Heritage Convention ended up in "a tyranny of states" notwithstanding its initial ambition to make a better world of peace and diversity (Meskell 2018, xvii, 26), I am afraid that also the Intangible Heritage Convention—despite being set-up to correct the monumental world heritage approach by the inclusion of the "living dimension" of heritage—is still not very well equipped to overcome the defining force of the nation state.

Although the scope of the Convention is universal and far from essentialist, it has come to frame culture and heritage in terms of identity and belonging, and defines globalization as the main threat to the sustainability of cultural diversity. This is problematic, as I will show below, first because it transforms intangible heritage from a "shared interest of humankind" into a cultural asset of national self-promotion; and second, because the Convention's discourse on cultural diversity intersects with a non-critical kind of "culturalism" (Eriksen 2013, 131–146)—which frames cultures as closed, homogeneous entities in a competitive framework of national identities instead of a dynamic, hybrid, conflictive construct to be assessed from a variety of interpretative, performative, discursive and spatial perspectives, such as perceived after the so-called "linguistic" and "cultural turns" in humanities and social sciences (Bachmann-Medick 2007). This has led to various criticism of UNESCO's "ideology", such as by Alain Finkelkraut in *La défaite de la pensée* (1987), who accused the Paris UN organization of betraying its initial Enlightenment spirit of universalism in support of a culturalization of politics, which he held for the West's self-accusing, mimetic response to the era of decolonization, characterized by parochialism and cultural relativism (see Finkelkraut 1987, ch. 'Portrait du décolonisé', 93–105). His later critique of consumer society, globalization and the multiculturalist discourse on diversity (in defence of universal humanism) brings him, however, also close to culturalist critiques of modernity (as noticed in Souillac 2011, 117–119). Such criticism presupposes, of course, a questionable *continuity* of a binary grand narrative of Europe's modern culture of an inherent antagonism of the late eighteenth century enlightened values of reason, universalism, and empiricism by what Isaiah Berlin has coined (with approval) a "Counter-Enlightenment" of romantic, historicist values of origin, uniqueness, and identity. Though mostly understood in an opposite way, the Counter-Enlightenment thesis actually held German Romanticism for more pluralist than the "totalitarian" monist Enlightenment (Berlin 1981, 25–79; see for a critique of this binary culture model van der Laarse et al. 1998, 1–14). As "distantly related to certain Counter-Enlightenment discourses about ethnic identity", also the anthropologist Adam Kuper in the late 1990s, recognized such anti-universalist values in today's (multi)culturalist politics of identity and difference, which to him should be regarded, however, as a "*new* [cultural] form of racism" (Kuper 1999a, b, 233–234, 241). The English anthropologist Susan Wright, participant in the 2002 Drafting Group of UNESCO's Convention on Intangible Heritage, noticed the same discursive renewal of post-racist neo-nationalism, though from the more dynamic assumption that "the New Right appropriated one of the founding inspirations of cultural studies, Gramsci's ideas of hegemony", and thereby "the *anti*-racist language about the need to respect cultural difference". The far-right was, in her view, successful rightly by not going into *politics* but into *culture*; by successfully manipulating words, redefining key concepts, and "reformulating the meanings of one semantic cluster – 'difference', 'nation', 'culture'" (Wright 1998, 10). The American sociologist Robert J. Antonio (2000, 51) even speaks of a new "postmodernism of the Right". This discursive bridge between the seemingly opposites of Counter-Enlightenment thinking and left-wing postmodernism might be seen as the main offspring of the post-war ethnic revival and its romantic equating of Enlightenment universalism with cultural homogenization. It is the rejection of the rational state's destruction of community and evaporation of cultural autonomy, which now unites all kind of populists, and heritage activists, in opposition to globalization, for "in matters of race and ethnicity, anti-universalist views range from support for affirmative action and recognition of minority differences to advocacy of racial separatism or from efforts to preserve local communities and local dialects to 'ethnic cleansing'" (Antonio 2000, 51).

Altogether, such contradictory statements on the intangible heritage turn, thus ask for a critical observation in the context of the current authoritarian revolt and the related revival of Identitarian discourses in large parts of Europe, both from the Left and from the Right (in defence of, respectively, minority cultures and national cultures). Sketching the past and current state of affairs in intangible heritage policy, and using examples from the Dutch postcolonial case of Black Pete to the Russian-Ukrainian culture war on Kolobok, I will argue how by highlighting cultural diversity, the Intangible Heritage Convention takes the risk of becoming a legitimizing instrument for groups and communities claiming *exclusive* rights and values in competition with others. In contrast to liberal "soft" pluralism, this advocating of collective cultural rights is described as "hard" multiculturalism by Eriksen and Stjernfelt (2012). The protection of cultural traditions and expressions might then lead to the result that what is safeguarded as intangible heritage may actually be a community's nostalgic brand identity, whereas such community values might at the same time be framed by populist governments and movements as being threatened by precisely the kind of cultural diversity, or the "creolization of the world",[3] which the Convention should help to support.

The Intangible Heritage Turn

Although almost everything can be transformed into heritage, the main thing heritage sites, artifacts, and traditions share is their rescue from imminent demise or external danger by being lifted out of their ordinary

---

[3]Creolization, it should be stressed, is not the same as homogenization (Burke 2009, 115).

context. The key result of the rhetoric of heritage is therefore the transformation into cultural property, even when it concerns something as strikingly ordinary as a toilet or as astonishingly horrible as a bombed car wreck after a terrorist attack. Far from a passive musealization of "rubbish" into artifacts, such a second life as heritage is only allowed for a select group of items and elements that can somehow claim authenticity or uniqueness, as heritage making and valuation is inevitably selective and exclusive (cf. Thompson 1979; Bendix 2007, 337–356). Against such rescue narratives, however, critics have since the 1980s argued that museums, archives, and sites turn living culture into dead objects with no other function than heritage tourism. The "heritage industry" has also been criticized as "bogus history" for its cleansing of the past from hard realities of labour, class, and inequality—both when dealing with castles and industrial heritage (see for the leading British debate Wright 1985; Hewison 1987; Mandler 1997, 415–416; Baillie et al. 2010, 51–71; Harrison 2010, 16–18), and for its silencing of cultural dissonances at musealized (some would say estheticized) "dark heritage" sites or "Holoscapes" (cf. Turnbridge and Ashworth 1996; van der Laarse 2018).

Yet this critical approach to so-called "authorized heritage discourses", focusing on "authenticity" and "uniqueness" as key values in state-controlled expert selection procedures (Smith 2006, 29–34) seem to have dissolved with the intangible heritage turn, which—partly in the wake of the Holocaust-memory boom—attributed new, empowering values to witnesses of war crimes and genocide and to long-suppressed subaltern voices from indigenous populations. Even though it is hard to unravel the conceptual and normative connotations of this Gramscian move from materiality to culture within the heritage apparatus, the attraction of the notion of intangible heritage might have had a lot to do with the way it assimilated Romantic, ethnographical, archaeological, and community approaches to a re-awakening of "forgotten" minority and pre-colonial cultures within a new, inclusive rhetoric of a "guilt of nations" (see for the underlying narratives of post-war dealings with World War II and Colonialism Barkan 2000). UNESCO's Intangible Heritage Convention seemed the outcome of this paradigm shift, as it explicitly stressed the dynamic character of intangible cultural heritage while connecting the protection of material heritage elements to the safeguarding of "living" cultural communities.

Thus safeguarding intangible heritage was not only held to be a *complement* but also an *alternative* to traditional notions of protecting material authenticity. The origin of this discursive break with traditional heritage approaches goes back to the late 1980s, when cultural-anthropological approaches came to dominate the social and historical sciences and the public human rights debate. This led to the inclusion of folklore in the Recommendation on the Safeguarding of Traditional Culture and Folklore (1989) from the 25th session of the General Conference of UNESCO in Paris, which stated "that folklore forms part of the universal heritage of humanity and that it is a powerful means of bringing together different peoples and social groups and of asserting their cultural identity". Framed as "the totality of tradition-based creations of a cultural community", folklore also includes the wealth of songs, rituals, myths, and traditions collected by generations of folklorists. As such, this 1989 Recommendation also introduced the concept of "safeguarding" (instead of protecting) cultural identities by means of a policy of heritage preservation. Thus heritage protection was no longer the goal but a *means* of cultural safeguarding. Yet how could such safeguarding of communal identities preserve the universal heritage of humanity—for are not identities by definition unique and dynamic, and are not communities often rivalling in the recognition of their identities? The explanation might be found in what the Recommendation in almost Hegelian terms defined as the "universal will" to safeguard "cultural diversity" (Recommendation on the Safeguarding 1989).

With the UNESCO Convention for the Protection of the World Cultural and Natural Heritage of 1972, cultural diversity became *en vogue* parallel to biodiversity (and sustainability), and with UNESCO's report Our Creative Diversity (World Commission on Culture and Development 1995) the UNESCO Universal Declaration on Cultural Diversity of 2001, it became a normative guideline for all European culture programmes. At that point, cultural diversity had already entered the cultural heritage domain as a conceptual power tool with the ICOMOS Nara Document on Authenticity (1994), which introduced cultural heritage in relation to "heritage diversity" in the same way as the 1989 Recommendation introduced heritage protection as a powerful means for the universal safeguarding of cultural identities. In advance of the later notion of intangible cultural heritage, however, the Nara Document advocated with respect to communities more explicitly that the concept of authenticity should no longer be regarded as an intrinsic quality of heritage properties, but as a transmitter of values and significance "to be judged within the cultural contexts to which they belong" (The Nara Document on Authenticity 1994).

This contextualized heritage approach looked at first glance modestly liberal, though as Cornelius Holtorf (2017, 1–14) recently put it, at this point the Nara Document's metacultural framing risked turning cultural diversity into relativism. Actually, the whole idea of safeguarding the cultural heritage of communities (against the threat of cultural homogenization) echoes a romantic, binary narrative of *Gemeinschaft* versus *Gesellschaft*. What this break with an object-oriented approach of heritage promoted, was actually a *culturalist* notion of diversity which closely touches an essentialist approach of identity. According to Wright, the 1995 Our Creative Diversity report might be held for the most symptomatic expression of this new "UNESCO ideology"; yet instead of a new, dynamic cultural perspective on multiple identities, fluidity, and contestation, it reveals still a 1930s anthropological concept of culture as *difference*, "the old idea of authentic culture" (Wright 1998, 7–15). Thomas Hylland Eriksen (2001, 129, 132, 135–136) held this classic view from cultural relativism for a conservationist, "archipelago view of culture" which regards cultures as isolated islands or bounded entities, esteems diversity as the highest value, and "naturalizes" traditions, and the idea of culture as a "way of life". In summary, the paradoxical outcome of UNESCO's attempt to protect "minority cultures" against the danger of cultural homogenization was a binary, essentialist view on "deep" (authentic) group cultures threatened by a "superficial" culture of modernity (or civilization), which, however, strikingly resembled the UN's own universal mission of protecting individual human rights and global ethics of respect, equality and tolerance.

When this discursive framework was fully included in the 2003 UNESCO Convention of the Safeguarding of the Intangible Heritage, these problems were discussed, but far from solved. New was nevertheless the replacement of the by-then outdated notions of folklore and tradition for that of intangible heritage. According to the ethnographer Valdimar Hafstein, who chaired the Icelandic Commission for UNESCO from 2011–2012, the replacement of "tradition" by "intangible cultural heritage" was actually the most significant of the paradigm change. In his view, the new, intangible heritage approach was basically born from a wide-shared theoretical disappointment with the universalist 1989 Recommendations. At the same time, however, it reflected a geopolitical shift in cultural hegemony. The Convention's intangible heritage rhetoric he characterized as a reorientation from a "European-inspired archival approach" to a more dynamic approach of heritage associated with Asian (in particular Japanese and Korean) programmes for "living national treasures". As a "shared interest of humankind" and as "a mainspring of cultural diversity", intangible heritage thus came to replace a conservationist, art-oriented policy with a future-oriented, ethnographical perspective. While introducing a more communitarian treatment of culture with new concepts like (cultural) identity and safeguarding, it disposed others, such as (material) authenticity (Hafstein 2004, 18, 37ff.; Hafstein, UNESCO Organization; Bortolotto 2013).

Most remarkably, the 2003 Convention also made a giant step beyond the 1989 Recommendation by proclaiming that safeguarding intangible heritage would be "a guarantee of sustainable development". By embracing both a (sustainable) development perspective and a policy of multiculturalism, however, the Convention could also be read as a powerless compromise. While recognizing the benefits of globalization and social transformation when referring to existing international human rights instruments, the Intangible Heritage Convention, at the same time, noted that "the conditions they create for renewed dialogue among communities, *also* give rise, as does the phenomenon of intolerance, to grave threats of deterioration, disappearance and destruction of the intangible cultural heritage".[4] In other words, the Convention pointed to the paradox that the same global trends and transformations which were assumed to counter intolerance and xenophobia might endanger the continuity of communities' living heritage and might even evoke new misuses of the past. Thus, the diversity of cultures may at the same time be preserved *and* endangered by processes of cultural globalization.

Yet might it be that this contradiction is inherently related to the Convention's own discursive framework? Following Hafstein, this is after all a metacultural mishmash of Western and Asian heritage approaches. Thus heritage values are, on the one hand, framed within Western human rights discourse, but, on the other, not primarily distributed on the level of citizens but on that of communities—which generally means

---

[4] Text of the Convention for the Safeguarding of the Intangible Cultural Heritage *ICH-UNESCO*; the italics by the author. As a first step after the 1989 Recommendations, UNESCO introduced the notion of intangible heritage as starting point for a new culture policy in 1993 (Tauschek 2010, 71).

national communities. Taking to the extreme, it follows that cultural diversity would ultimately lead to a compartmentalized homogeneity, as the right of individuals in post-plural, hybrid societies to choose their own lifestyle is implicitly framed as threatening the safeguarding of communal identities. In other words, the whole issue of cultural homogenization (and hybridization) is far more complex than assumed in UNESCO discourse. Although in global society more and more people share various identities, what we do see, as recently observed by Burke (2009, 104–105), is not an overall homogenization of culture, but a more complex variety of styles with more heterogeneity on the local and less diversity on a global level. Yet Burke neglects precisely the national level which is crucial for the legal protection of *individual* human rights of citizens. In UNESCO discourse on cultural diversity these might easily be violated by collective minority rights, for, as noticed also by Eriksen (2001, 135–136, 141) on the "official", national level individuals are still supposed to basically share the authorized heritage discourses of the cultural community to which they (are presumed to) "belong".

What's on the List?

Like the 1989 Recommendation, the 2003 Convention at first articulated the supposedly grave threats to intangible heritage to signal the urgency of providing still existing "living cultures", such as tribal communities in Africa or Latin America, with protection against globalization processes. Interestingly, this culturalist interpretation of heritage was initially also supported by some Western European countries dealing with a contested colonial past, of which the Netherlands is a good example. After the Indonesian decolonization war and the loss of the Indies in 1949 the Dutch' politics of regret took the form of a striving for moral leadership in human rights and international development cooperation. Thus Rieks Smeets, the secretary-general of the Dutch National Commission for UNESCO (The Hague) and secretary of UNESCO's Intangible Heritage Convention in Paris, argued in 2003 that Europe should not prioritize its own heritage, like what happened with World Heritage, but support underdeveloped countries, like those in Africa, which had less built heritage than the West but still had important living tradition to protect. Because of "the necessity of keeping the diversity of non-mainstream cultures alive", the intangible heritage convention should in this way compensate for a Western overrepresentation with material sites on the UNESCO World Heritage Convention list (1972) (Rieks Smeets Interviewed 2003).

Yet in the course of its implementation of the Convention for the Safeguarding of the Intangible Cultural Heritage took a more pragmatic direction, adjusting to existing heritage practices. The Dutch politics of regret was outvoted by other countries with a less paternalistic approach. Both some East-Asian countries as well as some other Western European countries, such as France and Belgium, were prone to promoting their own national treasures, like they had done in the 1972 World Heritage Convention. Thus, at the 2003s final expert meeting of the intangible heritage draft convention, a majority of the participants supported an initiative of Korea and Japan (with opposition from many Latin-American countries) to adopt the ninety "masterpieces" from the UNESCO Masterpieces of the Oral and Intangible Heritage of Humanity list (2001) as a starting point for a new intangible heritage list, modelled after the UNESCO's World Heritage List (cf. Hafstein 2008, 93–111).[5] As a result, the originally intended protection of endangered intangible heritage made way for a crucially important role of governments in nominating and showcasing their masterpieces, which—in a semantic attempt to remove the impression of national treasures—were now called "representations" (cf. Aikawa-Faure 2009, 13–44).

The 2003 text of the Convention then provided for three types of lists: the Representative List, the Urgent Safeguarding List, the Register of Good (or Best) Safeguarding Practices, and one or more inventories of the intangible heritage to be drawn up by State Parties, which as a first step of the registering procedure could be national as well as federal, regional, or transnational. After these instruments took shape in 2008, however, most State Parties opted to mainly register their more touristic items on the Representative List, and for instance, the Netherlands UNESCO committee's website simply states: "Just like world heritage also intangible heritage cannot do without an international Unesco list: the International representative List of Intangible Heritage of the Humanity" (Dossier Immaterieel-erfgoed). Martin Grandjean's

---

[5] Hafstein was also a member of the Icelandic delegation at the 2003 third UNESCO expert meeting on the Draft Convention, and gives a hilarious account of the discussion about the choice between 'list' or 'register' so as to avoid the resemblance with the World Heritage List or the "elitist" Masterpieces list.

geo-mapping of UNESCO's Intangible Cultural Heritage clearly shows how in 2014 Europe still made up a third of the 313 items of the Representative List (although it also indicated a rising representation of the Asian powers China, Japan, and South-Korea, and some countries in Latin America), which stood in striking contrast to a strong African under-representation (Grandjean 2016).[6] However, the number of items do not speak for themselves. Thus according to Filomena Sousa's geo-mapping of e-inventories three years later, Europe with 46 (of 198) countries still outnumbered the other continents on the intangible heritage country list, but Africa took with 42 countries the second position. Yet, the unbalance becomes more striking when Europe's new *online* domination is taken into account. With more than half (83) of a total of 158 registered ICH e-inventories in 2017, the European countries then again completely overshadowed the other continents. No less than 65% of the ICH member states (129) did even without any e-inventory; the largest number (38) in Africa (Sousa 2017).[7] As these figures concern mainly touristic items such as traditional dances, crafts, and folk music, it remains to be seen whether the original objective will ever be achieved. Safeguarding threatened elements of cultural diversity on the Urgent Safeguarding List (and the registration of Good Safeguarding Practices) was still not very popular among governments.

What explains the growing importance of the listing of world heritage sites and intangible heritage items? In heritage-making the most authentic, or iconic, thing is always valued above another as heritage inscriptions

[6] Browse the Lists of Intangible Cultural Heritage. A direct resemblance of both lists is complicated because some top scorers of the World Heritage list. The USA, Canada and Australia, all with strong indigenous cultures, are still no State Parties to the Convention, while The Russian Federation takes a special position as a 'State non-party' with two elements inscribed on the Representative list of which it accepts rights and obligations, https://ich.unesco.org/en/state/russian-federation-RU?info=periodic-reporting#pr-2015-2015.

[7] Sousa is a researcher funded by the Fundação Para a Ciência e Tecnologia at the UNESCO accredited Portuguese NGO Memória Imaterial. From the expressions "National Inventory of the Intangible Cultural Heritage [of country x]" and "Inventory of the Intangible Cultural Heritage [of country x]", in English and in the official language of the respective country, she came up to 158 e-inventories – 88 national, 41 regional/local and 29 transnational, 46 from Europe, 31 Latin America, 37 Asia, 42 Africa, 18 Arab States, while 24 countries not ratified the Convention; 129 (of 198) countries analysed show no record, and among the 69 countries with registered ICH e-inventories stands out Europe with 83 mapped inventories (53%) (Sousa 2017, 2–4).

are inevitably selective and exclusive. However, although favouring a dynamic and inclusive notion of intangible heritage which covers both "inherited traditions from the past" and "contemporary rural and urban practices in which diverse groups take part", the Intangible Heritage Convention's metaculture turned out to be selective also in a different, *political* way. For on the one hand, it came out that UNESCO's requirement for nominating intangible heritage elements as actively supported by "living communities" was hard to control, while on the other, the introduction of selective lists offered governments influential instruments to prioritize the promotion of national cultures over minority and transnational cultures This was already noticed in the evaluations of the 2001–2005 nominations for the Masterpieces list, about which the head of the supervising NGO, Anthony Seeger, concluded that minority traditions were often neglected and sanitized by national elites in control of the nomination procedure, who at the same time frequently claimed certain transnational elements as exclusively to be found within *their* nation's borders (Seeger 2001–2005, 112–128).[8] The process of inscription has therefore, just like with the World Heritage Convention, become an important tool for national identity politics as well as for intergovernmental "nations-to-nations transactions", as Meskell (2018, 130, 168) noticed. Her observation concerns the post-1972 world heritage committee, and her analyses of the committee's decision-making reveals strong mutual networking support from European countries like France and Germany as competing in particular with the Russian Federation and the rising group of BRICS countries (China, India, South Africa, Brazil), as well as the almost complete un-representation of the entire African continent (Meskell 2018, 127–128, 130–131). Likewise, as a result, the role of experts and intellectuals is taken over by diplomats and politicians in the ICH procedures and meetings, who lack however the space for critical opinions when facing the danger, not of the votes of other nations but of their own people, in defining the value of cultural heritage sites and elements. Sousa recently observed that most State Party reports on ICH recommendations still focus on listing elements on the Representative List with motivations "that hardly can be recognized as ICH or considered in line with the 'spirit of the Convention'".

[8] Seeger was Secretary-General of the International Council for Traditional Music (1997–1999), and supervisor of the scientific and technical evaluation of the Masterpieces nominations from 2001 to 2005 (Foster 2015, 10).

In contrast to the valid need for an Urgent Safeguarding List, it confirms the problematic meaning of the Representative List, which in her view is dangerous not only because of political misappropriation, "but also because this inscription promotes the distinction between the ICH elements that are on the list and those that are not [...] increasing the risk of privileging certain expressions to the detriment of others, hierarchizing or discriminating less recognized traditions" (Sousa 2018, 18).

This not only plays a role in "new" postcolonial and post-communist countries, but also in less divided "old" European countries. Thus in the Netherlands, politicians initially feared that an intangible heritage list could become a costly instrument to safeguard something difficult to control. Also, in a country where nationalism had been taboo since World War II, progressives did not like the idea that the government would decide what elements would be on or off the list. And, for opposite reasons, right-wing Dutch populists did not trust a government whose human rights regime was held to support multiculturalism, as was clear from the storm of criticism provoked in 2007 by a speech of Princess (now Queen) Máxima (born in Argentina), given at the press release of a report of the Scientific Council for Government Policy on Dutch people's identification with the nation. After summarizing the plural lifestyles resulting from globalization, Europeanization and individualization, she remarked on a personal note that after seven years in the Netherlands she had not found "*the* Dutch identity" and was convinced that the cliché Dutchmen did not exist (Toespraak van Prinses Máxima).[9]

I myself observed how fluid the professional debate on cultural heritage had become at a 2008 expert meeting in preparation of the Netherlands' decision on the ratification of the UNESCO Intangible Heritage Convention, where on the invitation of the Netherlands' UNESCO Committee some 30 experts and policymakers discussed the question if the Netherlands should ratify the 2003 Convention. The discussion based on a position paper[10] of the National UNESCO Committee was "fierce and fruitful" according to the organizers who

---

[9] Compare the (slightly suggestive) English subtitled YouTube video: Maxima—'The Dutchman Does Not Exist', and see *Identificatie met Nederland* (2007).

[10] I was one of 22 experts discussing this question on the basis of the position paper with the authors and policy makers, and the only participant voting against ratification whereas some other academic experts abstained from voting.

some months later processed a positive advice to the Minister of Culture (Verslag van werkzaamheden 2010, 23–24). Written in cooperation with the Dutch Secretary of the 2003 Convention in Paris, the position paper defined intangible heritage from an advanced perspective, as a transnational (including postcolonial) living heritage of which the valuation process would be all about the cultural dynamics of meaning and signification. Proclaiming "an active, participatory community approach" from a non-hierarchical perspective with respect for cultural diversity and creativity, it criticized the essentialist notion of authenticity, both in the sense of a single origin as an authentic primal form and in that of a typical national peculiarity. Though slightly critical towards the notion of listing "masterpieces" and a top-down approach of heritage, it accepted the Convention's call for State Party inventories (considered a national inventory of ICH), although reframed in a more dynamic way. Stressing the need for a continuing process, this was meant to prevent a fossilizing of "communities" which were, interestingly, defined by their active (and changing) identification with heritage activities—as to avoid any kind of essentialist "group" idea. Most remarkable, the Dutch position paper even anticipated critical doubts that things might move into another direction, and threw up the rhetorical question: "Suppose a state would use the Convention to define distinctive criteria of a certain 'people' (and thus exclude part of its population), would this not create enormous problems?" It was convinced that this risk would be eliminated by communicating new, inclusive practices, such as facilitating international cooperation on the safeguarding of transnational items like the Dutch-Indonesian and Surinamese cuisine, hip-hop culture, and bicycling. And finally, the National Committee warned the experts that by *not* ratifying the Convention, the Netherlands "would leave an opportunity for introducing the notion of *folk culture* in the sense of living heritage (within limits set by the human rights Convention) in the intercultural dialogue".[11]

---

[11] 'The Position Paper. Nederland en de Convention for the Safeguarding of Intangible Cultural Heritage' was written by the Nederlandse Unesco Commissie in cooperation with the KNAW Meertens Institute and the Nederlands Centrum voor Volkscultuur for the Dutch expert meeting of 25 June 2008. It is not printed, nor public accessible via the Internet, and was more widely distributed only as an attachment (1) to the Advisory Report 'Advies Nationale UNESCO Commissie over de Conventie betreffende de bescherming van het immaterieel cultureel erfgoed' (10 November 2008).

Although the position paper thus called the experts to ratify the Convention as to prevent a more nationalist intangible heritage interpretation from other countries dominating the international community, from the minutes of the meeting one gets the impression, though, that among policymakers also a more stately perspective played a role.[12] In contrast to the Netherlands, Belgium was already very active since 2006 with listing elements for State Party's inventories, which resulted in subdivided "national" inventories for its Flemish, French-speaking and German-speaking Communities, and one for the international Representative list. In a keynote during the Dutch expert meeting of 2008 the director of the Flemish Centre for Intangible Heritage (FARO) showed himself amazed about the Dutch reservations and advised to ratify as soon as possible, if only to strengthen the influence of North-Western Europe in the first (European) election group of the Paris Executive Committee (Keynote Marc Jacobs).[13] Many experts at the 2008 meeting shared doubts, however, about such Eurocentrism, and also the Secretary of the 2003 Convention admitted that the Netherlands had to compete with other countries which, like France or China, were more interested in masterpieces than in minority cultures. In agreement with international debate (cf. What is intangible heritage?; see also Blake 2009, 45–73), there was theoretical criticism of using binary categories like intangible (versus material) heritage, and in particular also of the notion of "folk culture" (*volkscultuur*) as a Dutch working definition of intangible cultural heritage, which was regarded as regressing from the Convention's more dynamic approach of popular culture (including pop, street, migrant, and web communities) to a more conventional (white) folklore interpretation associated with local community participation in traditional festival performances and craftsmanship.[14]

---

[12] The following is based on the 'Advies Nationale UNESCO Commissie, bijlage 2' (2008) and see also Smeets (2010), de Leeuw (2010), Margry (2010), and Kerkhoven (2010).

[13] The UNESCO ICH Committee's Group I consisted then of the Mediterranean state parties Cyprus, Italy and Turkey, and only in 2018 the Netherlands were admitted in addition to Austria and Cyprus, https://ich.unesco.org/en/members-00028.

[14] This participatory 'folklore' approach was introduced by the socialist Minister of Culture Ronald Plasterk, together with that of a national heritage canon, and a plan for heritage education, in the policy report Kunst van Leven (2007, 24–25). See also van der Zeijden (2010, 24–27).

Although the suggested dynamic inventories of the position paper were more advanced than UNESCO's already introduced system copied from the "statist" World Heritage List, there was disapproval of the epistemology of listing, and of the assumed downsizing of the Convention's goal of safeguarding cultural diversity to merely documenting popular practices by an authorized national execution agency.[15] Finally, some scholars believed that the essentialist approach of intangible heritage ran the risk of turning the key issue of cultural diversity into a cultural minefield, with the prospect of an opening of Pandora's box of identity politics.

Even though many participants felt uncomfortable and some abstained from voting, the national UNESCO committee could advise the government to ratify the Convention. On the grounds of protecting cultural diversity against the threat of globalization, as a clear signal towards the developing countries ("the South"), and in accordance with the Netherlands' self-proclaiming, leading European role in international cultural policy, ratification was expected "to foster the awareness of active citizenship and intercultural dialogue, on national, local, and international levels" (Advies Nationale UNESCO Commissie). Although the Dutch were, as we saw, deeply involved in the international drafting of the Intangible Heritage Convention, the country took, however, another four years to finally sign the Treaty as late as 2012.[16] Yet it was not only the critical tone of the 2008 Dutch expert meeting that explained the delay in ratification.

What really caused the delay was a fundamental change in political culture on the issues of internationalism and multiculturalism. After a decade of internal discussions on national identity and the canonization of national culture and history, the Netherlands had actually moved in the same direction as the aforementioned Asian countries. In contrast to the 2008 position paper, Dutch cultural policy by 2012 had come to focus on touristic masterpieces of the Dutch Golden Age "burger"

---

[15] The Ministry of Culture, in coordination with the Nederlandse Unesco Commissie, engaged in 2011 the Nederlands Centrum voor Volkscultuur (1984) of the Netherlands' Open Air Folklore Museum Arnhem to become the official national implementation body (NIB), renamed as Kenniscentrum Immaterieel Erfgoed (KIEN). See Dibbets et al. (2011) and Margry (2014, 56–66).

[16] Apart from Germany (which ratified in 2013), Ireland (ratified 2015), and the UK (not a party to the Convention), all EU countries accepted or ratified between 2004 and 2012 (UNESCO Intangible Cultural Heritage Lists; Convention for the Safeguarding).

culture and the national "water culture", just like with the World Heritage List.[17] Moving away from Third World Solidarity, the longing for national identity had thus penetrated deeply into the Dutch polder. This might explain why it was, as late as 2017, the traditional craft of operating wind- and watermills that was ultimately registered as the first Dutch element on UNESCO's representative list of the intangible cultural heritage of humanity.[18] Two years later the national inventory contained already 142 elements of almost exclusively traditional folklore and crafts, although something of the dynamic community approach of 2008 now had returned in the form of an additional bottom-up "network" holding some hundred items signed up by local communities, which included the Chinese-Indonesian Babi Pangang kitchen, the metropolitan hardcore Gabber culture, and Gay Pride Amsterdam![19] Thus a (critical) 2014 advisory report of the Netherlands' Council of Culture questioned the leading opinion of focusing for nominations on the representative list, and advised the minister of culture to reconsider her assumption that the urgency list would be best suited for endangered heritage in developing countries: "The Council would not like to withhold you the irony of this [urgency] list. For, precisely intangible heritage with a more contested character will most likely be expected to disappear, though is probably the least eligible for [national] nominations, or selection by the [international] UNESCO committee" (Advies Immaterieel Erfgoed).[20]

---

[17] Compare the 28 exclusively agrarian, regional folklorist items on the national inventory in 2013, https://www.unesco.nl/nationale-inventaris-immaterieel-erfgoed. As to compare, Belgium had already by 2014 some 42 elements (included in 4 inventories for its Flemish, and German-speaking communities, Wallonia, and Brussels Region), of which ten were selected for the international Representative list, and compare for the themes of listed World Heritage in the Netherlands, see Dossier: Werelderfgoed.

[18] Interestingly, Dutch cheesemaking lost the competition with the miller craft in the nomination competition for the 2017 intangible heritage list, failing the criterium of living heritage from a supporting community; van der Zeijden (2015, 191–202). See for critical assessments of the Dutch longing for identity ('het eigene') Legêne (2006), Rooijakkers (2005, 207–217), and van der Laarse (2011, 88–95).

[19] See for the (international) Register (national) Inventory, and (bottom-up) 'Network', Kenniscentrum Immaterieel Erfgoed Nederland.

[20] Author's parentheses and translation from Dutch. Head of the RvC report committee, which supported nomination with these reservations to the socialist Minister of Culture Jet Bussemaker, was Gerard Rooijakkers, though the irony was not well consumed on UNESCOs platform (Imhof 2014).

The Hyperreality of Heritage Communities

I do not want to dwell on this much further, but would like to focus more on the issue of diversity and its endangering. This brings me to the apparently harmless role of the Convention's disposed category of authenticity. Material heritage experts use complex provenance standards and preservation guidelines to trace and assess the origin, uniqueness and ageing of objects, but how to safeguard the authenticity of intangible heritage? Established practices of signification, valuation, conservation, and restoration can hardly serve as a model, if only because intangible heritage in UNESCO discourse is perceived as a dynamic, inclusive expression of cultural diversity which opposes folklorization, fossilization, and musealization. From a theoretical viewpoint, of course, there is probably nothing more fluid and transformative than heritage, which as a cultural mode of production commodifies the past by changing places into destinations and items in experiences (cf. Kirshenblatt-Gimblett 1998). One only has to compare historical photos of a street to find out that in this process of heritagization the material and intangible are inseparable, or as Elisabeth Tietmeyer puts it, heritage is both "a symbolic thingification and a materialization of the intangible" (Tietmeyer et al. 2010, 7; see also van Mensch and Meijer-van Mensch 2010). Yet this is not how heritage by most communities is perceived. Intangible, no less than material heritage, is regarded as "authentic", right because of its assumed role of representing their age-old "identity".

Such paradoxes then beg the question against what grave threats the intangible heritage of humanity should actually be safeguarded. Against a looming extinction of certain human communities perhaps, which, according to the logic of the Convention, would lead to the conclusion that there cannot be any "living" heritage without a viable heritage community to support it? Or should we focus more strongly on the dangers of mass tourism for vulnerable intangible heritage? Doubtlessly, the sustainability of living traditions may be enhanced by tourism, but it can at the same time be threatened by the tourist market. Mass tourism, as we have seen, was as one of the "grave threats of deterioration, disappearance and destruction of the intangible cultural heritage" which according to the Convention would endanger the cultural identity and diversity of living heritage communities. The endangering of urban monuments and historical landscapes through tourist overexploitation is also an established theme in cultural criticism, such as in the case of Umberto

Eco's postmodernist proposal for "hyperreal" replica tourist attractions of Florentine antiquities (as with the caves of Lascaux, Eco 1995, 2007) to keep the looky-loos away from the originals, which apparently assumes that only connoisseurs are entitled to enjoy the beauty of authenticity. "Taste, like class, becomes racist when the capacity for it is a matter of breeding, when it masquerades as the natural attribute of an elite", according to Barbara Kirshenblatt-Gimblett (1998, 12). Yet it is completely unclear how the Convention could protect any culture against mass tourism without having the "Western" category of authenticity as its core value. Authorities mostly safeguard intangible heritage to preserve the cultural value of economic investments in communities, which is evinced by the slogan of the Dutch landscape heritage programme Belvedere: "Safeguarding through development" (van der Valk 2010, 21–52). Quite removed from the original intention of the Convention, the positive response among policymakers to participatory community approaches might then have had a lot to do with the assumed transformation of industrial societies into experience economies, while using, or misusing, the past for a tourist consumption of places (cf. Ashworth 2005, 193–206; Urry 2002).

The gravest threat to intangible cultural heritage might therefore be its own transformative, mimetic nature. A living heritage community could easily turn into what Baudrillard called a simulacrum, a cultural model which only seems real because of its assumed authenticity, for economic and identity reasons (Baudrillard 1981). Kirshenblatt-Gimblett also defines cultural heritage as a mode of production that, instead of things, produces the whole range of period museums, ethnographic villages, recreated environments, re-enacted rituals, memorial museums, and in situ memorial sites in a process which can best be characterized as "the art of the metonym" or "the art of mimesis" (Kirshenblatt-Gimblett 1998, 20). This mimetic mode is a process already described in 1961 by the American historian Daniel Boorstin (1992) in *The Image* which also inspired Eco's critique of mass tourism, and the American anthropologist Clifford Geertz' interpretation of culture as both a "model of" and a "model for" reality, a normative framework fed by its own imagined representation (Geertz 1973, and compare Schilbrack 2005, 429–452).

Where such simulations of reality come to exist and even surpass the real in "realness", original folk culture (if it ever existed) is rapidly commodified as a staged image of a past that never was. A patrimony simply preserved becomes an intolerable burden, as Lowenthal (2002, 412) has mentioned: "We can use the past fruitfully only when we realize that to inherit is also to transform". While on the one hand tourism and heritage industries produce musealized material fragments detached from normal life, they create a performative *illusion* of "authentic" intangible heritage on the other. This paradox has created endless visual and affective possibilities to thematize folklore festivities, old crafts, country houses, military battles, bombings, migration, and even the Holocaust in a museum context. As noticed, such "experiencing" of the past can likewise be found in folklorist landscapes and touristy historic cities, where visitors in the age of mass culture have learned to identify past cultures through performative markers that help them to consume re-enactments as living heritage.[21] One may think of the virtual Yiddish folklore and klezmer music re-enacted in heritage quarters of today's European "cities without Jews" (cf. Gruber 2002, of which the last chapter is titled "Whose Music?"; van der Laarse 2018, 39–42), but the same art of the mimetic can be found in tourist experiences like the staged "ancient" shamanist rituals in Siberia with horse rides and drumming sessions.[22] It can also be traced in the nationalist urban reconstructions of ethnically (and spatially) cleansed Yugoslav heritage tourism cities like Vukovar and Serajevo after the 1990s "urbicides" [23] (cf. Mazzucchelli 2013, 379–402), or in the commodified touristic "homeland" archaeology of biblical Israel, like with the City of David project, which among Jerusalem's Jewish population creates the illusion of living upon the traces of their expelled ethnic forefathers (cf. Silberman 1991, 76–87; Bohstrom 2017; Rothman 2014; van der Laarse 2010, 321–328; Pullan and Gwiazda 2008, 25). Mass cultural forms like tourism, film, media, museums, and memorials not only fulfill the powerful desire to relive the past, but they are also held to deliver "prosthetic memories" of other people's experiences powerful enough to be embodied as one's own; a kind of simulated

---

[21] Compare some Dutch folklorist icons promoted in tourism and export campaigns and revived as living heritage Elpers (2005) and Grevers (2004, 207–220).

[22] Broekhoven (2011), and for an impression, the promotional website 'Shamanism and Horses', http://www.horsejourneys.com/shamanism.html. For staged authenticity in tourism's semiotics, see MacCannell (2011, 13–40). He introduced the concept in 1973.

[23] The term was already used for the destructive impact of city reconstructions in the USA and elsewhere before being used for violent destructions of cities with the 1990s Yugoslav Wars, later to be used in the double meaning of urban destructions and reconstructions.

empathy that is even considered supportive of progressive human rights discourse (see Landsberg 2004). Thus the ethical, commercial, and political borders of sightseeing and heritage consumption are hard to draw. Nonetheless, once turned into hyperreality, intangible cultural heritage becomes economically dependent on virtual identities revived as living cultures which could also be politicized by right-wing populists as something worth fighting for.

Our Way of Life

"We will fight everywhere: in Parliament, in Brussels, soon in the Senate and in our Provinces. Everywhere patriots are ready for action", thus the Dutch politician Geert Wilders in his militant speech in support of the regional candidates in Friesland for the provincial elections of 2 March 2011. Although his Freedom Party (PVV) was at first opposed to progressive plans for safeguarding cultural diversity, with this speech the right-wing populist leader recognized folklore as a powerful weapon against what he calls the "church of leftists" and its doctrine of multiculturalism. With the Trojan horse of folklore, Wilders used an ethnically charged notion of regional culture to mobilize a *Heimat* nostalgia among his supporters, declaring: "the Frisian traditions are something to be proud of. The Frisian flag is the flag of free people". In other words, in the only Dutch region with a regional language recognized by the EU, Wilders (himself born on the other end of the country, in Limburg) was combatively trying to revive nineteenth-century Romantic sentiments. "Better dead than enslaved!", he announced, quoting what is written in Frisian on the 1951 monument in Warns in remembrance of the Frisians' 1345 victory in a battle from the Frisian-Hollandic wars in their defence of regional freedom against the Count of Holland and Hainaut. As an effective populist, Wilders understood the strategic power of mobilizing regional pride over age-old freedoms in a Europe-wide battle against progressive multiculturalism and the supposed threat of migration and Islamism to local communities' culture and identity. "Friesland should be our inspiration when we are fighting to defend our way of life", as he put it (Wilders 2011).[24]

---

[24] Translated from Dutch by the author. For the organisers, critics, and fascist appropriations of the yearly commemorations, see *Stiftung Slach by Warns* (1345), Horling (2012), and de Mik (1993).

In many European countries, we can notice a similar politicizing of regional cultures centred around the notion of "our way of life"—traditional cultural values that are assumed to be threatened by Brussels, migrants, the Islam, "cultural Marxism", the animal-rights movement, or, more generally, globalization. In another example, the disputed Italian socialist prime minister Bettino Craxi offered the Italian population constitutional reforms in favour of regional autonomy in his "Declaration of Pontida" (1990). The location was carefully chosen: the medieval battle of the Lombards against the Habsburg empire, which had also inspired Garibaldi's nineteenth-century struggle for Risorgimento (cf. Gómez-Reino Cachafeiro 2002; Coen 1990).[25] Regional populists of Lega Nord held it for a direct provocation, however, as they were also inspired by the Lombards, in their fight for autonomy against "Rome". Soon after the Northern-Italian burgomasters of the successful Lega hijacked his message with the invented tradition of an annual oath in which they promise loyalty to their charismatic leader Umberto Bossi (like to his successor, Italy's current Deputy Prime Minister Matteo Salvini) in the struggle against "Roma Ladrona". Each year at the legendary sward of Pontida, where the Lombard League in 1167 united against the occupying imperial forces, they assemble in crusader's costume, pronouncing the sentence: "Today in Pontida our efforts for the freedom of our people converge with the sacrifice of our ancestors, who chose this place to swear their solemn duty to defend their freedom" (Pelgrom 2005, 208).

Similarly, the authoritarian Hungarian prime minister Viktor Orbán regards himself the new, "illiberal" leader of "21st-century Christian democracy", and succeeds to mobilize his followers in "peace marches" commemorating in a narrative of purity, degeneration, and victimhood the Hungarian freedom struggle against the Ottomans, the Habsburgs, the Bolshevists, and today against the European Union! Rallying up to 500,000 people at his 15 March 2018 celebration speech on the 1848–1849 Revolution for Independence in Budapest, he defined his supporters as the heirs of the freedom fighters of the 1848 revolution as well as of the Battle of Mohács (1526), and the 1956 Revolt, calling on them to prepare for a culture war against "an international network organized into a real empire". "Europe is being invaded", according to Orbán,

---

[25] Ironically, both Craxi and Bossi were sentenced to prison for political corruption in the 1995 *Mani Pulite* (clean hands), Enimont trial.

and "we have to deal with a displacement of people, which threatens our way of life" (Orbán 2018). His speech depicts Hungary as always having been the frontline of European culture, and it perfectly shows the connection of the crusader trope to that of the strongman prepared to take the lead in the struggle for the defence of Western Christian culture.

Such a politicization of culture closely relates to what the German Nazi theorist Carl Schmitt in *The Concept of the Political* (1932) defined as imposing authoritative decisions in "friend–enemy conflicts". More than ideological conflicts, such "total wars" were held by him for the most decisive factor in the creation of group identity, occurring at "the high points of politics" when enemies are recognized with "concrete clarity" as "other", "different", or "alien" (Schmitt 1996, 22–27, 53, 67–68, and see Antonio 2000, 59). Orbán borrowed a lot from Schmitt and his New Right followers when framing as his enemies, in the same speech: "Media supported by foreign consortia and local oligarchs, paid activists, agitators, NGOs funded by international speculators, things that the name of George Soros represents and embodies. It is this world that we must fight in order to preserve ours" (Orbán 2018). Seamlessly fitting into a fascist, anti-Semitic imagery of the cosmopolitan plutocrat, Soros, an Hungarian-born Jewish-American financier and philanthropist has become Orbán's perfect scapegoat.[26] His Open Society Institute supported dissidents in communist countries and black South African activists, whereas the Soros sponsored Central European University in Budapest has become an academic think tank for transitional justice and multiculturalism, the leading university in the region, and one of the wealthiest in Europe. Appealing to the Hungarian youth after his landslide 2018 victory, Orbán asked them to join his fight for their homeland in a long-awaited vengeance on Hungary's enemies, which will be no less than a total "moral, political, and legal revenge" (cf. Tharoor 2018). A year before, and faced with European and US protests, the Orbán administration had already issued new Hungarian legislation, known as the "Stop Soros" bill, against foreign-funded NGO's like the "Soros University". Immediately after the elections, a pro-government newspaper listed already two hundred CEU academics by name as Soros' "mercenaries", whereas the university, as unique for Europe,

---

[26] Orbán's defence against accusations of anti-Semitism (also from Hungary's Jewish community for praising the pro-Nazi Horthy regime), is his relation with Israel (Trew 2018).

faces the prospect of having to move its whole base abroad (cf. Kárath 2018; Walker 2018).

Nowadays, echoes of such authoritarian narratives from Orbán, or from his Russian ally Vladimir Putin, can be heard from right-wing political leaders in every part of Europe, even from Christian Democrats (who long cooperated with Orbán's political party in the EU parliament), for instance, when arguing for downgrading of the rights of Muslim organizations in defence of their nation's "way of life". Such Europe-wide repeated xenophobia also created the climate for Great Britain's majority vote in the Brexit referendum. And it was only a few years before that dramatic event that the Conservative English philosopher Roger Scruton asserted: "If we look at the big issues facing us today—the EU, mass immigration, the union, Islamic extremism, the environment—we will surely see that the Conservative view rightly identifies what is now at stake: namely the survival of our way of life" (Scruton 2014). It clearly illustrates Wright's observation how the New Right in England since the 1980s adopted the anthropological notion of culture as a "way of life" explicitly in lieu of its former racism, whereas the hegemonic core of "Englishness" stayed actually strongly class specific and white, as a clear marker of "one's own kind" (see Wright 1998, 10).

If culture took over the role of race and class, it was the politicization of nostalgia, even to a grim industrial past, which turned former trade-unionists into cultural conservatives, and migrants into "others" (for England in particular Hewison 1987; Reeve 2017, 65–76). I therefore agree with Bonefeld (2017, 747–761) that the authoritarian structure of the current EU's economic governance has "disarmed a whole tradition of left internationalism and reinforced earlier ideas about the nation as a force against globalization".[27] Like their non-European counterparts, such as the American white-nationalist alt-right movement and its figurehead Steve Bannon, who claimed to have delivered Donald Trump to world power in 2016, European parties succeeded in winning the popular vote for a heritage crusade against multiculturalism, refugees, and Islamism on behalf of Europe's "original", white *Leitkultur*,

---

[27] At the same time, one could say that the opposite is also true: the New Right is born out of the failure of Europe's social democracy to develop a defence strategy against growing class divisions, economic inequality, poverty, and the neoliberal destruction of the welfare state.

the 2015 Polish PiS government, with its successful "Orbánization" of media and state power; the rise to power of Austria's Freedom Party in 2017 (promoting a "culturally German" *Heimat* identity); the 2018s new Italian populist Lega-Five Star coalition government (refusing to ratify the EU's free trade agreement with Canada in support of farmers demanding specialty products like Parmesan cheese to be labelled "Made in Italy" as to defend the Italian economy against an invasion of cheap, foreign imitations)[28]; as well as many other supporters of Putin and Orbán's Eurasian model of authoritarian democracy.[29] What it shows, is how again and again a progressive culturalist discourse has been hijacked and step-by-step turned into its opposite. Volker Weiss has recently traced the discursive origin of these movements back to Alain de Benoist's French *Nouvelle Droit* movement and the German "national revolutionary" *Wir Selbst* activists, which since the late 1970s—in competition to "1968"—linked the decolonial "liberation struggle" against American (cultural) imperialism to the notion of "ethno-pluralism". By defending an *essentialist* notion of cultural diversity, they have sown the seeds of the current cultural struggle of Europe's *Eigenständiger Völker* to safeguard their traditions, heritage, folklore, community, and identity. This European "decolonization war" *against* the universalist, Western multicultural human rights discourse and the threat of globalization basically follows the Identitarian agenda of the "authoritarian revolt" (cf. Weiss 2017, 23, 187ff.).

From Black Pete to Kolobok

I believe UNESCO's conceptualization of cultural diversity in the Intangible Heritage Convention risks giving unexpected ammunition to such culture wars. It is as if the "universal will" of the 1989 Recommendation has been defeated from both the outside and the

---

[28] Both Lega and the 5-Star prime minister Luigi di Maio threatened to remove every Italian official defending treaties like CETA, even though Canada has actually recognized Italy's protected labels. See Hard Cheese (2018). The item seems not accidentally chosen, for immediately after UNESCO's inscription of the (transnational) Mediterranean diet on the Representative List (Mediterranean diet, ICH website 2013), the Unesco Club of Reggio Emilia filed the *Parmigiano Reggiano* for the Representative ICH list (Home of Parmigiano cheese 2013).

[29] Compare the Political Capital/SDI Report of Juhász, Györi, Krekó and Dezsö 2015, 53.

inside, on the one hand a geopolitical move from Western to Asian heritage approaches, and by an ideological move from progressive multiculturalism to New Right's identitarianism on the other. Together this has succeeded in redefining European nations as truly, hyperreal "imagined communities" in which it is no longer "diversity" but "identity" that is harmoniously integrated as the new normal (cf. Anderson 1983). Totally neglecting the New Right's move to culturalism, the New Left itself might be held partly responsible for this parallel development of cultural politicization. Adapted as it was, as we saw, from older scientific notions on race and biodiversity, UNESCO's mission of safeguarding cultural diversity by the preservation of intangible cultural heritage, came to frame culture in no longer empirical but normative categories. If this may seem self-evident to those who claim certain traditions as part of their endangered ethno-nationalist identity, such notions of cultural belonging should, however, never be taken for granted. For not only has heritage a complex, dynamic biography with many meanings for different communities, it is also easy to manipulate because of its fabricated character, which—in contrast to is aura of authenticity—is distinguished by a strong sense of "makeability" (cf. Lowenthal 1998, 1–16; van der Laarse 2005, 1–39; 2015, 345–346). Heritage is thus not only passively consumed, but *does* something to communities—it transforms virtual environments into experienced realities, just like a website algorithm filters personalized searches into compartmentalized, "common" lifestyles. Precisely this is what makes folklore and intangible heritage into such a powerful tools for cultural identity policies. Specifically, intangible heritage easily generates strong politics of affect when deployed as a marker of identity, but also, vice versa, transforms politics into "culturalism" (cf. Eriksen and Stjernfelt 2009). Probably, nothing evokes stronger feelings of "us" and "them" than an assumed threat to one's way of life. Activists therefore like to frame culture in terms of belonging and victimhood, as a heritage complex fundamentally endangered by outside forces of globalization, migration, capitalism, robbery, pollution, or "fake" media. This offers an enormous metacultural potential for exclusive, if not legally enforced, heritage claims, resulting in a growing overlap between left-wing and right-wing culturalist discourses.

The case of the Netherlands is again significant to demonstrate how both forms of culturalism with their different perspectives on diversity may clash on precisely the identification of intangible heritage. This strongly multicultural country witnessed an explosion of radical populism and the abandonment of multiculturalism as a political ideal after the assassinations of the anti-Islamic gay politician Pim Fortuyn by an animal-rights activist in 2002 and of the provocative right-wing filmmaker Theo van Gogh two years later by a radical Islamist (Saukkonen 2013). Remarkably though, it was actually in defence of freedom, secularization, and free speech that New Right politicians framed Islamic minorities and non-western refugees as a threat to what they regarded as quintessentially Dutch: the right to publicly criticize (or insult) minority cultures as inferior. Like in the US, England and other countries, populists hijacked progressive identity narratives to be transformed into an essentialist discourse in defence of a so-called "Judeo-Christian tradition". A concept originally constructed with an intention of inclusiveness, was now used for the exclusion of Muslims (not on racial but cultural grounds), from a historically bizarre, fabricated legacy of Christianity, Jewishness, and the Enlightenment (cf. Rosensaft 2013; and compare the negative opinions of Dutch Jews about its political use by PVV and Christian Democrats, see Voorn 2017).

In spite of a boom of ethnic hatred on the internet, and the opinions of some leading politicians, Dutch public opinion research clearly showed, though, that multicultural democracy since 2008 not really faced an electoral crisis, the majority continued to share multicultural values (cf. PVV-kiezer 2011),[30] and the country's long-term accommodationist traditions in public culture have thus far successfully prevented ethnic violence (cf. van der Laarse 2000, 50–76). What did change, however, was that Islamic communities lost their former political ties with progressive parties, which at the same time lost some support from Jewish and gay people attracted by the New Right's opposition to Islamic migration, though soon confronted with no less virulent anti-Semitism, anti-feminism, and homophobia among (5–15%) white right wing social media platforms as among Muslim communities. Nonetheless, the Dutch implementation of the Intangible Heritage Convention in political culture thus took place during a very visible, though strongly overrated, populist opposition to a progressive human rights discourse.

---

[30]The information is based on the Sociaal Cultureel Planbureau, which from 2008 produced a range of public opinion reports: 'Continu Onderzoek Burgerperspectieven', *Sociaal en Cultureel Planbureau*, https://www.scp.nl/Publicaties/Terugkerende_monitors_en_reeksen/Continu_Onderzoek_Burgerperspectieven.

This traumatic political climate might explain why difficult heritage issues around the Netherlands' most popular national ritual, the yearly *Sinterklaas* festivities, became the focus of a heated debate about the country's "forgotten" colonial past and the black page of its role in the global slavery trade.[31] This annual feast had never been strongly contested in Dutch society, and is still supported by 90% of the population.[32] This explains why, at the 2008 UNESCO expert meeting, a Dutch participant who demanded more attention for painful heritage, such as slavery, then pointed to the popular feast of Saint Nicholas as the opposite kind of safe and innocent folklore (Stam 2008, 6). A few years later, the country was deeply divided on what for long was regarded the most widely shared ritual in the Netherlands. After protests by black artists in 2011, the contestation focused on the release of an independent expert report by the Office of the United Nations High Commissioner for Human Rights' Working Group of Experts on People of African Descent, headed by the Jamaican Professor of Social History Verena Shepherd (Shepherd et al. 2013).[33]

The issue found its scapegoat in the jester-like type of Black Pete (*Zwarte Piet*), the popular servant of Sinterklaas, the legendary Catholic Saint Nicholas, patron saint of sailors. The bones of this Greek bishop were moved around 1000 CE from his Turkish town of Myra to the Italian town Bari (which later was briefly part of the Spanish empire). The Saint's name day (December 6) was very popular in the "Spanish" Low Countries, and has still a religious connotation in Belgium today.

---

[31] Dutch share in the European slave trade was 5–6% of 11 million African slaves transported to the New World, of which more than two-thirds (400,000) to Surinam, while many descendants are today living in the Netherlands (Emmer 2006; van Welie 2008, 1–2, 47–96).

[32] For background on the St. Nicholas cult and the contested heritage debate, see Rodenberg and Wagenaar (2016, 716–728), and for the late nineteenth century colonial iconography modelled on black courtiers and child slaves to be found on then rediscovered Dutch seventeenth century genre painting, see Kolfin (2012, 161–190) and Hondius (2014).

[33] Earlier protests went back to the 1980s, though the current controversy started when the Curaçaoan Dutch artist-activist Quinsi Gario in 2011 produced a theatre production called 'Zwarte Piet Is Racisme', which led to a media debate on a national scale, after which the debate was picked up again on an international scale with the Shepherd report; 'Zwarte Piet is Racisme-Campagne', Nederland wordt beter (2017), https://www.nederlandwordtbeter.nl/projecten/zwarte-piet-is-racisme-campagne/.

After the sixteenth-century Dutch Revolt against Habsburg Spain, the saint's name day in the protestant Netherlands (December 5) evolved into a national children's ritual, and most Dutch children are still growing up believing that once a year the "good holy man" blessed them with presents brought from his Cockaigne-like homeland of Spain. The figure of Black Pete was only introduced in a late nineteenth-century folklore book on national education, but the Saint's troops of young Moorish-looking helpers (who off the page were of course played by white people in blackface) have made this invented Spanish-colonial counter-image one of the strongest embodied figures of Dutchness. Despite nationwide support for the Sinterklaas festivities' nomination to the preliminary national inventory of intangible cultural heritage, the assessment procedure ran, however, completely different than expected. Because nominated heritage should not violate human rights, the traditional arrival of Saint Nicholas' ship, with its now presumed racist figure of Black Pete appeared to the UN's report in 2013 as no less than "a [yearly] Dutch return to slavery in the 21st century" (Shepherd et al. 2013).[34] Aware of the severity of the accusation, progressive city councils offered pragmatic solutions with rainbow colours, as had already been a tradition on one of the Dutch Caribbean islands (Op Curaçao 2013),[35] though some non-urban communities stubbornly defended "their" Black Petes against any outside interference. Even a Facebook page against the "abolition of Sinterklaas" was launched immediately after the release of the Shepherd report, and within two days earned in more than two million "likes" (just over one-eighth of the entire population), the highest number of likes ever reached in the country.[36] The culture clash divided towns and villages and strengthened the impression of a country-capital division. In the Frisian town Dokkum, where once the Anglo-Saxon missionary Saint Boniface was martyred for bringing Christianity, extreme-right activists raised roadblocks, with police support, to prevent buses with urban anti-Pete activists from protesting the festivities, whereas the orthodox

---

[34] See also the *YouTube* comments at 'Why Black Pete (Zwarte Piet) Is Racist'. Interview with Prof. Verena Shepherd (2013); and for a Dutch activist decolonial perspective, see Wekker (2016) and Weiner and Carmona Baéz (2018).

[35] On the Dutch Caribbean island of Bonaire, however, the black youth stayed loyal to a black-faced Black Pete and a white-faced Sinterklaas (Monna 2013).

[36] The slogan of the Facebook referendum was 'Don't let the Netherlands' most beautiful tradition disappear' (Zwartepietpetitie 2013).

protestant fishing village Urk began to rename some streets after seventeenth-century naval heroes like Michiel de Ruyter, who were accused of slave trading by anti-Black Pete activists (van Laarhoven 2018a, b).[37]

Apart from this internal Dutch conflict about intangible heritage, the Shepherd report also provoked debate among UN experts and UNESCO. The Flemish FARO director still wondered why the Dutch took so long to ratify the Convention, and accused black memory activists of using the Convention for their own agenda (Jacobs 2013). Like in the Netherlands, Belgium celebrates the annual entry by ship of Saint Nicholas around St. Martin's Day (11 November), broadcasted live on national television, and both the "Sinterklaas" and "Sint Maarten" rituals were registered in 2009, without any protest, on the Flemish Inventory for Intangible Heritage (Over Zwarte Piet). The Nederlands Instituut voor Volkscultuur (later renamed Kenniscentrum Immaterieel Erfgoed Nederland), however, hesitated to nominate the Feast for its national inventory intangible heritage as long as the Black Pete issue was unresolved (Posthumus 2013). Instead it called for expertise on the ritual's historical background, mediation, and consensus. Soon after, this approach was supported by the other four members of Shepherd's UN Working Group of Experts on People of African Descent, who called for an open dialogue in Dutch society and convinced the UN to drop its complaint of a human rights violation (van der Zeijden 2014; see also UN Experts Call for Dialogue 2013 and Waterfield 2013). Yet, after having published a historical study, an international report on the debate, educational material and even a comic book to guide debate among school children, while still receiving an average of some 1500 daily hate males, the Kenniscentrum in 2015 supported the nomination of *Sinterklaasfeest*, including Black Pete, for inscription on the Inventory Intangible Heritage in the Netherlands, while declaring that the tradition could still be changed according to the outcome of the debate (van der Ploeg 2015; Visser 2015; Wagenaar and Rodenberg 2018). Remarkably, a new network organization for the local Sinterklaas committees with the archaic name of "Sint en Pietengilde" (Saint Nicholas and Peters Guild) was made responsible for the heritage listing as well as the preservation and future of the tradition. On the website of this self-proclaimed "living

---

[37] Ironically, the same Dutch naval hero is honoured with a monument in the Hungarian town of Debrecen for his 1676 liberation of 26 protestant Hungarian ministers from Habsburg galley slavery.

community", however, the idea of Black Pete being a racist figure was in 2018 rejected in only a short text as nothing more than a proven historical falsification, under the heading of "solving debate?" (Oplossing debat?).

This Dutch case therefore is a good example of the inherent contradictions of the intangible heritage turn. Whereas the 2003 Convention was supposed to safeguard community identities against threats of globalization, it shows how precisely the heritagization of living cultures has after UN expert investigations of its relation to human rights violations, itself become perceived by local and national communities as a "grave threat" to their "way of life". Such outside interference may also transform existing cultural forms into easy targets for identity politics—both from national governments and minority activists. For, in the first place, neither the anti-Petes, nor pro-Petes were really considering universal values of cultural diversity. Even the UN experts were actually exchanging *civil* for *cultural* rights, and so did their opponents (with a white instead of black activist's agenda). In contrast to the Convention's metacultural assumptions of cultural debate and dialogue, essentialist assumptions of heritage and identity were dominating both sides of the "debate". Yet, such culture wars not only broke out by outside UN interventions; over the past decade, comparable intangible heritage conflicts can be found on the European continent between the EU and the rising forces of Western European Identitarianism and Eastern European authoritarianism, and between many ethnically revitalized communities, wanting to defend their cultures, territories, and borders. Because so many countries have in the past been part of the same empires (through what are now often regarded as "occupations"), they still share parts of the same popular culture.[38]

Yet such recognition of mutual heritage has hardly prevented claims of exclusive ownership. In 2010, for instance, a fairy-tale competition broke out between Russia and Ukraine (Rosenberg 2011; Osborn 2011) at the same time as the countries' more widely known political memory conflict on the Holodomor, the 1932–1933 Stalinist "terror famine", which the Ukrainian government now officially calls the "Ukrainian Genocide" (and claimed to have killed even more victims than the Holocaust), and on the posthumously proclaimed national hero

---

[38] See Plokhy (2015, 19–32) for a remarkable Russian-Ukrainian contested/shared religious heritage case of the US transferred holy remains of Prince Yaroslav the Wise.

Stepan Bandera. Although Israel, Russia, and Poland held Bandera, the Ukrainian fascist nationalist leader during World War II, responsible for genocide against Jews and Poles, Bandera statues, museums, and street names have replaced those of Lenin in many Ukrainian towns; this as a result of a new state-organized heritage regime after the decommunization policy since the 2014 Euromaidan revolt and the subsequent Russian–Ukrainian conflicts on the annexation of Crimea and the violent Donbass War (Snyder 2010; van der Laarse 2016b).[39]

Precisely as in Peeva's documentary *Whose Is This Song?*, the curiosity about each other's mutual folklore was initially related to the wish to strengthen the bond between what were then still "befriended nations". In 1997 Russia and Ukraine had signed an official Treaty on Friendship, Cooperation and Partnership, respecting the inviolability of their mutual borders and the principle of territorial integrity, as well as the rights and freedoms of minorities of the other countries within their borders (which is no longer in force since 1 April 2019). Yet soon each country started mapping its "own" folklore. Russia released a *Fairy Tales Map of Russia* with about thirty figures, such as the giant knight Muromets, Kurochka, the chicken with the golden eggs, and Kolobok, a smiling dumpling acting as a runaway bun (comparable to the Gingerbread Man), who were all attributed a Russian origin (cf. Fantastic Map of Russia 2011; Marshall 2004; Are There Any Secrets 2017). A university chair on Kolobocology (*Kolobkovedenie*) was even created at Ulyanovsk State University, held by Professor Sergei Petrov, while Kolobok's supposed hometown of Ulyanovsk (also Lenin's birth town, known as Simbirsk before 1924) had already chosen him in 2008 as the mascot for the 2018 FIFA World Cup in Russia. At the same time, the *Fantastic Tales of the Ukraine* appeared, with the same figures on display, and Ukrainian historians and linguists were convinced that the name Kolobok was derived from the Ukrainian *kolo*, meaning round, like the pastry's shape. Yet in Russia a ball of dough is called a *kolob*, and the traditional name for dough in Simbirsk (Ulyanovsk's region) should be *kolebyatka*, as stated by Professor Petrov. The Ukrainians are convinced that Russia stole their heroes, and folklorists complain that their fairy tales have not been listed in UNESCO's Memory for the World Register, like the early nineteenth-century Annotated Reference Copies of the

---

[39] This was at the end of Viktor Yushenko's government, which took over power with the 2004 Orange revolution. On the revived Bandera campaign, see van der Laarse (2016a, 2017, 143–168).

Kinder- und Hausmärchen (Children's and Household Tales) collected by the Brothers Grimm in 2005 (*Kinder- und Hausmärchen*; Hensen 2011; Rosenberg 2011). For some also economic interests are at stake. Countries can actually earn a lot of money by a touristic exploitation of their "own" fairy tales, such as the German city of Kassel with the Brothers Grimm's figure of the Pied Piper of Hamelin after the inscription of their Fairy Tales as UNESCO Memory of the World. In addition, in 2017 even the "telling of fairy tales", has been registered as a German tradition on a national inventory for the UNESCO Intangible Heritage list. The Russian-Ukrainian tales were less successful, although the Russians succeeded at least in commodifying their fairy-tale modelled kolobok as fried dough balls served as street food during the 2018 World Cup (Bunina 2018; Rennick 2018).

It is shocking to see how, like in former Yugoslavia before, folklore conflicts turned into violence between countries sharing the same empire's past. Thus, although many Russian and Ukrainian fairy tales had been shared for centuries (and also been known to other countries), within a few years they turned from a mutual heritage into a nightmare of competing commodified folklore. The nationalization of popular culture has in the present context of military conflict taken extremist geopolitical forms. Thus, after splitting from the Orthodox Church, nationalizing the Ukrainian language, and introducing political purifications and decommunization laws, Ukraine officially banned twenty popular fairy-tale books on *bogatyrs*, the traditional Russian knight errant, in 2018. This battle about folklore and fictional characters may continue with film and literature, and the whole apparatus of public archives, media, and memory.[40] It might be clear that it is actually not a fear of *someone else's* heritage, but that of sharing *the same* heritage, a fear of polluting a pure and proud identity, that is considered to be most threatening to what is held and defended as one's way of life.

Conclusion

Without any pretention to completeness, I hope to have shown how the safeguarding of representative intangible heritage contributed to heritage conflicts between countries and communities that claim the

---

[40] According to Russian fairy tales 2017 and from the official Russian perspective see Ukrainian Authorities (2017).

same traditions as their own. UNESCO's focus on representative and "neutral" intangible heritage items has actually supported an unexpected folklorization, nationalization, and politicization of culture. Against the "spirit" of the Convention, the traditionalist authorized narrative focusing on authenticity and traditions has succeeded to "contaminate" the State Parties ICH recommendations (Sousa 2018, 56). Even more, instead of safeguarding universal cultural values of diversity, its instruments are more and more used for cultural identity politics and exclusive national claims on shared heritage. Even the notion of safeguarding itself has fostered unwanted effects. Echoing the fin-de-siècle trope of the degeneration or decay of presumed pure and harmonious cultures, cultural safeguarding is portrayed as the last defence against "grave threats" to community identities. The vaguely defined threats of globalization and cosmopolitanism, which Hungarian-nationalist discourse embodies in the figure of George Soros, is in my opinion so powerful because it appeals equally to culturalists from the right and the left, both sharing the modernist assumption of a paradise lost and a strong belief in the makeability and regeneration of culture.

Yet what went wrong? Firstly, like the spatial, performative, and digital turn in cultural sciences, the intangible heritage turn initially seemed to provide a necessary alternative to authorized heritage discourses, but after the existing masterpiece lists were adapted, it now just looks like another branch of the same brand. Thus, instead of approaching culture as commons, the Convention came to protect cultural property and its assumed intangible values as community belongings, and not much is left of the original urgency of safeguarding endangered living cultures (cf. Benesch et al. 2015). And even in case of bottom-up ICH "webcommunities" sharing "web mapping" platforms, the support of ministries of culture is often needed to enhance their visibility and thus to strengthen the authoritative role of central governments up into the digital world (Sousa 2018, 45).

Secondly, the Convention's notion of cultural diversity lost its potential inclusive meaning encompassing minority cultures as well as the often "forgotten", dissonant heritage of twentieth-century diasporic communities in and beyond Europe. For not only are societies (national states as well as minority cultures) above all imagined communities with symbolic boundaries, in the digital age cultural borders have also become more fluid than ever before (Anderson 1983; Bauman 2000). Yet rightly among current generations of assimilated Jews, Armenians, and Blacks, for example, one finds a surge for "symbolic ethnicity", or virtual bonds based on identifications with traumatic pasts (Smith 1981, 157, and see also Gans 1979). People's diasporic identities are often more related to peers a hundred kilometers away than to their local communities. Far removed from their families' "original" countries, such "travelling memories" will not meet UNESCO's "living heritage" criteria while their remembrances will not be supported by local communities currently living in the houses, or among the traces, of their erased forefathers, even when virtually revived as heritage tourism destinations (cf. Mendelsohn 2006; Bartov 2007). In contrast to the World Heritage list, which registered Auschwitz-Birkenau in 1978, or the *Diary of Anne Frank* (2009) and the *Westerborkfilm* (2017) listed in the UNESCO's Memory of the World register, the Intangible Cultural Heritage lists, so far lacks any reference to such "heritage that hurts" (Uzzel and Ballantyne 2000, 503–508). Belgium, it is true, in 2016 nominated 20,000 newspaper articles from 1914 to 1919 for the World Memory Register programme, as well as the In Flanders Fields museum for the UNESCO World Heritage List and the impressive Last Post Ceremony at the Menin Gate Memorial for UNESCO's Register of Good Safeguarding Practices of the ICH, both in Ypres—Europe's first bombed city—but all these nominations have been either withdrawn or rejected.[41]

[41] Information from Prof. Marc Jacobs, director of FARO, the Flemish NGO for Intangible Cultural Heritage and temporary seat for the Flemish Memory of the World Committee, who was also a member of the Flemish UNESCO Committee (2010–2016), E-mail, 23 April 2018. And compare on the combined federal and Flemish application for the digitised collection of Belgium War newspapers (submitted 20 May 2016): 'De Belgische pers tijdens WO I en het Memory of the World programma van UNESCO', FARO, 6 November 2015, https://faro.be/nieuws/de-belgische-pers-tijdens-woi-en-het-memory-of-the-world-programma-van-unesco, and *100 Jaar Groote Oorlog in Vlaanderen, Vlaams Actieplan 2014–2018*, December 2016, 40, https://www.vlaanderen.be/de/nbwa-news-message-document/document/09013557801c296d; for the negative ICOMOS advice on the In Flanders Fields Museum: Kabinet Bourgeois, 'Unesco zet deur op een kier voor WO I Werelderfgoeddossier', 16 May 2018, Wereldoorlog I in *De Westhoek* – *Greatwar.be*, http://www.wo1.be/nl/nieuws/62747/unesco-zet-deur-op-een-kier-voor-woi-werelderfgoeddossier, and to the Last Post Ceremony: Examination of Proposals for Selection in 2017 on the Register (item 11.e on the agenda), *ICH website*, https://ich.unesco.org/en/11e-register-00940. To this might be added the negative ICOMOS advice of April 2018 on the nomination of the combined French, British, and German war graves for UNESCO's World Heritage program, on the argument

Thirdly, the biggest problem seems to be, however, that culture has turned into a list, and that lists categorize and suggest a hierarchy and a kind of completeness which can never be achieved, and will never be taken for granted because of this selectiveness (cf. Schuster 2002). For *who* decides what is on and off the list, and *whose* heritage should be rescued, shown, and commoditized by whom, and for what? Lists promote safe choices, i.e. beautiful, impressive, and intriguing national icons such as Spanish Flamenco, the Indonesian Wayang puppet theatre, the Peking Opera, the Belgian Carnival of Binche, or traditional Lithuanian crafts (cf. Tauschek 2010, 257–312; Vincent Winterman, coordinator of the Netherlands' UNESCO Committee speaks about symbol, see Chin-A-Fo 2010). They order things to consume, packaged in memoryscapes or soundscapes, because heritage is after all a cultural mode of production that commodifies virtual identities by way of folklorization, musealization, and mediatization within the context of a rising experience economy for which it has become a crucial agent.

This brings me, finally, to the question of (hyper)reality. The Cartesian distinction between spirit and matter is deceptive, because heritage- and memoryscapes are mindscapes, and the value of art lies in the eye of the beholder. What is lacking in the 2003 Convention is therefore a more critical reflection on theoretical key concepts like authenticity and identity, and related heritage dissonances (see Peckham 2003; Turnbridge and Ashworth 1996; Kisić 2017). The way in which "living heritage" has been framed as an intangible opposite to "static" materiality is problematic because of heritage's intrinsic dynamic nature and intermediality. For something to be perceived as a monument, one needs to have an idea, derived from a poem, a text, music, or ritual. Such cultural forms cannot be owned but circulate within many communities and cultures, being endlessly re-invented, delocalized, canonized, and re-mediated. Ironically, it is precisely those nationalist appropriations, like the Macedonian "Skopje 2014" project of a young Balkan country risen as an offshoot from the imploded Socialist Federal Republic of Yugoslavia, that show how every essentialist act of heritage localization

---

that safeguarding war heritage (although it concerns a site of transnational remembering) would be too politically contested (België verbijsterd 2018), although there is still a comparable application in the making by the French Association of Landscapes and Memorials of the Great War, http://www.paysages-et-sites-de-memoire.fr/association-of-landscapes-and-memorials-of-the-great-war/.

completely fails to understand its deeply virtual nature: this gigantic, neoclassicist architectonic facelift of a capital city basically tried to materialize a cultural image and historical tradition. In this case it concerned the "appropriation" of the Hellenistic heritage of its Greek neighbour who in turn prevented Macedonia's admission to the European Union until its renaming in 2018 as the Republic of North Macedonia (Janev 2016, 111–130; Smith 2018).

Heritage is always material and intangible at the same time. In the ICOMOS Declaration of San Antonio (1996) on the significance of authenticity for cultural heritage practices, the "comprehensive cultural value of our heritage" is therefore rightly considered as understandable both through a historical study of "the material elements inherent in the tangible heritage, and a deep understanding of the intangible traditions associated with the tangible patrimony" (The Declaration of San Antonio). However, even within such a dynamic dialectical framework, the old notion of authenticity comes back like a boomerang (for the Netherlands, see Margry and Roodenburg 2007, 1–10). This applies not only to a concept like cultural heritage, which implicitly assumes a genealogy or biography, but equally to, for instance, the human rights discourse of the UNESCO Convention on the Means of Prohibiting and Preventing the Illicit Import, Export and Transfer of Ownership of Cultural Property 1970, and the UNIDROIT Treaty of 1995 on the restitution of art and cultural heritage. It is hard to see how one can proceed with a dynamic intangible heritage approach when so much weight is given to the return of "authentic" objects to "countries of origin" without taking their fabricated character in consideration. Unfortunately, even local cultures will not be safeguarded by such safeguarding policies, as compensation generally works in favour of national elites and capital cities, even after a regime change or annexation, as in the current case of the "orphaned" Crimean treasures, which according to a Dutch court should "return" to Kiev, Ukraine—where they have never been before (van der Laarse 2016b, 15–52).

As it is hard to separate material from intangible values, in all such cases, I have argued that whereas material heritage is preoccupied with decay and authenticity, intangible heritage is obsessed with identity and ownership, and thus with cultural threats from "others". Yet both share the same metacultural production of heritage, and both compete as selective acts of preservation and safeguarding within a market of competing heritage claims. Most important though is the dominant role of states in the recommendations and implementation procedures which prevents a truly participatory approach. Anthropologists and ethnographers have already recorded how under the influence of UNESCO "living" traditions from Siberia to Indonesia have turned into staged folklore in state museums and tourism experiences, whereas from Bolivia to the Balkans multicultural complexities made way for hegemonic simplicities monumentalized in stories and stone. It confronts us with new ethical dramas, like that of heritage experts in the undesirable role of identity amplifiers (Adams 2009, 45–59, 57).

Acknowledgements This research was supported by funding from the European Union, through the Marie Skłodowska-Curie Innovative Training Network 'CHEurope: Critical Heritage Studies and the Future of Europe' H2020 Marie Skłodowska-Curie Actions 722416.

REFERENCES

SCHOLARLY PUBLICATIONS

Adams, K.M. 2009. Generating Theory, Tourism, and 'World Heritage' in Indonesia: Ethical Quandaries for Anthropologists in an Era of Tourist Mania. In *Tourism and Applied Anthropologists: Linking Theory and Practice*, ed. Tim Wallace, spec. issue *NAPA Bulletin* 23: 45–59.

Aikawa-Faure, N. 2009. From the Proclamation of Masterpieces to the Convention for the Safeguarding of Intangible Cultural Heritage. In *Intangible Heritage*, ed. L. Smith and N. Akagawa, 13–44. London and New York: Routledge.

Anderson, B. 1983. *Imagined Communities: Reflections on the Origin and Spread of Nationalism*. London and New York: Verso.

Antonio, R.J. 2000. After Postmodernism: Reactionary Tribalism. *American Journal of Sociology* 106: 40–87.

Ashworth, G. 2005. Heritage and the Consumption of Places. In *Bezeten van vroeger*, ed. R. van der Laarse, 193–206. Amsterdam: Het Spinhuis.

Bachmann-Medick, D. 2007. *Cultural Turns. Neuorientierungen in den Kulturwissenschaften*. Reinbeck bei Hamburg: Rohwolt.

Baillie, B., A. Chatzoglou, and S. Taha. 2010. Packaging the Past: The Commodification of Heritage. *Heritage Management* 3 (1): 51–71.

Barkan, E. 2000. *The Guilt of Nations: Restitution and Negotiating Historical Injustices*. Baltimore and London: John Hopkins University Press.

Bartov, O. 2007. *Erased: Vanishing Traces of Jewish Galicia in Present-Day Ukraine*. Princeton: Princeton University Press.

Baudrillard, J. 1981. *Simulacres et simulation*. Paris: Galilée.
Bauman, Z. 2000. *Liquid Modernity*. Cambridge: Polity Press.
Bendix, R. 2007. Kulturelles Erbe zwischen Wirtschaft und Politik. In *Prädikat Heritage. Wertschöpfung aus kulturellen Ressourcen*, ed. D. Hemme, M. Tauschek, and R. Bendix, 337–356. Münster: LIT.
Benesch, H., Feras Hammami, Ingrid Holmberg, and Evren Uzer (eds.). 2015. *Heritage as Common(s), Common(s) as Heritage*. Curating the City series. Gothenburg: Makadam.
Berlin, I. 1981. The Counter-Enlightenment. In *Against the Current: Essays in the History of Ideas*, ed. Roger Hausheer. Oxford: Oxford University Press.
Blake, J. 2009. UNESCO's 2003 Convention on Intangible Cultural Heritage: The Implications of Community Involvement in 'Safeguarding'. In *Intangible Heritage*, ed. L. Smith and N. Akagawa, 45–73. London and New York: Routledge.
Bonefeld, W. 2017. Authoritarian Liberalism. From Schmitt Via Ordoliberalism to the Euro. *Critical Sociology* 43 (4–5): 747–761.
Boorstin, D. 1992 [1961]. *The Image, a Guide to Pseudo-Events in America*. New York: Vintage.
Bortolotto, C. 2013. Authenticity: A Non-criterion for Inscription on the Lists of UNESCO's Intangible Cultural Heritage Convention. In *2013 IRCI Meeting on ICH—Evaluating the Inscription Criteria for the Two Lists of UNESCO's Intangible Cultural Heritage Convention, The 10th Anniversary of the 2003 Convention*. Final Report, 10–11 January 2013. Tokyo, Japan (International Research Centre for the Intangible Cultural Heritage in the Asia-Pacific Region [IRCI] in cooperation with Maison des Cultures du Monde, France), 73–79.
Broekhoven, J. 2011. Genealogy or Shamanism: Struggles for Power, Charisma and Authority. PhD dissertation RUG.
Burke, P. 1978. *Popular Culture in Early Modern Europe*. New York: Harper & Row.
Burke, P. 2009. *Cultural Hybridity*. Cambridge: Polity Press.
Crane, S. 2000. *Collecting & Historical Consciousness in Early Nineteenth-Century Germany*. Ithaca and London: Cornell University Press.
de Cesari, C. 2012. Thinking Through Heritage Regimes. In *Heritage Regimes and the State*, vol. 6, ed. R.F. Bendix, A. Eggert, and A. Peselmann, 399–413. Göttingen Studies in Cultural Property. Göttingen: Universitätsverlag Göttingen.
de Leeuw, R. 2010. Op weg naar ratificatie. De UNESCO Conventie en de Nederlandse overheid. *Levend erfgoed* (special issue *Immaterieel erfgoed*) 7 (1): 11–17.
Dibbets, H., S. Elpers, P.J. Margry, and A. van der Zeijden. 2011. *Immaterieel erfgoed en volkscultuur. Almanak bij een actueel debat*. Amsterdam: Amsterdam University Press.

Eco, U. 1995 [1986]. *Faith in Fakes: Travels in Hyperreality. Essays*, 1–58. New York: Vintage.
Elefterias-Kostakidis, E. 2013–2014. Whose Is This Song? Nationalism and Identity Through the Lens of Adela Peeva. *Modern Greek Studies: Crisis, Criticism and Critique in Contemporary Greek Studies* 16–17 (A): 21–43.
Elpers, S. 2005. *Frau Antje bringt Holland. Kulturwissenschaftliche Betrachtungen einer Werbefigur im Wandel*. Münster: Waxmann.
Emmer, P.C. 2006. *The Dutch Slave Trade 1500–1600*. Oxford: Berghahn.
Eriksen, T.H. 2001. Between Universalism and Relativism: A Critique of the UNESCO Concept of Culture. In *Culture and Rights: Anthropological Perspectives*, ed. J. Cowan, M.-B. Dembour, and R. Wilson, 127–148. Cambridge: Cambridge University Press.
Eriksen, J.-M. 2013. Culturalism: When Culture Becomes Political Ideology. *Telos* 163: 131–146 (earlier published in *Eurozine*, 9 January 2009).
Eriksen, J.-M., and F. Stjernfelt. 2009. Culturalism: Culture as Political Ideology. *Eurozine*, 9 January.
Eriksen, J.-M., and F. Stjernfelt. 2012. *The Democratic Contradictions of Multiculturalism*. Candor: Telos Press.
Finkelkraut, A. 1987. *La défaite de la pensée*. Paris: Gallimard.
Foster, M.D. 2015. UNESCO on the Ground. In *UNESCO on the Ground: Local Perspectives on Intangible Cultural Heritage*, ed. M.D. Foster and L. Gilman, 1–14. Bloomington: Indiana University Press.
Gans, H.J. 1979. Symbolic Ethnicity: The Future of Ethnic Groups and Cultures in America. *Ethnic and Racial Studies* 2 (1): 1–20.
Geertz, C. 1973. *The Interpretation of Cultures*. New York: Basic Books.
Geisler, M.E. 2005. In the Shadow of Exceptionalism: Germany's National Symbols and Public Memory After 1989. In *National Symbols, Fractured Identities: Contesting the National Narrative*, ed. M.E. Geisler, 63–100. Middlebury: Middlebury College Press.
Gómez-Reino Cachafeiro, M. 2002. *Ethnicity and Nationalism in Italian Politics: Inventing the Padania: Lega Nord and the Northern Question*. London and New York: Routledge.
Grevers, M. 2004. Visualisering en collectieve herinneringen. Volendams meisje als icoon van de nationale identiteit. *Tijdschrift voor Geschiedenis* 117: 207–220.
Gruber, R.E. 2002. *Virtually Jewish: Reinventing Jewish Culture in Europe*. Berkeley, Los Angeles, and London: University of California Press.
Hafstein, V.T. 2004. The Making of Intangible Cultural Heritage. Tradition and Authenticity, Community and Humanity. Unpublished PhD dissertation, University of California, Berkeley.
Hafstein, V.T. 2008. Intangible Heritage as a List: From Masterpieces to Representation. In *Intangible Heritage*, ed. L. Smith and N. Akagawa, 93–111. London: Routledge.

Harrison, R. 2010. What Is Heritage? In *Understanding the Politics of Heritage*, ed. R. Harrison, 5–42. Manchester: Manchester University Press.

Hewison, R. 1987. *The Heritage Industry: Britain in a Climate of Decline*. London: Methuen.

Holtorf, C. 2017. What's Wrong with Cultural Diversity and Archaeology? *Claroscuro* 16 (December): 1–14.

Hondius, D. 2014. *Blackness Inn Western Europe: Racial Patterns of Paternalism and Exclusion*. New Brunswick, NJ: Transaction.

Identificatie met Nederland. 2007. WRR Report No. 79. Amsterdam: Amsterdam University Press.

Janev, G. 2016. Skopje 2014: Erasing Memories, Building History. In *Balkan Heritages: Negotiating History and Culture*, ed. Maria Couroucli and Tchavdar Marinov, 111–130. London and New York: Routledge.

Judt, T., and T. Snyde. 2013. *Thinking the Twentieth Century*. London: Vintage Books.

Kerkhoven, J. 2010. Immaterieel erfgoed, wetenschappelijke belangen, kromme tenen. *Levend erfgoed* (special issue *Immaterieel erfgoed*) 7 (1): 47–51.

Kirshenblatt-Gimblett, B. 1998. *Destination Cultures: Tourism, Museums and Heritage*. Berkeley: University of California Press.

Kirshenblatt-Gimblett, B. 2004. Intangible Heritage as Metacultural Production. *Museum International* 56 (1–2): 52–64.

Kisić, V. 2017. *Governing Heritage Dissonance: Promises and Realities of Selected Cultural Practices*. Amsterdam: European Cultural Foundation.

Kolfin, E. 2012. Becoming Human: The Iconography of Black Slavery in French, British and Dutch Book Illustrations c.1600–c.1800. In *From Renaissance Trophy to Abolitionist Emblem: The Slave in European Art Publications of the Warburg Institute*, ed. E. McGrath and J.M. Massing, 161–190. London: Warburg Institute.

Kuper, A. 1999a. *Culture, the Anthropologists' Account*. Cambridge, MA: Harvard University Press.

Kuper, A. 1999b. Culture. In *The Evolution of Cultural Entities*, ed. M. Wheeler, J. Ziman, and M.A. Boden, 87–102. Oxford and New York: Oxford University Press.

Landsberg, A. 2004. *Prosthetic Memory: The Transformation of American Remembrance in the Age of Mass Culture*. New York: Columbia University Press.

Lévi-Strauss, C. 1952. *Race and History*. Paris: UNESCO.

Lévi-Strauss, C. 1994. Anthropology, Race, and Politics: A Conversation with Didier Eribon. In *Assessing Cultural Anthropology*, ed. Robert Borofsky, 420–425. New York: McGraw-Hill.

Lowenthal, D. 1997. *The Heritage Crusade and the Spoils of History*. Cambridge: Cambridge University Press.

Lowenthal, D. 1998. Fabricating Heritage. *History and Memory* 10 (1): 1–16.
Lowenthal, D. 2002 [1985]. *The Past Is a Foreign Country.* Cambridge: Cambridge University Press.
Lowenthal, D. 2005. Keynote Lecture at the Amsterdam Conference 'The Challenge of Heritage: Heritage and History. Rivals and Partners in Europe'. In *Bezeten van vroeger. Erfgoed, identiteit en musealisering*, ed. R. van der Laarse, 29–39. Amsterdam: Het Spinhuis.
MacCannell, D. 1989 [1976]. *The Tourist: A New Theory of the Leisure Class.* New York: Shocken Books.
MacCannell, D. 2011. *The Ethics of Sightseeing.* Berkeley, Los Angeles and London: Routledge.
Macdonald, S. 2013. *Memorylands: Heritage and Identity in Europe Today.* London and New York: Routledge.
Mandler, P. 1997. *The Fall and Rise of the Stately Home.* New Haven and London: Yale University Press.
Margry, P.J. 2010. SIEF, ICH, UNESCO en het curieuze NGO-wezen. De UNESCO-bijeenkomst in Abu Dhabi. *Levend erfgoed* (special issue *Immaterieel erfgoed*) 7(1): 4–17.
Margry, P.J. 2014. UNESCO en de paradox van bescherming. *Immaterieel erfgoed in Nederland. Ons Erfdeel* 1: 56–66.
Margry, P.J., and H. Roodenburg (eds.). 2007. *Reframing Dutch Culture: Between Otherness and Authenticity.* Aldershot: Ashgate.
Marshall, B.C. 2004. *The Snow Maiden and Other Russian Tales.* World Folklare Series. Westport, CT and London: Libraries Unilimited.
Mazzucchelli, F. 2013. (Post-)urbicide. Reconstruction and Ideology in Former Yugoslavia's Cities. In *Post-conflict Reconstructions: Re-mappings and Reconciliations*, ed. M. Rui Goncalves and F. Zullo. Nottingham: CCCP.
Mendelsohn, D. 2006. *The Lost: A Search for Six of Six Million.* New York: Harper.
Meskell, L. 2018. *A Future in Ruins: UNESCO, World Heritage and the Dream of Peace.* Oxford: Oxford University Press.
Müller-Will, S. 2010. Claude Lévi-Strauss on Race, History, and Genetics. *Biosocieties* 5 (3): 330–347.
Olick, J.K. 2007. *The Politics of Regret: On Collective Memory and Historical Responsibility.* New York: Routledge.
Peckham, R.S. 2003. Introduction: The Politics of Heritage and Public Culture. In *Rethinking Heritage: Cultures and Politics in Europe*, ed. Robert Shannon Peckham, 1–16. London and New York: I.B. Tauris.
Pelgrom, A. 2005. The Lombard League Traditions in Northern Italy. In *Statehood Before and Beyond Ethnicity: Minor States in Northern and Eastern Europe, 1600–2000*, ed. L. Eriksonas and L. Müller. Brussels: Peter Lang.

Plokhy, S. 2015. The Missing Skeleton: Understanding the Identities of Kyivan Rus. In *Religion, State, Society and Identity in Transition Ukraine*, ed. R. van der Laarse, M.N. Cherenkov, V.V. Proshak, and T. Mykhalchuk, 19–32. Oisterwijk: Wolf Legal Publishers.

Pullan, W., and M. Gwiazda. 2008. 'City of David': The Politicisation of Urban Heritage. *Conflict in Cities and the Contested State*. Working Paper No. 6, Cambridge University.

Reeve, M. 2017. Grim up North? Northern Identity, History, and Heritage. *International Journal of Regional and Local History* 12 (2): 65–76.

Rodenberg, J., and P. Wagenaar. 2016. Essentializing 'Black Pete': Competing Narratives Surrounding the Sinterklaas Tradition in the Netherlands. *International Journal of Heritage Studies* 22 (9): 716–728.

Rooijakkers, G. 2005. De musealisering van het dagelijks leven. In *Bezeten van vroeger*, ed. van der Laarse, 207–217. Amsterdam: Het Spinhuis.

Saukkonen, P. 2013. Multiculturalism and Cultural Policy in Northern Europe. *Nordisk kulturpolitsk tidsskrift* 16 (2): 178–200.

Schilbrack, K. 2005. Religion, Models of, and Reality: Are We Through with Geertz? *Journal of American Academy of Religion* 73 (2): 429–452.

Schmitt, C. 1996. *Der Begriff des Polischen* (1932), trans. G. Schwab. *The Concept of the Political*. Chicago: University of Chicago Press.

Seeger, A. 2001. Lessons learned from the ICTM (NGO) Evaluation of Nominations for the UNESCO Masterpieces of the Oral and Intangible Heritage of Humanity, 2001–2005. In *Intangible Heritage*, ed. L. Smith and N. Akagawa, 112–128. London and New York: Routledge.

Silberman, N. 1991. Desolation and Restoration: The Impact of a Biblical Concept on Near Eastern Archaeology. *The Biblical Archaeologist* 54 (2): 76–87.

Smeets, R. 2010. Twee nieuwe UNESCO erfgoedlijsten. De Conventie van het immaterieel erfgoed. *Levend erfgoed* (special issue *Immaterieel erfgoed*) 7 (1): 4–10.

Smith, A.D. 1981. *The Ethnic Revival in the Modern World*. Cambridge and New York: Cambridge Univeristy Press.

Smith, L. 2006. *Uses of Heritage*. London and New York: Routledge.

Souillac, G. 2011. *The Burden of Democracy: The Claims of Culture, Public Culture and Democratic Memory*. Plymouth: Lexington Books.

Sousa, F. 2017. Map of E-Inventories of Intangible Heritage, *Memoriamedia Review* 1, 1–13. http://memoriamedia.net/pdfarticles/ENG_MEMORIAMEDIAREVIEW_Mapa_einventarios.pdf.

Sousa, F. 2018. *The Participation in the Safeguarding of the Intangible Cultural Heritage: The Role of Communities, Groups and Individuals*. Alenquer, Portugal: Memória Imaterial CRL.

Steiner, W., and S. Benedik. 2005. *Kino, Kur und Kerksuppe. Leben und Gegensätzen in Oberzeiring 1920–1980.* Oberzeiring.

Tauschek, M. 2010. Wertschöpfung aus Tradition. *Der Karnaval von Binche und die Konstituerung kulturellen Erbes.* Berlin: LIT Verlag.

Tauschek, M. 2011. Reflections on the Metacultural Nature of Intangible Cultural Heritage. *Journal of Ethnology and Folkloristics* 5 (2): 49–64.

Thompson, M. 1979. *Rubbish Theory: The Creation and Destruction of Value.* Oxford: Oxford Univeristy Press.

Tietmeyer, E., et al. (eds.). 2010. *Die Sprache der Dinge. Kulturwissenschaftliche Perspektiven auf die materielle Kultur.* Münster: Waxmann.

Turnbridge, J.E., and G.J. Ashworth. 1996. *Dissonant Heritage: The Management of the Past as a Resource in Conflict.* Chichester: Wiley.

Urry, J. 2002 [1991]. *The Tourist Gaze.* 2nd ed. London, Thousand Oaks, and New Delhi: Sage.

Uzzel, D., and R. Ballantyne. 2000. Heritage That Hurts: Interpretation in a Postmodern World. In *The Heritage Reader*, ed. G. Fairclough, R. Harrison, J.H. Jameson, and J. Schofield, 503–508. London and New York: Routledge.

van der Laarse, R. 2000. Bearing the Stamp of History. The Elitist Route to Democracy in the Netherlands. In *European Democratization Since 1800*, ed. J. Garrard, V. Tolz, and R. White, 50–76. Houndmills and New York: Macmillan.

van der Laarse, R. 2005. Erfgoed en de constructie van vroeger. In *Bezeten van vroeger. Erfgoed, identiteit en musealisering*, ed. R. van der Laarse, 1–39. Amsterdam: Het Spinhuis.

van der Laarse, R. 2010. Gazing at Places We Have Never Been: Landscape, Heritage and Identity. In *The Cultural Landscape and Heritage Paradox*, ed. T. Bloemers, H. Kars, A. Van Der Valk, and M. Wijnen, 321–328. Amsterdam: Amsterdam University Press.

van der Laarse, R. 2011. De terugkeer van het eigene. *Boekman. Tijdschrift voor kunst, cultuur en beleid* (special issue *Volkscultuur?*) 88: 88–95.

van der Laarse, R. 2013. Archaeology of Memory. Holocaust Dissonances in East and West. In *Heritage Reinvents Europe*, ed. D. Callebaut, J. Mařik, and J. Mařiková-Kubková, 121–130. Budapest: Europae Archaeologiae Consilium/Archaeolingua.

van der Laarse, R. 2015. Fatal Attraction. Nazi Landscapes, Modernism and Holocaust Memory. In *Landscape Biographies*, ed. J. Kolen, H. Renes, and R. Hermans, 345–375. Amsterdam: Amsterdam University Press.

van der Laarse, R. 2016a. "Il nous l'ont fait": Muséographie des mémoires concurrentes après 1989. In *Muséographie des Violences en Europe centrale et ex-URSS*, ed. D. Bechtel and L. Jurgenson, 213–232. Paris: Sorbonne-Kimé.

van der Laarse, R. 2016b. Who Owns the Crimean Past? Conflicted Heritage and Ukrainian Identities. In *A Critical Biographic Approach of Europe's Past*, ed. D. Callebaut, 15–52. Gent: Provincie Oost-Vlaanderen.

van der Laarse, R. 2017. Bones Never Lie? Unearthing Europe's Age of Terror in the Age of Memory. In *Mapping the 'Forensic Turn'*, ed. Z. Dziuban, 143–168. Vienna: VWI.

van der Laarse, R. 2018. Tourism Conflicts and Conflict Tourism. Curating 'Holoscapes' in Europe's Age of Crisis. In *Heritage and Tourism: Places, Imageries, and the Digital Age*, ed. L. Egberts and M.D. Alvarez, 31–54. Amsterdam: Amsterdam University Press.

van der Laarse, R., A. Labrie, and W. Melching (eds.). 1998. *De hang naar zuiverheid. De cultuur van het moderne Europa*. Amsterdam: Het Spinhuis.

van der Valk, A. 2010. Planning the Past. In *The Cultural Landscape and Heritage Paradox: Protection and Development of the Dutch Archaeological-Historical Landscape and Its European Dimension*, ed. Tom Bloemers et al., 21–52. Amsterdam: Amsterdam University Press.

van der Zeijden, A. 2010. Betrokkenheid organiseren van onderop. De centrale rol van 'communities' in de Immaterieel Erfgoed Conventie. *Levend erfgoed* 7 (1): 24–27.

van der Zeijden, A. 2015. Cultural Tourism and Intangible Heritage: A Critical Appraisal and Policy Guidelines. In *Anthropology as a Driver for Tourism Research*, ed. W. Munsters and M. Melkert, 191–202. Antwerpen and Apeldoorn: Garant.

van Welie, R. 2008. Slave Trading and Slavery in the Dutch Colonial Empire: A Global Comparison. *New West Indian Guide* 82 (2): 47–96.

Wagenaar, P., and J. Rodenberg. 2018. Acting in a National Play: Governmental Roles During the Zwarte Piet Contestation. In *Cultural Contestation: Heritage, Identity and the Role of Government*, ed. J. Rodenberg and P. Wagenaar, 283–314. Palgrave Studies in Cultural Heritage and Conflict. New York: Palgrave Macmillan.

Weemaels, F. 1969–1970. Hoffmann von Fallersleben en de Nederlanden. *Ons Erfdeel*, 13: 146–148.

Weiner, M.F., and A. Carmona Baéz (eds.). 2018. *Smash the Pillars: Decoloniality and the Imaginary of Colour in the Dutch Kingdom*. New York: Lexington.

Weiss, V. 2017. *Die Autoritäre Revolt. Die Neue Rechte und der Untergang des Abendlandes*. Stuttgart: Klett-Gotta.

Wekker, G. 2016. *White Innocence: Paradoxes of Colonialism and Race*. Durham: Duke University Press.

Wright, P. 1985. *On Living in an Old Country: The National Past in Contemporary Britain*. Oxford: Oxford University Press.

Wright, S. 1998. The Politicization of Culture. *Anthropology Today* 14 (1): 7–15.

Websites and Newspapers

Are There Any Secrets in Russian Folk Tales? Kolobok and Repka. *Instant Advices*, 19 October 2017. http://instadvices.com/are-there-any-secrets-in-russian-folk-tales-kolobok-and-repka/.

Binder, A. 2018. 5 German Traditions Listed as UNESCO Intangible Cultural Heritage. *DW. Made for Minds*, 26 June. https://www.dw.com/en/5-german-traditions-listed-as-unesco-intangible-cultural-heritage/a-39542142.

Bohstrom, P. 2017. Did David and Solomon's United Monarchy Exist? Vast Ancient Mining Operation May Hold Answers. *Haaretz*, 21 November.

Bunina, M. 2018. The 2018 FIFA World Cup Russia: What Will Football Fans Feast on? *Russia Beyond*, 12 January. https://www.rbth.com/russian-kitchen/327239-2018-fifa-world-cup-russia-football.

Chin-A-Fo, H. 2010. Flamenco, de Franse keuken, de Peking Opera. Wat staat er op de lijst van immaterieel cultureel erfgoed? *NRC-Handelsblad* 27 November.

De Belgische pers tijdens WO I en het Memory of the World programma van UNESCO. *FARO*, 6 November 2015. https://faro.be/nieuws/de-belgische-pers-tijdens-woi-en-het-memory-of-the-world-programma-van-unesco.

de Mik, K. 1993. Faksisten' mogen het Frysk Flaggeliet niet meezingen. *NRC-Handelsblad*, 27 September.

Eco, U. 2007. Temples for the Tourists. *The New York Times*, 2 April. https://www.nytimes.com/2007/04/02/opinion/02iht-edeco.1.5111284.html.

Elina Psykou. Biography. *IMDb*. http://www.imdb.com/name/nm1841581/.

Europe, Oh Europe. *Anemon Productions*. http://www.anemon.gr/films/film-detail/europe-oh-europe.

'Fantastic Map of Russia' project from Alexey Kozlovsky. 2011. *Ria Novosty*. https://ria.ru/trend/fairytale_map_27042011/. [In Russian].

Grandjean, M. 2016. Mapping UNESCO Intangible Cultural Heritage. *MartinGrandjean Digital Humanities*, 28 April. http://www.martingrandjean.ch/mapping-unesco-intangible-cultural-heritage/m.

Hard Cheese: Italy Vows to Scupper EU Free Trade Deal with Canada. *The Guardian*, 13 July 2018. https://www.theguardian.com/world/2018/jul/13/say-cheese-why-italy-wont-ratify-eu-free-trade-deal-with-canada.

Hensen, C. 2011. Het koekemannetje en de boze buren. *NRC Weekend*, 7–8 May.

Home of Parmigiano Cheese Aims for UNESCO Recognition. *L'Italo-Americano*, 14 March 2013. https://italoamericano.org/story/2013-3-14/ReggioEmilia-WorldHeritage.

Horling, A. 2012. Friezen herdenken Slag bij Warns (1345). *Historiek*, 5 September. https://historiek.net/friezen-herdenken-omstreden-slag-bij-warns-1345/18190/.

Imhof, A. Het immaterieel erfgoed verdrag biedt alle ruimte. *Nederlandse UNESCO Commissie*. https://www.unesco.nl/artikel/het-immaterieel-erfgoed-verdrag-biedt-juist-alle-ruimte.

Jacobs, M. 2013. UNESCO heeft beslist: Sinterklaas kan geen werelderfgoed worden. *FARO.be*, 23 October. https://faro.be/blogs/marc-jacobs/unesco-heeft-beslist-sinterklaas-kan-geen-werelderfgoed-worden.

Kabinet Bourgeois. Unesco zet deur op een kier voor WO I Werelderfgoeddossier. *Wereldoorlog I in De Westhoek - Greatwar.be*, 16 May 2018 http://www.wo1.be/nl/nieuws/62747/unesco-zet-deur-op-een-kier-voor-woi-werelderfgoeddossier.

Kárath, K. 2018. Hungarian Scientists Are on Edge as Country Is Poised to Force Out Top University. *Science*, 10 May. http://www.sciencemag.org/news/2018/05/hungarian-scientists-are-edge-country-poised-force-out-top-university.

Kenniscentrum Immaterieel Erfgoed Nederland. https://www.immaterieel-erfgoed.nl/inventaris#eyJxcyI6IiIsInR5cGUiOiJsaXN0IiwiY3VzdG9tGl-2b3RzIjpbImltbWF0ZXJpZWVsZXJmmZ29lZF9pbmZvIl0sImZpbHRlcnMiOltbWyJpcl19zdGVwMSIsdHJ1ZV1dXSwiYW55a2V5d29yZCI6Wzg4OV0sInBhZ2UiOjUsImZhY2V0Y2I6e319.

Legêne, S. 2006. Laten we dus de herinnering herstellen. Autoriteit en collectieve constructies van het eigene. *Ketelaar-lezing 2006*, The Hague. https://anzdoc.com/laten-we-dus-de-herinnering-herstellen-autoriteit-en-collect.html.

Maxima—'The Dutchman Does Not Exist'. YouTube. https://www.youtube.com/watch?v=zt0pHmZuDz0.

Mediterranean Diet: Cyprus, Croatia, Spain, Greece, Italy, Morocco and Portugal Inscribed in 2013 (8.COM) on the Representative List of the Intangible Cultural Heritage of Humanity. *ICH Website*. https://ich.unesco.org/en/RL/mediterranean-diet-00884.

Monna, J. 2013. Op Bonaire schminkt de Sint zijn huid elk jaar wit. *Trouw*, 24 October. https://www.trouw.nl/home/op-bonaire-schminkt-de-sint-zijn-huid-elk-jaar-gewoon-wit~aa1cd495/.

Op Curaçao hebben ze al regenboogpieten, *AD*, 24 October 2013. https://www.ad.nl/buitenland/op-curacao-hebben-ze-al-regenboogpieten~a4022a1e/.

Oplossing debat? *Sint & Pietengilde*. http://sintenpietengilde.nl/vergeten-symboliek-binnen-maatschappelijke-debat/.

Orbán: We Must Fight Against an Organized International Network. *Visigrad Post*, 16 March 2018. https://visegradpost.com/en/2018/03/16/orban-we-must-fight-against-an-organized-international-network/.

Osborn, A. 2011. Russia and Ukraine Squabble over Fairytale Characters. *The Telegraph*, 29 April. http://www.telegraph.co.uk/news/worldnews/europe/russia/8481095/Russia-and-Ukraine-squabble-over-fairytale-characters.html.

Over Zwarte Piet en Immaterieel Cultureel Erfgoed. *LECA*. https://www.lecavzw.be/nieuws/over-zwarte-piet-en-immaterieel-cultureel-erfgoed.

Posthumus, N. 2013. Sinterklaasfeest niet op UNESCO-lijst vanwege Zwarte Piet. *NRC-Handelsblad*, 26 October.

PVV-kiezer negatiefst over homo's. *De Volkskrant*, 6 September 2011. https://www.volkskrant.nl/nieuws-achtergrond/pvv-kiezer-negatiefst-over-homos~b8465899/.

Rennick, L. 2018. Here's How the World Cup Is Putting Russia's Street Food on the Map. *SBS*, 21 June. https://www.sbs.com.au/food/article/2018/06/21/heres-how-world-cup-putting-russias-street-food-map.

Rieks Smeets Interviewed in Henk van Renssen, Monumentenzorg voor zang, dans en ambachten. *De Volkskrant*, 23 August 2003.

Rosenberg, S. 2011. Russia and Ukraine in Bun Fight over Fairy Tales. *BBC News*, 27 April. http://www.bbc.com/news/world-europe-13206871.

Rosensaft, M. 2013. Jewish Values and the Judeo-Christian Tradition Do Not Belong to the Fundamentalist Right. *Huffington Post*, 27 April. https://www.huffingtonpost.com/menachem-rosensaft/jewish-values-and-the-jud_b_2757928.html.

Rothman, M. 2014. 10 Reasons the 'City of David' Is Not the Wholesome Tourist Site You Thought It Was. *The Times of Israel*, 9 February.

Russian Fairy Tales About Bogatyrs Are Not Allowed in Ukraine, 112 International, 5 December 2017. https://112.international/society/russian-fairy-tales-about-bogatyrs-are-not-allowed-in-ukraine-23336.html.

Scruton, R. 2014. Why It's so Much Harder to Think Like a Conservative. *The Guardian*, 10 September. https://www.theguardian.com/commentisfree/2014/sep/10/why-its-harder-to-think-like-a-conservative.

Shepherd, V. et al. 2013. Request for Information on the Dutch Celebration of Black Pete, 17 January 2013. https://spdb.ohchr.org/hrdb/23rd/public_-_AL_Netherlands_17.01.13_%281.2013%29.pdf.

Smith, H. 2018. Macedonia Agrees to New Name After 27-Year Dispute with Greece. *The Guardian*, 12 June.

Snyder, T. 2010. A Fascist Hero in Democratic Kiev. *The New York Review of Books*, 24 February. http://www.nybooks.com/daily/2010/02/24/a-fascist-hero-in-democratic-kiev/.

Stiftung Slach by Warns. 1345. http://www.betinking-slachbywarns.nl/index_NL.html.

Tharoor, I. 2018. How Viktor Orbán Became the Real Threat to the West. *The Washington Post*, 6 April. https://www.washingtonpost.com/news/worldviews/wp/2018/04/06/how-victor-orban-became-the-real-threat-to-the-west/?utm_term=.40045aea8250.

The List of Intangible Cultural Heritage and the Register of Good Safeguarding Practices, UNESCO. https://ich.unesco.org/en/lists.

The Nobel Peace Prize. 2012. European Union (EU), The Norwegian Noble Committee. https://www.nobelprize.org/nobel_prizes/peace/laureates/2012/press.html.

Toespraak van Prinses Máxima. *Het Koninklijk Huis*, 24 September 2007. https://www.koninklijkhuis.nl/documenten/toespraken/2007/09/24/toespraak-van-prinses-maxima-24-september-2007.

Trew, B. 2018. Israel's Netanyahu Criticised for Wooing Hungary's Far-Right Prime Minister Orbán. *Independent*, 19 July. https://www.independent.co.uk/news/world/middle-east/netanyahu-orb-n-israel-welcome-hungary-prime-minister-antisemitism-a8454866.html.

Ukrainian Authorities Designate Russian Fairy Tales as National Security Threat. *Sputnik International*, 22 December 2017. https://sputniknews.com/europe/201712221060252657-ukrainian-ban-on-russian-fairy-tales/.

UN Experts Call for Dialogue on Controversy over Dutch 'Black Pete' Holiday Tradition. United Nations Human Rights Office of the High Commissioner. *UN News*, 21 November 2013. https://news.un.org/en/story/2013/11/456012-un-experts-call-dialogue-controversy-over-dutch-black-pete-holiday-tradition.

van der Ploeg, J. Sinterklaas (en Zwarte Piet) Immaterieel Erfgoed. *De Volkskrant*, 15 January 2015. https://www.volkskrant.nl/nieuws-achtergrond/sinterklaas-en-zwarte-piet-immaterieel-erfgoed-~b42822cf/.

van der Zeijden, A. 2014. Dealing with Black Pete. Media, Mediators and the Dilemmas of Brokering Intangible Heritage. *Volkskunde* 3: 349–360. http://www.albertvanderzeijden.nl/2014.3%20Albert%20van%20de%20Zeijden.pdf.

van Laarhoven, K. 2018a. In Dokkum had de politie alleen oog voor Zwarte Piet-tegenstanders. *NRC-Handelsblad*, 29 April. https://www.nrc.nl/nieuws/2018/04/29/de-hooligans-konden-gewoon-doorlopen-a1601268.

van Laarhoven, K. 2018b. Urk vernoemt straten naar zeehelden als tegengeluid. *NRC-Handelsblad*, 21 February. https://www.nrc.nl/nieuws/2018/02/21/urk-vernoemt-straten-naar-zeehelden-als-tegengeluid-a1592953.

Visser, Y. 2015. Sinterklaasfeest op lijst immaterieel Erfgoed. *Historiek*, 16 January. https://historiek.net/sinterklaasfeest-op-lijst-immaterieel-erfgoed/47448/.

Whose Is This Song? *Adela Media: Film and TV Production Company*. http://www.adelamedia.net/movies/whose-is-this-song.php.

Why Black Pete (Zwarte Piet) Is Racist. Interview with Prof. Verena Shepherd. *YouTube*, 26 October 2013. https://www.youtube.com/watch?v=AMuQtk0Reqo.

Wilders: Friesland Is boegbeeld van nationale trots en vrijheid. *Trouw*, 15 January 2011. https://www.trouw.nl/home/wilders-friesland-is-boegbeeld-van-nationale-trots-en-vrijheid~ad294c08/.

Zwartepietpetitie gaat 2 miljoen likes voorbij. *Het Parool*, 24 October 2013. https://www.parool.nl/kunst-en-media/zwartepietpetitie-gaat-2-miljoen-likes-voorbij~a3532658/.

Documents

100 Jaar Groote Oorlog in Vlaanderen. *Vlaams Actieplan 2014–2018*, December 2016. https://www.vlaanderen.be/de/nbwa-news-message-document/document/09013557801c296d.

Advies Immaterieel Erfgoed, Raad voor Cultuur, 3 April 2014, rc-2013.06814/2, page 8, on the request on international nomination for UNESCO lists (including selection criteria) of Min. of OCW Jet Bussemaker, 26 July 2013, rc-2013.06814/1. https://www.cultuur.nl/upload/documents/adviezen/advies-immaterieel-erfgoed.pdf.

Advies Nationale UNESCO Commissie over de Conventie betreffende de bescherming van het immaterieel cultureel erfgoed, Nationale UNESCO Commissie, Den Haag, 10 November 2008.

Coen, L. 1990. Craxi detta il decalogo di Pontida. *La Republica*, 4 March. http://ricerca.repubblica.it/repubblica/archivio/repubblica/1990/03/04/craxi-detta-il-decalogo-di-pontida.html.

Convention for the Safeguarding of the Intangible Cultural Heritage, Paris, UNESCO Legal Instruments, 17 October 2003. http://www.unesco.org/eri/la/convention.asp?KO=17116&language=E.

Convention on the Means of Prohibiting and Preventing the Illicit Import, Export and Transfer of Ownership of Cultural Property 1970, UNESCO Legal Instruments. http://portal.unesco.org/en/ev.php-URL_ID=13039&URL_DO=DO_TOPIC&URL_SECTION=201.html.

Dossier: Immaterieel Erfgoed, UNESCO Nederlandse Commissie. https://www.unesco.nl/nl/dossier/immaterieel-erfgoed.

Dossier: Werelderfgoed, Rijksdienst voor het Cultureel Erfgoed. https://cultureelerfgoed.nl/dossiers/werelderfgoed/werelderfgoed-in-nederland.

Examination of Proposals for Selection in 2017 on the Register (item 11.e on the agenda). *ICH Website*. https://ich.unesco.org/en/11e-register-00940.

Hafstein, V.T. UNESCO Organization. http://portal.unesco.org/en/ev.php-URL_ID=30438&URL_DO=DO_TOPIC&URL_SECTION=201.html.

Imhof, A. 2014. Het immaterieel erfgoed verdrag biedt alle ruimte, Nederlandse UNESCO Commissie, 17 April. https://www.unesco.nl/artikel/het-immaterieel-erfgoed-verdrag-biedt-juist-alle-ruimte.

Immaterieel Erfgoed. Nederlands Instituut voor Volkscultuur, Utrecht, 25 June 2008.

Keynote Marc Jacobs, Belgium UNESCO Representative of the Paris Committee at the Expert Meeting, *Verslag expert*.

Kinder- und Hausmärchen. Memory of the World. UNESCO.org. http://www.unesco.org/new/en/communication-and-information/memory-of-the-world/register/full-list-of-registered-heritage/registered-heritage-page-4/kinder-und-hausmaerchen-childrens-and-household-tales/.

Kunst van Leven. 2007. *Hoofdlijnen cultuurbeleid*. The Hague: Min. OCW.
Recommendation on the Safeguarding of Traditional Culture and Folklore, 15 November 1989. UNESCO.org. http://portal.unesco.org/en/ev.php-URL_ID=13141&URL_DO=DO_TOPIC&URL_SECTION=201.html.
Schuster, M.J. 2002. Making a List and Checking It Twice: The List as a Tool of Historic Preservation. Working Paper of the Cultural Policy Center, The University of Chicago, Version 2.2, 25 November. https://culturalpolicy.uchicago.edu/making-list-and-checking-it-twice-list-tool-historic-preservation.
Stam, D. 2008. Verslag expert meeting Immaterieel Erfgoed at the Nederlands Instituut voor Volkscultuur, Utrecht 25 juni 2008. Advies Nationale UNESCO Commissie, Den Haag, 10 November, bijlage 2.
Text of the Convention for the Safeguarding of the Intangible Cultural Heritage, ICH-UNESCO. https://ich.unesco.org/en/convention.
The Declaration of San Antonio. 1996. ICOMOS. http://www.icomos.org/docs/san_antonio.html.
The Nara Document on Authenticity. 1994. ICOMOS. https://www.icomos.org/charters/nara-e.pdf.
UNESCO Intangible Cultural Heritage Lists, Wikipedia. https://en.wikipedia.org/wiki/UNESCO_Intangible_Cultural_Heritage_Lists.
Unidroit Convention on Stolen or Illegally Exported Cultural Objects. 1995. UNIDROIT Instruments. https://www.unidroit.org/instruments/cultural-property/1995-convention.
van Mensch P., and L. Meijer-van Mensch. 2010. Collecting as Intangible Heritage. *Collecting Newsletter* 9. ICOM Museum. http://network.icom.museum/fileadmin/user_upload/minisites/comcol/Newsletter/Newsletter9.pdf.
Verslag van werkzaamheden van de Nationale UNESCO Commissie 2009. Den Haag, Nationale UNESCO Commissie, 2010, 23–24. https://www.unesco.nl/sites/default/files/dossier/verslag_werkzaamheden_natcom_2008-2009_def.pdf?download=1.
Voorn, J. 2017. Wat vinden Nederlandse Joden van de term joods-christelijk? *De Kanttekening*, 4 April. https://dekanttekening.nl/samenleving/wat-vinden-joden-van-de-term-joods-christelijk/.
Walker, S. 2018. Liberal Hungarian University warns Viktor Orbán could force it abroad. *The Guardian*, 15 May. https://www.theguardian.com/world/2018/may/15/central-european-university-ready-to-move-out-of-hungary.
Waterfield, B. 2013. UN drops Black Pete 'racism' charge against the Dutch, *The Telegraph*, 24 October. https://www.telegraph.co.uk/news/worldnews/europe/netherlands/10402662/UN-drops-Black-Pete-racism-charge-against-the-Dutch.html.
What Is Intangible Heritage? UNESCO Intangible Cultural Heritage. https://ich.unesco.org/en/what-is-intangible-heritage-00003.

Open Access This chapter is licensed under the terms of the Creative Commons Attribution 4.0 International License (http://creativecommons.org/licenses/by/4.0/), which permits use, sharing, adaptation, distribution and reproduction in any medium or format, as long as you give appropriate credit to the original author(s) and the source, provide a link to the Creative Commons license and indicate if changes were made.

The images or other third party material in this chapter are included in the chapter's Creative Commons license, unless indicated otherwise in a credit line to the material. If material is not included in the chapter's Creative Commons license and your intended use is not permitted by statutory regulation or exceeds the permitted use, you will need to obtain permission directly from the copyright holder.

PART II

Borders and Mobility

CHAPTER 5

Bodies Making Spaces: Understanding the Airport as a Site of Dissonance

Milica Trakilović

Amsterdam Airport Schiphol in the Netherlands is a veritable hub of networks, contact zones, and transfers. Boasting the title of third-largest airport in Europe in terms of number of passengers, it now processes approximately 60 million passengers yearly. Schiphol wants to be known for four intersecting qualities, being "efficient, reliable, sustainable, and inspiring" (Amsterdam Airport Schiphol). As a frequent flyer in and out Schiphol myself, I can attest to its fulfilling these aims: I always marvel at the speed and ease with which I am able to move through the airport, whether on my way to a gate or back from a trip. While going through many airports is a chore, being at Schiphol is almost a treat; as I effortlessly move from one section to the next, I am entertained by colourful and inviting shop displays, art objects, and informational posters and notices. Although this warm reception is part of Schiphol's aim to "provide smooth processes and good facilities and [do] everything in its power to guarantee its passengers a pleasant journey" and "to remain the preferred airport in Europe", (ibid.) my experience is not a universal

M. Trakilović (✉)
Graduate Gender Programme - Department of Media and Culture Studies, Utrecht University, Utrecht, The Netherlands

© The Author(s) 2019
T. Lähdesmäki et al. (eds.),
Dissonant Heritages and Memories in Contemporary Europe,
Palgrave Studies in Cultural Heritage and Conflict,
https://doi.org/10.1007/978-3-030-11464-0_5

one. Indeed, Schiphol, like all airports, is very much a site of (invisible) border zones that will allow easy entry to some subjects, while prohibiting free movement to others.

In January of 2017, I spoke to a young Syrian who had come to the Netherlands in 2015, seeking asylum. More specifically, his place of arrival was Schiphol, but his experience of the place differed drastically from mine. While I routinely experience almost uninterrupted movement in this large and seemingly open space, my interviewee's[1] stay at Schiphol was characterized by waiting and confinement. After introducing himself as a refugee to the Schiphol police, he spent seven days in the Schiphol detention centre while waiting for his request for asylum to be processed. During this time, his movement was severely restricted; he describes the detention centre as a "good prison", but a prison nevertheless. I take this personal account as the empirical starting point of my analysis, which will center on a phenomenological reading of the space of Schiphol Airport. I thereby join several other contributors to this book who have chosen to analyze particular spaces as sites of heritage dissonance, notably Iris van Huis and Sigrid Kaasik-Krogerus. In my analysis, Schiphol also emerges as a site of heritage dissonance.

Theorizing on the possibility of queering social spaces through the arrival of different bodies, Sara Ahmed writes that "the skin of the social might be affected by the comings and goings of different bodies, creating new lines and textures in the ways in which things are arranged" (2006, 9). At the same time, as Anssi Paasi notes, spaces are constantly being reworked and reconstructed based on unequal and hierarchical power relations, "in the sense that some actors are more actively participating in the production of space/scale while most people are 'consuming' and reproducing them" (2001, 13). In this chapter, I consider how the controlled movement of bodies in airports contributes to, and contests, both the European memory-heritage-identity complex (Macdonald 2013, 5) and the (Dutch) cultural archive (Wekker 2016). The former concept is useful in this analysis because it allows for an exploration of the airport as a historically, culturally, and politically entangled phenomenon, while the latter specifically addresses the ways in which the Dutch cultural canon, to which Schiphol belongs in my analysis, is built on an

---

[1] The interview was conducted in the context of the ERC project Bodies Across Borders in Europe: Oral and Visual Memory in Europe and Beyond on 14 January 2017 in Amsterdam, The Netherlands.

imperial and colonial legacy. I will provide a phenomenological account of Schiphol Airport based on my interviewee's experience of arriving in the Netherlands as a Syrian national and applying for asylum. In the process, I am guided by the following question: To what extent are European cultural and national politics of belonging being promoted and enforced at airports in general, and Schiphol Airport in particular, through processes of detainment and control, and to what extent does Schiphol emerge as a site of heritage dissonance through this dynamic?

METHODOLOGICAL FRAMEWORK AND CONCEPTUAL APPROACH

Space and Belonging

In this chapter, I ask how spatiality and belonging are negotiated at the airport and how they impact on identity formation. At the same time, in no way do I want to produce a unitary, simplified, or homogenous conceptualization of identity, or any conceptual category for that matter. In her chapter in this volume, Tuuli Lähdesmäki has noted that identity has become a rather weak analytical category, and instead proposes the concept of belonging, as that indicates a process rather than a fixed position. I join her in this approach, particularly drawing on Marco Antonisch's (2010, 645) argument that any analysis of belonging should contain considerations both of personal feelings of being "at home" (or not) somewhere and of the broader discursive dimension that "constructs" belonging according to a particular social and spatial ordering, and in so doing produces a "politics of belonging". My analysis of Schiphol consists precisely of these two dimensions. My interviewee's embodied experience of arriving at Schiphol and being detained represents the first set of empirical data and the starting point of my analysis. From there, I extend the analysis to a broader observation of Schiphol's spatial ordering, which includes Schiphol's camp-like detention centre and the "open" space of the airport. With the latter, I pay particular attention to how certain objects, visuals, and discourses are disseminated, and what kind of politics of belonging is attached to them. I am informed by Benedict Anderson's formulation of the nation as an imagined community that rests in the imagined union of its national subjects (2006, 7), as well as Anthony Easthope's insistence that nations exist in their discursive dimensions (1999, iix). All of this suggests that cultural and national identities are performative rather than absolute, which also means that I am less interested in pinpointing *what* a national space may be and more in *how* it is brought into being, i.e. what cultural, organizational, and ideological practices are at the heart of these conceptualizations. That being said, in this analysis I do understand Schiphol Airport as a specifically *European* space according to a critical postcolonial/decolonial scholarly framework.

To think about spaces is to think about the kinds of bodies that can inhabit them. In other words, the question of spatiality is largely a question of bodily presence. In this chapter, I take a phenomenological approach in looking at the connection between spaces and bodies, which means that I am interested in actual bodily practices that make up somebody's being-in-the-world and the inevitable affective experiences that accompany these. I agree with Sharon Macdonald when she says that:

> Giving attention to materialities not only recognizes the inevitably material nature of human existence but also opens up investigation of how the differential properties of particular materials, objects or technologies interact with human endeavour and understanding; in other words, what difference do the differences between things make? (2013, 84)

Indeed, what difference do the differences between bodies and the way that they are positioned in space make? First of all, it is important to note how spatiality and understandings of belonging are and have always been inextricably linked. As Anssi Paasi observes: "Identity is not merely an individual or social category, but also—crucially—a spatial category, since the ideas of territory, self and 'us' all require symbolic, socio-cultural and/or physical dividing lines with the Other" (2001, 10). Paasi here not only points to the importance of recognizing the spatial and territorial logic of identity formation, but also its inherent hierarchical ordering. Since "space" (as a concept and a physical structure) can only exist if it is in some way delineated or defined, then it follows that identities require boundaries as well, if they are to be comprehensible, "readable". In this chapter, drawing on the conceptual work by Sara Ahmed in *Queer Phenomenology* (2006) and *A Phenomenology of Whiteness* (2007), I am taking a phenomenological approach by looking at how a spatial makeup and the controlled movement of bodies in spaces (airports in particular) bring into being and enforce dominant notions of national and cultural heritage, keeping in mind how these may be contested as well.

Europe and Race

Many scholars have made the link between a European claim to colour blindness (notably El-Tayeb 2011; Goldberg 2006; Wekker 2016) and the dominant conception of spaces as (culturally, politically, and ideologically) "white". As Fatima El-Tayeb states in *European Others*:

> To reference race as native to contemporary European thought, however, violates the powerful narrative of Europe as a colorblind continent, largely untouched by the devastating ideology it exported all over the world. This narrative, framing the continent as a space free of 'race' (and, by implication, racism), is not only central to the way Europeans perceive themselves, but also has gained near-global acceptance. (2011, xv)

El-Tayeb here speaks of the way in which European spaces have been imagined, and of the dominant cultural and symbolic framings and perceptions which have followed from the idea that Europe is a continent that is not influenced or "touched" by race. Theo Goldberg points out how, in order to maintain this ideal of a racially homogenous space, Europe has historically purged its territories from those considered non-white and/or non-European, both in a symbolic and in a literal sense, "repeatedly making the Different different so as to sustain the Same" (2011, 357). El-Tayeb joins him in this line of thought by illustrating how "Europeans possessing the (visual) markers of Otherness" will always stand outside of a conceptualization of European authenticity and thus will always carry the notion of "arrival" with them, even if they belong to the descendants of migrants who arrived to Europe decades before (2011, xxv). This reinforces the racialized idea that there is a "proper Europeanness" (El-Tayeb 2011, xii), but the exclusionary logic on which this notion is built is difficult to critique or even point out.

Gloria Wekker comes to a similar conclusion with regards to the question of a racialized cultural identity in the Netherlands. She argues that identifying the "whiteness" of the dominant conception of Dutchness is "iconoclastic" (Wekker 2016, 2), because the racialized logic that is the foundation of this self-conception is completely disavowed. This dominant idea is part of the Dutch cultural archive, "an unacknowledged reservoir of knowledge and affects based on four hundred years of Dutch imperial rule" (ibid.) that informs the processes of making meaning on all levels (individual, institutional, and structural/symbolic).

The cultural archive for Wekker is not located in any particular place, but it does inform behaviours, rules, knowledge, and emotions because it works as "a repository of memory, in the heads and hearts of people" (2016, 19), and thus also inevitably influences the spatial ordering of bodies and objects.

Wekker's notion of the cultural archive as a highly elaborate system in some respects echoes Sharon Macdonald's theory of the European memory complex, which she in fact points out is better referred to as "the memory-heritage-identity complex" (2013, 5). Both concepts point to the interrelation between the workings of memory, the construction of belonging, and the preservation and building of heritage sites/spaces where memory and identity come together. In fact, both Wekker and Macdonald emphasize the foundational importance in the European imaginary of World War II and the centrality of the Holocaust "as the epitome and model of racist transgressions" (Wekker 2016, 4), resulting in the cosmopolization of the memory of the Holocaust in Europe and beyond as well (Macdonald 2013, 214). The centrality of the Holocaust in European memory is also responsible for a "displacement" of European colonialism "off" the European shores and from European historical consciousness, which invokes the notion of Europe as a separate space free of racism all the more (Wekker 2016, 4). Theo Goldberg notes how the Holocaust serves as a reference point in the European imaginary which results in a "racial erasure" and an "evaporation" of colonial history from European shores (2006, 336). Both the (Dutch) cultural archive and the (European) memory complex are heavily informed by this historical moment.

All of these accounts are not meant to contribute to a homogenization of "European space", nor to imply that the Dutch cultural archive and the European memory complex are interchangeable and easily comprehensible phenomena. Highlighting the similarities between these concepts, however, should contribute to a deeper understanding of the place (and displacement) of racial minorities in the European imaginary, as well as that of actual European spaces. Theo Goldberg's concepts of racial europeanization and racial regionalization are of central importance here. While racial europeanization signifies the particular ways in which race is being done in Europe (the centrality of the Holocaust and the subsequent erasure of race being a prime example), racial regionalizations "exemplify the regionally prompted, parametered, and promoted racisms in the form of 'racial europeanization'" (Goldberg 2006, 333).

What this means is that distinct local characteristics still contribute to the overall idea of racial europeanization, keeping the idea of Europe as a racially "pure" territory in place, and hence it makes sense to see how the particular situation of the Netherlands fits into a larger European framework. Sharon Macdonald, in her ruminations on Europe as a memoryland, or rather memorylands, arrives at similar conclusions: "The indeterminacy of the singular or plural here is indicative of what is at issue" (2013, 2). Macdonald recognizes that there is an overarching, although by no means unvarying way of understanding and doing the past in Europe, while there are also significant variations on more local levels (ibid.). This tension between the national and the European can also be found at airports, as they are complex sites where European and national (Dutch) heritage are simultaneously enforced and contested. When talking about heritage, I am drawing on Višnja Kisić's conceptualization of "heritage dissonance", noting that the meaning of heritage is always contingent and never stable, since dissonance is always presented as "a passive potential" (2017, 29). Considering Schiphol as a site of dissonant heritage is useful since, as, according to Kisić, heritage is both a unifier and a simultaneous producer of difference, respectively represented in my argument by the airport and its detention centre. It is important to note, however, that dissonance does not always stand for contradiction, but can also point to the instability and negotiation of political processes and power relations (2017, 57).

Bordering Processes

European understandings of national belonging have been significantly influenced by the irregular migration that has marked the beginning of the twenty-first century, acquiring a particularly central position in popular and political debates since the European migration/refugee crisis at the beginning of 2015. As Henk Van Houtum (2010, 960) observes, anxieties around uncontrolled migratory masses in Europe have resulted in bordering, ordering, and othering, all three going hand in hand. They especially operate in today's EU (which is popularly and routinely collapsed into Europe), where the openness of its internal borders—according to the Schengen principle, at least, although this openness has been modified in light of the migration crisis and become more controlled—is counteracted by fortifying its external borders. The rise of, and support for, right-wing populism across Europe reflects the wish to keep unwanted others at bay and fortify outer boundaries which are perceived as having been weakened and being in dire need of restoring, which the Brexit phenomenon is an exemplary case of. Anssi Paasi (2001, 22) has noted that, out of all the continents, Europe is the youngest in the sense that European national boundaries have been collapsed, redrawn, and reworked the most in the past century. In Europe, national and ethnic belonging typically carry much more weight in how subjects identify themselves than a broader and perhaps more elusive European identity, resulting in differing accounts and opinions about what exactly constitutes that identity (Paasi 2001, 21). Yet it can be argued that it is precisely because there is no official account of what constitutes Europe that the idea of a singular European identity has emerged so strongly in recent years, clearly outlined against the constant "threat" of migration.

Indeed, in *Memorylands*, Sharon McDonald (2013, 37) discusses European histories and observes that identity-building is often predicated on invoking an "oppositional 'Other'", especially the Muslim Other,[2] through different mechanisms of exclusion that can take various shapes: social, cultural, political, structural. In *White Innocence*, Gloria Wekker highlights "the fundamental impossibility of being both European, constructed to mean being white and Christian, and being black-migrant-Muslim-refugee" (2016, 21). Protecting the European space thus becomes synonymous with protecting an imagined European identity by erecting "a myriad of new invisible borders that are ideological, radicalized, and politicized" (Ponzanesi and Blaagaard 2011, 3). This means that the process of monitoring, controlling, and surveilling those who are deemed as outsiders extends far beyond the official national and geographic borders zones into "diverging social practices and discourses" (Paasi 2001, 16). In other words, *invisible* bordering practices, propagated and upheld by social and structural actors and institutions, are just as instrumental as visible, official mechanisms of border control in producing the kind of segregation that makes it possible to speak and think of Europeanness as a solid and unquestioned project. Official bordering practices interact with invisible borders as ideological parameters and come together in the complex site of the airport.

---

[2] The figure of the Muslim especially carries with it a threat of death (Goldberg 2006, 345) and therefore inspires particularly high levels of apprehension and fear in the post-9/11 moment.

Processes of bordering are considered in this chapter in their ideological dimension, as something that is actively being *done* rather than something that simply *is*. Considering them in their processual dimension moves us to an understanding of borders not as spaces marked on a map, or onto territory, but instead as "actions that must be performed by human beings in relation to one another. Borders can be made to exist, and must be made in order to exist" (Whitley 2015, 14). Conceptualizing borders not according to what they are but according to how they are being done, which is a change in understanding borders not as ontology but as function (ibid. 16), allows me to trace the processes of inclusion/exclusion at Schiphol Airport which need to be actively maintained in order to sustain a particular notion of cultural/national homogeneity. At the same time, understanding the processual logic of borders might even allow for a conceptualization of practices that challenge their exclusionary nature.

Politics of the Airport

Airports not (only) figure not as zones of transit, they also fulfil a political role. By looking at Amsterdam's Schiphol Airport specifically, I consider how this space represents a site of a specific and enforced notion of cultural heritage, a notion which is also always contested and under threat. While my observations could be extended to a broader analysis of airports as (European) cultural archives, I am following Sharon Macdonald's (2013, 6) "assemblage theory" approach of studying specific sites of knowledge and identity production so as to avoid generalizations and notice context specificities. This allows me to consider Schiphol Airport as a site where, first and foremost, the notion of the Dutch cultural archive is enforced, negotiated, and contested in a complex way, while Goldberg's conceptualization of racial Europeanization and racial regionalization allows me to still place these observations into a larger European framework and connect it to Macdonald's memory-heritage-identity complex.

I follow Debbie Lisle, who advocates for politicizing the airport as a site of "mediated power" (2003, 4). Understanding the airport as mediated means paying particular attention to how power relations there are always being negotiated, destabilized, challenged, and subverted. This Foucauldian strand of thinking allows us to see how an airport is never merely the site of extreme authority, control, and surveillance (although it is of course all of these things too). Rather, understanding power as mediated in airports makes it possible to consider how they are also sites of continually contested meanings, and this in turn allows me to see how the notion of cultural heritage *and* the practice of bordering take form and are challenged at this site. The point is that power, just like people, "never stays put at airports" (ibid.). At an airport, the border is, in Balibar's words (2002, 81), "polysemic" in the sense that it does not

> have the same meaning for everyone, and indeed this differential meaning is essential to the function of the border [...] Border law enables some to pass national frontiers, while denying others; it upholds the freedom of circulation of some, while depriving others of this same freedom. (Whitley 2015, 17)

Airports as border sites have different meanings for different people and also actively work to produce those meanings: they can be sites of both national belonging and forced alienation. Although my own reading of Schiphol Airport pays more attention to the way in which power is used to control, monitor, and detain unwelcome bodies, as a tool of cultural hegemony, it is important to keep in mind how and where these mechanisms fail to exert their control. In what follows, I provide a phenomenological analysis of the airport, starting with my interviewee's experiential account.

Phenomenology of the Airport

Peripheral Imaginaries

In January 2017, I interviewed a young Syrian who recounted his journey coming to the Netherlands, and I draw here on his experiential account of arriving at Schiphol as an asylum seeker. As he had been working in Dubai for years before his departure, he describes his trajectory in light, easy terms, saying how he and the friend who was accompanying him were "laughing all the way". However, upon their arrival at Schiphol Airport, they spent an hour in front of the police office, paralyzed by the idea that they would have to introduce themselves as asylum seekers: "You know, your pride cannot allow you to say 'We're asking for asylum'". I would like to consider the disorienting experience that occurs once a request for asylum is uttered, and how this disorientation takes place on a discursive and phenomenological level. In other words, I am looking at where the category of asylum seeker or refugee places one in the social and cultural European fabric, but also at what it means *spatially* to move from traveller to asylum seeker; in this case, my interviewee was literally removed from the "open"[3] space of the airport into the closed space of the Schiphol detention centre, where he spent seven days while waiting for his case to be processed. He was removed from the airport the moment he "became" an asylum seeker; this social category precluded him from inhabiting the same cultural space as other travellers. Of course, this was done according to the official asylum procedure[4] in the Netherlands, but in this analysis I am more interested in the symbolic and cultural dimension of these bordering practices. He was not taken to the detention centre prior to his request. In other words, there was nothing in particular about his physical appearance that coded him as somebody seeking asylum. Rather, it was the utterance of the request that marked his body as one that should be removed from the premises of the open airport zone. The airport emerges in this case not as a site of empty signification, but very much as a national and even European space in which anxieties surrounding the collapse of cultural homogeneity routinely result in the removing and containment of undesirable bodies from public spaces, an ideology which I have already outlined above with the discussion of El-Tayeb, Wekker, Macdonald, and Goldberg. The asylum seeker in this case comes into being through a discursive (verbalizing the need for asylum) and spatial dimension (being removed from the airport to the airport detention centre).

[3] I am aware that classifying airports as 'open' is somewhat of an oxymoron, especially considering how airports are becoming sites of ever more sophisticated mechanisms of surveillance, control, and restricted movement. However, in this case I contrast the relative openness of Schiphol Airport (mainly designed to facilitate travel) with the containment that characterizes the Schiphol detention center, where movement is controlled and restricted to a very high degree.

[4] One can apply for asylum at a Dutch border by reporting to the Immigration and Naturalization Service (IND). In case the person who is applying for asylum is arriving by either plane or boat from a non-Schengen zone, they are detained and must apply for asylum immediately, before crossing the external (Schengen) Dutch border, at the Application Centre of Schiphol Amsterdam airport (Aanmeldcentrum Schiphol, AC). The person arriving at Schiphol Airport will in most cases be detained by the Royal Military police. As those who are detained at Schiphol are not officially on Dutch territory, they can be expelled should their application be rejected (Ammeraal et al. 2014, 7, 22).

Mark Salter (2006, 168) has noted that the global passport and visa regime is built on a confessionary logic that urges subjects to willingly present their bodies and data for scrutiny in order to be granted mobility. In this particular case, the confession is quite literal, since it is not stored in document but in a verbalization. Both the airport and the detention centre function as spaces with particular meanings: the airport is a space of transit because it is (presumably) made up by travellers, while, conversely, the detention centre is a space of (temporary) confinement because it is inhabited by asylum seekers/migrants/refugees.[5] As Sara Ahmed points out in *Phenomenology of Whiteness*, "likeness is as an effect of *the proximity of shared residence*" (2007, 155). Spaces are coded in a certain way by the kind of bodies that (are allowed to) inhabit them. There is nothing intrinsically or fundamentally similar about these bodies, but it is their (forced) proximity that creates a certain kind of reading of that space. Accordingly, the Schiphol detention centre is a place of detention because it is inhabited by people coded as asylum seekers, while Schiphol Airport is a place of transit because it is inhabited by presumably cosmopolitan (inter)national subjects. The movements of these people are controlled and steered by biopolitical apparatuses (Foucault and Senellart 2008), managing the circulation of bodies through strategies of governance that are always political and power-laden. Yet, as power at the airport is mediated, this also means that it is possible to challenge these spatial orderings, however minutely. My interviewee was also aware of the fact that his request for asylum would effectively move him into the category of asylum seeker. However, in the hour he had spent working up to this moment, his presence was innocuous and undisturbed, and he was able to "pass" as one among many travellers. Although he was removed from the premises once he requested asylum, this turn of event also highlights to what extent seemingly homogenous national and cultural spaces are not "natural" but rather the result of selective processes that actively produce the notion of difference. As Salter notes, "passage through airports condition and normalize particular identities, certain authorities, and normalize ways of managing the mobility of a population" (2008, xii). As such, the existence of the detention centre in close proximity to the international airport becomes

---

[5] I do not mean to suggest that the terms migrant, refugee, and asylum seeker are interchangeable, but I cluster them together here to point to the classification of "undesirable others" in light of the 2015 European migration crisis.

a condition upon which the smooth functioning of the airport is predicated, even if the existence of the detention centre is invisibilized.

The detention centre is, in other words, part of Schiphol's well-oiled machine; the openness of the airport is predicated on the detention centre functioning like a prison camp in which the movement of the contained subjects is monitored and controlled. The creation of camps is not only a way of ordering and containing an undesirable population, but, importantly, also a means of separating them from the "authentic" subjects (Van Houtum 2010, 971). Detention centres are routinely placed in remote and rural areas,[6] reminiscent of the "out of sight, out of mind" principle: they are not really *here* if we do not see them or interact with them, or if we do not inhabit the same spaces. Interestingly, the Schiphol Application Center is located in the close vicinity of Schiphol Airport, and both are situated in the most densely populated area in the Netherlands, the metropolitan Randstad area. Here, detainment and "free" movement happen side by side, albeit in two distinctly separate spaces. Although the physical proximity between the two spaces is small, the space of the airport occupies a central position in the national imaginary (I will elaborate on this below), while the detainment centre is symbolically peripheral, and this distinction is upheld and enforced by the state. This is evinced, for instance, by the response to the fire at the Schiphol detention centre in October 2005 that claimed the life of eleven detainees. Although subsequent investigations ruled that the death toll was due to negligence of the guards on duty and the poor construction of the facilities, then-Minister for Integration and Immigration Rita Verdonk found that the staff had behaved "appropriately". Although the events sparked national outrage, the only party who was prosecuted was the inmate whose discarded cigarette was ruled to have started the fire. The state and government officials were not held responsible. Over the following years, a group of activists made efforts to commemorate the Schiphol fire and raise awareness of the events surrounding the deaths of the eleven detainees. In 2010, however, the final official commemoration of the victims took place, which was attended

---

[6]My interviewee told me that after his seven-day detainment at Schiphol he was transported to an asylum center in the north-east of the country. He describes it as being "in the middle of nowhere" but nevertheless "the biggest one in the Netherlands," which is illustrative of the tendency to place large migrant populations in the least densely populated areas in the Netherlands.

by some forty people. The annual commemorations were discontinued due to the public's lack of engagement and waning interest. For Judith Butler (2009), those whose deaths have occurred on the periphery of Europe constitute "ungrievable lives". My claim here is that the lives lost in the Schiphol fire are also peripheral in the sense that they do not occupy any significant component in the dominant national imaginary.

Mark Salter writes that: "Public and private authorities have taken advantage of the liminal character of airports to conduct policing and border functions, which take place inside the state but at the margins of the law. At the same time, more and more airports have accelerated lanes for the elite, transnational class and invisible corridors for the 'deportation class'" (2008, xi). Schiphol Airport and its detention centre also operate according to this duality. My interviewee describes the process immediately following his request for asylum as follows:

> It took like half an hour for the IND guys to come. They came. They took us. We walked like ten to fifteen minutes and then they took us to another building. No, first we did the fingerprints, and then they took us to another building which is in Schiphol but like a five-minutes drive. Which is the prison. I don't know if you've heard about this prison: There are drug dealers, there are criminals, there are asylum seekers who've been there a week if they're Syrians or Palestinians, or a few months if they're another [nationality]. Yes, it was like five days. At 9 p.m. they'd close all of us in a room. Then at seven in the morning they'd wake us up and then we got the one meal for the day, which is like breakfast and lunch. And then you can go out for an hour to play football or something. Yes, it's a prison. It's like a good prison, but it's a prison.

Here, the proximity of the detainment centre to Schiphol Airport is emphasized ("a five-minute drive") together with the distance between the bodies inhabiting the two spaces. Whereas the movement of people in the airport is relatively free (albeit organized), the movement of the people in detention is highly controlled and monitored. Moreover, the lumping together of different categories of unwanted others (drug dealers, criminals, asylum seekers) establishes a relationship of resemblance based on their physical location, as Ahmed has pointed out, and I find this also links to Balibar's conceptualization of "the duplication of the notion of the border" (Balibar 2002, 83). In that way, the asylum seeker-illegal-criminal emerges as a complex construct that has no place inside the nation. As Charlie Hailey points out in *Camps*, these places of detention only serve to amplify concerns around unrestricted movements by foreign bodies. Such spaces can have an "open" or "closed" policy (the former refers to places that host people with very limited administrative and social rights, while the latter forcibly detain persons in one place). However, as Hailey states: "Less the resurgence of an authoritative political power, the camps are symptoms of a state's weakness and a resulting need to demonstrate the semblance of a policy of control" (2009, 244). What this means is that anxieties around uncontrolled migration prompt the building of special zones of confinement, which, when erected, prompt a fresh new wave of fear as they become the concrete embodiment of foreign bodies crossing European territories, perpetuating a vicious cycle. Meanwhile, the camps themselves become semi-permanent places of impermanence that some bodies can enter and leave freely (people like aid workers, camera crews, researchers, and reporters), while others cannot (the detainees themselves). Van Houtum (2010, 958) therefore speaks of

> a constant border-work trying to separate the wanted from the unwanted, the barbarians from the civilised, and the global rich from the global poor in the territorial society. In so doing the EU increasingly is not only defining itself via its internal affairs, its ordering practices, but also by the production of new border rules and legislation towards its incoming migrants.

In other words, amplified anxieties around a "new" Other bring into being new ideas about a European culture that needs protection, which promotes the fortification of borders on all levels: social, cultural, political, institutional, territorial. While this bordering apparatus works according to particular structural orderings in each European nation state, they all promote the idea of a specific European space/identity union, as these bordering practices are specifically aimed at detaining and controlling people from outside of Europe. As Paasi notes: "The emergence of right-wing movements in European Union countries—and in many of those that are negotiating to get into the EU—shows that the links between (a bounded) space, culture, and politics are still full of political dynamite. It also shows how various spatial scales come together in the changing geographies of inclusion and exclusion" (2001, 23). Although Paasi's observations date back to 2001, they still astutely describe the political climate in many European countries after 2015. Detainment centres across Europe therefore contribute to "long-nurtured" European "civic drive to identify the foreign, to uphold the possibility of keeping the foreign, of permanently foreignizing the '(racially) non-European'" (Goldberg 2006, 354), an imperial gesture that is still being implemented in order to control the imagined migratory masses' movement into both imagined and actual European spaces.

The Airport: Non-place or Heritage Site?

Airports may be popularly considered as sites of "empty" signification because of the (visual, auditory, spatial) excess that characterizes them. This way, the airport is a "supermodern" site (Augé 2008), essentially devoid of meaning because it is *too full* of meaning; it represents too much, all at once (Lisle 2003, 6). However, this reading of the airport overlooks the ways in which these sites are imbued with cultural and national symbols that communicate specific meanings. Of course, national symbols at airports have a touristic and commercial value, and are typically found as items in souvenir shops, but they also "spill out of the souvenir shops" (Lisle 2003, 13). As I move through the different areas of Schiphol Airport, I am struck by the promotion of "typically" Dutch imagery that depicts commercialized aspects of Dutch culture: tulips, windmills, flat agricultural planes, and waterscapes. Typical and commercialized though they may be, Lisle describes these and other symbols as national heritage "at work" because of the "'official' narratives of nation they encourage" (ibid.). It must also not be forgotten that airports are the first and last impressions of a place (Iyer 1995, 54), and for national subjects, airports are the last and first impressions of "home" when they travel abroad. At Schiphol, there are now large screens installed at several locations, in- and outside the airport, showing videos with a goodbye or welcome-home message for a traveling loved one. These visuals amplify both the idea of "home" as well as that of the "homeland", and together with other symbols create the idea of Schiphol not only as a zone of transit but as a cultural space too. Sharon Macdonald (2013, 166) argues that ideas of national heritage in Europe have typically been disseminated through public institutions such as museums and monuments. A significant aspect of such objects and places is that they are "gathering grounds" for people to meet and experience "the nation" together. A current example of this is the Schiphol library. Opened in 2010, the first of its kind, the library houses books, movies, music, and small exhibitions by Dutch artists. These materials are offered to travellers on intercontinental flights so that they can learn more about Dutch history and culture, but they also serve to promote a particular politics of belonging, one connected to the Dutch past and its cultural canon. In this way, the airport also becomes a site of national heritage. This is also evinced by the fact that Schiphol occupies an important position in Madurodam, a popular park that showcases miniature replicas of Dutch heritage sites and landmarks of cultural significance. Schiphol has been featured in the park since 1952. This information can be found at the Schiphol website as well, which has a comprehensive overview of Schiphol's 100-year "rich history". A notable portion of this overview is dedicated to the occupation and destruction of Schiphol by German forces during WWII. The subsequent reclaiming and rebuilding of Schiphol is framed as Schiphol's phoenix-like rise from the ashes of destruction. Once again, the memory of WWII is centralized as defining moment. All of this points to the fact that Schiphol is not merely a transit zone (non-place), but a space with specific cultural roots tied to Dutch soil. Both its inception as well as its development to the international hub that it is now have always received great national attention and been well documented.

This way, the airport might be considered as one of the zones where cultural heritage and the cultural archive are made, negotiated, enforced, and contested. Wekker understands the cultural archive not as a single place or phenomenon where documents are stored, but rather as an accumulation of thoughts, feelings, and affects that shape the—in this case Dutch—cultural consciousness and canon. Importantly, Wekker notes that the cultural archive is built on a select body of memory that is frequently informed by the ways in which dominant understandings of Dutch colonial history are configured. Wekker states that the archive is to be found "in the heads and hearts of people in the metropole, but its content is also silently cemented in policies, in organizational rules, in popular and sexual cultures, and in commonsense everyday knowledge, and all of this is based on four hundred years of imperial rule" (2016, 19). My claim is that the airport does not stand outside of this logic; indeed, national and cultural markers are amplified here, making it a highly complex site where the cultural archive is played out.

Conclusion

In this chapter, I have sought to answer the question of how notions of European national and cultural heritage and belonging are controlled, secured, and contested through the controlled movement, detainment, and separation of foreign bodies at airports. To do so, I have situated my analysis at Schiphol Airport in Amsterdam, basing it on the detainment experience as recounted by one of my interviewees. Taking a phenomenological approach propounding that the organization of spaces is made up by the bodies inhabiting them, I have sought to establish the link between space, materiality, and belonging, while not advocating for unitary conceptions of any of these concepts. Following this, I have drawn on the work of Fatima El-Tayeb, Gloria Wekker, and Theo Goldberg to point out how European spaces have been imagined as white/colour blind and are thus built on exclusionary practices. These practices largely take shape through the bordering processes that invoke the image of the "oppositional Other" who, in recent years, has been imagined as the (Muslim) migrant/refugee/asylum seeker. Following this, I have taken a closer look at how airports work as complex sites where power and belonging are constantly mediated.

Contrary to much of the literature on this topic, in this chapter airports do not feature as non-sites, but rather as places where notions of nationhood and cultural belonging are constantly enforced (and contested). The proximity between Schiphol Airport and the Schiphol detention centre forwards this enforced logic. Detaining difference in the name of cultural and national homogeneity then becomes a question of spatial ordering. The national subject or the undesirable Other are both very much shaped by the spaces they (are allowed to) inhabit, and this logic of inclusion/exclusion has the same imperial/racial roots that shape many European spaces; i.e. it is part of a European cultural heritage. However, this is not to claim or invoke Europe as a homogenous space where notions of heritage and the cultural archive are not and cannot be contested—rather the opposite. I agree with Sharon Macdonald when she emphasizes the need to recognize and acknowledge "cultural alternatives" since they "can not only unsettle assumptions but can also open up new possibilities by highlighting other routes—other ways of doing memory, heritage, and identity—that we might choose to take" (2013, 3). In this regard, it is important to keep in mind just how contested and multifaceted the notions of Europe and airports can be, both as concepts and as physical structures (airports, for instance, have been theorized to be either sites of no signification or with an abundance of signification). Finally, the chapter highlighted some of the dissonances and restrictions that shape the ordering of Schiphol as a site of heritage dissonance: the close proximity of the airport as an open space and the detention centre as a controlled space; the politics of belonging that is encouraged or discouraged in these places; and the peripheral or dominant memory practices that characterize both spaces.

Acknowledgements This work received funding from the European Research Council under the European Union's Seventh Framework Programme (FP/2007–2013), ERC Grant Agreement number 29585 (BABE).

References

Ahmed, S. 2006. *Queer Phenomenology: Orientations, Objects, Others.* Durham and London: Duke University Press.
Ahmed, S. 2007. A Phenomenology of Whiteness. *Feminist Theory* 8 (2): 149–168.
Ammeraal, S., F. Borekhof, and A. van Kampen. 2014. Asylum Information Database National Country Report. The Netherlands. AIDA Project. http://www.asylumineurope.org/sites/default/files/report-download/aida_-_netherlands_second_update_final_uploaded.pdf.
Amsterdam Airport Schiphol. 2017. http://www.schiphol.nl/en/schipholgroup/page/amsterdam-airport-schiphol/. Accessed 7 April 2017.
Anderson, B. 2006. *Imagined Communities: Reflections on the Origin and Spread of Nationalism.* London and New York: Verso.
Antonsich, M. 2010. Searching for Belonging—An Analytical Framework. *Geography Compass* 4 (6): 644–659.
Augé, M. 2008. *Non-places: An Introduction to Supermodernity.* London: Verso.
Balibar, É. 2002. What Is a Border? In *Politics and the Other Scene*, ed. É. Balibar, 75–86. London: Verso.
Butler, J. 2009. *Frames of War: When Is Life Grievable?* London: Verso.
Easthope, A. 1999. *Englishness and National Culture.* London and New York: Routledge.
El-Tayeb, F. 2011. *European Others: Queering Ethnicity in Postnational Europe.* Minneapolis: University of Minnesota Press.
Foucault, M., and M. Senellart. 2008. *The Birth of Biopolitics: Lectures at the Collège de France, 1978–79.* Basingstoke: Palgrave Macmillan.
Goldberg, D.T. 2006. Racial Europeanziation. *Ethnic and Racial Studies* 29 (2): 331–364.
Hailey, C. 2009. *Camps: A Guide to 21st Century Space.* Boston: MIT Press.

Iyer, P. 1995. Where Worlds Collide. *Harper's Magazine* (August): 50–57.
Kisić, V. 2017. *Governing Heritage Dissonance: Promises and Realities of Selected Cultural Policies*. Amsterdam: European Cultural Foundation.
Lisle, D. 2003. Site Specific: Medi(t)ations at the Airport. In *Rituals of Mediation*, ed. C. Weber and F. Debrix, 3–29. Minneapolis: University of Minnesota Press.
Macdonald, S. 2013. *Memorylands: Heritage and Identity in Europe Today*. London: Routledge.
Paasi, A. 2001. Europe as a Social Process and Discourse: Considerations of Place, Boundaries and Identity. *European Journal of Urban and Regional Studies* 8 (1): 7–28.
Ponzanesi, S., and B. Blagaard. 2011. In the Name of Europe. *Social Identities* 17 (1): 1–10.
Salter, M.B. 2006. The Global Visa Regime and the Political Technologies of the International Self: Borders, Bodies Biopolitics. *Alterantives* 31 (2): 167–189.
Salter, M.B. 2008. *Politics at the Airport*. Minneapolis and London: University of Minnesota Press.
Van Houtum, H. 2010. Human Blacklisting: The Global Apartheid of the EU's External Border Regime. *Environment and Planning D: Society and Space* 28 (6): 957–976.
Wekker, G. 2016. *White Innocence: Paradoxes of Colonialism and Race*. Durham and London: Duke University Press.
Whitley, L. 2015. *More Than a Line: Borders as Embodied Sites*. PhD dissertation, Goldsmiths College, University of London.

Open Access This chapter is licensed under the terms of the Creative Commons Attribution 4.0 International License (http://creativecommons.org/licenses/by/4.0/), which permits use, sharing, adaptation, distribution and reproduction in any medium or format, as long as you give appropriate credit to the original author(s) and the source, provide a link to the Creative Commons license and indicate if changes were made.

The images or other third party material in this chapter are included in the chapter's Creative Commons license, unless indicated otherwise in a credit line to the material. If material is not included in the chapter's Creative Commons license and your intended use is not permitted by statutory regulation or exceeds the permitted use, you will need to obtain permission directly from the copyright holder.

CHAPTER 6

Politics of Mobility and Stability in Authorizing European Heritage: Estonia's Great Guild Hall

Sigrid Kaasik-Krogerus

"Europe starts here". At first sight the sentence seems simple and clear, signaling the starting point of Europe. Looking closer, however, the three words that form this claim enable us to make a variety of interpretations. To start with the last word, "here", gives the sentence a strong spatial dimension, implicitly drawing boundaries between "here", where Europe starts, and "there", when it ends. This boundary drawing also implicates a European space of which "here" is a part. Locating Europe "here" paradoxically both concretizes this sentence and Europe and increases confusion about the "here", since meanings of Europe are continuously (re)-negotiated in political and cultural processes in which "Europe" is entangled with a variety of other partly overlapping geographical scales like the local and national ones. Furthermore, as used in this sentence, "starts" can, besides geographically, also be interpreted

S. Kaasik-Krogerus (✉)
Department of Music, Art and Culture Studies,
University of Jyväskylä, Jyväskylä, Finland
e-mail: sigrid.kaasik@helsinki.fi

© The Author(s) 2019
T. Lähdesmäki et al. (eds.),
Dissonant Heritages and Memories in Contemporary Europe,
Palgrave Studies in Cultural Heritage and Conflict,
https://doi.org/10.1007/978-3-030-11464-0_6

from a temporal perspective, denoting the very first moments of Europe. In sum, while aiming to fix the spatial and temporal starting point of Europe, the sentence concurrently indicates mobility in time and space.

"Europe starts here" is the slogan of the newest heritage initiative of the European Union, the European Heritage Label (EHL). This flagship initiative was launched in 2011, and twenty five member states have now confirmed their participation.[1] Apart from in the EU policy documents, the slogan is used on the EHL webpages and at the awarded sites. According to the European Commission (EC) webpage, the objective of the EHL is to use cultural heritage to bring to life a European narrative of identity and belonging—a task that is at least problematic due to the EU's internal controversies and diversity (see the more detailed description of the EHL by Mäkinen and Turunen in this volume). By 2018, 38 sites with "European significance"—as they are framed in EHL terminology—have been awarded with the label. The sites form a system of meanings of what is "European" heritage, and the process simultaneously shows how the EU believes it has a special claim over the term "Europe". Therefore, the EHL can be scrutinized as a discourse, that is, as simultaneously a system of meanings and a social practice of meaning-giving (cf. Fairclough 1995, 2; Raik 2003, 27–28; cf. Kaasik-Krogerus 2016, 16).

Critical heritage studies distinguishes between the dominant, authorized heritage discourse (AHD) and other, competing discourses, like the ones representing the heritage of various communities (Smith 2006; see also Waterton and Smith 2009). Laurajane Smith (2006) writes that, as a social construct, AHD is closely associated with nationalism and national narratives, heritage-related expert knowledge, and an endeavour to "conserve and preserve" heritage for future generations. Taken for granted on national scale, this discourse is experienced as "normal" part of social reality, leaving its dominant position hidden (Waterton and Smith 2009). As Laurajane Smith (2006) and Vsenja Kisić (2017) point out, all heritage, including AHD, is inherently processual and dissonant. AHD's intrinsic attempts to conform to what appears to be normal, however, make it imperceptible and homogeneous (Waterton and Smith 2006, 13). As Tuuli Lähdesmäki writes in this volume, since AHD promotes common views and consensus, its idea and concept of heritage are not problematized. AHD has thus been criticized for lowering

[1] Non-participating countries are Sweden, Ireland, and the United Kingdom.

dissonance, avoiding conflict, and consequently diminishing the transformative potential of heritage (Harrison 2013; see also Turunen in this volume).

The EHL carries some characteristics of an AHD: the awarded sites are embedded in the national and/or local narratives of the EU-member states, and various heritage experts hold key positions in the process of awarding and managing the sites. However, instead of showing up as self-evidently European heritage, the EHL mixes local, national, and European scales in an endeavour to reconcile their dissonance and make the heritage suitable for constructing European identity narratives. Therefore, instead of a taken-for-granted European heritage, the EHL can be depicted as an authorization process, AHD in the making (cf. Smith 2006, 100; Kaasik-Krogerus 2019). The EHL sites are situated in the EU member states, whereas the system of meanings of what is European heritage is formed in interactions between European, national, and sometimes also local scales. Mobility between these intertwined scales as a combination of Europeanization (of the national and local) and domestication (of the European) forms the very essence of the EU.

Europeanization is defined as an international socialization (Schimmelfennig 2000) and used to depict the spheres of integration where formal and informal rules, procedures, policies, and norms are constructed at the European scale and then diffused to domestic institutions (Radaelli 2000, 4; Sassatelli 2008, 225; see also Schimmelfennig 1998, 198–200; 2000, 109–112; see also Kaasik-Krogerus 2016, 43–44). The domestic institutions and actors then incorporate the "European" with national and/or local conditions, a process that has been called "domestication" (Alasuutari 2009, 67). This process does not occur without struggle and conflict, if not against Europeanization then over the contents of policies, informal rules, as well as representations and constructions of heritage. Hence, as entangled processes of mobility and stability related to different scales, Europeanization and domestication create and reinforce the dissonance of European heritage, while at the same time attempts to manage that dissonance are also embedded in those same processes.

In this chapter, I focus on what can be called a "politics of mobility and stability". I scrutinize how a politics of mobility and stability is conducted as part of the EHL with the aim to manage dissonance related to local, national, and European scales. By politics, I refer to the attempts and/or abilities of the EHL-related actors to have certain meanings legitimized at the expense of others (cf. Smith 2006, 81). This politics of mobility and stability plays a crucial role in the EHL as an AHD in the making and consequently also in constructing EU narratives of identity and belonging as the cultural-symbolic foundation for political purposes (cf. Karlsson 2010, 38; Kraenzle and Mayr 2017, 2; see also Sassatelli 2002, 436; Delanty 2005, 409–410).

As empirical data I use the exhibitions at one of the EHL sites: the Great Guild Hall (the site is discussed also in the Turunen chapter). The site is situated in Tallinn, Estonia, and was awarded with the EHL in 2014. Since the Estonian History Museum is located in this medieval building situated in the old town of Tallinn, it offers rich data for analyzing the dissonance of entangled mobility and stability on local, national, and European scales. Furthermore, Estonia was one of the Central and East European (CEE) countries that joined the EU during the Eastern enlargement.[2] As the EU's relation to the CEE countries, simultaneously depicts them as being and becoming European (for example Mälksoo 2006; Kaasik-Krogerus 2016; see also Jones and Subotic 2011, 544–546), this offers an additional nuance to the politics of mobility and stability conducted by the displays in the process of constructing knowledge at the site (see also Moser 2010, 22; De Cesari 2017). The study asks: How do the exhibitions conduct their politics of mobility and stability and with what effects? I also discuss the consequences of this politics for the EHL and the European identity narratives that the EC is attempting to construct.

The chapter starts with a closer look at the politics of mobility and stability in relation to the formation of an AHD, paying special attention to the dissonance of Europeanization and domestication. After introducing the empirical data, this chapter's analysis appears in a section scrutinizing two Great Guild Hall exhibitions: "Spirit of Survival. 11,000 years of Estonian History" and "Medieval pleasures. Festivals of the Great Guild in the fifteenth and sixteenth centuries".

POLITICS OF MOBILITY AND STABILITY IN FORMING AHD

Mobility is defined as movement ascribed with meaning: quality of being mobile, that is, an ability to move or being moved freely or in forced ways, whereas stability stands for the quality of not being likely to move

---

[2] Estonia joined the EU in 2004 together with nine other countries, and the so called Eastern enlargement continued in 2007 when Bulgaria and Romania joined the EU.

or change but remaining stable (Oxford Living Dictionaries; Cambridge Dictionary). Both terms are also widely used in academic analysis. While Tim Cresswell (2001) writes that mobility refers to movement saturated with meanings that make that movement significant and bring along power dimensions, I would say the same about stability: it, too, brings along power dimensions and is saturated with meaning.

The essential nature of mobility in contemporary societies is captured in scholarly references to the "mobile turn" (Urry 2007, 6) or the "new mobilities paradigm" (Sheller and Urry 2006). Academic discussions debate the current condition of constant mobility within the framework of modernity (for example Bauman 2000; Sheller and Urry 2006; Urry 2007). Scholars tend to agree that, within the progress-oriented framework of modernity, mobility is widely seen as a social good, whereas stability (immobility)[3] acquires a connotation of defeat, of failure, and of being left behind (for example Morley 2000, 202; see also Bauman 1998, 2). That division between mobility and stability is analytical, however, since apart from advancing mobility, modernity is also invested in stability in the ways that it orders and classifies matters in order to tackle chaos, minimize risks, and withstand uncertainty (Harrison 2013, 227). Mobility and stability are therefore largely intertwined in modernity, and no strict boundaries between them can be drawn.

At the EU level, the four freedoms—free movement of people, goods, services, and capital—offer a good example of such a politics of mobility and stability. The EU promotes mobility for example in its programmes on culture and citizenship that stimulate transnational cooperation and exchange (Mäkinen 2014, 133). Furthermore, the policies and programmes of "everyday" mobility related to travel for work, education, tourism, and so on aim to bring Europeans closer in terms of common experiences (Delanty 2005, 410, 415; Karlsson 2010, 38). Nevertheless, during the EU's Eastern Enlargement in the beginning of the 2000s, it was debated whether or not the EU should temporarily restrict the mobility of the soon-to-be EU citizens on the labour market of the "old" EU countries. The transition periods some EU member states put in place for the new EU citizens are good examples of a politics that endeavours to manage the entangled notions of mobility and stability.

---

[3] As the term "immobility" refers to an absence of mobility and thus clearly contributes to valorizing mobility, I use "stability" in this chapter, since that word does not have such a negative connotation.

A similar example can be found in the current fences built on the borders of some EU countries to restrict the mobility of people who seek refuge in the EU. These policies are conducted at the same time as these member states appreciate and benefit from the mobility options offered *inter alia* by the above-mentioned programmes of culture and citizenship. In the current volume, the chapters by Proglio and Trakilović provide solid analyses of this controversy.

In the context of heritage as a modern phenomenon, mobility and stability are also profoundly entangled. In temporal terms, an overall idea of AHD is to create stability by conserving and safeguarding sites, objects, and artefacts and by preserving intangible phenomena. By making the sites and phenomena durable, heritagization is supposed to protect and safeguard them from temporal decomposition. However, as critical heritage studies shows, even material or "fixed" heritage is continuously being constructed over time. This mobility in time can be grasped using Sharon Macdonald's term "past presencing", that is, selectively remembering and using pasts in the present (2013, 15–17; see also Lähdesmäki in this volume). When what is and what is not worth preserving is being decided, the past is accordingly divided into valuable and valueless sections. Although heritage is a contemporary phenomenon, the key objective of the selective fostering of the past is to influence future developments (Harrison 2013).

In spatial terms, intertwining heritage with a physical location aims to place it and therefore stabilize it in space (for example McDowell 2008). Especially in (nation) states this fosters an understanding of them as self-sufficient and autonomous "containers" with a clear "inside" and "outside" (Beck 2000; about Europe, also see De Cesari 2017, 26). Thus, AHD often functions to make and maintain a distinction between the people who are accepted and those who are excluded. Seen from an alternative, heterotopic perspective, states are revealed to be not actually self-sufficient, instead being formed in interrelations with other, similar actors. Instead of self-sufficiency, what characterizes the modern state is its ongoing mobility of meanings and social relations (see Massey 1991, 2005, 118; Lehtonen 2004, 2013, 15–17). Consequently, this heterotopic perspective widens the spatial scale of heritage as well as the variety of actors involved. On the EHL application form (2017), for example, applicants are asked to describe how they "foster the mobility of European culture professionals, artists and collections, stimulate intercultural dialogue and encourage linkage between heritage and contemporary creation", emphasizing the importance of diverse social relations.

Dissonance of Europeanization and Domestication

In this chapter I approach mobility and stability between local, national, and European scales as an interplay of Europeanization and domestication. This interplay both contributes to heritage dissonance and seeks to handle it through its politics of mobility and stability. In the context of Europeanization, norms, procedures, policies, and rules are first defined and consolidated at the European level, and then delivered to the national scale to incorporate them into domestic institutions and policies (Radaelli 2000, 4; Sassatelli 2008, 225; see also Schimmelfennig 1998, 198–200; 2000, 109–112; see also Kaasik-Krogerus 2016, 43–44). Discourses and practices related to EU policy are adapted to the domestic context, thus interpreting what is "European", and as a result national and local politics in different countries can largely differ from "original" European policy. The Eastern Enlargement presents a good example of domestication, as the states' national interpretations of EU policies also contribute to what is understood as "European" at the EU level. Yet, domestication is not an entirely domestic (national and local) process: since the same process takes place in different countries simultaneously, the domestic agenda in policy spheres tends to get synchronized with analogous political alignments in other countries (Alasuutari et al. 2013).

Different but interrelated processes of cultural Europeanization and the Eastern enlargement are fruitful cases to explore the interplay between Europeanization and domestication from the perspective of heritage. These interrelated processes started in the 1990s after the collapse of the Soviet Union. Cultural Europeanization is defined as a process that aims to strengthen a "sense of shared European identity amongst citizens of the various member states" (Kraenzle and Mayr 2017, 2). Although the very existence of any such single European identity narrative is questioned in this volume, endeavours to authorize European cultural heritage and use it to constructing common narratives deserve attention. While several authors write that cultural Europeanization followed the waves of economic and political integration (Karlsson 2010, 39; see also EU 2014, 4; Lähdesmäki 2019), the EU accession process—a key part of Europeanization—covered all three: political, economic, and cultural integration. Although both cultural Europeanization and the EU enlargement contribute to authorizing European heritage, they do this in opposite ways.

During the Eastern enlargement, the "Europeanization" of the political and economic spheres of the candidate countries (their "becoming

European") was accompanied by a rhetoric according to which these countries culturally and historically formed an integral part of Europe ("being European"). References to a common past were used by both the EU and the candidate countries to legitimize EU membership as simultaneously a suitable scenario for the future and a "return to Europe" (Feldman 2001, 9) to which the countries had supposedly truly belonged to since at least the Middle Ages (see also Kaasik-Krogerus 2016). While this politics aimed to paint the Communist past as a rupture in a centuries-long continuity of belonging to Europe, it also strengthened the idea of a common European heritage and of CEE countries as part of that (see also Lähdesmäki et al. 2019). Since the assumption of such a centuries-long continuity that is embedded in European identity narratives is often legitimized with reference to a shared Christian background, on a European scale the argument strengthens the importance of Christian religions as a key part of this common heritage.

According to Klas-Göran Karlsson (2010, 38, 44), in the context of cultural Europeanization, the European cache of cultural valuables temporarily becomes a site of negotiation between actors from different scales. During the accession process, common European heritage was used as an argument to legitimize the membership of the CEE countries, yet the EU also needs to authorize this common heritage without provoking the reactions of national-scale institutions (cf. Sassatelli 2002, 440; see also Kuus 2017, 3). As scholars write, this dissonance between the European and national scales is especially apparent after the latest accessions, when Central and East European countries have aspired to broaden "the store of collective memories" (Checkel and Katzenstein 2009, 3; see also Mälksoo 2009, 656; see also Jones and Subotic 2011, 554).

The EU's EHL action is a good example of this dissonance, as it also illuminates how actors who are related to different scales attempt to manage this dissonance by conducting a politics of mobility and stability. The sites apply for the label, whereas the decisions about "locating" European heritage at the sites are made by the EC. The chosen sites are introduced through videos that all follow a similar format and are available at the web page of the EC (see also Kaasik-Krogerus 2019). However, since the sites maintain their own daily practices "at home", they also choose how to Europeanize. Their chosen imaginaries of Europe impact the selection of their exhibitions, the viewpoints, and the angles taken when introducing historical events and persons, as well as the substance and format of the guided tours organized on the sites. This process clarifies why the "normalcy" and "taken for grantedness" characteristic of national AHD are not directly conveyable to the EHL.

THE GREAT GUILD HALL AS EMPIRICAL DATA

Framed on the EHL website as "one of the most distinguished societal buildings" in Tallinn, the Great Guild Hall was built in 1410, and is an example of Hanseatic architecture from the Middle Ages. In the EHL Panel Report, medieval Hanseatic history and the idea of continuity created on the basis of that is used to argue the European significance of the site. Since 1952, Estonian History Museum has operated in the hall, which was completely renovated in 2010–2011. The Great Guild that gives the Hall its name is characterized as a social, religious, and professional association intended for Tallinn's most important merchants of German origin during the Middle Ages, while important representatives of some other professions were also accepted. Remarkably, Estonians had no right to belong to the guild.

My analysis here focuses on the two exhibitions on the first floor of the Great Guild Hall. On the museum webpage and flyer, these are introduced as the core displays: the permanent "Spirit of Survival" exhibition which focuses on Estonian history as the "story of Estonians" over the past 11,000 years and is located in the great hall, and a temporary exhibition called "Medieval Pleasures",[4] which was located in the small guildhall and dealt with the Great Guild Hall festivals in the fifteenth and sixteenth centuries. The other floors and their displays are out of the scope of this chapter.[5]

Since the "Spirit of Survival" has been up since 2011, it was not designed as an EHL exhibition. According to the museum flyer, the exhibition tells colorful stories of Estonian history and helps to understand the extraordinariness of the people who have lived "here". To tell these stories, the exhibits use text plates in Estonian and English as well as humorous interactive multiple-choice questions. Since texts

---

[4] The temporary exhibition was open from 25 May 2016 to 4 June 2017.

[5] They concern the history of the Great Guild Hall itself ("Power of the Elite") plus rooms focused on certain topics, like the Armory ("Wars through Estonia's History"), the "Experimentarium" education center ("Spirit of the Thing") as well as the Coin Room ("Striking it Rich?! Money in Estonia through the ages").

dominate the displays, my analysis also focuses on those. The texts were made attractive for visitors by combining facts and figures with funny sayings and small jokes. Apart from those, my data consists of two videos displayed in the exhibition: "Spirit of Survival" and "Is Estonia a Nordic country?" Since the permanent exhibition is more extensive than "Medieval Pleasures", it also gets more attention in the empirical analysis.

The "Medieval Pleasures" focuses on the local scale and deals with the medieval festivals held at the Great Guild, which functioned as the main fora for communication between the guild members and strengthened their sense of community. As the title indicates, the exhibition does not claim to give a comprehensive overview of medieval times, but focuses on a single aspect of medieval life—partying and having fun. This choice makes the tone and the themes of this exhibition different from the familiar take on the Middle Ages as a dark era. Though based on facts, the story is told in a fictional and a joyful manner, mostly through the key figure of Urban Dene. Master of the Mint, Dene was a member of the Great Guild and probably the richest man in Tallinn at the time. He is introduced in the exhibit as a first-person narrator: "Around 1530, I arrived in Tallinn from Jülich in Germany. After six years I became a citizen and took a wife". Since the exhibition does not elaborate gender relations any further, they remain largely suspended.

The Politics of Mobility and Stability in the Exhibitions

The empirical data was gathered through observation during my visits to the Great Guild Hall in October 2016 and September 2017. Apart from explicitly/concretely emphasized representations of mobility and stability, both also appear implicitly/abstractly in the exhibitions (cf. Palonen 2014; see also Lähdesmäki et al. 2019). Since the explicit and implicit layers are intertwined, I make no further distinction between them in the analysis.

By focusing on the representations in the displays, I analyze the Great Guild Hall as an actor that attempts to influence people by constructing knowledge through its exhibitions (see also Moser 2010, 22; De Cesari 2017). In this volume, Milica Trakilović analyses airports as sites where heritage and belonging are negotiated, and I apply similar approach to this museum. In the spirit of Sharon Macdonald (2013, 166), I analyze how the museum constructs identity stories in a three-dimensional space on the basis of cultural heritage. As part of an AHD in the making, the EHL site enables me to research the interplay and dissonance between local, national, and European scales, including its domestic intentions and consequences on European scale. I scrutinize how the displays of the Great Guild Hall construct mobility and stability in time and space to find out how the exhibitions' politics of mobility and stability handles dissonance. These politics work in two controversial ways: simultaneously legitimizing mobility and stability as natural and challenging them as problematic.

Depoliticizing and Naturalizing Stability and Mobility

> The farm was headed by the man of the house; the oldest son usually inherited this position, and the farm was not divided. The younger siblings often stayed on the farm and worked as farmhands.

This quotation from the "Spirit of Survival" display is supposed to characterize the situation in Estonia until World War II. It provides an illustrative example of naturalizing stability. The text portrays people as very static in their everyday: the man of the house occupied[6] a leading position, and the younger siblings stayed on the farm. The hereditary system and the fact that the farm was not divided exemplify the stability of the societal structures, including the clear role and labour division between men and women in the countryside at the time. The display also tells visitors how the changes in the twentieth century "significantly changed the roles of men and women, both in society and in the family" so that "the expression 'man of the house' has lost its original meaning".

In addition to farms other spatial scales are also used to indicate location-based stability. Visitors are told that Estonia is situated "on the outskirts of Europe". The claim that Estonia "found its place on the world map" in the fifteenth century, when some of its parts were mentioned on a Scandinavian map, shows that others have also recognized its long history. While the first ancestors of the people living on this land came from Africa, the claim that some of them were molded "into Estonians by time" contributes to the idea of Estonia as a formative "container". In this process, the symbolic value of the Estonian language as "the heart

---

[6] Literal translation of the Estonian verb, *seisis* (headed) would be 'was standing'.

of this land and the people living here" is emphasized especially. One exhibit states that, while people from many nations have lived in Estonia, those "who have learned Estonian and can communicate with the natives in their language have always been loved most of all". Language thus works as a stabilizing factor that offers foreigners access to the container.

The "Is Estonia a Nordic country?" video provides a good example of how materiality and natural phenomena like climate, flora, and soil are used to promote the idea of stability. Though the video claims that the "Estonian ski mecca Otepää" has been around since the Ice Age, it should be noted that neither was the place always called Otepää, nor was the ski mecca open to skiers in the Ice Age. The video's conclusions about the ski mecca are drawn on the basis of the hilly landscape formed at the time. Creating this age-old connection gives both the place as well as the ski slopes (a rather recent phenomenon) a firm and long-lasting basis. As the title of the video implies, it also legitimizes Estonia as a Nordic country, with all the supposed stability that entails (more about this in Kaasik-Krogerus 2017).

The "roots" metaphor also forms a strong basis for stability in the display: it "places" (even "plants") people and therefore makes a firm (almost organic) container of the country and its people. Among those who are "inside", this setting supposedly evokes pride (of maintaining stability no matter what) and safety (experience shows that roots will last), whereas from the ones "outside" respect and compassion is expected. Accordingly urging stability of people and the country is not related to the idea of them being left behind in terms of development.

By claiming that the "Estonian spirit's meant for survival", the permanent exhibition depicts a struggle between the community and their harsh circumstances as one where "[t]he Lord helps those who help themselves". Although the saying might seem religious, it actually takes an ironic stand towards God and religion, indicating that it is naïve to hope that somebody else is going to solve your problems. This continuous "struggle for survival" is depicted as taking place amidst a hard climate, rocky soil, not to mention plagues and famines. These conditions are shown not to intimidate Estonians, however, as the exhibition states that they have been loyal to their home country throughout history despite these hardships. Thus, they can be depicted as "winners".

On the individual level, temporal context is used in the "Spirit of Survival" to frame the phases of human life from birth to death. In this path, "natural" rituals like weddings are claimed to contribute to stability. Rituals also structure the temporary exhibition "Medieval Pleasures", which is built around annual festivities, the biggest and most important of which being two very different events: the Shrovetide (Carnival) and the Christmas Festival. The exhibits introduce rituals related to the structure and content of the events. The display presents Carnival entertainments like wearing masks or costumes representing animals, devils, or the opposite sex. Additionally, attention is paid to the games that were played and the food and drinks that were consumed during the festivities. While the exhibits note that masked people were also seen as a potential threat to the public order during the Carnival, the measures, such as fines, for handling potential violations, are presented as well. Implicitly, however, the exhibition communicated a more abstract interpretation of the Carnival as an event that challenged societal stability and the prevailing order. In the spirit of Bakhtin (1984), the masks and Carnival activities can be interpreted as a performance of temporal liberation empowering disadvantaged people by turning the world upside down for a short time period and building a frame within which the powerful could be mocked and ridiculed.

There were also points where mobility was naturalized in the exhibitions. In the permanent exhibition, mobility inside the country through phenomena like urbanization is legitimized by showing it as a "normal" societal evolution. Certain forms of mobility from other places to Estonia, like borrowing words from other languages, are justified by praising foreign influence as being beneficial from the local perspective.

As the permanent exhibition tells the visitors, factories were built while the Industrial Revolution "reached Estonia". Concerning religion, the display claims that the Orthodox Church arrived in Estonia in the eleventh century, whereas Lutheran ideas "spread and made the local population receptive to the Protestant Reformation in the sixteenth century". "Medieval Pleasures", meanwhile, emphasizes the German background of the guild, as the guild members, starting from Urban Dene, are *from* Germany. These examples show how mobility is naturalized by detaching the processes from human agency, blurring it and releasing it from responsibility. Consequently social and political phenomena "reach" and "spread" similarly to weather conditions, and therefore smoothly become part of "normal" reality.

Examples of such "naturalized" mobility also show up *from* Tallinn and Estonia to the world. Since the Great Guild Hall was a brotherhood of merchants, "Medieval Pleasures" emphasizes the importance of trade. "Spirit of Survival" also presents Estonia's exports as an ordinary form of mobility since ancient times. As the permanent exhibition tells the visitors, iron exports were replaced by grain in the Middle Ages, and in the nineteenth century by linen, amber, foodstuffs, and alcohol. Nowadays, the focus is largely on services: "Estonians have given the world the Internet telephone service Skype and several different innovative e-services".

That idea of "giving something to the world" is widened to the world-famous people who have been born and/or lived in Estonia. The permanent exhibition states that: "Tiny Estonia has had an influence [...] that is much greater than its territory", since various internationally known figures "have emerged from Estonia's multicultural and ethnically diverse history". Unlike the vague way agency appears in accounts of mobility *to* Estonia, here the agency of both Estonia as well as several famous individuals is emphasized. This creates a paradox of simultaneous superiority and inferiority. The famous people are implicitly represented as superior to the domestic community and Estonia as superior to "the world", to whom it has "given" key e-services. On the other hand, the need to leave your homeland to become known and famous elsewhere refers to a certain kind of intellectual exile (cf. Camurri 2014); the display does not elaborate on whether these exiles were voluntary or forced. The idea that in order to become world famous you have to leave your country itself, however, is constituted by and maintains a setting of periphery (Estonia) and centre ("the world"). As the exhibition states, famous people emerged "despite unfavorable conditions such as Estonia's small population and location on the periphery of Europe". By becoming "the Eastern border of the EU" in 2004, Estonia itself also "moved" symbolically. The idea of "becoming European" is therefore embedded in the exhibits' representation of natural mobility.

In sum, while in "Medieval Pleasures" rituals create stability, in "Spirit of Survival" different spheres of life are stabilized in various ways. As a result, Estonia stands for a self-sufficient, largely natural, and material container of a tightly interlinked soil/country and people, without much interaction with the rest of the world (including Europe). This bears similarities to the idea of "from-here-ness" or "people from here" as a survival strategy for making a distinction between oppressors and oppressed nation (cf. Pershai 2008, 86–87). The permanent exhibition naturalizes mobility by combining stories about the societal processes that reach Estonia and contribute to its development with ones about Estonian agency impacting "the world". Although the connections between "in-" and "outside" are valorized, their interaction remains rather vague, since the counterparts of Estonia remain unknown or are mapped in an abstract way (for instance by talking about "the world"). Though the focus is first and foremost on the city (Tallinn) or country (Estonia), it is also widened to include the European scale, since Estonia is implicitly or explicitly situated with regards to Europe. Portraying stability as a natural order of things means that no changes are foreseen to the idea of "being European", whereas the mobility between Estonia and Europe is related to "becoming European" in a process of Europeanization and domestication.

Problematizing and Politicizing Stability and Mobility

"Spirit of Survival" problematizes mobility and stability in cases when Estonia and "the world" are interrelated but do not interact. As a result, Estonia is seen to be affected by the other actors through ambiguous processes. Like the exhibition crystallizes, Russians and Germans "have oppressed Estonians the most but have also enriched the history and culture". Estonia here becomes an arena for oppressive mobility and "target of pillaging and military campaigns" like crusades, invasions, occupations, wars, and conquests. As the permanent exhibition explains, over ten foreign powers have ruled Estonia in the past 800 years, "dislocating" the country by incorporating it into different states (the Russian Empire) or dividing its territory between powers (the king of Denmark, a German military order, and the bishops of Western and Eastern Estonia). Little by little, this oppressive mobility develops into to an oppressive stability, like being incorporated into the Soviet Union for fifty years.

Soldiers and armies, but also powerful, coercive foreign immigrants like the German-speaking nobility, are represented as agents who entered the country, shook the landscape and the borders, shaped the land, and diminished agency of the local individuals. "Spirit of Survival" tells visitors that the German-speaking nobility who ruled the country for centuries "regarded Estonians as nothing but peasants and servants" and described them as "pitiful and pathetic, barbaric, dirty, lazy, and promiscuous". Accordingly, documents from the sale of an Estonian peasant are showcased as artefacts that prove the country's extreme state of both forced stability and mobility (Fig. 6.1). These handwritten pieces of paper with red stamps concreticize the meaning of oppression on a micro level and offer a personalized perspective (see also Macdonald 2013, 235).

While various authors in this volume discuss current immigration issues (see the chapters of Trakilović and Proglio), the Estonian case enables me to elaborate on the relations between the exhibitions' narratives about the past and the current attitudes towards immigration. During the country's EU accession process, some fear of immigration from the EU to Estonia was expressed (Kaasik-Krogerus 2016, 184), but most attention was targeted towards preventing immigration from Russia by keeping EU's eastern border strong. Currently, 62% of Estonian respondents (compared to 38% of the EU average) mention immigration as one of the main concerns at the European level (Standard Eurobarometer 87, 2017). According to the government of Estonia, 226 applications for international protection were received in 2015, and protection was granted to 78 people. By the end of 2017, 171 refugees who arrived in other EU countries had been relocated to Estonia. Hence, the Estonians' concern seems to be mostly fueled by the mediated transnational "refugee crisis" discourse rather than rooted in the current social reality in the country. Simultaneously, the situation is interpreted in the context of the historical migrations, like the one that took place during the Soviet period, that resulted in local people being put in a subordinate position.

The exhibition's examples of problematized mobility also depict the mobility of Estonian people who were forced to leave their home/country. As the permanent exhibition explains, during the Middle Ages people escaped serfdom by leaving the countryside to become free in towns. During mass deportations in 1940s, thirty thousand people were taken from their homes and sent to Siberia, tens of thousands escaped to the West, and many fled to the woods to continue fight against Soviets as guerillas. Consequently, World War II is depicted as having left Estonians "fearful and distrustful":

> Both World War II and the occupations brought brutal repression against landowners and their property. Most of the farms were absorbed into collective farms (known as *kolkhozes*) – an act from which country people still have not fully recovered.

And yet the exhibits do not paint Estonia as a place without a future, since the permanent exhibition also depicts people's resistance as a mixture of victimhood and heroism (see also Bogumił et al. 2015, 80).

Resistance means finding appropriate methods and tools to persist under oppressive conditions and undermine the regime. Humour is an important tool of resistance, and the exhibition notes that a "sarcastic sense of humour" is a crucial part of Estonians' self-perception, helping them deal with serious and painful issues as well as depicting themselves through a humorous prism. Broadly speaking, irony is seen to add strength to arguments (Pettersson et al. 2017, 633). Irony also helps to regain a sense of agency as an observer who reflects things. As the exhibition states, Estonians make fun of their neighbours and rulers, and show off their own superiority as being more clever.

The exhibitions also use humour in their displays. In "Spirit of Survival", this first and foremost occurs in carnivalesque forms of textual and visual self-irony. In a video in which famous historical figures alternate to "tell" the story of Estonia, apart from a few well known actors as a poet Lydia Koidula and a former president of Estonia Konstantin Päts, figure also fictional characters such as the Spirit of Survival and a giant amphibian from a local fairy tale, the Dragon of the North.[7] In fact, the video installation gives a funny impression of all its characters, since animation is combined with historical footage. From the visitors' perspective these elements make the display fun and entertaining, even though the issues and events it deals with, like wars and oppression, are not funny at all. While on the one hand this humorous approach helps visitors to digest this difficult past, on the other hand the video also is a great example of how humour is used for political purposes against holders of power from oppressive regimes.

In "Medieval Pleasures", joyful humour is combined with playfulness as an example of escaping the worries of everyday. Visitors are encouraged through exclamations like "Let's play something!" and "Fun hasn't been lost!" The festivities are described in an exaggeratedly careless manner, emphasizing the importance of the joy of the moment, if necessary even at the expense of the future. The mask of the devil that can be tried on is an example of how visitors are urged to participate. Hence, while "Spirit of Survival" uses irony to problematize and make visible oppressive mobility and stability, "Medieval Pleasures" uses humour and joy to keep away everyday problems as well as the presupposed darkness of the Middle Ages. At the same time, the exhibition communicates a rather

---

[7] The Estonian name for the creature is *Põhja konn*.

timeless message, telling visitors that no political regime is capable of preventing or banning humour.

In sum, while it was relatively easy to make a distinction between naturalized mobility and naturalized stability, problematic mobility and problematic stability are tightly intertwined in the exhibition, since problematic mobility (as evinced by wars, for instance) is "finalized" through oppressive stability in a form of occupation. In this process, the exhibits depict clear positions of agency. The permanent exhibition points to certain countries, particularly Russia and Germany, as responsible for centuries-long oppression, whereas larger entities like "Europe" are missing from this "dirty business". While the scholarly debate increasingly demands that not only single EU-member states, but also the union (as "Europe") should take responsibility for its dark history, for example with regards to colonization (for example Heinze 2012, 211; Schmidt-Gleim and Wiesner 2014, 12; see also Turunen and van Huis in this volume), in the permanent exhibition "Europe" implicitly forms a bright spot in the darkness as a potential positive story among many negative ones.

Discussion and Conclusions

The Great Guild Hall presents a great example of negotiating the boundaries of pluralization in the context of the EHL. Since the Great Guild Hall houses the Estonian History Museum, its permanent exhibition can be studied for its "past-presencing" of narratives of the nation and the country. The permanent exhibition introduces Estonia and its history as an integral part of Europe and museum experts see that this understanding does not need to be explicitly emphasized.[8] This way, any dissonance between the national and European scale is managed by removing it from the authorization process.

However, this management is noted and criticized in the EHL documents. The EHL Panel report[9] encourages the Great Guild Hall to use the recent history of Estonia to present "the narrative of Estonia and Estonian people within the context of European history and integration" (2013).

---

[8] Author's research interview with the experts of the Great Guild Hall, 7 September 2017.

[9] The panel reports include recommendations for the attribution of the EHL and provide explanations for its conclusions.

Later, the Monitoring Report[10] urges "a thorough rethinking [...] on how to contextualize the mainly Estonian national history narrative in a wider European perspective" (2016, 15).

This interaction between the national and European scale illustrates the controversies and complexities related to identity construction well. On one hand, the claims of being an "integral part of Europe" counter the EHL documents' Othering claims that state the current narratives of the Great Guild Hall are not "European enough". Yet on the other hand, the same claims of being European enable a different kind Othering by making an implicit distinction between Europe and what is left outside. Therefore, any attempts to tackle exclusion simultaneously also evoke it towards others. This illuminates the dissonance between the intentions at the national scale and their consequences on the European one. In what follows, I will draw conclusions about this dissonance with regards to power relations, spatial scales, and future imaginaries of AHD in the making from the perspective of constructing European identity narratives.

First, to return to the EHL slogan, starting points of Europe ("here") can be located in the Great Guild Hall building and the city of Tallinn ("Medieval Pleasures") as well as in Estonia ("Spirit of Survival"). The depictions of country's difficult past are also used more widely in Estonian public discussions to justify a depoliticized longing for stability. What gets obscured, however, when this narrative of external oppression is extended from the past to today, is that although the arguments remain unchanged, their consequences alter, and empowering the powerless thus turns into excluding Others. This is due to a change in power relations, since the same tools and means have very different consequences depending on whether they are used by oppressed people or by a EU member state. The same politics might thus lead towards empowerment or exclusion, and it is scarcely perceptible where or when one turns into the other. Hence, instead of studying who does or does not exercise power, what deserves attention is the complexity of the process of (re)gaining power. In the case of Estonia, new narratives depicting it as a leading information society (for example Mäe 2017) appear right alongside ones that are dominated by its oppressive past. The war in

---

[10] 2016 was the first year when the sites awarded in 2013 and 2014 were examined by the European Monitoring Panel. Sites are monitored to ensure that they continue to meet the criteria for which they were selected.

Ukraine evoked fear throughout the Baltic countries, and despite being "officially European" through their membership in the EU and NATO, a dark future was (silently) imagined on the basis of the countries' past experience. Political debates at the European scale often reduce this puzzle either to a narrative of victims or one of the intolerance and ignorance of the "Eastern Block countries". Ironically, public discussion about the EU who is "hit" or "flooded" by the refugee crisis, repeats similar victim position on the European scale.

Second, in spatial terms, the heritage discourse of the Great Guild Hall is an example of multi-scalarity, covering everything from farms and small towns to Estonia and Europe. However, while Huot et al. (2014, 330) map out multi-scalarity on the basis of different, partly overlapping scales of communities (city, nation, region, etc.), in the current case the scales are also contradictory. The exhibitions are an example of simultaneously displaying common heritage and dissonant multiheritage (Macdonald 2013, 162). This holds true particularly when we compare the two exhibitions: the exclusion of Estonians from the Great Guild is not problematized in "Medieval Pleasures", for example, whereas "Spirit of Survival" talks about Estonians as one of the most unhappy people in Europe, "second-class citizens in their own land for a long time, starting from the thirteenth century". In the EHL's site video of the Great Guild Hall, the museum representative says that on the basis of the exhibition visitors could understand how Estonian identity is connected to European identity. This is especially clear in the permanent exhibition, which domesticates Europe by elaborating it in relation to Estonia. Here, Europe as a stable context is interlinked with the national scale (of the EU's member states), obscuring how the agency of "Europe/the EU" impacts a variety of scales, including the global one.

Third, since heritage is formed in the present with an aim to influence the future, the key question is what kind of future is imagined to and for whom. On the basis of the video "Is Estonia a Nordic country?", the "Europe starts here" slogan can be domesticated as a (supposedly permanent) end to oppression that was sealed by Estonia's joining the EU in 2004. In this setting, the EU stands for a survival that enables the country to move on. However, a context described in the permanent exhibition where "Happiness is being alive" does not facilitate bright imaginaries of the future. Since most of the stories from the past do not offer "happy endings", hope is instead communicated by a silence around the future. From an Estonian perspective, this silence shows an attempt to have a story (independence followed by the country's EU

Fig. 6.1 This document of the sale of an Estonian peasant from the eighteenth century is an example of both oppressive stability and oppressive mobility from one owner to the next

accession) that could lead towards a "normal" future. A lack of explicitly plotted future imaginaries means that visitors are given some specs to conclude the story by themselves. Consequently, the exhibition posits the EU as more or less fixed to the year 2004, the "good old times" before the current crises of the union, as the latter are outside the scope of the permanent exhibition. The Hall's setting resembles fairy tales that end with a wedding (EU accession), not with a depiction of a married couple's daily life. In the background, though, the EU (and tacitly Europe) is a "good guy" in the story (vis-à-vis the Russian and German "bad guys" from history). This implicitly rejects any potential criticism against the EU.

Acknowledgements This work was supported by the European Research Council (ERC) under the EU's Horizon 2020 Research and Innovation Programme under Grant 636177 (EUROHERIT). The content of this chapter does not reflect the official opinion of the European Union. Responsibility for the information and views expressed in the chapter lies entirely with the author.

References

Alasuutari, P. 2009. The Domestication of Worldwide Policy Models. *Ethnologia Europaea* 39 (1): 66–71.
Alasuutari, P., E. Mikola, M. Rautalin, J. Syväterä, and L. Valkeasuo. 2013. Globaalien kehityslinjojen luominen ja kotoistaminen. In *Liikkuva maailma*, ed. M. Lehtonen, 7–29. Tampere: Vastapaino.
Bakhtin, M. 1984. *Rabelais and His World*, trans. H. Iswolsky. Bloomington: Indiana University Press.
Bauman, Z. 1998. *Globalization: The Human Consequences*. Cambridge: Polity Press.
Bauman, Z. 2000. *Liquid Modernity*. Cambridge: Polity Press.
Beck, U. 2000 [1997]. *What Is Globalization?* Cambridge: Polity Press.
Bogumił, Z., J. Wawrzyniak, T. Buchen, C. Ganzer, and M. Senina. 2015. *The Enemy on Display: The Second World War in Eastern European Museums*. New York and Oxford: Berghahn Books.
Cambridge Dictionary. https://dictionary.cambridge.org. Accessed 16 August 2017.
Camurri, R. 2014. The Exile Experience Reconsidered: A Comparative Perspective in European Cultural Migration During the Interwar Period. *Transatlantica* 1. http://journals.openedition.org/transatlantica/6920. Accessed 2 February 2018.
Checkel, J.T., and P.J. Katzenstein. 2009. The Politicization of European Identities. In *European Identity*, ed. J.T. Checkel and P.J. Katzenstein, 1–28. Cambridge: Cambridge University Press.
Cresswell, T. 2001. The Production of Mobilities. *New Formations* 43: 11–25.
De Cesari, C. 2017. Museums of Europe: Tangles of Memory, Borders, and Race. *Museum Anthropology* 40: 18–35.
Delanty, G. 2005. The Idea of a Cosmopolitan Europe: On the Cultural Significance of Europeanization. *International Review of Sociology* 15 (3): 405–421.
EC (The European Commission). 2013. European Heritage Label. 2013 Panel Report. Brussels: European Commission.
EC (The European Commission). 2016. European Heritage Label. Monitoring Report. Brussels: European Commission.
EC (The European Commission). 2017. European Heritage Label. Application Form. Brussels: European Commission.
EC (The European Commission). 2017. Standard Eurobarometer 87. http://ec.europa.eu/commfrontoffice/publicopinion/index.cfm/Survey/getSurveyDetail/instruments/STANDARD/surveyKy/2142. Accessed 3 September 2017.

EP&C (The European Parliament and the Council of the European Union). 2014. Proposal for a Decision of the European Parliament and of the Council Amending Decision. No. 445/2014/EU Establishing a Union Action for the European Capitals of Culture for the Years 2020 to 2033. *Official Journal of the European Union*, L 132.

Fairclough, N. 1995. *Media Discourse*. London: Edward Arnold.

Feldman, M. 2001. European Integration and the Discourse of National Identity in Estonia. *National Identities* 3: 5–21.

Harrison, R. 2013. *Heritage: Critical Approaches*. London: Routledge.

Heinze, E. 2012. The Reality and Hyper-Reality of Human Rights: Public Consciousness and the Mass Media. In *Examining Critical Perspectives on Human Rights*, ed. R. Dickinson, E. Katselli, C. Murray, and O.W. Pedersen, 193–216. Cambridge: Cambridge University Press.

Huot, S., B. Dodson, and D.L. Rudman. 2014. Negotiating Belonging Following Migration: Exploring the Relationship Between Place and Identity in Francophone Minority Communities. *The Canadian Geographer/Le Géographe canadien* 58 (3): 329–340.

Jones, S., and J. Subotić. 2011. Fantasies of Power: Performing Europeanization on the European Periphery. *European Journal of Cultural Studies* 14 (5): 542–557.

Kaasik-Krogerus, S. 2016. *Normative Stories of the Formative Moment: Construction of Estonian National Identity in Postimees During the EU Accession Process*. Helsinki: Unigrafia.

Kaasik-Krogerus, S. 2017. Kuvitellut Pohjoismaat Viron presidenttien puheissa. *Idäntutkimus* 24 (2): 18–32.

Kaasik-Krogerus S. 2019. Identity Politics of the Promotional Videos of the European Heritage Label. *Contemporary Politics*. https://doi.org/10.1080/13569775.2019.1611207.

Karlsson, K. 2010. The Uses of History and the Third Wave of Europeanization. In *A European Memory? Contested Histories and Politics of Remembrance*, ed. B. Strath and M. Pakier, 38–52. New York and Oxford: Berghahn Books.

Kisić, V. 2017. *Governing Heritage Dissonance: Promises and Realities of Selected Cultural Policies*. Amsterdam: European Cultural Foundation.

Kraenzle, C., and M. Mayr. 2017. Introduction: The Usable Pasts and Futures of Transnational European Memories. In *The Changing Place of Europe in Global Memory Cultures: Usable Pasts and Futures*, ed. C. Kraenzle and M. Mayr, 1–21. Basingstoke: Palgrave Macmillan.

Kuus, M. 2017. Locating Europe's power, or the Difference Between Passports and Passporting. In Interventions in Europe's Political Futures (with F. McConnell, A. Jeffrey, A. Smith, N. Vaughan-Williams, and H. Crawley). *Political Geography* 60: 261–271.

Lähdesmäki, T. 2019. Taide, paikka ja kuulumisen politiikka EU:n Eurooppa-projektissa. In *Kuulumisen reittejä taiteessa*, ed. K. Hiltunen and N. Sääskilahti. Turku: Eetos.
Lähdesmäki, T., S. Kaasik-Krogerus, and K. Mäkinen. 2019. Genealogy of the Concept of Heritage in the European Commission's Policy Discourse. *Contributions to the History of Concepts* 14 (1): 115–139.
Lehtonen, M. 2004. Johdanto: Säiliöstä suhdekimppuun. In *Suomi toisin sanoen*, ed. M. Lehtonen, O. Löytty, and P. Ruuska, 9–28. Tampere: Vastapaino.
Lehtonen, M. 2013. Miten tutkia liikkuvaa maailmaa? In *Liikkuva maailma*, ed. M. Lehtonen, 7–29. Tampere: Vastapaino.
Macdonald, S. 2013. *Memorylands: Heritage and Identity in Europe Today*. London: Routledge.
Mäe, R. 2017. The Story of e-Estonia: A Discourse-Theoretical Approach. *Baltic Worlds* 1–2: 32–44.
Mäkinen, K. 2014. Constructing Europe as an Area via EU Documents on Citizenship and Culture. In *The Meanings of Europe: Changes and Exchanges of a Contested Concept*, ed. C. Wiesner and M. Schmidt-Gleim, 130–143. London: Routledge.
Mälksoo, M. 2006. From Existential Politics Towards Normal Politics? The Baltic States in the Enlarged Europe. *Security Dialogue* 37: 275–297.
Mälksoo, M. 2009. The Memory Politics of Becoming European: The East European Subalterns and the Collective Memory of Europe. *European Journal of International Relations* 15 (4): 653–680.
Massey, D. 1991. A Global Sense of Place. *Marxism Today*, June: 24–29.
Massey, D. 2005. *For Space*. London: Sage.
McDowell, S. 2008. Heritage, Memory and Identity. In *The Ashgate Research Companion to Heritage and Identity*, ed. B. Graham and P. Howard, 37–53. Burlington (VT): Ashgate.
Morley, D. 2000. *Home Territories: Media, Mobility and Identity*. London: Routledge.
Moser, S. 2010. The Devil Is in the Detail: Museum Displays and the Creation of Knowledge. *Museum Anthropology* 33 (1): 22–32.
Oxford Living Dictionaries. https://en.oxforddictionaries.com. Accessed 16 August 2017.
Palonen, E. 2014. Assigning Meaning to (EU-)Europe Through Cultural Policy. In *The Meanings of Europe: Changes and Exchanges of a Contested Concept*, ed. C. Wiesner and M. Schmidt-Gleim, 144–159. London: Routledge.
Pershai, A. 2008. Localness and Mobility in Belarusian Nationalism: The Tactic of Tuteishaść. *Nationalities Papers* 36 (1): 85–103.
Pettersson, K., K. Liebkind, and I. Sakki. 2017. You Who Are an Immigrant—Why Are You in the Sweden Democrats? *Discourse & Society* 26 (6): 624–641.

Radaelli, C.M. 2000. Whither Europeanisation? Concept Stretching and Substantive Change. *European Integration Online Papers* (EIoP) 4 (8).
Raik, K. 2003. *Democratic Politics or the Implementation of Inevitabilities? Estonia's Democracy and Integration into the European Union*. Tartu: Tartu University Press.
Sassatelli, M. 2002. Imagined Europe: The Shaping of a European Cultural Identity Through EU Cultural Policy. *European Journal of Social Theory* 5 (4): 435–451.
Sassatelli, M. 2008. European Cultural Space in the European Cities of Culture. *European Societies* 10 (2): 225–245.
Schimmelfennig, F. 1998. NATO Enlargement: A Constructivist Explanation. *Security Studies* 8: 198–234.
Schimmelfennig, F. 2000. International Socialization in the New Europe: Rational Action in an Institutional Environment. *European Journal of International Relations* 5: 109–139.
Schmidt-Gleim, M., and C. Wiesner. 2014. The Meanings of Europe: Introduction. In *The Meanings of Europe: Changes and Exchanges of a Contested Concept*, ed. C. Wiesner and M. Schmidt-Gleim, 1–15. London: Routledge.
Sheller, M., and J. Urry. 2006. The New Mobilities Paradigm. *Environment and Planning A* 38: 207–226.
Smith, L. 2006. *Uses of Heritage*. London: Routledge.
Urry, J. 2007. *Mobilities*. Cambridge: Polity Press.
Waterton, E., and L. Smith. 2009. There Is No Such Thing as Heritage. In *Taking Archaeology Out of Heritage*, ed. E. Waterton and L. Smith, 10–27. Cambridge: Cambridge Scholars Publishing.

Open Access This chapter is licensed under the terms of the Creative Commons Attribution 4.0 International License (http://creativecommons.org/licenses/by/4.0/), which permits use, sharing, adaptation, distribution and reproduction in any medium or format, as long as you give appropriate credit to the original author(s) and the source, provide a link to the Creative Commons license and indicate if changes were made.

The images or other third party material in this chapter are included in the chapter's Creative Commons license, unless indicated otherwise in a credit line to the material. If material is not included in the chapter's Creative Commons license and your intended use is not permitted by statutory regulation or exceeds the permitted use, you will need to obtain permission directly from the copyright holder.

PART III

Colonial Pasts in the Present

CHAPTER 7

A Geography of Coloniality: Re-narrating European Integration

Johanna Turunen

Although the interlinkages of European integration and colonialism have been increasingly acknowledged in academic circles (e.g. Ahmed 2000; Bhambra 2009; Hansen and Jonsson 2015; Kinnvall 2016), colonialism continues to be a difficult topic in many forums in and around Europe. In the general narratives on Europe, "colonialism has been framed as the past property of individual nation states to be displaced by a new narrative of European integration free from the stain of colonialism" (Bhambra 2014, 155; see also Passerini 2012). This shifting of responsibility to the EU's member states has been coupled with academic attempts to frame postcoloniality as an issue of the formerly colonized regions and thereby firmly outside of the European polity (for critiques, see e.g. Bhambra 2016; Goldberg 2006; Passerini 2012). This chapter, however, seeks to look beyond former imperial states and colonies to imagine what kind of a role the European Union (EU), as a transnational

J. Turunen (✉)
Department of Music, Art and Culture Studies,
University of Jyväskylä, Jyväskylä, Finland
e-mail: johanna.k.turunen@jyu.fi

© The Author(s) 2019
T. Lähdesmäki et al. (eds.),
Dissonant Heritages and Memories in Contemporary Europe,
Palgrave Studies in Cultural Heritage and Conflict,
https://doi.org/10.1007/978-3-030-11464-0_7

European institution, could have in contributing to dismantling colonial legacies, especially in the realm of European cultural heritage.

It is true that Europe itself is not postcolonial in the same sense that the formerly colonized regions are. As the centre of the former European empires, its position is quite different. This, however, does not mean that Europe, nor the EU are somehow free or detached from the effects of colonialism. As Ahmed has stated, "the colonial project was not external to the constitution of the modernity of European nations" (2000, 10). Indeed, colonialism and the connected processes of slavery (e.g. Gikandi 2011) and racialization (e.g. Goldberg 1993, 2002, 2006) came to define European modernity and also had implications for the development of its political systems, especially in the former imperial states (e.g. Tully 2002). The influence of these processes is not, however, limited to the former imperial states. Through their entanglement with ideas of modernity, the effects of colonialism can be perceived to have wider effect across a wide variety of European states. This colonial foundation is not only embedded in structures of rule and power, but it also has vast cultural influence (e.g. Said 1993 on cultural imperialism) and is deeply infiltrated in Europe's cultural archive (e.g. Wekker 2016; Milica and Van Huis in this volume). Cultural heritage, especially when combined with its ability to create narratives, is an important part of this cultural archive.

To analyze the remnants of colonialism in the context of European cultural heritage, the relationship between modernity and "coloniality" is central. The idea of coloniality stems from the Latin American decolonial school (e.g. Quijano 2007; de Sousa Santos et al. 2007; Mignolo and Escobar 2010). Although drawing from different epistemologies and canons of knowledge, postcolonial and decolonial thinking have many connections and overlaps, and this study draws on both traditions. The decolonial school's emphasis on understanding colonialism and modernity as deeply entwined processes, however, has many advantages for the study of heritage, a concept which itself is a product of European modernity too. In reference to this connection between modernity and coloniality, Mignolo has noted that they "go hand in hand, and you cannot have modernity without coloniality; the unfinished project of modernity carries over its shoulders the unfinished project of coloniality" (2006, 312). Through acknowledging modernity/coloniality as two aspects of the same process, we can move beyond merely analyzing postcolonial heritage (or heritage directly connected to colonialism), towards analyzing the traces of coloniality within the larger context of all European heritage. Additionally, the broader approach that coloniality enables through its linkage to modernity allows us to shift our focus from the former imperial states to the broader context of the contemporary EU.

As a concept, coloniality "refers to long-standing patterns of power that emerged as a result of colonialism, but that define culture, labor, intersubjective relations, and knowledge production well beyond the strict limits of colonial administrations" (Maldonado-Torres 2007, 247). According to Grossfoguel (2004, 320), this coloniality is a manifestation of the long history of European colonialism and is deeply embedded in the modern capitalist world system. Though there are significant differences between the national and regional experiences of this coloniality, coloniality's effects can be detected in almost every sphere of our lives. Although mindful of this diversity, the aim of this chapter is not to analyze or map these different overlapping experiences of coloniality. Rather, this chapter aims to unearth the coloniality that exists beyond these diversities—a deeper level of coloniality embedded into the European project of the European Union.

Many contemporary narratives of modern Europe are still inherently products of the same cultural processes, power relations, and discourses of Western hegemony that were used to legitimate colonial rule. Despite the end of formal colonialism and the disenfranchisement of official colonial and racial discourse, some traces of these ideas are still embedded in contemporary understandings of Europe and of the rest of the world. It is exactly this, Eurocentric understanding of Europe and the ways it manifests through cultural heritage that this chapter seeks to engage. I argue that this coloniality of the European project is deeply embedded in Eurocentric and Western notions of European heritage, not only influencing the ways Europe deals with its many "external" others, but also distorting the internal dynamics of the European Union. As a result, like much of the rest of the world, Europe is posited inside a geography of coloniality—a spatial narrative of the expansion of Eurocentric notions of Europeanness.

This chapter sets out from the understanding, that "colonialism never left Europe unaffected and is still part of European reality" (Kinvall 2016, 153). Accordingly, Europe is analyzed as a profoundly postcolonial space as well as a construct heavily influenced by coloniality. I approach this coloniality and its relationship to the idea of Europe through one cultural construct that heavily draws on the cultural archive mentioned above: the idea of European cultural heritage. I especially focus on the ways this idea is promoted in the European Union's heritage actions. Empirically, this chapter focuses on the European Heritage Label (EHL)—an EU cultural heritage action that seeks to nominate European heritage sites that represent the history of European integration and common European values.

More specifically, this chapter seeks to analyze the following: how the "European significance" of the EHL sites is narrated in the selection process; how notions of Eurocentrism are integrated into these narratives of Europe; and, finally, what kind of a spatial dynamic these narratives produce as a side-product of the process narrating European heritage. The analysis especially draws on the interconnection of European values and European integration, arguing that, in the context of the EHL, integration is intricately linked to spreading common values which itself is further entangled with the ideas of "European significance".

Although I especially focus on the EU's cultural heritage initiatives, I acknowledge that there is significant overlap between notions of Europe and notions of the EU. As I argue more extensively below, the political entity of the EU seeks to connect itself with wider cultural notions of Europe by promoting the idea of European cultural heritage, which to some extent blurs the limits of these two entities.

The European Heritage Label and Authorized Heritage Discourse

The European Heritage Label (EHL) was first launched as an intergovernmental cultural scheme in 2006. In 2011, the EHL was reinstituted as a European Union action—one of the flagship initiatives of the EU. Along with the renewal of the program, the grounds for granting the label were also renewed. The new criteria placed more emphasis on the European dimension of the sites—as opposed to the more national or regional interpretations that were possible during the intergovernmental phase (see EC 2010). The newly founded European Panel of Experts (see EC 2013, 2014, 2015, 2016) was put in charge of the evaluation of the sites, and the final decision-making power was given to the European Commission.

My primary data consists of different official documentation produced by the European Parliament, European Commission, and the actors coordinating the European Heritage Label. These consist of documents related to the founding of the Label as well as documents related to the selections of the sites.¹ In the panel reports, all applications are evaluated based on three criteria: the European significance, the proposed project to communicate this significance, and the management capacity of the site. My analysis focuses on the period between 2011 and 2016, when a total of 29 sites in 16 member states had been awarded the label. During that period, an additional 10 sites were evaluated as meeting the criterion of European significance, but not nominated for the actual Label due to deficiencies elsewhere in the application. Although the analysis takes into account all the successful and unsuccessful candidate sites (64 sites in total), the analysis is especially focused on the 39 sites (see Appendix 1) evaluated as meeting the criterion of European significance.

My analysis especially focuses on how the sites' "European significance"—a term used in the EHL documents—is narrated in the panel reports. These narratives of European significance are understood as tools to create, promote, and sustain the sites' perceived—yet fuzzy and ambiguous—ideas of "Europeanness". Although they summarize, re-articulate and reference the original applications, the short descriptions in the panel reports are analyzed as a representation of the applicant sites that has been produced by the European Panel of Experts. The methodology for the analysis is made up of a thematic close reading of the documents that uses postcolonialism as a reading strategy (Ashcroft et al. 2002). By highlighting dissonances, this chapter seeks to re-evaluate the ways we interpret European pasts. Postcolonial approaches can

---

[1] These documents include Decision No 1194/2011/EU of the European Parliament and of the Council (EP 2011). This is the official founding decision passed by both the European Parliament and Commission. Secondly, the Commission Staff Working Document SEC (2010) 197 (EC 2010), Impact Assessment—Accompanying document to the Proposal for Decision of the European Parliament and of the Council establishing the European Union actions for the European Heritage Label. The Impact Assessment is a comprehensive compilation of documents that was produced as a Commission staff working document to support the founding process of the EHL as an EU action. In addition to the actual Impact Assessment, the document includes several annexes, including the meeting summaries of several public consultations. Additionally, the data comprises of four reports produced by the European Panel of Experts. These reports include the European Heritage Label Panel Reports from 2013, 2014, and 2015, as well as the first Panel Report on Monitoring, published in 2016. All documents have been published by the European Commission. These reports make reference to the original applications of the candidate sites, but mainly consist of the European Panel of Experts' evaluations and commentaries. Finally, as supplementary data I will use the information on the EHL website (https:// ec.europa.eu/programmes/creative-europe/actions/heritage-label_en).

offer tools for this process that can tackle issues even beyond analyzing Europe's colonial past. For, as Bhambra (2014, 117) has claimed, "[p]ostcolonial and decolonial arguments have been explicit in their challenge to the insularity of historical narratives and historiographical traditions emanating from Europe". By bringing European heritage and the coloniality of Europe closer together, this postcolonial approach can allow us to make hidden power hierarchies, exclusions, and biases more visible. As such, it can be used to challenge "the universals of European narratives constructed, as they are, on the basis of marginalizing and silencing other experiences and voices" (Bhambra 2009, 81).

Before going into the analysis, I want to reflect on the relationship between this data and the idea of an "authorized heritage discourse" (AHD) proposed by Laurajane Smith (2006; cf. inclusive heritage discourse e.g. Kisić 2017). This approach, along with a larger discursive turn in critical heritage studies, sees heritage as a process of knowledge production. As has been noted by Smith, "[t]here is, really, no such *thing* as heritage" (2006, 11, emphasis added). A specific site, historical phenomenon, tradition, or value is not automatically heritage through some im- or explicit link to the past; rather heritage is a social construct. Objects, places, and landscapes become heritage only through the meanings attached to them in a process of labeling, defining, and ordering. As a result, heritage is "a set of values and meanings" (Smith 2006, 11) as well as a cultural practice seeking to control and regulate these values (ibid.). As a social construct, the meanings we assign to heritage can be altered, reinterpreted, or contested, which makes heritage not only open to change, but also a potential tool for change. However, as Smith criticizes, different kinds of heritage experts hold a predominant role in this process of defining heritage and selecting heritage sites. The resulting authorized heritage discourses that rely on expert opinion are problematic, as they tend to not only distance the public and the visitors from the knowledge production around meanings attached to heritage, but also to exclude or disenfranchise specific historical, cultural, and social experiences. As such, these AHDs also diminish or disguise the transformative potential that heritage could possess as a future-oriented idea (e.g. Harrison 2013, Lähdesmäki 2017).

In terms of the role given to expert opinions, the EHL can be considered as a super-AHD due to its three-layer system of expert evaluation—first at the site, then at the national level, and lastly at the European level. This also leads us to the potential fracture point between the many narratives of the EHL and the authorized heritage discourses of the EU. The sites, after having received the label, have the potential to challenge the narrative created by the coordinating actors of the EHL and, in many cases, they actually also seek to do this. There is a constant negotiation between the official narrative envisioned in the EU documents and the many narrative strategies used by the sites themselves (on the intergovernmental phase, also see Lähdesmäki 2014). The narratives of European significance that are used as grounds for nomination as an EHL site represent only one aspect of the overall narratives offered by the sites and not always the one most actively communicated to the public.

It would be tempting to label the narrative analyzed here as an authorized heritage discourse of the European Union (EU-AHD). The narrative created through the official documents of the EHL especially reveals the agency of the European Panel of Experts. Through its connections to wider EU policy discourses, however, it is also embedded in the wider political project of the EU and reflects the values and understandings of this wider political construct. As such, it is not a narrative describing European history nor the totality of European heritage, but a politically motivated narrative that the EU in the context of the EHL has produced of itself. As such, there are many grounds for conceptualizing the official narrative and discursive practices of the official documents of the EHL as an authorized heritage discourse of the EU (EU-AHD). However, it also needs to be remembered that in addition to being challenged by the actors within the EHL, this authorized heritage discourse is also challenged by actors both in- and outside the institutional frame of the EU. The European Parliament's own history project, the recently opened House of European History (HEH) is one such attempt. Although engaging with the conceptual frame of history rather than that of heritage, the HEH does offer an alternative interpretation of the story and values of Europe.

With these limitations in mind, this chapter uses the term EU-AHD as a shorthand for the official narrative and/or discursive practices of the official documents of European Heritage Label. What must be emphasized is that the data used for analysis do not represent the totality of what could be the EU-AHD, nor is it able to discuss the narratives the EHL sites themselves choose to use in their everyday practices. It is thus not able to bring forth the agency of the sites themselves. What is analyzed here instead is very much an authorized heritage discourse in the making (see also Kaasik-Krogerus in this volume).

Modernity/Coloniality and Lingering Eurocentrism

The importance of ideas associated with modernity should not be understated when debating European cultural heritage and the values that this heritage embodies. For, as noted by Delanty (2017, 54), "[m]odernity is the constitutive matrix that gave to Europe a direction and meaning". Despite this long and entangled connection between the ideas of Europe and modernity, Europe can no longer be considered as "the vanguard of modernity" (Passerini 2012, 123–124; see also 2002). However, as Passerini continues, even though this identification no longer carries the same meanings, ideas of modernity have continued to maintain a strong Eurocentric tone (ibid.). It is this enduring nature of Eurocentrism that reminds us that modernity should not be reduced to European Enlightenment (see also Chakrabarty 2000), as the connections between modernity and colonialism, and the implications they have for the ideas of Europe, are far deeper. Enrique Dussel (2000)—a central thinker among the decolonial school—has criticized the Eurocentric understanding of modernity "for it indicates intra-European phenomena as the starting point of modernity and explains its later development without making recourse to anything outside of Europe" (ibid., 471; see also Dainotto 2007). This disregards the very material impact the colonies had in the creation of European modernity (e.g. Fanon 1963, 81), and also hides the many historical and cultural entanglements between Europe and the regions European imperial states controlled overseas.

Coloniality as the entwined counterpart of modernity especially manifests in Eurocentrism. According to Quijano (2000, 549), Eurocentrism "does not involve all of the knowledge of history of all of Europe […] It is instead a specific rationality or perspective of knowledge that was made globally hegemonic, colonizing and overcoming other previous or different conceptual formations and their respective concrete knowledges, as much in Europe as in the rest of the world". The central factor of Eurocentrism is the tendency to position specific cultures and forms of knowledge in hierarchical positions. Though these hierarchies played a central role in legitimating colonialism (e.g. Tully 2002), they are not only limited to historical relations, as similar hierarchies can also be found in early documents related to European integration. In her analysis of the Declaration on European Identity (1973) signed by the nine Western European states that formed the European Economic Community (EEC) at the time, Luisa Passerini (2012) commented on the fundamental hierarchies that the document created in terms of the relations between the EEC and the external states. These hierarchies prioritized Western connections over relationships with Eastern Europe, but also posited former European colonies in a subordinate position. The document can be seen as profoundly influenced by the Cold War and the long colonial histories of many of the signatories. Passerini's analysis shows how deeply Western norms were embedded in the EEC documents, which also form the foundation for the European Union. As the rest of this chapter will show, tendencies towards similar hierarchies, both between Europe and its former colonies, as well as between Western and Eastern Europe, can also be identified in the EU-AHD.

A second key aspect of Eurocentrism (and one directly related to the cultural hierarchies) is the incentive for "spreading" culture with little consideration for other pre-existing cultures and forms of knowledge production. In the founding documents of the EHL, the spread of Eurocentric ideals is evident especially in the Impact Assessment (EC 2010), in which the EHL is aligned with core European values and the promotion of a preconceived and unproblematized joint European heritage. It is important to note that the document is convinced the EHL would have only positive impacts, mainly in terms of social/societal challenges. Any concerns that the promotion of European heritage would downplay or silence other heritages are not actively discussed. As the Impact Assessment states:

> European common values are at the core of the EHL and one of the foundation stones for the initiative concerns the building of a shared European identity based on democratic values and human rights. It should therefore be noted that the label is likely to have positive impacts (and certainly no negative ones) and thereby make a contribution to the objectives of the Charter of Fundamental Rights of the European Union. (EC 2010, 26)

Within this framework, the spread of central ideals and values is narrated as a positive and desirable development, or as progress, with very limited room for alternative interpretations, criticism, or any acknowledgement of the domination, abuse, and control that might have been associated with it. It presumes that, since these values are depicted as positive, benign, or even universal, anything that is associated with these values is thought to have positive implications. Additionally, as it fails to acknowledge "European domination over much of the world through colonialism, dispossession, appropriation, and enslavement as significant to that history" (Bhambra and Narayan 2017, 2), it also fails to create space for discussing or dismantling the baggage left by this difficult history. Furthermore, it posits European heritage at the top of a hierarchical system through which Europeanness becomes measurable by the level of adaptation to these values and cultural norms. In the empirical section below, it will become clear that this incentive for spreading a preconceived, yet fuzzy idea of Europe is entangled in the ways integration and expansion are narrated in the EU-AHD.

Narrating European Significance in the European Heritage Label

The EHL website declares that the "European Heritage sites are milestones in the creation of today's Europe. Spanning from the dawn of civilization to the Europe we see today, these sites celebrate and symbolize European ideals, values, history and integration". Already from this basic definition, it is evident that through the EHL sites, the EU-AHD seeks to create a progressive, continuous narrative of Europe, spanning from the first steps of what is termed as "European civilization" to the contemporary European Union. Through this narrative, the EU-AHD not only seeks to take credit for a number of European historical developments, but also posits EU as the final state of this continuous process of European integration. This is a problematic foundation for any type of conceptualization for European memory. Although some EHL sites also represent ruptures or difficult periods of European history, the overall narrative remains one of continuity. Passerini (2011, 48) has strongly criticized this "illusion of continuity" and rather advocates for the acknowledgement of "radical discontinuity". By acknowledging important ruptures and discontinuities, Passerini argues, we can "conceptualize the kind of European memory that might allow for a break with Eurocentrism and hierarchies between European countries and regions" (ibid.). Acknowledgement of this type of ruptures has become more commonplace in the general narratives of Europe (e.g. Delanty 2010), but these discontinuities are not given adequate space and importance in the EU-AHD. Rather, the implied continuity increasingly blurs the separation between cultural and geographical understandings of Europe and the political entity of the EU. This is hardly representative of the reality of European history and downplays the interpretations that emphasize the plurality of Europe and the plurality of European heritage (see for example Hall 1999; Delanty 2017). It also stands in stark contrast with the rhetoric of diversity that dominates both the founding decision of the EHL (EP 2011), as well as the wider EU policy discourses (e.g. Lähdesmäki 2012; Kraus and Sciortino 2014).

The Idea of "European Values"

As the idea of "European values" is a central aspect of the EHL, it is therefore perhaps unsurprising that "values" are also given a central position when narrating "European significance" in the EU-AHD. These European values are only defined in the EHL documents in terms of abstract references to "values" or by listing typical value mantras of freedom, democracy, human rights, diversity, tolerance, and solidarity. When we look at the way specific sites are narrated, peace and democracy seem to hold a central position. Sites directly related to peace, for example, are the Peace Palace in Hague (Netherlands), the Sites of the Peace of Westphalia (Germany), and several sites related to the First and Second World Wars (see Mäkinen in this volume). In the narrative sites related to democracy and the development of the rule of law include sites like the Archive of the Crown of Aragon (Spain) and the 3 May 1791 Constitution (Poland). References to human rights (e.g. the Charter of Law of Abolition of the Death Penalty 1867, Portugal, and Franja Partisan Hospital, Slovenia), the Enlightenment (e.g. Residencia de Estudiantes, Spain), and solidarity (e.g. European Solidarity Center, Poland) are also prominent.

Despite the ample references to "values", this linking is only rarely done directly. Rather, any references to values are often vague and abstract. Grand, abstract phrases like being a "symbol of the pursuit of democracy" (EC 2014, 12), being "central to strengthening of human rights and to the defense of democratic values and the rule of law" (EC 2015, 14), the fostering of "religious toleration and cultural diversity as well as democratic values" (EC 2014, 8), "highlighting the Enlightenment values" (EC 2014, 10), or being a "beacon of progressive ideas" (EC 2015, 10) were common in Panel reports' descriptions of the EHL sites. Interestingly, a resistance to values that are seen to counter these European values, especially those of democracy and peace, can also be seen as markers of European significance, as evidenced by several sites nominated through their role in the resistance of either communism,

Nazism, or other forms of authoritarian rule. The reports' emphasis on abstract references could be a result of the explicit focus on the sites' symbolic importance that can be derived from the founding decision of the EHL (EP 2011). However, there seems to be only limited discussion on what these values in fact mean or how they should be applied when defining the European significance of the potential EHL sites. As a result of their constant repetition, the connection between the values and Europe seems to hold a normative position in the EU-AHD, yet this connection goes largely unattested. Furthermore, there is clearly an attempt to make these values more concrete by adding a material aspect through connecting abstract European values to specific heritage sites.

This normative position of "values", however, is not unproblematic. The connection between Europe and/or EU and these values has been questioned on numerous accounts. Chakrabarty (2000) and Sen (1999), for example, have challenged the idea of Europe as the home of democracy by highlighting democratic practices in different parts of Africa and India that predate Greek democracy. On the other hand, Bhambra (2009) has highlighted the discrepancies in the idea of the EU as an institution of peace in her analysis of the decolonization-related wars of former European empires during the formative years of the founding of the EU. In terms of human rights, both Delanty and Rumford (2005) and Suárez-Krabbe (2013) have questioned the implicit equality and inclusiveness of human rights and democracy by making the deeper linkages between these values and European racism visible. Finally, El-Tayeb (2011) has sought to highlight the investment in "whiteness as a norm against which ethnicization is read as a tool of differentiation between insiders and outsiders" (ibid., xiv). The relevance of these values is also questioned by many contemporary political and social phenomena, such as the continued structural racism, the discourses around the "immigration crisis", as well as the rise of the right-wing populist parties across Europe. All these processes seem to fundamentally challenge the connection between ideas of Europe and the values it seeks to represent.

Furthermore, as noted by Passerini (2012) the references to these values in official statements are not a particularly European phenomenon, but rather one that is repeated in the official narratives of almost all contemporary political entities. The prominent role of these values in the EHL should thus not be seen as indicative of the connection between these values and Europe per se, but rather as being due to the repetition of a typical global political rhetoric. Passerini identifies the reliance on these abstract value mantras as a "constant characteristic of Eurocentrism" (ibid., 124) and further points out that "definitions of identity based on such conceptions run the risk of reproducing rhetorical formulae which are either empty or suspect" (ibid.). She has also shown how the disproportionate emphasis on Christianity and the Enlightenment in the narratives of European value mantras makes it possible "to exclude the Judaic and Islamic worlds from this [European] cultural community" (ibid., 136), thus further narrowing the legitimate basis on which to build forms of European identification. The entangled nature of heritage and identities (e.g. Graham and Howard 2008) is also reflected in the founding decision of the EHL, which posits the promotion of belonging as the primary aim of the EHL. These problematic linkages between values and identities force us to reconsider the type of identities that can be built on conceptualizations of heritage focused primarily on abstract values.

Narrating Integration

I will now discuss the EU-AHD in the context of the relationship between "European significance" and integration. The narrative of integration promoted by the EU-AHD starts from the EHL-nominated site called the Heart of Ancient Athens, which represents "a rich historical landscape where events fundamental to the formation of essential aspects of European culture and identity took place" (EC 2014, 5). Next, the Archeological site of Carnuntum in Austria, which represents: "The Roman Empire [which] is considered by some 'as a predecessor of Europe'" (EC 2013, 7). Following the temporal foundation of Europeanness through the Ancient Greeks and Romans, many following sites are represented as sites of early integration. This includes sites that were historical centres of power which then "integrated" new areas under their influence, both in the political (for example The Union of Lublin, Poland, and the Imperial Palace in Vienna, Austria) and the cultural sense (for example the Abbey of Cluny, France). There are also sites that represent integration through submission to foreign political rule (for example the Great Guild Hall in Tallinn or Carnuntum, Austria).

This overall narrative could be criticized for many of its aspects, but a central flaw is the fact that it sidesteps crucial questions of power. More precisely, it fails to contemplate who is being integrated into what and under what conditions. Contributing to these power relations, the promotion of common values is identified as a tool to legitimate integration. This is not only the case in the EU-AHD, as the below quote from the founding decision of the EHL appears in numerous EU declarations and decisions starting from the Maastricht Treaty.

> For citizens to give their full support to European integration, greater emphasis should be placed on their common values, history and culture as key elements of their membership of a society founded on the principles of freedom, democracy, respect for human rights, cultural and linguistic diversity, tolerance and solidarity. (EP 2011, 1, preamble)

Instead of focusing on aspects of concrete integration, these attempts to narrate integration by focusing on abstract symbols of either European integration or European values are common. This tendency to focus on the internal symbolic value of the site is based largely on the way the EHL has been designed. The EHL is primarily interested in nominating heritage sites which can claim some role in the founding of the European Union or in the wider European project. As such, the sites should not only communicate "about the sites but also about the European project" (EC 2010, 46; see also Mäkinen in this volume). The notions of "European integration" and "European values" are used repeatedly to connect the sites' narratives to the broader European project. However, integration is often narrated in relation to the spread of "common European values" such as peace, democracy, or human rights, making it difficult, if not impossible, to always distinguish between European values and European integration, as adaptation to European values is treated as a sign of integration, and integration is understood to imply adaptation to European values.

In the official documents, these symbolic meanings attached to the sites were also identified as a way to ensure the sustainability and lasting significance of the EHL. According to the Impact Assessment, "the EHL would be awarded mainly on the basis of the symbolic value of sites and that this symbolic would not diminish over time" (EC 2010, 12–13). The monitoring report already departed from this view significantly in 2016, however, stating that it is up to the monitoring panel to determine "whether the European significance was fully understood, well-articulated and conveyed by the sites" (EC 2016, 8). This evinces the regulatory tendencies of authorized heritage discourses. The lasting symbolic meaning of the nominated EHL sites was quickly transformed into an aspect that needed to be managed, presented, and in some cases improved. For some sites, this meant that the narratives of their European significance were in need of revision to better align them with the core messages of the EU-AHD.

The Great Guild Hall in Tallinn (see also Kaasik-Krogerus in this volume) is an interesting example of this aspect. The panel reports position the site in two roles: as representative of the influence of the Hanseatic merchants in Estonia and the Baltic region at large, and of Estonia as a state emerging from the history of communist rule to re-enter the European polity:

> The Great Guild of Tallinn merchants was the important organization in the city for centuries. The Hanseatic League reveals the intriguing story of European "integration" in medieval times. [...] The recent history of Estonia creates an opportunity to present the narrative of Estonia and Estonian people within the context of European history and integration; the Panel encourages all efforts towards such contextualisation. (EC 2013, 6)

The exhibitions in the Great Guild Hall—part of the Estonian History Museum—broaden that scope, however. Although the Great Guild Hall has space allotted to its history and the Hanseatic merchants, the permanent exhibition, "Spirit of Survival", depicts the 11.000 years of Estonian resistance and survival under the German and Russian attempts to rule them. The dissonance between the narrower role posited in the EU-AHD and the broader interpretation presented by the Great Guild Hall was not lost on the European Panel of Experts. The idea that what was thought to be "early integration" would be narrated as hostile foreign rule was not appreciated. In fact, the first ever monitoring report on the nominated EHL sites comments;

> The Panel recommends that within the framework of the European Heritage Label, the story of Tallinn's role in the Hanseatic League – an example of early medieval North European trade and defense organization – be better articulated in the narrative offered by the museum. [...] The Panel recommends that during the 2017–2020 period the museum team looks into ways to better articulate and emphasise the European significance of the Great Guild Hall in the site's narrative. (EC 2016, 15)

In light of the often cited rhetoric of "contributing to the flowering of culture of the Member States" (EP 2011, 1, preamble), noted also in the preamble of the Founding Decision of the EHL, the attempts to repress the Estonian interpretation of their history as one of survival when faced with foreign domination is questionable. The case of the Great Guild Hall reveals the problematic power hierarchies embedded at the core of attempting to build a joint European heritage as well as the equally problematic regulatory tendencies of the EU-AHD.

Spreading Europeanness Beyond Europe

In addition to narrating integration within Europe, the idea of spreading European values is tightly intertwined with colonialism on a more global scale. Although there are no sites within the EHL framework that engage with colonialism directly, the sites related to the conquest of the Americas (and the onset of European imperialism) allow us to approach the topic in the context of EHL. Examples of these sites are the Sagres Promontory in Portugal and the Cape Finisterre in Spain.[2] In the EU-AHD, Sagres Promontory is described as one of the central harbors of the "Age of Discoveries", whereas Cape Finisterre, a harbor further north on the Atlantic coast, is identified as "the Westernmost point of civilized territory in Europe" and "the End of the Known World" (EC 2014, 26). I do not want to claim that the importance of these sites or their "European significance" would in itself be problematic. On the contrary, these sites have been fundamental in shaping not only European history and realities, but they have also been instrumental in a global sense through their role in the establishment of the nearly global colonial system. Crucial here are the narratives that are produced about these sites and the ways these narratives are able to connect the historical reality of these sites with contemporary European processes. In critical heritage studies, understandings of heritage have been shifted from being associated with the past towards notions that emphasizes contemporary and future motivations (see for example Harrison 2013; Lähdesmäki 2017; Macdonald 2013; Smith 2006). If we accept this basic principle, sites such as the Sagres Promontory could be powerful avenues to start sustained critical discussions of Europe's colonial past and slavery, as well as their connection to contemporary European racism (e.g.

---

[2] Please note that although the application of Cape Finisterre was not nominated for the EHL, the European Panel did note that the site met the requirements for "European significance". The application was rejected based on deficiencies in the proposed project and the organizational capacity of the site.

Grosfoguel 2004; Goldberg 2006; El-Tayeb 2011) and wider European identity politics. Based on my analysis, however, this potential is not for the time being acknowledged nor made use of in the official discourses that characterize the EU-AHD. Quite to the contrary, the EU-AHD proudly paints Sagres Promontory as a prime example of the expansionist Eurocentric cultural heritage.

> [Sagres Promontory] became the privileged scenario for the accomplishments of the Age of Discoveries in the fifteenth century, a key historical moment that marked the expansion of European culture, science and commerce both towards the Atlantic and the Mediterranean, setting European civilisation on its path to the global projection that came to define the modern world. [...] Sagres Promontory is a rich cultural landscape testifying to the remote origins of European civilisation and its universal expansion in the Age of Discoveries through science, commerce and exploration. (EC 2015, 8)

That quote is a powerful example of the type of Eurocentric rhetoric being used and it exemplifies the ways cultural hierarchies and the tendency towards expansion is embedded at the heart of the EU-AHD. In addition to the Eurocentric tone, it is impossible not to note that there are no direct references to imperialism or colonialism, let alone to any negative effects thereof, in the overall description of these sites. Passerini (2012, 133) has linked the silence over European colonialism to the need for a positive European identity. This has led to a "tendency to privilege a Eurocentric perspective" as well to a "reluctance to approach colonialism as a European rather than a national experience" (ibid., see also Bhambra 2014). However, it should be questioned to what extent colonialism was merely a national experience limited to the former European empires. The many cultural, political, and economic connections and structures of rule that existed during European colonialism were not limited to those between imperial states and their colonies. Many smaller European states also actively participated, for example through trade, military, or missionary work within the ruling, exploitation, and subordination of the colonies. Moreover, those same smaller states were also deeply influenced by the racist colonial discourses of the time that were used to legitimate European rule in the colonies. Approaching colonialism through the prism of imperial states alone is therefore too narrow (cf. Bhambra 2014; Passerini 2012) and will, in Catarina Kinnvall's words, only "feed the illusion that Europe can be disconnected from its imperial past" (2016, 153). I believe there is a need to also engage with colonialism on a European level, and cultural heritage actions such as the EHL could provide space for these engagements.

Before the EHL can form a sustainable platform to discuss the coloniality of European heritage, it needs to broaden the narratives it offers and especially challenge their embedded Eurocentrism (see also Suaréz-Krabbe 2014). Once more, I return to Passerini (2011), who, in connection to her critique of the tendencies to highlight the continuity of European history, also critiques the idea of an essential "European Spirit" as proposed by Zygmunt Bauman: "if anything of the sort has ever existed, our memory must see it for what it was, a drive towards capitalism and imperialism, while the passion for discovery must be remembered as a passion for conquest and exploitation" (ibid., 49). Although we cannot expect these narratives of "conquest and exploitation" to become the primary narrative of European cultural heritage, there is an urgent need to challenge and replace Eurocentric narratives with narratives that offer a more balanced and less biased narrative of Europe. Breaking the cultural hierarchies between (Western) Europe and its Others and challenging notions of continuity are central steps in this process. In addition to sites connected to colonialism, sites located in Eastern Europe could be important actors in this process. Otherwise, there is a significant risk that the idea of European heritage proposed by the EU-AHD, instead of contributing to the promotion of belonging and multicultural dialogue (the two main aims of the EHL initiative), will continue to the exclude a number of Europeans from being considered as equal members of the wider European community.

A Geography of Coloniality

We have already examined the many entanglements of Eurocentrism and the idea of European cultural heritage in the EU-AHD. In this final part, I want to both summarize some of what has been discussed so far and take one final step forward in the analysis. As we have seen, there have been many ways the "European significance" of the EHL sites has been narrated in the EU-AHD. There is an explicit focus on the symbolic importance of these sites, and using this narrative is a common aspect of almost all the EHL sites analyzed here. When it comes to the ways European values and integration are narrated in the EU-AHD, however, we are faced with crucial questions of power. For once we let go of the normative notion that integration is inherently good, integration can also be conceptualized through expansion or even further through domination and submission. I have argued above that there is a dynamic of spreading "Europeanness" embedded in the EU-AHD that is reminiscent of Eurocentric notions of European excellence. In the internal dynamic of Europe, however, this spread or expansion is hidden under neutral terms of integration, much as the sites that were complicit in the onset of European colonialism are narrated through the more neutral rhetoric of discoveries and trade. When integration is removed from its normative basis, it can be analyzed through three components: spread of values, resistance of non-European values, and submission. When these three aspects are placed in a spatial context (see Fig. 7.1), a broader underlying structure starts to emerge. This structure has been conceptualized here as a geography of coloniality.

Like the sites' symbolic importance, ideas of expansion or spreading "Europeanness" are similarly central and typical ways to narrate the EHL sites in the EU-AHD, and this type of narratives is spread quite evenly across Europe. The narratives dealing with resistance and submission, however, appear to be disproportionately located in Eastern parts of Europe. As is evident on the map, there is also more overlap of narratives in the sites located in Eastern and Central Europe. Although many of these sites are narrated through their symbolic importance as well as through narratives of spreading of values, the overall European significance of these sites is complemented and strengthened by narratives of resistance to values seen as contradictory to European values, as well as by narratives that emphasize the process of becoming European through interaction with other European powers (i.e. submission).

In terms of resistance, there is a tendency in the EU-AHD to describe sites as having a symbolic importance in the fight against values/ideologies that are seen as somehow countering or opposing "European values". These especially include sites related to the two World Wars and the Holocaust, as well as sites connected to a broader resistance of communism, fascism, and other forms of authoritarian rule. Yet although there are several sites that engage with human rights (for example the Peace Palace, The Netherlands, or the Charter of Law of Abolition of the Death Penalty 1867, Portugal), this resistance of countering or contrasting values is not extended towards, for example, resistance to racism or discrimination. Instead, this resistance is reserved for fighting

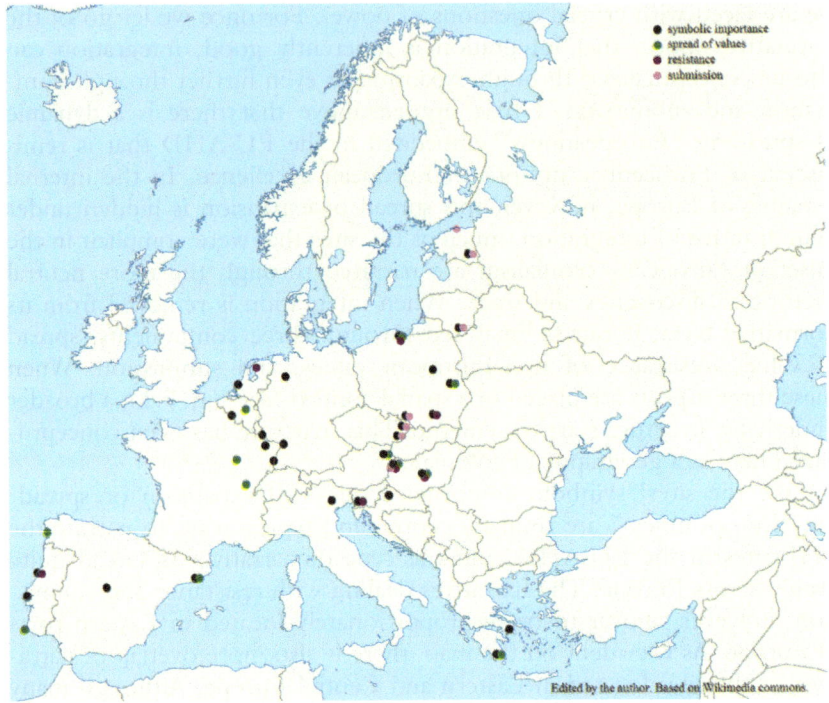

Fig. 7.1 Spatial dispersion of different narrative dynamics among the 39 sites that have either received the EHL (29) or were evaluated as meeting the criterion of European significance (10) between 2011 and 2016 (At the moment, the EHL is not open to countries who are not EU members. Additionally, some member states are currently not involved in the initiative, which explains the apparent "emptiness" in, for example, Northern Europe)

the authoritarian regimes of the World War II—or the "new forms of the Other [that] were found inside, in Europe's own history" (Passerini 2012, 121). This notion of resistance of values and ideals that are seen threatening those of Europe substantially participates in the creation and management of the discursive borders of Europe within the EU-AHD.

In terms of submission, the Great Guild Hall that was discussed earlier is perhaps the strongest example. Additionally, there are also several sites related to the adaptation of Western European technology in the industrialization of the region (for example the Hlubbina Mine and Vitkovice

Ironworks, Czech Republic, and the Industrialisation in Upper Silesia, Poland), as well as sites like the Kaunas of 1919–1940, which is narrated through the modernization (and westernization) of the city in line with "European interwar modernism". This took place during the 21 years Kaunas acted as the temporary capital of independent Lithuania, more precisely during the years between the rule of the Russian Empire and the occupation by the Soviet Union. Interestingly, the case of Kaunas plays into both submission, but also implies that its Europeanness relies on its ability to escape the influences of both Russian and Soviet rule. Although not representations of violence, these sites bring out a narrative of showcasing external influences in the region. With a few notable exceptions, especially the sites related to the development of parliamentarianism and democracy in Poland, and the sites related to the resistance of communism, the EU-AHD deposits Eastern European heritage as being European to the extent it is in relationship with a preconceived Western notion of Europe. As was already noted above, this process of being or becoming European is not stable but rather subject to monitoring and improvement. This becoming is akin to the idea of "waiting room of history" coined by Chakrabarty (2000; see also Mälksoo 2009), a state of constant liminality.

The way the narratives of both resistance and submission are expressed bring out the effects of coloniality. Although in the case of Eastern Europe, we must acknowledge that the form the modernity/coloniality relationship takes in this internal dynamic is of a very different nature than in the relationship between Europe and its former colonies. Instead of violence and direct dominance, the coloniality of the East–West division in the EU-AHD rather takes a conceptual or cultural form. As such a conceptual and value-based form of dominance, its effects in the real world are harder to determine. Despite the long history of European wars, this internal dynamic is largely lacking the history of direct rule, physical violence, and appropriation that is descriptive of the relationships between the European Empires and their colonies. In this sense, Eastern Europe is in fact in many cases more affected by the actions of the Russian Empire and the Soviet Union, and the remaining effects of Soviet colonization in the region (e.g. Annus 2018; Tlostanova 2018). Additionally, although the processes of racialization in Europe have become increasingly versatile, this internal dynamic between Western and Eastern Europe misses the crucial racial aspect that characterizes the more global dynamics of coloniality. Though these aspects make the coloniality in Eastern Europe much more ambiguous, its many dimensions have been actively engaged by academics from a wide variety of fields (e.g. Kuus 2004; Mälksoo 2009; Imre 2014; Mayblin et al. 2016). These critical tones should also be better reflected in the idea of European heritage that is being created through the heritage actions of the EU. For, as Delanty states, "Europe is now 'post-Western' in the sense that it is not reducible to the category of the West and [...] can no longer be defined exclusively in terms of the historical experience of its founding Western European nations" (2017, 21; see also 2003). In light of the analysis in this chapter, the EU-AHD seems to still privilege the Western European experience when defining European heritage, leaving Eastern European experiences in a liminal position. Unless these implicit biases are taken seriously, and effort is taken to balance the narratives used within the EU-AHD, there is a risk of producing tensions and conflicts that challenge not only ideas of joint European heritage, but also European identity politics at large.

Concluding Remarks

The EHL initiative is still in its early stages, and the number of selected sites is still relatively small. It is likely that in a few years the initiative will look significantly different. The first monitoring panel report on the EHL sites states that by "presenting their narrative in a historical and wider European context, the sites invite us and our leadership to visit them, to reflect on these problems and on our values, which in turn will, hopefully, contribute to better informed decisions for our society" (EC 2016, 5). In contrast with this optimistic tone, the chapter's analysis has shown that on the institutional level of the EHL, at least for the time being, there are several causes for concern behind this optimistic mission. Pakier and Stråth (2010) have noted the tendency to find common ground on the "positive sides of an argued European heritage" (ibid., 2), whereas the difficult history of violence, catastrophes, and atrocities is often only discussed in national terms. Yet this reliance on the good hides the darker side of European history (e.g. Mazower 1998)—what MacDonald (2009) has called "difficult heritage" (cf. Tunbridge and Ashworth 1996)—and clouds the role that the European Union could have in dismantling this historical baggage. The Holocaust has constituted Europe's ultimate difficult past, but Goldberg (2006) has argued that it is precisely this reliance on the Holocaust as the European symbol of racialized violence that makes discussions on colonialism and contemporary racism so difficult in Europe. There are increasing academic calls to also engage with Europe's dark heritage beyond the Holocaust, especially concerning slavery (for example Chalcraft and Delanty 2015), the war and ethnic cleansing in the former Yugoslav region (e.g. Kisić 2017), and colonialism (for example Delanty 2017). This chapter joins those calls.

In their book *EURAFRICA: The Untold history of European Integration and Colonialism* (2015; see also Hansen and Jonsson 2011), Peo Hansen and Stefan Jonsson intricately analyze the entanglement of the impulses behind European integration and the desire to continue to colonize the African continent both during and after the two World Wars. According to their analysis, European integration was never simply motivated by peace and economic cooperation in Europe, but always to a certain degree by the need to cooperate in order to continue to control European colonies, especially in Africa. At the time of the founding of the EEC in 1957, France, Belgium, and Italy all still had significant colonies in Africa. Controlling the resources of the European colonies in Africa was identified as one of the crucial components for the rebuilding of post-war Europe. Given these colonial motivations that were entangled with the early impulses for European integration, the continued Eurocentrism and entrenched coloniality of the EU-AHD and the ways it relates to integration do not come as a surprise. As my analysis has shown, the Eurocentric understandings of Europeanness embedded in the EU-AHD posit European cultural heritage as a process of mapping and displaying the spread of a hierarchical Eurocentric value system—or as a manifestation of the geography of coloniality. It displays the spread of, and integration into, Europeanness through positing certain regions in a position of becoming. For them, becoming European is a matter of relation, adaptation, and submission. Furthermore, their Europeanness is suspect to monitoring, development, and re-articulation. As we saw above through the example of the Great Guild Hall in Tallinn, the site's peripheral narrative of suffering and resistance seems to counter the underlying narrative of benign modernity that underpins the EU-AHD. As a result, the coloniality of the Estonian experience seems to have limited legitimacy in the European authorized heritage discourse and the spread of this narrative thus is subjected to regulation.

Similar to the discourse of integration that seeks to downplay or hide the resistance and submission that this integration also entails for those being integrated, the discourse of "Age of Discoveries" expands these processes to a global scale. The discourse of the "discoveries" that seems to be hardwired into the EU-AHD not only conceals the true nature of European colonialism, but also enforces a view that Europe should be celebrated for its role in manufacturing a new modern world. Furthermore, it fails to make use of the potential for social change that is embedded in critical engagement with the sites related to Europe's colonial past. It is worth remembering that European history is "not simply about past events, because the past of Europe continues to haunt its present in quite powerful ways" (Yegenoglu 2017, 18). The history of European colonialism lives on in capitalism and European racism, as well as in the exclusionary narratives of Europeanness and in Eurocentrism at large. It prevails in the disconnect between colonialism and the "immigration crisis", which is not so much a crisis of immigration, but a crisis of postcolonial Europe coming to grips with its colonial past. The migrants dying at Europe's borders are powerful examples of the extent to which the EU is ignoring the fundamental dissonance between its values and its actions. Through critical engagement with Europe's colonial past, actions like the EHL could fundamentally contribute to opening up space for solidarity. Many of the EHL sites themselves have engaged in this process, but this should also be reflected in the narratives produced around the EHL on the institutional level in the EU-AHD.

I noted earlier that acknowledging the ruptures and discontinuities in Europe's past and memory would be an important avenue to challenge the Eurocentrism of the EU-AHD. Another approach would be to focus on entanglements between Europe and its Others (e.g. Said 2003; Hall 1999; Delanty 2017). Through emphasizing entanglements and ruptures, the narratives of Europe could be opened up to create space to the silenced or hidden aspects of our past. This, however, would also require breaking away from old power hierarchies that prioritize a Eurocentric understanding of the world. Through approaches like these we can attempt to form paths towards more equal and inclusive narratives of Europeanness that are not only diverse in rhetoric, but also in practice.

Acknowledgements This work was supported by the European Research Council (ERC) under the EU's Horizon 2020 Research and Innovation Programme under Grant 636177 (EUROHERIT). The content of this chapter does not reflect the official opinion of the European Union. Responsibility for the information and views expressed in the chapter lies entirely with the author.

Appendix 1:
List of European Heritage Label Sites 2011–2016

- Abbey of Cluny, France
- Archaeological Park Carnuntum, Austria
- Archive of the Crown of Aragon, Barcelona, Spain
- Camp Westerbork, The Netherlands
- Charter of Law of Abolition of the Death Penalty, Lisbon, Portugal
- European District of Strasbourg, France
- Franja Partisan Hospital, Slovenia
- General Library of the University of Coimbra, Portugal
- Great Guild Hall, Tallinn, Estonia
- Hambach Castle, Germany
- Historic Ensemble of the University of Tartu, Estonia
- Kaunas of 1919–1940, Lithuania
- Krapina Neanderthal Site, Croatia
- Liszt Ferenc Academy of Music, Budapest, Hungary
- Mundaneum, Mons, Belgium
- Museo Casa Alcide De Gasperi, Pieve Tesino, Italy
- Münster and Osnabrück—Sites of the Peace of Westphalia, Germany
- Olomouc Premyslid Castle and Archdiocesan Museum, Czech Republic
- Pan-European Picnic Memorial Park, Sopron, Hungary
- Peace Palace, The Hague, The Netherlands
- Residencia de Estudiantes, Madrid, Spain
- Robert Schuman's House, Scy-Chazelles, France
- Sagres Promontory, Portugal
- The Heart of Ancient Athens, Greece
- The historic Gdańsk Shipyard, Poland
- The Imperial Palace, Vienna, Austria
- The May 3, 1791 Constitution, Warsaw, Poland
- Union of Lublin, Poland
- World War I Eastern Front Cemetery No. 123, Łużna—Pustki, Poland

The additional sites meeting the criterion of "European Significance"

- Archeological site of Movemvassia, Greece
- Cape Finisterre, Spain
- Congress Hall of Vienna, Austria
- Coudenberg, Former Palace of Brussels, Belgium
- Hlubbina Mine and Vitkovice Ironworks, Czech Republic
- Industrialisation in Upper Silesia, Poland
- Royal Palace of Visegrád, Hungary
- Schengen, France
- Troyes, France
- Zling city conservation zone, Czech Republic

Data

EC. 2010. *Impact Assessment: Commission Staff Working Document SEC (2010) 197, March 9, 2010*. Brussels: European Commission.
EC. 2013. *European Heritage Label: 2013 Panel Report*. Brussels: European Commission.
EC. 2014. *European Heritage Label: 2014 Panel Report*. Brussels: European Commission.
EC. 2015. *European Heritage Label: 2015 Panel Report*. Brussels: European Commission.
EC. 2016. *European Heritage Label: Panel Report on Monitoring*. Brussels: European Commission.
EP. 2011. Decision No. 1194/2011/EU of the European Parliament and of the Council of 16 November 2011 Establishing a European Union Action for the European Heritage Label. *Official Journal of the European Union* L 303: 1–9.

Bibliography

Ahmed, S. 2000. *Strange Encounters: Embodied Others in Post-coloniality*. London: Routledge.
Annus, E. (ed.). 2018. *Coloniality, Nationality, Modernity: A Postcolonial View on Baltic Cultures Under Soviet Rule*. London: Routledge.
Ashcroft, B., G. Griffiths, and H. Tiffin. 2002. *The Empire Writes Back: Theory and Practice in Post-colonial Literatures*. London: Routledge.
Bhambra, G. 2009. Postcolonial Europe or Understanding Europe in Times of the Postcolonial. In *The SAGE Handbook of European Studies*, ed. C. Rumford, 69–86. London: Sage.

Bhambra, G.K. 2014. *Connected Sociologies.* London: Bloomsbury Academic.
Bhambra, G.K. 2016. Whither Europe? *Interventions* 18 (2): 187–202.
Bhambra, G.K., and J. Narayan. 2017. Introduction: Colonial Histories and the Postcolonial Present of European Cosmopolitanism. In *European Cosmopolitanism: Colonial Histories and Postcolonial Societies,* ed. G.K. Bhambra and J. Narayan, 1–14. Abingdon: Routledge.
Chakrabarty, D. 2000. *Provincializing Europe: Postcolonial Thought and Historical Difference.* Princeton, NJ: Princeton University Press. Princeton studies in culture/power/history.
Chalcraft, J., and G. Delanty. 2015. *Can Heritage Be Transnationalised? The Implications of Transnationalism for Memory and Heritage in Europe and Beyond.* Cultural Base. http://culturalbase.eu/documents/1.%20 CHALCRAFT%20&%20DELANTY.%20Can%20Heritage%20be%20 Transnationalised.pdf.
Dainotto, R.M. 2007. *Europe (in Theory).* Durham: Duke University Press.
de Sousa Santos, B., et al. 2007. Introduction: Opening Up the Canon of Knowledge and Recognition of Difference. In *Another Knowledge Is Possible: Beyond Northern Epistemologies,* ed. de Sousa Santos, xix–lxii. London: Verso.
Delanty, G. 2003. The Making of a Post-western Europe: A Civilizational Analysis. *Thesis Eleven* 72: 8–25.
Delanty, G. 2010. The European Heritage from a Critical Cosmopolitan Perspective. *Europe in Question Discussion Paper Series of the London School of Economics (LEQs),* No. 19/2010.
Delanty, G. 2016. Multiple Europes, Multiple Modernities: Conceptualising the Plurality of Europe. *Comparative European Politics* 14 (4): 398–416.
Delanty, G. 2017. *The European Heritage: A Critical Re-interpretation.* Abingdon and New York: Routledge.
Delanty, G., and C. Rumford. 2005. *Rethinking Europe: Social Theory and the Implications of Europeanization.* London: Routledge.
Dussel, E. D. 2000. Europe, Modernity and Eurocentrism. *Nepantla: Views from South* 1 (3): 465–478.
El-Tayeb, F. 2011. *European Others: Queering Ethnicity in Postnational Europe.* Minneapolis: University of Minnesota Press.
Fanon, F. 1963. *The Wretched of the Earth.* London: Penguin books.
Gikandi, S. 2011. *Slavery and the Culture of Taste.* Princeton, NJ: Princeton University Press.
Graham, B., and P. Howard. 2008. Heritage and Identity. In *The Ashgate Research Companion to Heritage and Identity,* 1–18. Burlington: Ashgate.
Goldberg, D.T. 1993. *Racist Culture: Philosophy and the Politics of Meaning.* Oxford: Blackwell.
Goldberg, D.T. 2002. *The Racial State.* Malden, MA: Blackwell.

Grosfoguel, R. 2004. Race and Ethnicity or Racialized Ethnicities? Identities Within Global Coloniality. *Ethnicities* 4 (3): 315–336.
Goldberg, D.T. 2006. Racial Europeanization. *Ethnic and Racial Studies* 29 (2): 331–364.
Hall, Stuart. 1999. Un-settling 'the Heritage', Re-imagining the Post-nation. Whose Heritage? *Third Text* 13 (49): 3–13.
Hansen, P., and S. Jonsson. 2011. Bringing Africa as a 'Dowry to Europe': European Integration and the Eurafrican Project, 1920–1960. *Interventions* 13 (3): 443–462.
Hansen, P., and S. Jonsson. 2015. *Eurafrica: The Untold History of European Integration and Colonialism.* London: Bloomsbury Academic.
Harrison, R. 2013. *Heritage: Critical Approaches.* Abingdon and New York: Routledge.
Imre, A. 2014. Postcolonial Media Studies in Postsocialist Europe. *Boundary 2* 41 (1): 113–134.
Kinnvall, C. 2016. The Postcolonial Has Moved into Europe: Bordering, Security and Ethno-Cultural Belonging. *JCMS: Journal of Common Market Studies* 54 (1): 152–168.
Kisić, V. 2017. *Governing Heritage Dissonance: Promises and Realities of Selected Cultural Policies.* Amsterdam, The Netherlands: European Cultural Foundation.
Kraus, P.A., and G. Sciortino. 2014. The Diversities of Europe: From European Modernity to the Making of the Euroepan Union. *Ethnicities* 14 (4): 485–497.
Kuus, M. 2004. Europe's Eastern Expansion and the Reinscription of Otherness in East-Central Europe. *Progress in Human Geography* 28 (4): 472–489.
Lähdesmäki, T. 2012. Rhetoric of Unity and Cultural Diversity in the Making of European Cultural Identity. *International Journal of Cultural Policy* 18 (1): 59–75.
Lähdesmäki, T. 2014. Transnational Heritage in the Making: Strategies for Narrating Cultural Heritage as European in the Intergovernmental Initiative of the European Heritage Label. *Ethnologica Europaea* 44 (1): 75–93.
Lähdesmäki, T. 2017. Narrativity and Intertextuality in the Making of a Shared European Memory. *Journal of Contemporary European Studies* 25 (1): 57–72.
Macdonald, S. 2009. *Difficult Heritage: Negotiating the Nazi Past in Nuremberg and Beyond.* Abingdon: Routledge.
Macdonald, S. 2013. *Memorylands: Heritage and Identity in Europe Today.* New York: Routledge.
Maldonado-Torres, N. 2007. On the Coloniality of Being: Contributions to the Development of a Concept. *Cultural Studies* 21 (2): 240–270.
Mälksoo, M. 2009. The Memory Politics of Becoming European: The East European Subalterns and the Collective Memory of Europe. *European Journal of International Relations* 15 (4): 653–680.

Mayblin, L., et al. 2016. 'Other' Posts in 'Other' Places: Poland Through a Postcolonial Lens? *Sociology: The Journal of the British Sociological Association* 50 (1): 60–76.
Mazower, M. 1998. *Dark Continent: Europe's Twentieth Century*. London: Allen Lane.
Mignolo, W. 2006. Citizenship, Knowledge, and the Limits of Humanity. *American Literary History* 18 (2): 312–331.
Mignolo, W., and A. Escobar (eds.). 2010. *Globalization and the Decolonial Option*. London: Routledge.
Pakier, M., and B. Stråth. 2010. A European Memory? In *A European Memory? Contested Histories and Politics of Remembrance*, ed. M. Pakier and B. Stråth, 1–20. New York: Berghan Books.
Passserini, L. 2002. From the Ironies of Identity to the Identities of Irony. In *The Idea of Europe: From Antiquity to the European Union*, ed. A. Pagden, 191–208. Washington, DC, Cambridge and New York: Woodrow Wilson Center Press, Cambridge University Press.
Passerini, L. 2011. The Ethics of European Memory: What Is to Be done? *Moving Worlds* 11 (2): 48–56.
Passerini, L. 2012. Europe and Its Others: Is There a European Identity? In *The Oxford Handbook of Postwar European History*, ed. D. Stone, 120–138. Oxford: Oxford University Press.
Quijano, A. 2000. Coloniality of Power, Eurocentrism, and Latin America. *Nepantla: Views from South* 1 (3): 533–580.
Quijano, A. 2007. Coloniality and Modernity/Rationality. *Cultural Studies* 21 (2–3): 168–178.
Said, E. W. 1993. *Culture and Imperialism* (7th pr.). New York: Knopf.
Sen, A. 1999. *Development as Freedom*. Oxford: Oxford University Press.
Said, E.W. 2003. *Orientalism*. London: Penguin. Penguin Classics.
Stråth, B. 2000. *Europe and the Other and Europe as the Other*. Bruxelles: PIE Lang.
Smith, L. 2006. *Uses of Heritage*. New York: Routledge.
Surez-Krabbe, J. 2013. Democratising Democracy, Humanising Human Rights: European Decolonial Social Movements and the "Alternative Thinking of Alternatives". *Migration Letters* 10 (3): 333–341.
Suárez-Krabbe, J. 2014. Pluriversalizing Europe: Challenging Belonging, Revisiting History, Disrupting Homogeneity. *Postcolonial Studies* 17 (2): 155–172.
Tlostanova, M. 2018. *What Does It Mean to Be Post-Soviet? Decolonial Art from the Ruins of the Soviet Empire*. Durham and London: Duke University Press.
Tully, J. 2002. The Kantian Idea of Europe. In *The Idea of Europe: From Antiquity to the European Union*, ed. A. Pagden, 331–358. Washington, DC, Cambridge and New York: Woodrow Wilson Center Press; Cambridge University Press.

Tunbridge, J.E., and G.J. Ashworth. 1996. *Dissonant Heritage: The Management of the Past as a Resource in Conflict.* Chichester: Wiley.
Wekker, G. 2016. *White Innocence: Paradoxes of Colonialism and Race.* Durham: Duke University Press.
Yegenoglu, M. 2017. Cosmopolitan Europe: Memory, Apology and Mourning. In *European Cosmopolitanism: Colonial Histories and Postcolonial Societies*, ed. G.K. Bhambra and J. Narayan, 17–30. Abingdon: Routledge.

Open Access This chapter is licensed under the terms of the Creative Commons Attribution 4.0 International License (http://creativecommons.org/licenses/by/4.0/), which permits use, sharing, adaptation, distribution and reproduction in any medium or format, as long as you give appropriate credit to the original author(s) and the source, provide a link to the Creative Commons license and indicate if changes were made.

The images or other third party material in this chapter are included in the chapter's Creative Commons license, unless indicated otherwise in a credit line to the material. If material is not included in the chapter's Creative Commons license and your intended use is not permitted by statutory regulation or exceeds the permitted use, you will need to obtain permission directly from the copyright holder.

CHAPTER 8

Contesting Cultural Heritage: Decolonizing the Tropenmuseum as an Intervention in the Dutch/European Memory Complex

Iris van Huis

INTRODUCTION

Much of what is considered cultural heritage in Europe—especially in Western and Southern European countries—originates from a past in which these countries were substantial colonial powers. Though the Netherlands has a 400-year history of colonialism, it has long received little attention in terms of the national commemoration and education of that colonialist history (van Stipriaan 2007; Essed and Trienekens 2008; Weiner 2014a; Wekker 2016). The rare times that colonialism is mentioned in educational programs, there is usually hardly any reflection on the way colonial history has affected the current privileged position

I. van Huis (✉)
Faculty of Social and Behavioural Sciences, University of Amsterdam, Amsterdam, The Netherlands
e-mail: iris@vanhuis.com; i.vanhuis@uva.nl

© The Author(s) 2019
T. Lähdesmäki et al. (eds.),
Dissonant Heritages and Memories in Contemporary Europe,
Palgrave Studies in Cultural Heritage and Conflict,
https://doi.org/10.1007/978-3-030-11464-0_8

of Europe or the global West (Weiner 2014a; Wekker 2016). This is an issue that is found in many colonizing countries, as can be seen in studies of school curricula.[1] There is also a lack of attention for the colonial past and its consequences in art and ethnographic museums, both in what they present and in how art and ethnographic material is distinguished. Art museums have long shown the grandeur of the colonizing nations, while ethnographic museums highlighted exotic difference. Generally, when attention is given to the colonial past, it is still often done in a positive way, emphasizing the nation's (former) greatness or showing how the international orientation of a country is grounded in the past. For the Netherlands, this can be exemplified by a speech of Dutch Prime Minister Jan Peter Balkenende, who in 2006 encouraged the Dutch to regain their "VOC mentality" and attempt a "return" to that era's strong work and business ethics and economic prosperity.[2] Balkenende was criticized, for example by Socialist Party MP Jan Marijnissen, for praising an era in which the Dutch colonized and acted brutally towards other people (Dutch Parliament, 28 September 2006). This example shows that, besides the widespread uncritical ways of remembering the past, there is also a long, ongoing debate on this topic in politics and the media. Historians have long been doing historical research on colonialism and slavery. Historian Gert Oostindie, however, states that in a broad sense "one cannot speak of active silencing, but neither of a broad understanding" (2011, 149).

The currently dominant way in which the Dutch colonial past is simultaneously remembered and non-remembered has consequences for the in- and exclusion of postcolonial (post-)immigrants who migrated to the Netherlands from its former colonies, or whose parents, grandparents, or earlier ancestors migrated to the Netherlands, whether through voluntary or involuntary trajectories. As discussed by Johanna Turunen in this volume, colonialism has not only affected the former colonies, but also the very constitution of modernity in Europe (Ahmed 2000, 10), its Eurocentric views, and the lives of its (post-)immigrants.[3]

---

[1] For the Netherlands, see: Weiner (2014a); for Italy: De Michele (2011); for Spain and France: Pousa and Facal (2013); and for Portugal: Errante (1998).

[2] The VOC, or Dutch East India Company, was a trading company and military-political-economic complex that dominated trade as well as many parts of the world for 200 years (starting in 1600), after which it was nationalized.

[3] How this specifically accounts for the way slavery has contributed to European modernity is discussed by Gikandi (2011).

From a postcolonial-theory perspective, a lack of attention for the colonial past or uncritically representing that past is problematic, as it ignores power positionings that were created in the past, not to mention the way these privilege white people and negatively impact (post-)migrants, particularly people of colour, preventing diverse societies from being more equal, just, and inclusive (Gilroy 2004). In that sense, decolonizing is a practice aimed at rethinking heritage in a way that exposes such processes of power (as well as otherness, or alterity) in order to foster more equal and just societies and connections, even if a truly just society is hard, if not impossible, to achieve. Delmos Jones (1997) writes: "The just society is never achieved; instead it is a continual process of becoming, and this always involves struggles" (cited in Allen and Jobson 2016, 139). Similarly considering the goal of postcolonial thought and decolonization, Hawley (2015) writes: "As a central post-colonial concept, alterity seeks to move beyond the objectification of others (and beyond the objectively inaccurate imagination of them) to a moral leap of imagination that sees the distinction between oneself and the other, but also intuits enough similarity so that a true dialogue (which does not simply homogenize all difference) is truly possible". In other words, one of the aims of postcolonial thought is to rethink distinctions that are made (e.g. in or by heritage), not in order to dissolve them but to create new conversations.

In recent years, change agents with postcolonial, (post-)migrant backgrounds, people of colour, and white allies have all struggled to counter the dominant Dutch ways of (non-)remembering the past. Though there were many earlier protests (van Stipriaan 2007; Balkenhol 2010, 77; Oostindie 2011; Esajas 2014), in recent years these protests have become visible to a wider public as they started to push for changes on a national level and perhaps beyond. In this chapter, I analyse one of these interventions as a counter-narrative and tentatively explore to what extent and how they change Dutch/European heritage and the attendant memory complex—the latter referring to the way the past is remembered in the present in a broad sense, including memory, heritage, and identity (Macdonald 2013), which, as I will argue, happens in a way that is not unified but inherently contested. The intervention I tackle here concerns recent protests by an activist group called Decolonize the Museum regarding the way colonial history is portrayed in Amsterdam's Tropenmuseum. Studying these interventions at this ethnographic museum can help understand (potential) other interventions in the national as well as European contexts.

First, though, I will discuss key concepts in discussing the way we remember the past, which leads up to my main questions. After the empirical section of this chapter, I will then contextualize the interventions both nationally and in the larger European space.

Conceptualizing Contested Heritage and Introducing the Research Questions

By (cultural) heritage, I mean physical objects, the immaterial meanings and memories attributed to these objects, as well as other immaterial culture, that are all seen as worthwhile to display, preserve, and pass on to future generations. Although one can say heritage is always dissonant (Kisić 2013, 29), heritage is more visibly contested and more rapidly changing at certain moments in time than at others. The concept of dissonant heritage (Tunbridge and Ashworth 1996) can therefore highlight disharmonies and power relations within heritage at times that might seem harmonious from the perspective of more privileged subjects, as well as at times when interventions take place that can enable more radical or structural change. Highlighting social interventions by change agents who have (post-)migrant and postcolonial backgrounds and who protest against colonial ways of remembering is also intended to oppose dominant and dominating discourses within the Dutch/European memory complex and beyond. In reference to the Netherlands, Guno Jones (2012) sees a conflict between two main discourses: a dominant ethno-nationalist discourse and a postcolonial discourse. The first assumes an unambiguous representation of the past that presumes and reproduces a division between "real Dutch people" and "the other". This is part of a geographically wider discourse which Goldberg (2006, 352) has identified as part of a process he calls "racial europeanization" that also implies a silencing of race, and it is comparable with the preoccupation with autochtony, or (racial) belonging to the soil, which Geschiere (2009) identifies in other parts of the globe as well.[4] Postcolonial discourse, in

---

[4] The ethno-nationalist discourse is furthermore strongly anchored in, and overlaps with, the dominant neoliberal discourse. Both discourses neglect historically constructed structural inequalities. For neoliberalism, this is based on individualism and the idea of ahistorical individual merit and responsibility. In case of ethno-nationalist discourse, in its extreme, both the perceived disadvantage and privilege of the "other" (or just their "otherness") can be the basis of claiming their non-belonging.

contrast, refers to "a critical rereading of history, heritage, cultural practices, national symbols and representations against the backdrop of colonial history and its inherent power-relations".[5] It includes diverse ways of revealing and critiquing knowledge production in which essentialist notions are (re)created that rigidify cultures as fixed bordered entities and perpetuate global social inequalities. Postcolonial discourse and its dissonance with ethno-nationalist discourse is also not limited to the Netherlands, nor to Europe, postcolonialism being articulated in extensive international and interdisciplinary academic and activist work (Said 1978; Spivak 1999; Wekker 2016). To be sure, Jones does not see the two discourses as strict opposites and notes overlapping positivist epistemologies within these discourses: both engage with representing "the truth", and critique other, older, or newer representations as biased.[6] Yet there is also a difference in where these discourses are primarily positioned. Ethno-nationalist discourse is strongly articulated in populist right-wing politics and in left and centre political parties that are shifting towards the right, whereas postcolonial discourse is more strongly located in academia and left-wing activism (although these domains are not free from ethno-nationalist discourse either).

Ethno-nationalist discourse, furthermore, strongly resonates with the content and shape of the Dutch "cultural archive" (Wekker 2016; see also Trakilović in this volume). Wekker defines a cultural archive as "'a repository of memory' (referring to Stoler 2009, 49), in the heads and hearts of people in the metropole, but its content is also silently cemented in policies, in organizational rules, in popular and sexual cultures, and in commonsense everyday knowledge, and all of this is based on four hundred years of imperial rule" (Wekker 2016, 19). Wekker sees that the history of colonialism and slavery has profoundly affected the dominant meaning-making processes concerning race (2016, 3; referring to Gilroy 1993, 178). The Netherlands specifically has a cultural archive that rejects race as a meaningful concept. This is paradoxical, as the use of the concept of race invokes passionate responses, including aggression,

---

[5] I have translated this quote from the Dutch (Jones 2012, 59): "'kritische' 'herlezing' van geschiedenis, erfgoed, culturele praktijken, nationale symbolen en representaties tegen de achtergrond van het kolonialisme en de daaraan inherente hiërarchische verhoudingen."

[6] Guno Jones (2012) analyses overlapping epistemologies within these discourses, showing how positivist arguments prevail in public discussions on a Dutch documentary about slavery.

in these white Dutch people, while they at the same time "innocently" see themselves as tolerant and free from racism (and sexism, ableism, homophobia, etc.) (Stoler 2011; Weiner 2014b; Wekker 2016). For the Netherlands, this reluctance to criticize racism has been connected to WWII, after which strict distinctions were drawn between collaborators and those who resisted, between good and evil, creating a false understanding of the Netherlands as a nation of resistance during the war (van den Broek 2014, 269; Hondius 2014, 273). In this process, being called racist became a grave accusation, implying one would be on the wrong side of history or support the Holocaust, making it hard to address subtle but still highly constraining forms of racism (van den Broek 2014, 269). The collective remembrance of WWII also overshadowed the memory of earlier, colonial forms of violence, as well as the remembrance of the decolonization war with Indonesia (1945–1950). Many veterans, former colonizers, and people of mixed Dutch and Indonesian descent who migrated to the Netherlands after decolonization, were reluctant to, or actively protested against, discussing the "old wounds" of colonialism and decolonization, or preferred to entertain nostalgic memories of the colonial past. These forces prevented a more open critical discussion of the colonial past. Similar processes are seen in other European colonizing countries as well (Buettner 2016).

The relation between national (Dutch) heritage and European heritage in that sense is constituted by the way European countries deal with their colonial heritage in similar ways and in the way European colonial history has affected current societies (Buettner 2016, 498), including geopolitical structures, ethnic/racial inequality, and conceptions and hierarchies of race (Goldberg 2006). Contestations of cultural heritage should therefore not be seen as taking place in isolation within the Dutch nation state. This does not mean that there is one unified European colonial heritage, or memory complex, as there are also many differences in the way colonialism was and is part of nations and regions within and beyond Europe, the way this has affected current societies, and the way this is criticized. Yet it is useful to examine the interventions studied here within both the national and transnational historical contexts to understand Europe's continuing privileged position on a global scale, its continuing and increasing interconnectedness, as well as hierarchies within Europe.

The way heritage, discourses, the cultural archive, memory, as well as identity are intertwined in their material and immaterial forms can be captured by the term memory complex (Macdonald 2013; also discussed in this book by Mäkinen and by Trakilović). A memory complex is a loosely interwoven whole consisting of different elements that have to do with collective and individual pasts. It therefore entails a wider understanding of remembering than what is generally understood as heritage. The term encompasses memory, heritage, and identity in "non-exhaustive patterned combinations and relationships" (Macdonald 2013, 5). Though helpful in combining several ways of conceptualizing the way the past is remembered, it is important to be cautious of some potential problems. Macdonald does highlight diversity and fluidity within "the" (European) memory complex, but conflict, inequality, power, and resistance should also be part of the conceptualization. Furthermore, because MacDonald identifies "the" European memory complex, even if not strictly bordered or characterized in an essentialist way, this still runs the risk of representing memory, heritage, identity, and their internal connections in a falsely harmonious way, especially when conflict is not explicitly mentioned. I therefore suggest a use of the term that explicitly highlights contestation and dissonance, which is especially needed in a European memory complex with a cultural archive that silences the violent sides of colonial history and its consequences. I will consciously use the term in a way that highlights dissonance by also discussing the cultural archive and contesting discourses.

In order to understand changes that occur in dominant ways of remembering, and to further explore the aforementioned concepts, I ask the following questions in this chapter: How do recent interventions in ways of remembering the past impact (Dutch) cultural heritage and its cultural archive and memory complex? How do the interventions' (in)visibility, materiality, and conceptions of intersectional positionings (in this research: race, gender, and disability) contribute to their impact? Lastly, I will reflect on how the interventions and changes can be seen as part of a broader (European) transnational process and whether changes at the Tropenmuseum can be indicative of further change.

As data, I use written and visual material that is accessible on activist websites and on social media (352 tweets starting from the introduction of the hashtag #Decolonizethemuseum until the end of the fieldwork: October 2015–November 2017). I also interviewed six change agents—activists and curators[7]—and conducted observations in the Tropenmuseum before and after recent changes (January 2017–November 2017). I then compared these observations and have related them to the interventions and the changes as proposed on webpages, in interviews, and on Twitter, and to the national and international context.

The Tropenmuseum: A Short History and Observations from Early 2017

Before moving to Amsterdam, the Tropenmuseum first opened in Haarlem in 1871 as "the Colonial Museum", with colonial propagandistic motives: to convince people of the benefits of the colonies and of participating in colonial trade (van Dartel 2009, 29). The collection consisted of trade products as well as artefacts originated from private collections of Dutch colonizers and missionaries who brought back "curiosities" from the colonies. The museum moved to Amsterdam in 1910 and has since then changed its objectives several times (ibid.). The museum was also a centre for the study of physical anthropology, importing human remains from the Dutch Indies in order to study and display them. It was also briefly called the *Indische Museum*, referring to the Dutch Indies. After the formal decolonization of Indonesia,[8] the museum tried to back away from "the colonial association" and focused on collecting artefacts from the rest of the tropics, showcasing the daily lives of ordinary people there (ibid.; van Dartel 2008, 32). In 1949, the museum was therefore renamed the Tropenmuseum (which translates to the Tropics Museum). In the 1970s, there was a shift towards exhibitions of development projects and contemporary societal issues, such as water management, disease control, and agricultural issues.

Arguably, the Dutch colonial legacy had consequences for the museum's collection of colonial artefacts and representations of people of

---

[7] In this chapter I use the term curator for curators of exhibition, curators and conservators, who have different roles in creating the exhibition.

[8] Indonesia proclaimed itself independent in 1945, but the Dutch only acknowledged it as independent in 1949, after a war of independence. Only in 2010 did the Dutch government acknowledge 17 August 1945 as Indonesia's independence date.

the Global South[9] as "the other". Since the 1990s, the museum more actively started to develop ideas about (re)exhibiting colonial history, including the role of the museum itself. The temporary exhibition *White on Black*, for example, which ran from December 1989 until August 1990, showed stereotypical images of black people in popular European culture, this in an attempt to criticize by exposing these images, but not very explicitly (Pieterse 1990; van Dartel 2009). In 2003 a permanent exhibition on colonial history has been created, called *Oostwaarts!* (meaning *Eastward!*). The curation of this exhibition was headed by Susan Legêne, a scholar in postcolonialism.

Still on display at the beginning of 2017, the *Oostwaarts!* exhibition represents colonialism by showing objects that were collected in Asia (mainly in Indonesia, but also in India), as well as objects, images, and memories of the everyday life of colonizers (representing the beginning of the twentieth century). A display of life-sized wax statues, called "Colonial Theater", shows archetypes of white (Dutch) characters who lived in the colonies: a Governor-General, a military officer, a missionary woman, a tobacco planter, and a scientific explorer. They are placed in a jungle-like environment including bird sounds.[10] Audio devices enable visitors to hear the colonizers' stories. A native Indonesian man and woman who worked for the Dutch also appear, revealing complicit or in-between positions, and showing how inequality was constructed in complex ways, yet it does so without explicitly offering such context or problematization. The scientific explorations of the Dutch are also represented, including in the form of a head-measuring device (craniometer) that was used to "measure" anatomical differences between ethnic groups. According to curator[11] Pim Westerkamp

---

[9] The Global South is a term that is used as an alternative to the "Third World" or "developing world" (i.e. Africa, Latin America, and parts of Asia; but there are also "southern" sectors of the prosperous north, and "northern"/"western" sectors in the south) (Braveboy-Wagner 2003, 11). The term is used here because the other two terms have Eurocentric connotations.

[10] Simone Zeefuik from Decolonize the Museum has publicly critiqued these sounds, because she saw it as a colonial representation of the former Dutch Indies as primarily a jungle (interview, 14 August 2017).

[11] For legibility reasons I refer to all who are professionally involved in creating exhibitions curators, whereas the Tropenmuseum differentiates between curators, exhibition builders, and conservators.

(interview, 7 December 2017), displaying this object was intended as a critical representation of currently outdated scientific practices, but such a problematization was not included in the text accompanying the object.

The representations reveal memories of colonialism that were previously hardly ever visually represented in museums, nor in Dutch education in general. Though the wax statues are in fact a critical reaction to the objectifying way people from the Indonesian archipelago were represented in a 1938 exhibition organized in honour of the 40-year jubilee of Dutch Queen Wilhelmina (in an exhibition called *De Symbolische Troon*, Dutch for "the symbolic throne"), neither the display nor the rest of the exhibition offers such an explanation. The images and texts also do not show or help understand the violence and exploitation colonialism entailed, nor how colonized people resisted. Whereas white colonizers are shown as complex human beings with status, there are no such representations of colonized people.[12] A film showing white people on the streets and cafes of Batavia (current Jakarta) even looks like a commercial for colonial life. There are some exceptions. A displayed letter by Kartini, a feminist activist for independence and women's rights (1879–1904), evinces resistance against the colonizers (see also Connell 2015). Both sides of the 1825–1830 Javanese war, in which the Javanese fought against Dutch rule, is also represented in *wayang* shadow-puppet form, including general Diponegoro on the Javanese side (now a national hero in Indonesia).[13] Lastly and crucially, though the struggle for independence (1945–1949) is mentioned, no images are shown that represent this war, making it seem less relevant. Not showing this part of colonial history exemplifies how the struggle for independence has been silenced in the Netherlands; an issue that can be seen in other European

---

[12] This issue is also brought up in a presentation by Hodan Warsame and Simone Zeefuik on 12–13 November 2015, https://vimeo.com/164082870, consulted 7 November 2017.

[13] According to the museum text, the puppets portray nationalist and anti-Dutch sentiments, which is conveyed by giving the Javanese/Indonesian puppets traditionally noble features and status symbols. The widespread and highly varied Indonesian puppet theatre, or *wayang*, tradition, has proven to have great contesting potential within and outside its borders. Wayang puppets have been used to criticize or ridicule colonizers; they have also inspired Afro-American artists such as Kara Walker (e.g. in her work entitled "Silhouettes"), as well as South African artist William Kentridge.

colonizing countries as well (e.g. Great Britain, France, Belgium, and Portugal) (Buettner 2016).

Beside these representations of colonialism, the exhibition also features many objects that the museum has collected over the years, and a special section presents objects from New Guinea: masks, musical instruments, clothing, statues, and decorated boats. An introductory text states that "rituals and ceremonies" were important in everyday life, yet it does not distinguish between New Guinea's cultural groups and developments over time, thereby homogenizing and essentializing New Guinean culture, making it seem like the objects belong to one "fixed" culture that is foremost different from Europe or "the West". The introduction also highlights that the Western part of New Guinea used to be Dutch, which disregards the longer history of New Guinea.

The section on Suriname (which I also visited at the beginning of 2017), which was a Dutch colony from 1667 to 1975, did note the violence performed by Dutch colonizers, but in a way that offered little space for commemoration. Contemporary Surinamese artist Marcel Pinas traced the contours of an arch-shaped doorway with human figures taken from period blueprints made to maximize the number of enslaved people "loaded" in a slave ship. Other references to violence are a shackle, a whip, and a famous print of a black woman undergoing torture (from Stedman 2016 [1790]), all shown in one small display on corporal punishment.[14] In another small, somewhat hidden space, a list of one of the slave-trading companies' 62 ships is shown, next to a cross section of a slave ship. The list showed ships that transported enslaved Africans between 1740 and 1795, which falsely suggests the Dutch participation in the slave trade was limited to that brief period (van Stipriaan 2006, 72; Weiner 2014a, 8). Altogether, the images and information given are limited and cramped between other objects that show the history of various ethnic groups in Suriname.

These issues and more were criticized by the Decolonize the Museum activist group and by others who started using the #Decolonizethemuseum hashtag in support of their cause.

---

[14] Balkenhol (2010, 77) reflects on the historic use of this image, and the changing aesthetics of violence, in the abolition movement and in more recent protests in 1998, when Barryl Biekman showed the image in Dutch Parliament in a plea for a slavery monument (which was eventually successful).

Decolonizing the Tropenmuseum: Interventions by an Activist Group and Critical Curators

In 2015, the Tropenmuseum invited a diverse group of experts and activists for a brainstorming session about how the museum could change its exhibitions to reach and connects with a more diverse audience.[15] Three women in the group, Simone Zeefuik, Hodan Warsame, and Tirza Balk,—in their own words: "black women, women of colour" who have "different colonial histories" and grew up in the Netherlands[16]—decided to open a Twitter account and coin the hashtag #DecolonizetheMuseum by which they and others posted criticism of the ways the museum represented the colonial past, people of colour, and the Global South. By actively using the hashtag to flag what they regarded as problematic in the museum, the growing group collected and disseminated criticism of the objects on display, the way they were displayed, and the museum texts. Besides the direct contact and the use of social media, the Decolonize the Museum group started writing open letters to the boards of other museums. They exposed examples of uncritical, Eurocentric, and harmful representations. The growing group consisted of mainly people of African descent between the ages of 20 and 35.[17] Except for criticism of the way colonialism was (not) remembered, they also criticized the lack of accessibility of the museum for people with disabilities and called for more attention to gender and sexuality, showing an intersectional perspective in their inequality activism.[18] Warsame described the background of the intervention thus:

> In our activism and organizing, we critique and challenge what bell hooks calls the white supremacist capitalist, imperialist, ableist, hetero patriarchy

---

[15] Zeefuik and Warsame point out that Wayne Modest (head of the research centre for material culture) and Laura van Broekhoven (head of curators) initiated this conversation (12–13 November 2015, https://vimeo.com/164082870, consulted 7 November 2017; interview Zeefuik, 14 August 2017).

[16] Presentation of #Decolonize the Museum at Global Annual Event: On the Poetics and Politics of Redress, by Hodan Warsame and Simone Zeefuik on 12–13 November 2015, https://vimeo.com/164082870, consulted 7 November 2017.

[17] Hodan Warsame and Simone Zeefuik on 12–13 November 2015, https://vimeo.com/164082870, consulted 7 November 2017.

[18] Interview Simone Zeefuik, 14 August 2017.

[the group added "ableist" and "hetero" to hooks' quote]. (....) We are not academics, we do not have a background of working in museums, but we work from an embodied experience of being confronted with the everyday effects of colonial thinking in its many forms; from our own experiences as visitors of the Tropenmuseum, which before this project has been absolutely essential in reproducing that colonial thinking. (Hodan Warsame, 12–13 November 2015)

On social media (Twitter), there were particularly many comments on texts, for example on a text that stated that people with a mixed European and Indonesian background (called Indos) were considered equal to (white) Dutch and Europeans: "Were Indos really equal to Europeans?? Tell the whole story please" (@Thifa, 3 April 2016). The use of maps and their lack of contextualization were also criticized. A map of North Africa in an exhibition on Africa, for example, showed straight borders, prompting someone to comment: "Are we really talking history without discussing ruler straight borders like these?" (@simbuktu, 3 April 2016). There are comments on words that are used in the texts without being problematized, such as "coolie" and "bush negro" (@Ernestine98270332, 16 April 2016). Furthermore, commentators also noted what was *not* shown or articulated: "The land grab, the slavery, the genocide are shamelessly hushed up" (@MarjanBoelsma, 10 October 2015). Several voices on social media asked whether there were people of colour working at the Tropenmuseum, or how many of them were responsible for writing the wall texts: "You need structural change: Hiring policy? Critical curators? Critical focus groups?" (@SamoraMakonnan, 23 September 2015).

There was also criticism of the prominent portrayal of colonizers in the exhibition on the Dutch Indies. The aforementioned craniometer was criticized in a Twitter post too. A picture of the craniometer shows the museum text, which says that "physical anthropologists" carried out expeditions, encountered "unknown peoples", and measured racial characteristics. The post criticized the museum for representing the "exploring" of European physical anthropologists as an unproblematic "Disney-like adventure" (@uniofcolour, 12 September 2015).

Social-media comments also addressed issues the Decolonize the Museum group discussed in brainstorm sessions with the museum, for instance, "Words like 'contact' need to be put in perspective", which points to the unproblematized power relations that the (first) "contact" between Europeans and people in the Global South entailed. Suggestions made during these group sessions were also posted on Twitter: "Offer a critical tour that focuses on the colonial nature of the museum"; "You'll reach communities by including communities"; "Book launches!"; "Offer your space!" (These are all tweets by Zeefuik quoting other people in the meeting, @simbuktu, 10 October 2015).

The initiatives led to a conference at the Tropenmuseum in April 2016, organized by the group and also titled Decolonize the Museum. The panellists were Dutch and international curators, artists, activists, scholars, and museum professionals.[19] Issues were raised regarding ethnographic museums in the Netherlands and beyond. Eurocentrism, white supremacy, and the museum's assumed neutrality were the main issues, as well as the issue "We base this critique on the museum experience of ourselves and our friends whose heritage is studied and analysed, but who, ourselves, are seldom the target group of ethnographic museums". The articulated aim of the conference was to prevent the "neoliberal conceptions of 'diversity' [to] become the limit of change".[20]

During the conference, words that made an impact were cited on social media, sometimes by several users of the hashtag. The following quoted analogy represents the aim of decolonizing efforts from the perspective of a visitor with a postcolonial background: "to walk into your own family album without finding that all your pages are ripped out" (@SYFUCollective, 16 April 2016, quoting Simone Zeefuik). A quote from an unknown speaker wishes that the agency of colonized and enslaved people were represented: "Agency is distributed so falsely; this is a misrepresentation of history" (@SYFUCollective, 16 April 2016). The comments also reveal an activist stance and a drive for agency in future activism: "Put your foot down. Don't ask for permission, but put your foot down" (@uniofcolour, 16 April 2016). Similarly, another commentator writes: "Change will come quicker when we realize that we don't need to accept the position of 'underdog' given to us" (@SimeonRGreene, 16 April 2016).

During the April 2016 conference, the Decolonize the Museum group placed six text panels next to older wall-text panels, offering

---

[19] https://tropenmuseum.nl/nl/pers/gedeeldegeschiedenis-2017 (3 November 2017).
[20] Website conference, http://afromagazine.nl/agenda/decolonize-museum-conference-april-16th-2016 (25 July 2017).

criticism of the exhibition alongside alternative, more critical texts. These highlighted violence, exploitation, and the role of the museum itself in acquiring objects that were stolen or otherwise taken as trophies:

> Museums like the Tropenmuseum, ethnographic museums, were meant to display the wealth of the colonies and they were also meant to show how strange, different and primitive colonized people were, justifying the hierarchy that placed the colonizer above the colonized. Thereby justifying the violence of colonialism. (Written by Hodan Warsame)

The group's texts were displayed in the museum for several months, after which they were removed by the museum. According to Zeefuik, the museum planned to take their comments into account in changes to be made to the permanent collection, and the group therefore agreed on removing them. A second conference was organized on 9 February 2017, this one specifically about the (Dutch) history of slavery. At this conference, Lonnie Bunch of the National Museum of African American History and Culture was guest of honour, showing that this museum was seen as offering good practices.

The already mentioned interventions were followed by an intensive cooperation between curators and the Decolonize the Museum group (especially Simone Zeefuik) in writing and editing museum texts. According to the curators, Decolonize the Museum had a significant impact on the way texts were formulated in editing sessions, as well as over email. The curators believe that this working process had a more direct impact on the museum than what was posted on social media, which they hardly followed. The output on Twitter did help the group develop their ideas, sift out what was important, and connect. To indirectly quote political scientist Olivia Rutazibwa, who spoke at the Decolonize the Museum conference: "Social media helps with structural organizing" (@simbuktu quoting Rutazibwa, 16 April 2016) and provides "support and helps to structure the conversation" (@Ernesti98270332 quoting Rutazibwa, 16 April 2016). The conferences and working groups helped the Tropenmuseum develop general directions for change: according to the curators, they confirmed their ideas about the importance of being more explicit about power relations and how these are reproduced in the ways objects were displayed and described (interview Pim Westerkamp and Rik Herder, 7 December 2017; interview Richard Kofi, 7 December 2017).

Observed Changes in the Tropenmuseum

In combination with the museum officials' growing interest in change since the 1990s (apparent in the hiring of more critical curators with postcolonial and more critical academic backgrounds),[21] the interventions have resulted in crucial changes to the way the museum (re)presents cultural heritage. Based on the suggestions of the Decolonize the Museum group, and on their own changing ideas, the curators have added new texts to the older exhibits, while a new exhibition especially offers a more critical voice on Dutch colonial heritage.[22]

I will discuss three sections of the first floor of the museum—where the permanent exhibitions are found—and show how recent interventions affected the issues highlighted above. I chose these three sections because they can be seen as representing different ways of displaying the past.[23]

The first section concerns a display of objects from New Guinea (previously part of *Oostwaarts!*). The masks, statues, drums, shields, weaponry, and so on are still all in a large glass display, which has a somewhat homogenizing effect. Although the organization of the objects in the display has not changed here, texts have been added that show the objects from another perspective. A new introduction explains that New Guinea is a diverse island, and that its diversity of agricultural and naval

---

[21] In tweets posted during the conference, attendees noted the curators' critical involvement in the discussion, including self-criticism about the (historical) role of museums, for example quoting curator Wayne Modest: "We have a responsibility to undo some of the violence done by the institution." (@tevree, 16 April 2016). According to accounts on social media, he also said that it is not a "one-off fix", but something that needs to be done over and over, and that future generations need to keep it up (@nadine0tha, 16 April 2016). Additionally, three of the five curators have a post-colonial background, with roots in Jamaica, Indonesia, Ghana, and Europe.

[22] Wayne Modest, Richard Kofi, and Martin Berger were in charge of the *Afterlives of Slavery* exhibition. The curators in charge of the changes to the *Oostwaarts!* exhibition were Pim Westerkamp and Rik Herder. The opening of the *Afterlives of Slavery* exhibition (13 October 2013) also marked the changes to the permanent exhibitions. The temporary exhibition is meant as a prelude to major changes to the entire permanent exhibition planned for 2021.

[23] Liliana Ellena and Leslie Hernandez, fellow members of the Bodies Across Borders in Europe research team, joined me on one of the visits for observations in October 2017 and had considerable input.

techniques developed over tens of thousands of years. While the old introduction made it seem like there was one essentialized culture, stating that "rituals and ceremonies" used to be important in everyday life, the new text highlights diversity, technology, and change. Another new text informs the visitor that ceremonies are important in New Guinea, but that they have gained a new role as they have become embedded within Protestant, Catholic, and, recently, increasingly into Islamic religious calendars. This shows how cultural practices change and objects are given new meanings over time, liberating the presented objects and "cultures" from their more essentialist presentation and revealing the hybridity of culture. An added text, entitled "Only for Men?", discusses how men underwent initiation rites in the men's houses where many of the presented objects would be located, thereby showing a gendered aspect of the collected objects and indicating how objects from women's lives are absent from this collection. Another text mentions that some of the objects might have been stolen during the colonial period and that this issue is currently being considered, while the previous text said they had been "bought and given".[24] A separate text now explains the shared history between the Netherlands and New Guinea, formulating the colonial past as the Dutch "occupation" (1884–1962, with the exception of the WWII years, when Japan occupied New Guinea). Unlike in the previous introductory text, colonial history is neither ignored nor presented as of primary importance to the presented objects. Also new and de-essentializing is the work of art by Dutch artist Roy Villevoye that has been added to this section. His work displays photographs of Asmat people from New Guinea wearing t-shirts that they customized with patterns made up of tears and holes. Some of the t-shirts are exhibited as well. This form of cultural reinterpretation of material culture by customizing "Western" t-shirts shows the creative agency of Asmat people and functions as a crossover of ethnographic artifacts and art within the museum.

In other words, the recontextualization with new texts and objects allow the objects to cross previously rigid categorizations and temporal

---

[24] The Tropenmuseum moreover possesses a collection of human remains, mainly from the former Dutch colonies. These remains are currently not exhibited, and the museum wants to return them to their ancestors or country of origin. How this will happen and to whom they will return is still an ongoing struggle (Vrij Nederland, March 2018, https://www.vn.nl/dekolonisatie-kasten-vol-schuldgevoel/, consulted 14 May 2018).

borders and reveal their intersectional dimensions of inequality (gender and ethnicity/race). As this first section's changes mostly concern text and not in the objects' presentation—with the exception of the works by Villevoye and the Asmat—there is some friction between the text and the way objects are displayed. The experience of seeing objects displayed together, even if explained and contextualized separately, still has a somewhat homogenizing effect.

When moving to the second section, formerly also part of *Oostwaarts!* and now called "Indonesia", the objects are displayed in more thematic and diversified ways. After the interventions by Decolonize the Museum and the curators, the title of the exhibition was removed, which addresses that title's suggested celebration of conquering "the East"[25] and its orientalist connotations. Though this exhibition still displays colonizers and what they collected rather than the colonized, extra texts put objects in a new, critical perspective by explicitly highlighting oppression: "Colonialism refers to the practice whereby one country conquers and occupies another, using force, deception and betrayal. The original inhabitants are politically, economically, culturally and socially dominated, exploited and oppressed".

There have also been changes to the texts explaining specific objects. Next, to the craniometer, it now says: "Photographs, body measurements and parts of skeletons they had collected were used to develop a hierarchical classification of people's intelligence and character. [...] Research and science were clearly being used to justify colonialism". This new text offers a more critical perspective than before, and is more in line with contemporary academic ways of understanding such practices (Adas 1989, 293; Pieterse 1990, 96; Gikandi 2011, 6).

Although the added texts offer a more critical perspective and reveal the violence that came with colonialism, resistance against oppression still gets little space in this part of the exhibition; and neither do the positioning and narratives of people with mixed Indonesian-Dutch descent, although they formed the majority of people who migrated

---

[25] *Oostwaarts* (which translates to "eastward") is the title of a book by Louis Couperus (1924) that collects 41 travel letters from the Dutch Indies. The book is an acclaimed work of literature, but he writes in denigrating terms about the indigenous population and he is uncritical of Dutch colonizers.

to the Netherlands after decolonization. (As noted earlier, these were points of criticism by the users of the #Decolonizethemuseum hashtag). Additionally, objects are still often explained from a European perspective. Despite breaking with the "innocence" (Wekker 2016) and silence around Dutch colonial heritage, the agency and voice of the colonized are still hardly represented, especially visually, because of the absence of objects or images that embody colonial violence and resistance against it.

The third section I want to discuss is a new exhibition called *Afterlives of Slavery*.[26] Compared to the previous two sections, this exhibition pays more attention to violence and resistance, thereby adding a critical voice to the Dutch/European memory complex. Entering this exhibition, the visitor is confronted by a screen showing either Onias Landveld or Dorothy Blokland, depending on from which side you enter, reciting a poem. Both poems are compelling, personal, and critical, remembering slavery and resistance from a personal as well as a collective perspective. Shot in stark and static black and white in the Tropenmuseum's main hall, this lends the videos a (colonial) grandeur. At the same time, their fast editing resembles contemporary music videos, giving them a contemporary look, while also alternatingly bringing the viewer close up to the artist and farther away, offering a personal and a more distant view. Collective remembrance is represented by a button both poets wear that says "1873". This openly criticizes the official narrative of remembrance: Though the official year of abolition is 1863, "freed" enslaved people in the Dutch Caribbean were forced to work for their former owners for ten more years, whereas the latter were granted financial compensation by the Dutch state for the loss of their workers.[27]

Compared to the other sections of the museum, resistance and agency are more strongly embedded in this exhibition, presented in forms as far back as the time of transatlantic slave trade, including the Middle Passage, all the way to present-day protests. The museum walls bear accounts of revolts on board of slave ships, and there are short texts on rebels and abolitionists in the Dutch West Indies such as Tula, who led

---

[26] The Dutch title is *Heden van het slavernijverleden*.

[27] In the Dutch Indies, slavery was formally abolished in 1860 but continued until 1914 (Baay 2015).

a month-long revolt on Curacao in 1795, and Jan Houthakker, who was formerly enslaved and strived for abolition in Suriname and who bought the freedom of other enslaved people. There are accounts of communities of Maroons, escaped enslaved people who tried to free people who were still enslaved (but who, after signing a treaty, returned new escapees to their "owners" in exchange for being left alone themselves). Though there are few extant objects to visually support these histories, they help tell a strong narrative of resistance. Books and pamphlets on display by critical black writers and activists from the early twentieth century show that there was continuous criticism of colonialism and that black writers strived for workers' rights (e.g. Anton de Kom). Objects used in more recent protests are also shown, including signs and T-shirts from recent protests against Black Pete (a Dutch holiday tradition that includes blackfacing that has been highly contested since 2011). A book by Gravenberch and Helder (1998) shows that there had been earlier protests against Black Pete, which actually dates back to the 1930s (see also Esajas 2014; Rodenberg and Wagenaar 2016). Furthermore, video interviews on large screens with famous members of the Dutch black community (e.g. cultural anthropologist Gloria Wekker and activist Marian Markelo) explain the relation between the precolonial/colonial past and current forms of inequality as well as resistances against these inequalities.

The exhibition also shows the same shackles and branding iron that were displayed in the previous exhibition on Suriname, but they are now recontextualized as part of a different narrative. The exhibition forms a context through which these objects are not just visuals in a tangent of the previous Suriname exhibition, but crucial physical pieces that connect the past to the present, embedded in narratives of protest. They function as reminders of the widespread physical oppression and dehumanization in the past. They are physical remnants that embody a link to the violence, suffering, and dehumanization that was integral to slavery and has implications for the present. Such physical connectivity to the past is also incited by the display of a photograph of Johannes Kodjo, a thirteen-year-old black boy playing on drums who was on display on Amsterdam's Museumplein in 1883, surrounded by white people watching him behind a fence, as if he were in a zoo. It reminds us that even after abolition of slavery (in 1863/1873 in the Netherlands), acts of dehumanization continued. The same drums that are seen on the photograph (part of the museum's collection) are now on display, for the first time in this more critical context.²⁸ The drums offer us a physical connection with the boy who was forced to play them. These are forgotten histories that the objects and images help to collectively remember.

The exhibition also shows art and (other) cultural and religious forms of expression (mostly through video), and explains how these developed, tracing them back to places in West Africa, but also showing their influences from the United States and Latin America; this results in a display that depicts both a rich culture and the complex ways through which it develops. These cultural forms and their contextualizations through text also emphasize that the history of diverse black communities in Europe and the Americas did not start with encounters with Europeans and show that there is more to black history²⁹ than slavery. Furthermore, by showing various forms of art and culture, the exhibition crosses the border between arts and crafts that usually divides "art", made by white Europeans, usually men with individual authorship, and "craft", made by non-Europeans and/or women without any such authorship (Macdonald 2012, 30).

Altogether, the interventions have resulted in an exhibition that first of all represents a process. Moving through the three sections offers a mobility through time as well as space, through the history of ethnographic curation and related academic fields. Yet there are also overlaps, as new texts comment on objects that are still presented in "older" ways. The last and newest section I discussed showed ways in which heritage and memories have implications for the present and current decolonizing initiatives, which resonates with other interventions that might change

---

[28] The photograph was also shown in the temporary *Black & White* exhibition curated by Van Stipriaan (1 November 2013–15 June 2014). According to Kofi, *Afterlives of Slavery* builds on *Black & White*, with the difference that the current exhibition has a stronger black-history narrative, paying more attention to the history of identity and "mental slavery": "We wanted to show the unequal relationships that are hard to abolish" (interview, 7 December 2017).

[29] I use the same terminology (terms like black history, black heritage, and black archives) as used on activist webpages and in interviews. Notably, these terms are used in English and not in Dutch, showing a strong connection with American black activism. I want to clarify that the people involved do not necessarily see that there is a single black identity or black history that is strictly separate from "white" history. It is a way of articulating a counter-narrative to dominant "white" ways of remembering, and a unifying language that incites belonging and potential for collective resistance.

the way the past is remembered. I will discuss my observations in the Tropenmuseum in the context of other local and international interventions, noting what this means for changes in Dutch/European heritage and its cultural archive and memory complex.

Contextualizing Changes to the Cultural Archive and Memory Complex: Success or Failure?

The interventions by Decolonize the Museum and the curators resulted in an exhibition that offers a more critical view on Dutch and European heritage than the museum's previous exhibitions.[30] The exhibition now offers a more critical view in the sense that it enables reflection on history, including violent exploitation by the Dutch and Europeans and the way this has been opposed by colonized and enslaved people and their descendants.

The more critical view that the new exhibition offers is due to changes to visual representations and the positioning of objects in the museum space, but even more by verbally "unmasking" power relationships in heritage, including violence and resistance against colonial rule. The change agents present this display of resistance as an objectively more correct way of representing the past, one that makes it possible for people with postcolonial backgrounds to experience belonging (without having "pages ripped out of the family album", as Zeefuik pointed out).[31] This way of seeing the way the past is remembered, is comparable to what Guno Jones (2012), in public discussions about a slavery documentary, indicated: a certain positivist epistemology prevails, in combination with a critical engagement with how memories of the past are selected and represented.

At the same time, the new exhibition uses cultural material and text to bring the past closer without inducing a strong sense of (collective) victimhood, instead producing strong empowered postcolonial identities that intersect with an awareness of other dimensions of identity

---

[30] As said, there have been attempts to be critical, or to address racial and intersectional inequalities since the 1990s. The permanent exhibition, before the intervention, was however not perceived as such by the postcolonial visitors of the Decolonize the Museum group.

[31] @SYFUCollective, 16 April 2016.

and inequality (such as gender, sexuality, and disability). Especially in the third section, *Afterlives of Slavery*, this is achieved through showing examples of agency and resistance. According to curators Martin Berger and Richard Kofi, this was done consciously, following the example of the National Museum of African American History and Culture, which they visited before changing the exhibition.[32] The curators have chosen to not create a strong "dramatization" of history, but mainly "to inform" (conversation with Berger, 2 November 2017; interview with Kofi, 7 December 2017). By not choosing dramatization and depicting victimhood, the exhibition also arguably does not induce a strong sense of guilt in visitors who are white Europeans and descendants of colonizers. From a critical perspective, not wanting to induce such guilt can be seen as a compromise born of a fear of backlash, or of "uneasiness",[33] or of losing paying visitors. This issue has been discussed within the Tropenmuseum (for example on 2 November 2017) and outside the museum (Young 2011; Balkenhol 2014). Balkenhol points out that guilt and victimhood can induce "disavowal", while a sense of responsibility for "never forgetting" can create a common ground, a sense of solidarity (2014, 43; conversation with Balkenhol, 6 November). In the case above, this sense of responsibility is taken up by the museum, which embodies the wrong/violence done in the past and now encourages change (a rethinking of history) inside and beyond its walls. However, one has to be cautious of "successful" changes. One of the curators of the new exhibition, the head of the research institute of the Tropenmuseum (and postcolonial scholar) Wayne Modest stated that: "On the day of the opening the exhibition has already failed", as it is impossible to aim for a perfect solution. He said this to make clear that there is a need to continuously reflect on the exhibition and to plan new changes through communication with diverse audiences. As it concerns heritage that is itself always a process, exhibitions will always

---

[32] The curators took other museums into consideration as well, for example the Red Star Line museum in Antwerp and the Van Abbemuseum n Eindhoven (interview Kofi, 7 December 2017), but these did not have the same influence.

[33] In a presentation in October 2016. Zeefuik stated that the Dutch concern with maintaining a sense of "gezelligheid" (cozyness or comfort) is standing n the way of change: "[White visitors] want to do something 'cultural' with the children, but don't want to feel uncomfortable. (...) So [they] go to the Tropenmuseum, where nobody is held responsible".

have dissonances which require regular adjustments (discussion after presentation by Simon Gikandi at the Tropenmuseum, 2 November 2017). Modest's view on the need for regular adjustments actually aligns with that of Susan Legêne, who was involved in curating *Oostwaarts!* in 2003. Regarding the recent changes, she states that it is up to new curators to make adjustments and create new exhibitions, which according to her takes place in the context of "changed institutional and societal contexts" (email exchange, 15 February 2018).

Nevertheless, there are some "successes" (though, admittedly, distinguishing between failure and success somewhat oversimplifies matters). The interventions, especially the new exhibition on the afterlives of slavery, form a postcolonial counter-narrative to an ethno-nationalist discourse, thus helping visitors understand their/our cultural archive (Wekker 2016)—the way conscious and subconscious thoughts, images, feelings, and actions are formed collectively by colonial history and the way this is remembered—while this archive is at the same time opposed and broadened by the intervention. Radical changes to a cultural archive are of course neither simple nor self-evident, as this archive has been constituted over the course of 400 years and is embedded in everyday experiences. Moreover, visitors might oppose changing their mind about anything at all. Reflecting on the role of the museum in a meeting at the Tropenmuseum, Simon Gikandi stated: "You don't have racists entering the museum who leave baptized" (2 November 2017). Only certain people will visit the museum in the first place, plus there are limitations to what museums can do. Gikandi sees possibilities for change in the reasons why people visit the museum: "Rather than a radical intervention it can be seen as a pedagogical project. People expect to be educated. They come out of curiosity". Though the changes at the Tropenmuseum cannot decolonize the Dutch cultural archive overnight, they present an important counter-narrative that actively opposes ethno-nationalist discourse.

Except for the interventions' (limited) individual impact on museum visitors, there is potential for further changes within the memory complex because there are now changes planned in other major (Dutch) museums. In 2014, the Tropenmuseum merged with two other ethnographic museums, the Afrika Museum in Berg en Dal and the Museum Volkenkunde in Leiden. Through this fusion (a state austerity measure), the two other museums can learn from the interventions in the Tropenmuseum: Decolonize the Museum has already presented in the other museums, and there is a great deal of knowledge and opinion exchange between the curators. There are also plans to make changes within the Rijksmuseum in Amsterdam, starting with a temporary exhibition on slavery in 2020. Wayne Modest, head of the Research Centre for Material Culture of the Tropenmuseum and curator of the Afterlives of Slavery exhibition, will be involved in creating that exhibition,[34] which shows that recent changes within the Tropenmuseum are seen as a way forward. Such major museums with many local and international visitors (especially the Rijksmuseum) are important in building the imaginary of the national and European past (not to mention world history), therefore affecting how power structures are imagined at national and international levels. Interestingly, the Dutch government (at the time of writing a coalition of right-wing, conservative, and centrist parties) plans to make visits to the Rijksmuseum mandatory for children in an embrace of nationalist discourse that leans towards ethno-nationalism. The government's coalition agreement states that: "It is of great importance that we actively foster [our] history and [our] values. They are anchors of Dutch identity in times of globalization and insecurity" (Coalition Agreement, 10 October 2017).[35] In an effort to strengthen national citizenship, the Dutch government wants to oblige Dutch schoolchildren to visit the Rijksmuseum at least once in their school career (Coalition Agreement, 10 October 2017). As part of this (ethno-)nationalist intervention, schoolchildren might thus encounter postcolonial narratives and imagery in the museum. Countering this observation is that the shift towards stronger ethno-nationalism might also mean that the critical postcolonial rethinking of the past is in danger. Currently, however, there are many plans to change and decolonize museums, and a "slavery museum" is being planned in Amsterdam. According to curator Richard Kofi, there is still a risk of not following through or doing only "cosmetic" projects, however (interview, 7 December 2017).

[34] https://museumactueel.nl/2020-expositie-slavernijverleden-rijks/, consulted 7 December 2017.

[35] The shared histories and values that the government sees as crucial were canonized in a 2006 document in the form of 50 themes, including: "The Dutch East-India Company", "Slavery", "Indonesia", and "Suriname and the Dutch Antilles". The National Institute for the Study of Dutch Slavery and its Legacy (NiNsee) has advocated for taking up specific topics concerning slavery (van Oostindie 2012), but the canon has also been criticized for its lack of attention to the implications of slavery in the present and for reproducing colonial imagery (Weiner 2014a; van Oostrom 2007).

The changes at the Tropenmuseum also have a larger impact on the memory complex and cultural archive because they coincide and strongly resonate with other recent (and older) protests and changes. The interventions should thus be seen in the context of, and as a contribution to, many forms of activism and resistance, not necessarily carried out by the same change agents but with a great deal of overlap in their networks and discourse. A group of Afro-Surinamese Dutch activists, for instance, successfully pleaded for a National Slavery monument in Amsterdam, unveiled in 2002. According to Kofi, there are many young curators and activists who inspired his work in the Tropenmuseum. He lists fourteen names, twelve of whom, he says, have postcolonial backgrounds. According to him, they are creating exhibitions and art that "change the cultural landscape", noting that without them the recent changes in the Tropenmuseum would not have occurred: "they are my backup and give me confidence". He specifically singles out Imara Limon of the Amsterdam Museum, Amal Alhaag, an independent curator and researcher, and Dyonna Bennett for her research on inclusivity in museums. The movement, however, is broader than just the fields of curation and art in which these fourteen people work. Since 2013, there are protest groups in the Netherlands that aim to decolonize the university (e.g. a group called University of Colour, also a participant in the Twitter conversations), which has impacted the curricula of some educational programs, as well as codes of conduct, and instigated the a monitoring committee for diversity at the University of Amsterdam (Wekker et al. 2016). There have regularly been protests against Black Pete that are highly visible nationwide (and abroad), slowly resulting in changes to the celebration in schools, especially in the more densely populated areas of the Netherlands, but also leading to a very strong backlash (Esajas 2014; Rodenberg and Wagenaar 2016). Additionally, tourists can now go on a Black Heritage Tour through the canals of Amsterdam; there is a growing archive on (Dutch) black history (The Black Archives[36]); books on racism are being written and debated in Dutch media by black (women) writers, specifically addressing colonial memory and the responsibility of white Dutch people (Wekker 2016; Nzume 2017;

---

[36]The Black Archives is a publicly accessible archive that shows "black and other perspectives that are under-exposed in other places" (my translation, www.theblackarchives.nl, consulted 31 May 2018).

Sherif and Rouw 2018). Furthermore, two political parties have recently formed that address racism as a main societal issue, of which one also addresses intersecting dimensions of inequality. One party won three seats in Dutch Parliament in the 2017 election, and both are very vocal in Dutch media. Together, all these efforts (and many more) form a strong counter-narrative against an even stronger dominant ethno-nationalist discourse that aims to keep the way the past is remembered the same. The ethno-nationalist discourse, however, is more strongly represented in politics. The political parties that most strongly articulate this discourse, the Freedom Party (PVV) and Forum for Democracy (FVD) earned 15% of the votes in the 2017 elections; while, with 38% of the votes, the conservative coalition parties—People's Party for Freedom and Democracy (VVD), Christian Democrats (CDA), and Christian Union (CU)—also strongly lean towards such an ethno-nationalist discourse.[37]

The changes at the Tropenmuseum can have a larger impact on the (Dutch) memory complex as they testify to a change in the way change agents intervene in less compartmentalized ways. Although Oostindie (2012) has argued that there is no such thing as a postcolonial community in the Netherlands, and that organizing happens mostly along pluralist lines by which certain communities have stronger voices than others, the interventions in the Tropenmuseum were carried out by a diverse group of postcolonial migrants and people of colour who present themselves as such, crossing borders of ethnic "compartments". Not only does this group cross borders of ethnic and racial communities, it is also involved in anti-neoliberal, feminist, LGBTQ, and disability activism. It does so, additionally, in predominantly white and elitist spaces. By crossing borders between minority categorizations and moving beyond their compartmentalized spaces, there is more potential for change within the memory complex, including the cultural archive of the majority population, especially because the white population is explicitly addressed (Wekker 2016; Nzume 2017).

Lastly, the changes in the Tropenmuseum are part of an international movement[38] that is learning from experiences beyond the Dutch borders and possibly serving as an example for other museums internationally,

---

[37] The more progressive liberal party Democrats '66 completed the coalition.

[38] There is a sense of alliance with the Black Lives Matter movement in the US, as could be witnessed by the protests held in solidarity in Amsterdam, consulted 10 July 2016.

changing the memory complex even further. Opened in 2012, the Memorial to the Abolition of Slavery in Nantes, France, is known for its critical exhibition on slavery and resistance against it in a public space. France is also planning a slavery museum. Belgium, meanwhile, has a large ethnographic museum (KMMA) in Tervuren that famously did not change its main exhibition for 50 years. It closed its doors in 2013 to open again in 2018 after thorough adjustments, because "the setup was often not much critical about the dominant 20th century colonial imagery".[39] Altogether, decolonization is becoming a way forward for ethnographic museums, slavery museums, and other institutions.

The interventions and changes in the museum thus do not stand on their own but are part of a larger international postcolonial movement or project that is grounded in international (black) activism aiming to rethink the way the past is remembered, while taking intersectional dimensions of inequality into account. Because of the resonance with other interventions, both nationally and internationally, structural changes in the memory complex and cultural archive are more likely to take place, while opposition against these changes might grow as well. Both discourses are part of a globalized and highly connected world in which political issues and perspectives travel easily through (social) media, albeit with nationally and locally specific articulations.

Conclusion and Theoretical Reflection

In recent years, the way the past is remembered in the Netherlands has seen some interesting changes that were initiated by change agents actively trying to create a more inclusive and critical way of remembering an often troubled past. In their efforts to create a more inclusive and critical (Dutch/European) heritage, they exposed (embodied) experiences of dissonant heritage.

Though the changes in the Tropenmuseum have been local and limited, they resonate with a wider movement and therefore have the potential for further change, serving as an example and motivation for changes elsewhere. At the same time, they take place in a strong ethno-nationalist context, which makes intervening in heritage a very fragile endeavour (Jones 2012).

---

[39] http://www.africamuseum.be/renovation/renovate/index_html?set_language=nl&-cl=nl, consulted 17 November 2017.

The Tropenmuseum, and therefore on the (Dutch/European) cultural archive and memory complex, has been impacted by showing dissonance on social media through images and texts, writing open letters, communicating with the museum directly, recontextualizing objects and images through alternative texts, and organizing conferences. The dissonances mainly concerned an experienced lack of visibility of the oppression and violence of colonialism and slavery in public spaces, an absence of articulated thoughts on the implications of colonialism for the present, and a lack of visibility of the agency and resistance among the colonized, perpetuating colonial notions and images of global and racial inequality. In this case, curators, researchers, and exhibition makers welcomed the input from Decolonize the Museum and were open to discussing these dissonances and making changes. The case study has shown how a museum—here personified by their curators and other staff in charge of exhibitions—changed the way the past is remembered, not only by what it chooses to display, but also by deciding on who chooses what is being displayed and how this is contextualized in text. The current exhibition shows agency and resistance throughout history, including the intervention itself, and thereby posits a way of remembering in which stereotypical images of Europe's conquests as active and the colonized as passive are debunked, without forgetting the injustices and violence in history.

The interventions, as well as the curators' actions in response, furthermore started taking "cultures" and their objects out of their essentialized boxes. Objects and artworks are now (re)contextualized in different times and places, showing how culture develops over time, never being fixed. It is not only geographical and temporal borders that are crossed, but also those between ethnic/racial categories, creating "de-compartmentalized" spaces. More fluid understandings of culture also arise from crossing the borders between what is considered art and what craft. Interventions and changes in the exhibition not only evince racial/postcolonial inclusiveness in the act of remembering, but they also engage with (intersecting) gender justice and the experiences of disabled persons, crossing borders between categorizations or inequality dimensions that are often viewed separately. Change agents thereby enacted an intersectional perspective that built on African American feminist activism dating back as far as the nineteenth century. Though this intersectional perspective was certainly grounded in diasporic connections, the change agents also actively represented these memories, embodying and materializing them through their activism in order to ensure a strong, resistant identity now and in the future, while at the same time opposing essentialism and fixed categories.

It is still unsure whether the recent changes at the Tropenmuseum and other (ethnographic) museums will prove to be exceptional and temporary, ultimately being crushed by the prevailing cultural archive of innocence (described by Wekker 2016) and the raging ethno-national discourse, or whether they actually form an example and point the way for changes at more museums in the Netherlands and beyond, altering the cultural archive profoundly; it will all depend on whether forms of resistance continue and whether people who get to make decisions over what is remembered continue to make more inclusive and critical choices. The dominant ethno-nationalist discourse currently shows no signs of abating. At the same time, change agents are still pushing for more inclusive ways of remembering, which has shown to have an impact, though it remains an ongoing struggle.

I would like to leave you with one last theoretical reflection. I have studied these interventions with the aim of understanding how changes take place within the cultural archive and memory complex. I have intentionally combined many key concepts in remembering the past—cultural archive, memory complex, dominant discourse, and (dissonant) heritage—in order to best understand the changes I studied, but I have also explored how these concepts relate to each other. After concluding my analysis, I can see that both cultural archive and memory complex are useful as overarching concepts in that they indicate the similarity in the way the past is remembered within and between countries with similar pasts, in this case a colonial past which is still relevant for the present. These concepts can also help reveal the complex connections between memories, physical objects, images, and emotions, and situate other key concepts in more helpful constellations. As part of the overarching memory complex, these other concepts—memory, identity, (dissonant) heritage, counter-narrative, dominant discourse—and what they refer to can all question or confirm the cultural archive. I furthermore noticed that the cultural archive has a strong relation to dominant discourses. The former is more historically and emotionally grounded, whereas discourse has a strong basis in language production, values, and norms, but also in the actions and policies that are perpetuated through them, mostly in ways that reproduce the status quo. In that sense, the cultural archive actually consists of strongly historicized and (also) embodied dominant discourse. Since memory complex is such an overarching term, it sometimes has little meaning; as it can contain discourses and collectivities that oppose each other, it can be hard to point out where exactly the power relations are. Therefore it is only useful as a concept in combination with (some of) the other concepts, especially dissonant heritage and dominant discourse, as they unearth and reveal conflict and dissonance, identifying a *dissonant* memory complex. What speaks in its favour is that is relatively new and free from strong connotations. What speaks against it is the risk of drawing borders around "a complex" within societies that are mostly imagined as nationally bordered, while these borders actually are porous (as also shown in my discussion). The concept of dissonant heritage, lastly, exposes the fact that the way the past is collectively remembered involves power relations which can be exposed through social interventions by change agents who can question/oppose the cultural archive and dominant discourse, and thereby change "the" memory complex.

Acknowledgements This work received funding from the European Research Council under the European Union's Seventh Framework Programme (FP/2007-2013), ERC Grant Agreement number 29585 (BABE).

References

Adas, M. 1989. *Machines as the Measure of Men*. Ithaca: Cornell University Press.
Ahmed, S. 2000. *Strange Encounters: Embodied Others in Post-Coloniality*. Hove: Psychology Press.
Allen, J.S., and R.C. Jobson. 2016. The Decolonizing Generation: (Race and) Theory in Anthropology Since the Eighties. *Current Anthropology* 57 (2): 129–148.
Baay, R. 2015. *Daar werd wat gruwelijks verricht: slavernij in Nederlands-Indië*. Amsterdam: Singel Uitgeverijen.
Balkenhol, M. 2010. The Changing Aesthetics of Savagery: Slavery, Belonging, and Post-Colonial Melancholia in the Netherlands. *Etnofoor* 22 (2): 71–89.
Balkenhol, M. 2014. *Tracing Slavery: An Ethnography of Diaspora, Affect, and Cultural Heritage in Amsterdam*. PhD thesis, Vrije Universiteit, Amsterdam.
Braveboy-Wagner, J.A. (ed.). 2003. *The Foreign Policies of the Global South: Rethinking Conceptual Frameworks*. Boulder, CO: Lynne Rienner Publishers.
Buettner, E. 2016. *Europe After Empire: Decolonization, Society, and Culture*. Cambridge: Cambridge University Press.

Coalition Agreement. 10 October 2017. *Vertrouwen in de toekomst, Regeerakkoord 2017–2021.* VVD, CDA, D66, ChristenUnie, The Hague.

Connell, R. 2015. Meeting at the Edge of Fear: Theory on a World Scale. *Feminist Theory* 16 (1): 49–66.

De Michele, G. 2011. 'A Beautiful Moment of Bravery and Hard Work': Italian Colonialism in Post-1945 History High School Textbooks. *Modern Italy* 16 (2): 105–120.

Dutch Parliament. 28 September 2006. De algemene politieke beschouwingen naar aanleiding van de Miljoenennota voor het jaar 2007 (30800), Vergaderjaar 2006–2007, Vergaderingnummer 6.

Errante, A. 1998. Education and National Personae in Portugal's Colonial and Postcolonial Transition. *Comparative Education Review* 42 (3): 267–308.

Esajas, M. 2014. Beyond Blackface: Emancipation Through the Struggle Against Black Pete and Dutch Racism. You Are Here. http://stopblackface.com/beyond-blackface-emancipation-through-the-struggle-against-black-pete-and-dutch-racism/. Consulted 11 July 2017.

Essed, P., and S. Trienekens. 2008. 'Who Wants to Feel White?' Race, Dutch Culture and Contested Identities. *Ethnic and Racial Studies* 31 (1): 52–72.

Geschiere, P. 2009. *The Perils of Belonging: Autochthony, Citizenship, and Exclusion in Africa and Europe.* Chicago: University of Chicago Press.

Gikandi, S. 2011. *Slavery and the Culture of Taste.* Princeton: Princeton University Press.

Gilroy, P. 1993. *The Black Atlantic: Modernity and Double Consciousness.* Cambridge: Harvard University Press.

Gilroy, P. 2004. *After Empire: Melancholia or Convivial Culture.* Abingdon: Routledge.

Goldberg, Theo D. 2006. Racial Europeanization. *Ethnic and Racial Studies* 29 (2): 331–364.

Gravenberch, S., and L. Helder. 1998. *Sinterklaasje, kom maar binnen zonder knecht.* Antwerp: Uitgeverij Epo.

Hawley, J.C. 2015. Postcolonial Theory. In *Oxford Handbook of Archaeological Theory,* ed. U. Sommer and A. Gardner, 1–12. Oxford: Oxford University Press.

Hondius, D. 2014. Black Dutch Voices: Reports from a Country That Leaves Racism Unchallenged. In *Dutch Racism,* ed. P. Essed and I. Hoving, 273–294. Amsterdam and New York: Rodopi.

Jones, D. 1997. Epilogue. In *Decolonizing Anthropology: Moving Further Toward an Anthropology for Liberation,* ed. F.V. Harrison, 2nd ed., 192–200. Arlington, VA: American Anthropological Association.

Jones, G. 2012. Slavery Is (Not) Our History: On the Public Debate and Divergent Meanings of the NTR Television Series Slavery. *BMGN: The Low Countries Historical Review* 127 (4): 57–82.

Kisić, V. 2013. *Governing Heritage Dissonance: Promises and Realities of Selected Cultural Policies*. Amsterdam: European Cultural Foundation.

Macdonald, S.J. 2012. Museums, National, Postnational and Transcultural Identities. In *Museum Studies: An Anthology of Contexts*, ed. B.M. Carbonell, 273–286. Hoboken, NJ: Wiley.

Macdonald, S.J. 2013. *Memorylands: Heritage and Identity in Europe Today*. London: Routledge.

Nzume, A. 2017. *Hallo Witte Mensen*. Amsterdam: Amsterdam University Press.

Oostindie, G.J. 2011. *Postcolonial Netherlands: Sixty-Five Years of Forgetting, Commemorating, Silencing*. Amsterdam: Amsterdam University Press.

Oostindie, G.J. 2012. Postcolonial Migrants in the Netherlands: Identity Politics Versus the Fragmentation of Community. In *Postcolonial Migrants and Identity Politics*, ed. U. Bosma, J. Lucassen, and G. Oostindie, 95–126. Oxford and New York: Berghan Books.

Pieterse, J.N. 1990. White on Black: Notes for the Exhibition of Images of Africa and Blacks in the Tropenmuseum, Amsterdam (NL). *The Journal of Ethnic Studies* 18 (1): 93.

Pousa, M., and R.L. Facal. 2013. Eurocentric History in Spanish Textbooks. *International Journal of Historical Learning, Teaching and Research* 12 (1): 107–120.

Rodenberg, J., and P. Wagenaar. 2016. Essentializing 'Black Pete': Competing Narratives Surrounding the Sinterklaas Tradition in the Netherlands. *International Journal of Heritage Studies* 22 (9): 716–728.

Said, E. 1978. *Orientalism*. New York: Pantheon.

Sherif, V., and E. Rouw (eds.). 2018. *Zwart: Afro-Europese Literatuur Uit de Lage Landen*. Amsterdam: Atlas Contact.

Spivak, G.C. 1999. *A Critique of Postcolonial Reason*. Cambridge, MA: Harvard University Press.

Stedman, J.G. 2016. *Narrative of Five Years Expedition Against the Revolted Negroes of Surinam: Transcribed for the First Time from the Original 1790 Manuscript*. New York City: Open Road Media.

Stoler, A.L. 2009. *Along the Archival Grain: Epistemic Anxieties and Colonial Common Sense*. Princeton, NJ: Princeton University Press.

Stoler, A.L. 2011. Colonial Aphasia: Race and Disabled Histories in France. *Public Culture* 23 (1): 121–156.

Tunbridge, J.E., and G.J. Ashworth. 1996. *Dissonant Heritage: The Management of the Past as a Resource in Conflict*. Hoboken, NJ: Wiley.

van Dartel, D. 2008. Dilemmas of the Ethnographic Museum. In *Can We Make a Difference? Museums, Society and Development in North and South*, 29–39. Bulletin 387. Amsterdam: Tropenmuseum.

van Dartel, D. 2009. *Tropenmuseum for a Change! Present Between Past and Future: A Symposium Report*. Bulletin 391. Amsterdam: Tropenmuseum.

van den Broek, L.M. 2014. Neither With, Nor Without Them—Ethnic Diversity on the Work Floor: How Egalitarianism Breeds Discrimination. In *Dutch Racism*, ed. P. Essed and I. Hoving, 255–271. Amsterdam and New York: Rodopi.

van Oostrom, F. 2007. *A Key to Dutch History: The Cultural Canon of the Netherlands*. Amsterdam: Amsterdam University Press.

van Stipriaan, A. 2006. Slavery in the Dutch Caribbean: The Books No One Has Read. In *Beyond Fragmentation: Perspectives on Caribbean History*, ed. J. De Barros, A. Diptee, and D. Trotman, 69–92. Leiden: Brill.

van Stipriaan, A. 2007. Disrupting the Canon: The Case of Slavery. In *Beyond the Canon*, ed. M. Grever and S. Stuurman, 205–219. Basingstoke: Palgrave Macmillan UK.

Weiner, M.F. 2014a. (E)Racing Slavery: Racial Neoliberalism, Social Forgetting, and Scientific Colonialism in Dutch Primary School History Textbooks. *Du Bois Review: Social Science Research on Race* 11 (2): 329–351.

Weiner, M.F. 2014b. The Ideologically Colonized Metropole: Dutch Racism and Racist Denial. *Sociology Compass* 8 (6): 731–744.

Wekker, G. 2016. *White Innocence: Paradoxes of Colonialism and Race*. Durham, NC: Duke University Press.

Wekker, G., M. Slootman, R. Icaza, H. Jansen, and R. Vázquez. 2016. *Let's Do Diversity: Report of the University of Amsterdam Diversity Commission*. Amsterdam: University of Amsterdam.

Young, I.M. 2011. Guilt Versus Responsibility: A Reading and Partial Critique of Hannah Arendt. In *Responsibility for Justice*, ed. I. Young, 75–94. Oxford: Oxford University Press.

Open Access This chapter is licensed under the terms of the Creative Commons Attribution 4.0 International License (http://creativecommons.org/licenses/by/4.0/), which permits use, sharing, adaptation, distribution and reproduction in any medium or format, as long as you give appropriate credit to the original author(s) and the source, provide a link to the Creative Commons license and indicate if changes were made.

The images or other third party material in this chapter are included in the chapter's Creative Commons license, unless indicated otherwise in a credit line to the material. If material is not included in the chapter's Creative Commons license and your intended use is not permitted by statutory regulation or exceeds the permitted use, you will need to obtain permission directly from the copyright holder.

CHAPTER 9

Geography of Emotions Across the Black Mediterranean: Oral Memories and Dissonant Heritages of Slavery and the Colonial Past

Gabriele Proglio

Introduction

Every day, news about tragedies and shipwrecks in the Mediterranean are broadcast to our houses through different "black mirrors"—to quote the name of a dystopian TV series dedicated to the relationship between human beings and machines (Garofalo 2017). Yet the real life happening between the two shores appears tragically more dystopian than the sci-fi tv series created by Charlie Brooker: people who flee fighting, war, terrorism, political instability, and famine in African, Asian, and Middle Eastern countries are rejected and turned away by European institutions and Libyan naval forces (De Genova 2010, 2012); several thousands die in the Mediterranean each year (De Genova 2013; Cuttitta 2014); every

G. Proglio (✉)
Centre for Social Studies, University of Coimbra,
Coimbra, Portugal

year social sciences scholars reveal an increase in xenophobia and islamophobia in Europe (Alietti et al. 2014; Declich 2016; Grosfoguel 2017); and slave markets have even emerged in Libya (Amnesty International 2017; Elbagir et al. 2017).

These events could be interpreted as signs of a daily and ongoing catastrophe, a disaster that makes immanent the end of the world (Benjamin 1999; Kosellek 2007), especially when we consider the transformation and precarisation of everyday life (jobs, social relations, time, mobility, etc.) into a state of emergency (Butler 2004a, b). Indubitably, the availability of real-time information also contributes to the spreading spatial awareness of the elsewhere and otherness into the public sphere. Donna Haraway's ironic dream of a common language for human beings and integrated circuits (1984) seems to have become a nightmare, at least when we look at the media broadcasts about the refugee shipwrecks. In fact, she theorized the cyborg as space for the renegotiation, reinvention, and re-signification of women: "The cyborg is a matter of fiction and lived experience that changes what counts as women's experience in the late twentieth century. This is a struggle over life and death, but the boundary between science fiction and social reality is an optical illusion" (Haraway 1984, 4).

This was not a failed prophecy, it is a way for Haraway's ideas to cross over. Haraway's writings talk to us about her "here" and "now" yet propose a new insight that can call into question our past, present, and future at the same time. The cyborg—just like Gloria Anzaldua's "mestizia" (1987) and Teresa De Lauretis' "eccentric subject" (1999)—is an intellectual invention able to theorize an entity/subjectivity on the border of Western culture (human being, land, humanity). These devices perform the idea of space and aim to reach a specific goal, as pointed out by Haraway: "liberation rests on the construction of consciousness, the imaginative apprehension, of oppression, and so of possibility" (1984, 4).

My intention in this chapter is to bestow upon intersubjectivity the specific transgressive, out-of-place, floored positionalities of other figurations such as those quoted before, namely those of migrants in Italy. Within the BABE project headed by Luisa Passerini, my research was particularly dedicated to collecting oral memories through interviews with people coming from, or culturally connected with, the Horn of Africa. The chapter will raise questions about what I call the "geography of emotions", an imaginative geography concerning the perception of space, time, and temporalities dealing with shared ideas of the world.

In this case, the role of border (see Mezzadra and Nielson 2013) is not only to split or to connect, to show or to hide: the border is a marker of a liminal space—thought, planned, and made operative to divide and produce dichotomies, to create new forms of exploitation—which is used by migrant and diasporic people to, on the one hand, rethink the configuration of the world starting from more "ambiguous" subjectivities and, on the other, create new subjectivities from unordinary insights and perceptions of the world's geography.

In the first part of this chapter, this concept of a geography of emotions will be discussed in connection with the debate about the idea of "dissonant heritage" formulated by Tunbridge and Ashworth in 1996, in particular paying attention to dissonant memories in and of Europe, and with reference to reflections by Stuart Hall, Edward Said, David Harvey, and key cultural geographers. In the second part, I will introduce three different interviews in which a geography of emotions about migration from the Horn of Africa (Eritrea, Somalia and Ethiopia) to Europe emerges. The last part will be devoted to proposing a few considerations about the role of intersubjectivity in the production of meaning and a larger reflection on how these geographies of emotions are changing Europe and other territories with a stake in narratives and usages of memory by the interviewees.

Before starting, it is important to point out the vocabulary I will use. I will use the notion of "archive" in the theoretical sense proposed by Ann Laura Stoler (2010). In particular, I am interested in studying how the archive of the Black diaspora in Europe reshapes the private and public memory of the past, specifically those of colonialism and slavery. As Paul Gilroy described it, the slaves' journey was a "middle passage" symbolic for understanding the experience of transnational black modernity. Like the image of a ship, remembering the boat journey to Europe evokes, through a chronotope, memories, and positionalities between present and past. A set of emotions produces new transnational and intersubjective geographies which disclose a new idea of Europe.

Dissonant Memories and Imaginative Geographies

In this book, all the contributions have analysed what heritage is, who decides what it is and why, and for whom heritage is created. These questions were at the core of J. E. Tunbridge and G. J. Ashworth's analysis. Their book *Dissonant Heritage* (1996) investigates "how the past can be used as a resource in present conflict situations" (Johnson 1996, 584). They define dissonance as a condition of "discordance or lack of agreement and consistency as to the meaning of heritage" (Tunbridge and Ashworth 1996, 21). Brian Graham, G. J. Ashworth, and J. E. Tunbridge continued the collaboration in *A Geography of Heritage*, reworking the idea from a new perspective:

> This condition refers to the discordance or lack of agreement and consistency as to the meaning of heritage and should not be regarded as an unforeseen or unfortunate by-product. First, dissonance is implicit in the market segmentation attending heritage – essentially place products which are multi-sold and multi-interpreted by touristic and 'domestic' consumers alike; that landscapes of tourism consumption are simultaneously people's sacred places is one of the principal cause of heritage contestation on a global scale. Second, dissonance arises because of the zero-sum characteristics of heritage, all of which belongs to someone and logically, therefore, not to someone else. The creation of any heritage actively or potentially disinherits or excludes those who do not subscribe to, or are embraced within, the terms of meanings defining that heritage. (Graham et al. 2000, 24)

In *Uses of Heritage* (2006), Laurajane Smith, who worked on cultural heritage starting from the theoretical approach proposed by Graham, Ashworth, and Tunbridge, considered heritage as a construct of cultural identities and values in the present. In her book, she used a cultural approach in order to propose a reading of the past as a field where different subjects find meanings for the interpretation of the present. The year after, in 2007, Ashworth, Graham, and Tunbridge reconsidered the idea of dissonant heritage from a global perspective and in a wider sense, proposing to take into account the multiform dimension of heritage in connection with various identities and the ongoing revision and reinterpretation of the past.

Another debate about the relationship between place and heritage opened at the beginning of the 1970s. Human geography tried to propose a new approach to the study of the traces individuals and groups leave on the landscape—the city as mark of modernity. In 1973, David Harvey proposed the concept of "geographical imagination" in order to consider the close connection between narrative production and the meaning of a place:

> This imagination enables the individual to recognise the role of space and place in his own biography, to relate to the spaces he sees around him, and to recognise how transactions between individuals and between organisations are affected by the space that separates them. It allows him to recognise the relationship which exists between him and his neighbourhood, his territory, or, to use the language of the street gangs, his 'turf'[...] it allows him to fashion and use space creatively and to appreciate the meaning of the spatial forms created by others. (Harvey 1973, 24)

His work animated a vast, years-long debate involving scholars such as Brian Berry, John T. Coppock, William Bunge, Eliot Hurst, and Peter Kropotkin. Harvey's idea of the geographical imagination is very close to that proposed by Edward Said in *Orientalism* (1978) who describes the production of narratives concerning the past which are shared with people who have the same beliefs and cultural background. In particular, he presents imaginative geographies as the outcome of a triangulation of power, knowledge, and geography. Said claims:

> It is perfectly possible to argue that some distinctive objects are made by the mind, and that these objects, while appearing to exit objectively, have only a fictional reality. A group of people living on a few acres of land will set up boundaries between their land and its immediate surroundings and the territory beyond, which they call "the land of the barbarians". In other words, this universal practice of designating in one's mind a familiar space which is "ours" and an unfamiliar space beyond "ours" which is "theirs" is a way of making geographical distinction that can be entirely arbitrary. I use the word "arbitrary" here because imaginative geography or the "our land-barbarian land" variety does not require that the barbarians acknowledge the distinction. It is enough for "us" to set up these boundaries in our own minds; "they" become "they" accordingly and both their territory and their mentality are designated as different from "ours". (Said 1978, 54)

Influenced by Foucault, Said, and Soja, Derek Gregory proposed his own idea of the relationship between spatiality and the use of the past and memory. In his *Geographical Imaginations* (1994) and in "Imaginative geographies" (1995), Gregory used the concept of space using Said's categories. He proposed to move forward the discussion about geography by describing it as "will-to-power" disguised as the "will-to-map". For him, imaginative geography is a generalized practice involved in the construction of identity and usage of the Other through the representation of forms of otherness. In reason of this, the production of narrative is based on some aspects Said did not pay attention to, such as anxiety, desire, and fantasy. In a wider perspective, imaginative geography is a specific way to represent non-European subjects, as Said explains:

> The imaginative geographies that were used to display the Middle East were different from those that displayed south Asia, Sub-Saharan Africa or South America, for example, and the power of their representations – their effectivity in devising, informing and legitimating colonial practices – was guaranteed by more than metropolitan assertion. (Said 1978, 454)

In an essay published in *Critical Inquiry* (2000), Said focused on the connections between invention, memory, and place. Memory and its representations touch "questions of identity, of nationalism, of power and authority" (Said 2000, 176). It is not "a neutral exercise in facts and basic truths", but "the study of history, which of course is the underpinning of memory [...] is to some considerable extent a nationalist effort premised on the need to construct a desirable loyalty to and insider's understanding of one's country, tradition, and faith" (ibid.). Memories of the past are "shaped in accordance with a certain notion of what 'we' or, for that matter, 'they' really are" (Said 2000, 177). After introducing the *Invention of Tradition*, by Eric Hobsbawm, Said extends the reflection to the use of the past in the public sphere:

> My point in citing all these cases is to underline the extent to which the art of memory for the modern world is both for historians as well as ordinary citizens and institutions very much something to be used, misused, and exploited, rather than something that sits inertly there for each person to possess and contain. Thus the study and concern with memory or a specifically desirable and recoverable past is a specially freighted late twentieth-century phenomenon that has arisen at a time of bewildering change, of unimaginably large and diffuse mass societies, competing nationalisms, and, most important perhaps, the decreasing efficacy of religious, familial, and dynastic bonds. People now look to this refashioned memory, especially in its collective forms, to give themselves a coherent identity, a national narrative, a place in the world, though, as I have indicated, the processes of memory are frequently, if not always, manipulated and intervened in for sometimes urgent purposes in the present. (Said 2000, 179)

According to Derek Gregory, "the past is always present, of course, in precarious and necessarily partial forms: it has material presence, as object and built form, as archive and text, and it also haunts the present as memory and even as absence" (Elden et al. 2011, 314–315). In fact, it can be said that the past is always fragmentary and it casts shadows over our own present. In Gregory's theoretical approach, the usage of the past is constantly reconstructed and interrogated: it is the outcome of what Donna Haraway called "situated knowledge", the space "in which and through which knowledge is produced" (Haraway 1984, 320). In Gregory's opinion, that is similar to Haraway's, every knowledge is produced by someone from somewhere. He adds that conversation is the only way to fuse horizons: the interaction between two subjects and the resulting intersubjectivity is a tool.

Harvey, Said, and Gregory each in different ways tried to find ways in which the past could be considered as a symbolic place where fragments of memory could be gleaned for narratives used to recognize and distinguish the coupled notion of self and Other. They point out how each subject selects and uses part of a public memory for their ongoing own representational process which elaborates a position of the subject in relation with a group and the whole world. This usage of the past is compatible with the dissonant heritages scheme proposed by Ashworth, Graham, and Tunbridge. In this chapter, the idea of imaginative geography will be connected to that of dissonant heritage to consider the geographies of emotions emerging from the interviews collected in the BABE project. Before presenting a few key cases dealing with the Black Mediterranean—the repository of memories from black people who crossed the sea from Africa and the Middle East—the next section will theorize the "geography of emotions" as a tool for interpreting oral memories.

Theorizing a Geography of Emotions

In the introduction to their edited volume *Emotional Geographies*, Joyce Davidson, Liz Bondi and Mick Smith affirm their aim to reconsider geography through emotions, since they matter: "They affect the way we sense the substance of our past, present and future: all can seem bright, dull and darkened by our emotional outlook" (2007, 1). These emotional geographies are dynamic, transformed by the age, and typology of relationship. Their goal is to demonstrate that a spatially engaged approach to the study of emotions is capable of "bringing new insights to geographical research" (ibid., 2). The term "emotional geographies" should not be understood narrowly, though, since emotions slip through and between disciplinary borders. Bondi, Davidson, and Smith clarify that their intention is not to propose another sub-discipline: their concern is to introduce a new question about how emotions could be relevant in defining the spatiality and temporality of certain places. "Much of the symbolic importance of these places", they state, "stems from their emotional associations, the feelings they inspire of awe, dread, worry, loss or love. An emotional geography, then, attempts to understand emotions – experientially and conceptually – in terms of its socio-spatial mediation and articulation rather than as entirely interiorised subjective mental states" (ibid., 3).

Their work is very relevant in changing the geographic paradigm, introducing emotions as a relevant topic in the study of the space production. The emotional turn, as it was called in the field of geography, involved several scholars who studied emotional experiences such as phobias (Bankey 2002; Davidson and Smith 2003; Davidson 2003), psychotic illnesses (Parr 1999), the relation between anorexia and cyberspace (Dias 2003), and the role of the body in the construction of space (Bell and Valentine 1997; Crewe 2001; Colls 2004). All these scholars, who were influenced by Bondi, Davidson and Smith's writing, investigate the role of subjects or groups in a sociocultural context.

I would like to shift the attention from subject to subjectivity for the following reasons. Firstly, by using the term subjectivity one can not only map the movement of memory in chronological and spatial terms, but also highlight the production of new temporalities in the history. This allows me to unpack a new geography as elaborated by the subjects during the interview process. Secondly, paying attention to subjectivity would assist in investigating how shared memories of migration and/or diaspora connect places, people, and memories, disclosing another representation, perception, and experience of the world. This double attention for subjectivity can on the one hand show how the mobility of memory precedes the movement of people and is elaborated as a shared memory in a specific group (on a national, ethnic, gender, and/or skin colour basis) with the specific goal of completing and realizing a migrant project. On the other hand, the meeting between two subjectivities maps the geography of a migration anew, especially when emotions are relevant to characterize a place.

With "geography of emotions", I mean the way shared memories of an emotion connect subjects to a place (such as Lampedusa), crisis situation, or social condition (i.e. refugees or so-called illegals in Italy Europe[1]) and the way they affect the intersubjective sphere, reshaping, most of the time indirectly, the canonized geography of Europe. I would like to consider the idea of dissonant heritages from these two different perspectives, as memory processes—analysing the intersubjective field—which deal with human geography as a space of dialogue, connection, and mobility for subjects. Yet the dissonance produced by the meeting of voices will not be defined as a counter-geography (i.e. video artist Ursula Biemann uses this concept in her work), and I have several reasons for this approach. The most important, in my opinion, is about the definition of what is "counter", who can counter, and how to define this opposition. The category "counter" implies an emphasis on the role of geographies in juxtaposition with a hegemonic narrative. This insight could come from a dichotomous division/production of the world, which ultimately is one of the marks of Western modernity. The concept of dissonant heritages, in this sense, seems useful to show how memory, and heritages more generally, could be used to propose geographies which are not based on ideas of nations or continents, starting from the frontier which reiterates the Westphalian model or using the border as a device to invent a globalized unequal world. The geography of emotions is both a point of view and a method in investigating how (inter)subjectivity—and the use of memory—can reshape places, relationships, and representations.

From a philosophical perspective on the production of space through narratives, it could be useful to look at the relationship between dissonant heritages and the geography of emotions in light of Deleuze and Guattari's reflections on Kafka, particularly the idea of a *minor literature*, as it is interesting in order to rethink the role of subjectivities in reshaping and re-signifying the idea of Europe and being European. According to Deleuze and Guattari, "A minor literature is not the literature of a minor language but the literature a minority makes in a major language. But the primary characteristic of a minor literature involves all the ways in which the language is affected by a strong co-efficent of

---

[1] I use the formula "Italy Europe" to assign a specific positionality to subjectivities/memories (i.e. Italy as part of Europe), while allowing for the analysis of the oral interviews from a global and transnational perspective.

deterritorialization" (1975, 16). The second feature of minor literatures is that "everything in them is political". The two philosophers state:

> In "great" literatures, on the contrary, the question of the individual (familial, conjugal, etc.) tends to be connected to other, no less individual questions, and the social milieu serves as environment and background. None of these Oedipal matters is particularly indispensable, absolutely necessary, but all "form a unit" in a wide space. Minor literature is completely different: because it exists in a narrow space, every individual matter is immediately plugged into the political. Thus the question of the individual becomes even more necessary, indispensable, magnified microscopically, because an entirely different story stirs within it. [...] What goes on down below in great literature and constitutes a not indispensable cellar of the edifice, takes place here in the full light of day; what is of passing interest to a few over there is a matter of life and death here. (Deleuze and Guattari 1975, 16)

We can consider the official and canonized geography as "great" literature and the geography of emotions as a "minor" one. In this sense, it is possible to assume the geography of emotions as a dissonant heritage *in* and *of* Europe, coming from non- or new-European people, and dealing with colonialism and slavery. Finally, minor literature "has a collective value", which is crucial in order to rethink another possible community. Deleuze and Guattari (1975, 17) affirm:

> If the writer lives on the margin, is set apart from his fragile community, this situation makes him all the more able to express another, potential community, to force the means for another consciousness and another sensibility.

Read in the context of the topic at hand, this sentence could be reinterpreted in two different ways: firstly, the meaning is elaborated on the intersubjective field; secondly, the writer, or in our case the interviewee, is considered as part of a group of people who glean fragments of memory from a migration/diaspora archive which has been created by decades of migrant experiences and through thousands of narrative processes concerning the geography of emotions.

The next part of the chapter will be dedicated to a specific geography of emotions: that of the Black Mediterranean for people who fled Eritrea, Somalia and Ethiopia or for people born in Italy to parent(s) from the Horn of Africa.

Dissonant Heritages of the Black Mediterranean

Several scholars, as we will see below, have used the term "Black Mediterranean" in order to describe the condition of the thousands of people who have made the Mediterranean crossing "illegally". Innumerable shipwrecks have happened there over the last twenty years alone. More than thirty thousand people are estimated to have lost their lives among the waves between Libya and Lampedusa. Alessandra Di Maio introduced the term Black Mediterranean with a specific meaning: she was interested in comparing the situation of the African diaspora in the United States—as described by Paul Gilroy in his famous *The Black Atlantic* (1993)—with the present and ongoing condition of African people who have fled from North Africa to the south of Europe (Di Maio 2012, 2014). Other scholars focused on these people from the point of view of the controlling systems (Raeymaekers 2014), citizenship and Black Italy (Hawthorne 2017), the legacy of the history of slavery in Turkey (Kayagil 2004) and France (Otele 2018a, b), the epistemological debate about the humanitarian condition (Danewid 2017), and the "politics of policing" (Saucier and Woods 2014, 2015). In previous writing (Proglio 2018, 145), I theorized the Black Mediterranean as "space of representation" for people newly arrived in Europe. This approach aims to map the use of memory in the diasporic context: my suggestion is that we read the Mediterranean as an excess space for signification, moving beyond the dichotomies of national and colonial, Africa and Europe, North and South, progress and backwardness, civilization and barbarism. By "excess", I "mean that this space, such as others of extraterritoriality to the national and supranational entities, can be used as an empty and meaningless space by non-European people in order to rethink their subjectivities and their connections both with Africa and Europe" (Proglio 2018, 145). The Black Mediterranean is not Europe's "internal" sea: its space belongs to those who left Africa and Asia permanently without finding a new home, in Europe or elsewhere.

According to several historians, the Mediterranean Sea has been used by colonial nations to represent their interests and as legitimization to conquer North African and Asian territories (Proglio 2017). These narratives particularly represented the Mediterranean Sea as a space through which the white and modern European civilized societies had to act to extend their power, through colonialism, to other territories. This European rhetoric used the theme of the civilizing mission—the White

Man's burden, to quote Rudyard Kipling—in order to justify their conquests. The legacy of this insight on the world outside Europe, and in the Mediterranean basin after the end of the French, Italian, and English empires, originated a politics of border control and a resulting public perception of a line between Europe and the rest of the Mediterranean territories. European countries were and are considered the North and the rest became and remain the South—the multiplication of the border beyond geographical frontiers in Europe, Africa, and the Middle East provokes differential inclusions and several forms of exclusion. If we look at it from another perspective, it becomes clear that European countries still define themselves as North through the invention and production of narratives concerning the South and its multiform representations, just they had before and during the colonial period. From a decolonial point of view, finally, it is possible to talk about the Global South (de Sousa Santos 2016) as a social condition of hundreds of thousands of people both out- and inside the European borders. The markers of this state of exploitation—discrimination, exclusion, and segregation—are intersectionally elaborated by the hegemonic discourse on the basis of race, class, gender, and ethnic group affiliation. This last interpretation will be used in considering and interpreting the geographies of emotions about the Black Mediterranean.

In this chapter, I examine the Mediterranean as a repository/archive of memory for those people coming to Europe from the Horn of Africa, or who culturally linked with it while living in Europe. During my fieldwork in several Italian contexts (Turin, Milan, Rome, Padua, Bologna, 2014–2018), I collected 70 interviews with first-generation migrants from Ethiopia, Eritrea, and Somalia or second-generation people born in Italy to (mixed) families culturally connected with the Horn of Africa. I have asked my interviewees to talk about their and their family's journey, particularly about the crossing of the sea. My aim was to pinpoint how the memories of this experience—also when experience is not direct but shared in the diasporic community—elaborates new cultural identities and geographic views through emotions. It is possible to consider these elaborations of memory as dissonant heritages due to the interviewees' liminal positionality as non-European black people from Africa. On this basis, emotions elaborate a transnational and diasporic geography which, among other things, proposes other and new representations of Europe. My approach to the interviews was informed by the role of the intersubjectivity, as elaborated by Luisa Passerini (2007), that is to say, to regard the historical source as being produced in the social exchange between interviewer and interviewee(s).

The dissonant heritage I would like to investigate is related to a past of slavery and colonialism (see Turunen and van Huis in this volume) and could be seen as the source for the reconsideration of the dichotomous European narratives on these topics. This approach questions the discourse around who is considered heir to the European society and who is associated with the rest of the world. It should be added, for the sake of completeness, that this theoretical reflection starts out by considering the "production of space" as the result of the work of borders: the dichotomous division can be explained as the production of categories, based on Europe, between meanings which are part of the Self and meanings which are considered part of the Other. The Black Mediterranean shows a geography of emotions based on the intersubjective field which reshapes this scheme. In fact, black people's memories of the Mediterranean crossing reuse both the colonial archive and the archive of resistance to the European powers which was active from the heyday of colonialism to the present moment.

ORAL MEMORIES OF THE BLACK MEDITERRANEAN

In this section, I would like to focus my attention on transcripts of the interviews I collected in several Italian cities. As noted before, one of the main topics that emerged during the interviews was the illegal crossing of the Mediterranean Sea. These stories—and of course these oral memories—deal with the horrific experience of migrant crossings and sheds light on a phenomenon that is both invisibilized and hyper-visualized.

Robert was 42 when I met him in a famous square in Bologna. He escaped from Sawa, the city where young Eritreans spend several years of their life on their military service. He states—during the interview—that Europe is responsible for what is happening in the Mediterranean Sea because "Europe has the capacity to change, while nothing has been done". In his opinion, "Europe is a great country, better, a great culture". After listing several reasons for believing in a future of freedom and along the route for reaching Europe (the route connects Libya, Sudan, and Ethiopia), he started to talk about negative matters in which Italy has been involved. "Italy is part of Europe"—he asserted. In this case, the act of belonging to Europe could be interpreted as sign of civilization and progress, yet, as he says, "Italy colonized Eritrea for 50 years and left the country without doing anything. They [the Italians] owned enterprises and economic businesses: more than 2.000 Italians lived in Eritrea". He continues changing the topic and returns to the idea that Italy has other responsibilities: "Italy left dangerous chemical waste in the Eritrean soil. And Italy is the country of Beretta, the most used gun in Africa". These two sentences have to be interpreted from a memory perspective. Both, such as that dealing with colonialism, explain the present situation in Africa as the consequence of a terrible European heritage, of Italy's occupation of Eritrea. Robert talked about Eritrea as similar to Somalia—there, journalist Ilaria Alpi and cameraman Miran Hrovatin uncovered illegal trafficking of weapons and chemical waste—with Beretta as the arms manufacturer responsible for wars in Africa.

"Africa is not there anymore; it doesn't exist": this phrase is connected to Robert's memory of crossing the Ethiopian/Sudanese border. It is a controversial emotion: he lost his Africa for another world. He continues to talk about the bad things that happened during his journey, such as several corpses found in the Sahara Desert, violence and jails in Libya. After 45 days of waiting, he started the travel by boat to Lampedusa. "I was frightened, but you have no choice. Luckily, I arrived after that first journey". Crossing the Mediterranean—as he recounts the memory—provokes shifting emotions, from fear to anxiety of expectation. He says:

> After Lampedusa, Crotone, a refugee camp. Then, there [...] your expectations were high, because once you arrive in Europe. and then obviously in Italy [...] you expect everything to be positive, but there are so many things missing: the hosting is lacking, even the dormitories were a temporary solution [...] anyway when you see it [...] when you think of the whole journey you've made, even if your expectations were very positive, you're still satisfied with what you find, because you've survived a terrible journey.

I met Sonia in a garden in Quartiere San Donato, one of the most popular areas in Bologna. Her father is Eritrean, her mother Italian. She was involved with a group of other Eritrean people trying to help people who had just arrived from Lampedusa. I started the interview asking about her identity. She confessed to me she felt composed of two parts:

one Eritrean and the other Italian. Immediately after this description, though, she pointed out that the two parts do not divide her body or her identity: they constitute part of a unique entity. When we started to talk about European responsibilities in the Mediterranean, she explained: "there is a heritage of the Italian colonial period which is used by institutions to manage the postcolonial condition". She then added:

> We are facing an event of epochal dimensions; probably we do not realize it. It's an event that started so many years ago, it's not going to end in the short term surely, we are trying to plug holes, to find a remedy rather than looking for a broader, long-term solution/view. Starting from this assumption, what moves the European Union in general and not only that – because we have to say that it is the condition of almost all the states that face this type of reception problem; I think of Israel for example – is the principle of non-humanity, that is, a lack of humanity in looking at these people. There is a depersonalization, dehumanization of the human mass that is moving, as if it were a thing, as if it were a process, as if it were […] I do not know, something not real, something to face like a budget, like a mad cow crisis, I don't know; something […] against which […] must be legislated.

Due to this lack of humanity, people are legitimized to be racist, as it "provokes anti-human behaviour". In her opinion, what is happening in the Mediterranean is "unconstitutional, and it is the consequence of a total indifference from the institutions". But immediately afterwards, she says: "I am wrong, it is not indifference, it is to face up to this event inhumanly". In her opinion, the problem is not the immigrant traffickers, because "if there were no the immigrant traffickers, people would find other ways to reach Italy". The problem is not the so-called new slavery, because—she asserted—"there is no a new slavery". The depersonalization of these people is the problem. At this point, I asked her what she meant. She replied:

> This is not slavery because you voluntarily entrust yourself to a person; you pay the person. It's illegal, but it's called something else; it's not called slavery: you pay a person, there are two consenting entities. I take your money to give you a service – even if you cannot call that a service – I pay to reach Europe's threshold and then, once landed, there is no longer any kind of relationship, there is no relationship of subsistence, it is not slavery.

Salem was 24 at the time of the interview. She was born in Eritrea in a small countryside town not far from Asmara. She arrived in Italy with her parents and lives in Bologna. She is part of an Eritrean association fighting the Eritrean regime from Europe, a group that is part of the constellation of political parties called the opposition. She felt melancholic remembering her country and house. When we started to talk about migration from Eritrea to Europe, she began by saying: "Here, all are responsible and no one is responsible". She continues with a Biblical image: people such as Nero "all want to wash their hands. Then, if you pay attention, the countries involved in this human trafficking are Ethiopia, Eritrea, and Libya: three countries colonized by Italy. In my opinion, several things are due to the condition in which Italy left these countries – think, for example, of the frontier between Eritrea and Ethiopia which was the reason for a war". The condition of instability is for

> dirty interests: you don't care if a human being dies in the desert or at sea, because on the television news they don't say: "Ah, poor people, these persons are dying"; No, they say: "These people are invading our country. I will say that if they die in Libya, I do not care about this: the important thing is they do not come to Italy, do not enter Europe! That gives me the opportunity to reflect on the situation… if 10.000 black people die, I don't care about this; if a French man dies, you start a war".

I asked her about the meaning of this last sentence, if she was referring to the terrorist attack on the Charlie Hebdo office, to which she replied:

> Yes, I was. Now makes it easy to say: "There are many, we do not know where to put them, this one and that other". If you had properly behaved from the beginning, if you did the border as it should… Instead, you acted like you were not interested in this situation, you arrived, you have done what you wanted to do, your own choice, but then you're gone. Who cares if ethnic groups come into conflict with each other. Now that problems start to arrive at your house, you change your behaviour.

I would like to compare these three transcripts from the perspective of the geography of emotions. To start with their similarities, all three use cultural memories of past—concerning colonization and slavery—in order to describe the present situation in which the crossing of the Mediterranean Sea presents a physical and symbolical border. In this sense, it is also possible to consider them as so-called "postmemories", as they belong to generations of black people since the times of colonialism and slavery (Hirsch 2012). Robert experienced the terrible journey from Libya to Europe via Lampedusa; Sonia and Salem, however, had two different positionalities (the first was born in Italy, the second in Eritrea). In all these cases, talking about the Mediterranean crossing provokes a sort of double-consciousness: on the one hand, memory of slavery and colonialism are used to describe the postcolonial conditions in both Africa and Europe; on the other hand, the process of belonging to and recognizing of the "Self" in a group is marked by skin colour, place of origin, and ethnic group identification. Furthermore, that "being part" of a group which is not only European is characterized by a sort of "movement of emotions". By this I mean the process through which memory is used to describe a mobility from different times and conditions: from colonial Africa to postcolonial Europe. This process of moving from emotion to emotion in describing both colonial past and postcolonial condition is an analogue to that of migration and crossing borders. Robert's remembered fear when he recounted the journey and the Mediterranean crossing was replaced by hope (and delusions) about a future in Europe. Sonia moved from worry over the conditions of her people in Eritrea to rage over the dehumanization and depersonalization of migrants. For Salem, then, melancholia over losing her country changed to anxiety and rage over a world where black people are not considered equal to white ones. These movements of emotions are part of a geography elaborated in the intersubjective field.

Each subjectivity proposed a representation closely connected with positionalities, experiences, identities. In the case or Robert, for example, the Black Mediterranean represents the disappearance of Africa—"Africa is not there anymore, it doesn't exist", he said—and the appearance of a new unique scenario: Europe as place of duplicity and ambiguity, where he converges hopes and finds disillusions and frustration. Robert reuses the image of Africa as a dark continent—which owes much to the colonial archive of the likes of Rudyard Kipling, Emilio Salgari, and Jules Verne—to give relevance to the process of invisible bodies becoming hyper-visible when they arrive in Europe. He has discussed the loss of his homeland and his betrayed expectations about a dream called Europe in terms of the visibility regime. In order to give power to his dejections, he used two images, one of Italy's colonial domination and one of its postcolonial presence in the Horn of Africa: the Italian use of gas during the Ethiopian war and Beretta's arms manufacturing. According to his geography of emotions, Italy is part of Europe: it is a nightmare that started in the past, before his birth, and has now reached him after having swallowed his ancestors.

Sonia, on the other hand, uses European categories to describe how institutions consider "migrants" as aliens without applying the international legal categories for humans. We can consider her geography as marked by two words, one overlapped by the other: human beings and dehumanized people. The body is the territory of her reflections: a body which has been created by the colonial power; a body as a place of resistance to power during colonialism and in the postcolonial condition. It is always a black body: it is not the object of European people's desires and fears; it is a subject of self-narratives, cultural identities, and positionalities which elude narrative cages and domain practices such as those about categories and the colour, ethnic, race and gender divisions formulated by European discourses. For instance, Sonia asserts to be half-Italian and half-Eritrean, clarifying that she has a unique identity. Starting from this point of view, her analysis of what happened and is happening in the Mediterranean is directly connected to the categories reformulated by the colonial archive: who is human and who is not. In doing so, she has pointed out some connections in terms of continuity—she feels angry about the persistence of power relations—and discontinuity—when she asserts that contemporary migration is not like slavery, she associates black bodies with a self-agency.

Lastly, Salem's geography of emotions is based on identification by skin colour. The body becomes the tool around which a specific geography is built for black people—both on the African side of the journey and the European one. Salem's gaze shows how the difference between these two positionalities involves both life and death—because the value attributed to (the end of) a life differs. According to her recounted memories, the genealogy of power relations has built a world centred on white people and Europe. She is melancholic remembering her country. This feeling could be interpreted, as in the case of Robert, as a sign of delusion. Differently to him, though, her "journey" does not involve physical movement or migration. Hence, this is a double sort of sign: on one hand it makes evident her membership of the black diasporic community; on the other, she expresses her deception about being born in Europe without being considered properly European because she is black. In order to explain her disappointment, she uses the image of Nero washing his hands to describe how white Europeans were and are reacting to the shipwrecks and deaths in the Mediterranean. The reactivation of this public and popular image is, in this context, characterized by the responsibilities of former colonial countries with regards to the ongoing maritime disaster. In this sense, Nero is a symbol that brings my analysis to the colonial imaginary of the Italian Empire and the myth of Rome. According to Salem's attribution of meaning to this trope, Nero has been re-signified, moving from the disaster that occurred in Rome to another in the Mediterranean: it is used by those who, like Salem, want to underline the real, violent face of the civilized Europe and its heritage in Africa.

If we move to the topic of diversities, we may consider dissonant heritages as multiple ways in which the archive of memory (see Trakilović and van Huis in this volume) concerning colonialism and slavery is (re)used during these interviews. From a theoretical point of view, there are two, or perhaps more, archives at work during this process or scrutinized by the interviewees. It is possible to highlight a variation in the reproduction of narratives on a specific theme. For instance, the Black Mediterranean has several facets that are all part of the same matter, with many voices trying to use them as the basis of self-trajectories, positionalities, personal and collective imaginaries, experiences, and cultural backgrounds. As I said before, each geography of emotions can engender a narrative. Hence, there are several dissonances in this work of voices and subjectivities: (a) a dissonance in terms of the individual and intersubjective re-signification of memories of the past (colonialism and slavery) in order to describe the postcolonial condition in Europe; (b) the dissonance of emotions and geographies mobilized to describe the movement of memory and bodies across the Mediterranean and in Europe; and (c) the dissonance of narrative exchanges between two or many archives of memory, of dialogic connections and interactions concerning subjectivities.

Conclusions

I started this chapter analysing the idea of dissonant heritage from an intersubjective perspective. Before applying this interpretation to the collected interviews, I introduced the notion of the Black Mediterranean.

As argued above, the Black Mediterranean is an excess space of (re)signification used "to reinvent the individual and collective condition of refugees and asylum seekers in Europe" (Proglio 2018). From a global perspective, this excess space of signification allows for imaginative geographies marked by the role of emotions. In this perspective, the Black Mediterranean does not only involve the Mediterranean region or remembering the crossing, but also other geographies between Europe and Africa, past and present, white and black. It is important to make it clear how every subject uses memory to elude cartographic borders, proposing other representations of the space through their subjectivity. Finally, from an intersubjective point of view, the Black Mediterranean is at the same time a way to use memories of the past to take up new positionalities in Europe and in the context of diasporas and the evidence of how several subjectivities—through their emotions—are changing the face of Europe.

In the cases studied here, dissonant heritages are based on two different practices. Firstly, archives of colonialisms and slavery are re-used by diasporic and black subjectivities to produce narratives and practices against border devices in the Mediterranean. Salem's use of the story of Nero—and her re-elaboration of the story of Rome as a symbol of decadence—is extremely efficient. Secondly, other archives—which have been elaborated by resistances to the European power relations in- and outside its borders—are scrutinized for memories which are able to support new ways of opposing and fighting European racialized narratives. This is the case proposed by Sonia: she considers her identity unique and autonomous. The accessibility of these different archives results from the liminal position of the interviewees and always has strategic uses in opposition to categories produced by racial discourses in Europe.

These geographies of emotions point out the complex system of elaboration of space based on self-positionalities. The usage of specific images indicates a set of perceptions of the relationship between Self and Europe. From this point of view, each personal and collective life trajectory is described through a set of emotions. Focusing on the Black Mediterranean as a space of self-representation—in relation to the interviewer's subjectivity—it is possible to move from the description of migrations to the state of the subjectivities in Europe. Analysing these movements of emotions makes it possible to show how new identities are reshaping the canonized geography of Europe, beyond frontiers, boundaries, and borders.

Acknowledgements This work received funding from the European Research Council under the European Union's Seventh Framework Programme (FP/2007-2013), ERC Grant Agreement number 29585 (BABE).

Bibliography

Alietti, A., D. Padovan, and C. Vercelli. 2014. (eds.). *Antisemitismo, islamofobia e razzismo. Rappresentazioni, immaginari e pratiche nella società italiana*. Milano: Franco Angeli.

Amnesty International. 2017. *Report: The State of the World's Human Rights*. London.

Anzaldúa, G.E. 1987. *Borderlands/La Frontera: The New Mestiza*. New York: Aunt Lute Books.

Ashworth, J.G., B. Graham, and E.J. Tunbridge. 2007. *Pluralising Pasts: Heritage, Identity and Place in Multicultural Societies*. New York: Pluto Press.

Bankey, R. 2002. Embodying Agoraphobia: Rethinking Geographies of Women's Fear. In *Subjectivities, Knowledges, and Feminist Geographies*, ed. L. Bondi, 44–56. Lanham, MD: Rowman & Littlefield.

Bell, D., and G. Valentine. 1997. *Consuming Geographies: We Are Where We Eat*. London and New York: Routledge.

Benjamin, W. 1999. *Selected Writings*, vol. 2, Part 2, 1931–1934, ed. N. W. Jennings, trans. Rodney Livingston et al. Cambridge, MA, and London: The Belknap Press of Harvard University Press.

Butler, J. 2004a. *Frames of War: When Is Life Grievable?* London: Verso.

Butler, J. 2004b. *Precarious Life: The Powers of Mourning and Violence*. London: Verso.

Colls, R. 2004. When We Lived in Communities: Working-Class Culture and Its Critics. In *Cities of Ideas: Civil Society and Urban Governance in Britain, 1800–2000*, ed. R. Colls and R. Rodger, 283–307. Aldershot: Ashgate.

Crewe, L. 2001. Progress Reports. The Besieged Body: Geographies of Retailing and Consumption. *Progress in Human Geography* 24 (4): 629–641.

Cuttitta P. 2014. Borderizing the Island Setting and Narratives of Lampedusa "Border Play". *ACME: An International E-Journal for Critical Geographies* 2 (13): 196–219.

Danewid, I. 2017. White Innocence in the Black Mediterranean: Hospitality and the Erasure of History. *Third World Quarterly* 7 (38): 1674–1689.

Davidson, J. 2003. *Phobic Geographies: The Phenomenology and Spatiality of Identity*. Aldershot: Ashgate.

Davidson, J., and M. Smith. 2003. Bio-Phobias/Techno-Philias: Virtual Reality and Exposure as Treatment for Phobias of Nature. *Sociology of Health & Illness* 25 (6): 644–661.

Davidson, J., L. Bondi, and M. Smith (eds.). 2007. *Emotional Geographies.* New York: Routledge.
De Genova, N. 2010. Migration and Race in Europe: The Trans-Atlantic Metastases of a Post-colonial Cancer. *European Journal of Social Theory* 3 (13): 405–419.
De Genova, N. 2012. Bare Life, Labor-Power, Mobility, and Global Space: Toward a Marxian Anthropology? *CR: The New Centennial Review* 3 (22): 129–152.
De Genova, N. 2013. Spectacle of Migrant 'Illegality': The Scene of Exclusion, the Scene of Obscene Inclusion. *Ethnic and Racial Studies* 7 (36): 1180–1198.
De Lauretis, T. 1999. *Soggetti eccentrici.* Milano: Feltrinelli.
de Sousa Santos, B. 2016. Epistemologies of the South and the Future. *From the European South* 1: 17–29.
Declich, L. 2016. *Islam in 20 Parole.* Roma: Laterza.
Deleuze J., and F. Guattari. 1975. *Kafka. Pour une literature mineure.* Paris: Les Éditions de Minuit.
Di Maio, A. 2012. Il Mediterraneo nero. Rotte dei migrant nel millennio globale. In *La città cosmopolita,* ed. G. de Spuches, 143–163. Palermo: Palumbo Editore.
Di Maio, A. 2014. The Mediterranean, or Where Africa Does (Not) Meet Italy: Andrea Segre's a Sud di Lampedusa. In *The Cinemas of Italian Migration: European and Transatlantic Narratives,* ed. S. Schrader and D. Winkler, 41–52. Newcastle upon Tyne: Cambridge Scholars Publishing.
Dias, K. 2003. The Ana Sanctuary: Women's Pro-Anorexia Narratives in Cyberspace. *Journal of International Women's Studies* 4 (2): 31–45.
Elbagir, N., R. Razek, A. Platt, and J. Bryony. 2017. People for Sale. CNN, November 19, 2017.
Elden, S., D. Gregory, and A. Sevilla-Buitrago. 2011. Spaces of the Past, Histories of the Present: An Interview with Stuart Elden and Derek Gregory. *ACME: An International E-Journal for Critical Geographies* 2 (10), 313–339.
Garofalo, D. 2017. *Black Mirror.* Roma: Edizioni Estemporanee.
Gilroy, P. 1993. *The Black Atlantic: Modernity and Double-Consciousness.* Harvard: Harvard University Press.
Graham, B., J.G. Ashworth, and J.E. Tunbridge. 2000. *A Geography of Heritage: Power, Culture and Economy.* London and New York: Oxford University Press.
Gregory, D. 1994. *Geographical Imaginations.* New York: Blackwell.
Gregory, D. 1995. Imaginative Geographies. *Progress in Human Geography* 19 (4): 447–485.
Grosfoguel, R. 2017. *Rompere la colonialità. Razzismo, islamofobia, migrazioni nella prospettiva decoloniale.* Milano: Mimesis.

Haraway, D. 1984. Cyborg Manifesto: Science, Technology, and Socialist-Feminism in the Late Twentieth Century. In *Simians, Cyborgs and Women: The Reinvention of Nature*, ed. D. Haraway, 149–181. New York: Routledge.

Harvey, D. 1973. *Social Justice and the City*. Baltimore: John Hopkins University Press.

Hawthorne, C. 2017. In Search of Black Italia: Notes on Race, Belonging, and Activism in the Black Mediterranean. *Transition* 123: 152–174.

Hirsch, M. 2012. *The Generation of Postmemory: Writing and Visual Culture After the Holocaust*. New York: Columbia University Press.

Johnson, L. 1996. Flexing Femininity: Female Body-Builders Refiguring the Body. *Gender, Place and Culture* 3 (3): 327–340.

Kayagil, A. 2004. *The Construction of Cultural Boundaries in Turkey*. PhD thesis defended in 2004 at the Koç University.

Kosellek, R. 2007. *Futuro Passato*. Bologna: Clueb.

Mezzadra S., and B. Neilson 2013. *Borders as Method: Or the Multiplication of Labor*. Durham: Duke University Press.

Otele, O. 2018a. *Afro-Europeans: A Short History*. London: Hurst.

Otele, O. 2018b. Race, Politics and Memory of Slavery in 21st Century France. In *Slavery, Memory and Power in France*, ed. A. Diptee and M. Cattias. Ottawa: University of Ottawa.

Passerini, L. 2007. *Memory and Utopia: The Primacy of Intersubjectivity*. London: Equinox.

Proglio, G. (ed.). 2017. *Decolonizing the Mediterranean: European Colonial Heritages in North Africa and the Middle East*. Newcastle upon Tyne: Cambridge Scholar Publishing.

Proglio, G. 2018. Is the Mediterranean a White Italian-European Sea? The Multiplication of Border in the Production of the Historical Subjectivity. *Interventions: International Journal of Postcolonial Studies* 20 (3): 406–427.

Raeymaekers, T. (ed.). 2014. The Mediterranean Migration Frontier. Special issue in *ACME: An International E-journal for Critical Geographies* 13 (2): 163–172.

Said, E. 1978. *Orientalism*. New York: Penguin.

Said, E. 2000. Invention, Memory, and Place. *Critical Inquiry* 26 (2): 175–192.

Saucier, K.P., and P.T. Woods. 2014. Ex Aqua: The Mediterranean Basin, Africans on the Move and the Politics of Policing. *Theoria: A Journal of Social and Political Theory* 61 (141): 55–75.

Saucier, K.P., and P.T. Woods. 2015. Slavery's Afterlife in the Euro-Mediterranean Basin. *OpenDemocracy*. 19 June 2015. https://www.opendemocracy.net/beyondslavery/tryon-p-woods-p-khalil-saucier/slavery%E2%80%99s-afterlife-in-euromediterranean-basin.

Smith, L. 2006. *Uses of Heritage*. New York: Routledge.

Stoler, A.L. 2010. *Along the Archival Grain: Epistemic Anxieties and Colonial Common Sense*. Princeton: Princeton University Press.

Tunbridge, J.E., and G.J. Ashworth. 1996. *Dissonant Heritage: The Management of the Past as a Resource in Conflict*. Chichester: Wiley.

Open Access This chapter is licensed under the terms of the Creative Commons Attribution 4.0 International License (http://creativecommons.org/licenses/by/4.0/), which permits use, sharing, adaptation, distribution and reproduction in any medium or format, as long as you give appropriate credit to the original author(s) and the source, provide a link to the Creative Commons license and indicate if changes were made.

The images or other third party material in this chapter are included in the chapter's Creative Commons license, unless indicated otherwise in a credit line to the material. If material is not included in the chapter's Creative Commons license and your intended use is not permitted by statutory regulation or exceeds the permitted use, you will need to obtain permission directly from the copyright holder.

CHAPTER 10

Epilogue

Luisa Passerini

This book is centered on a thematic cluster of theoretical and practical relevance: heritage, dissonance, and memory. Placed in the European context, these notions and practices presuppose the wider debate on European identity that has occurred in the last three decades, radically deconstructing this concept. The critique has been twofold: attacking, in general, the very concept of identity as a fixed and exclusionary notion, and, more specifically, refuting the claim to a cohesive and linear European sense of belonging throughout the centuries (Pagden 2002). Attributing continuity to the history of Europe and to European identity has always been, and still is, a heavy anachronism, dictated by religious and political motivations and/or intended to assert cultural exclusivity/superiority.

In the course of this long debate, a wide range of materials and practices, ranging from the consideration of official documents of the European Union to various forms of popular and academic culture, has come under the spotlight (Stone 2012). This process has entailed the

L. Passerini (✉)
Department of History and Civilization,
European University Institute, Florence, Italy
e-mail: luisa.passerini@eui.eu

deconstruction of the notion of European identity in many fields, including the history of emotions (Passerini 1999, 2012a), thus extending from the private to the public sphere, and vice versa, in a direction parallel to one that is modifying and expanding the prevailing concept of the public sphere centered in Europe towards a transnational public sphere (Kaelble and Passerini 2002; Fraser et al. 2014). "European identity" has thus not only been pluralized and "opened up" through an endeavor that unfolded during the initial phases of the process extending up to the 1990s, but it has also been turned upside down in terms of many of its implications. Its history has been shown to be discontinuous and contradictory, reflecting the history of the continent and the extra-European origins of its very name from the mythical Europa traveling west from Phoenicia, that is, present-day Lebanon.

The traditional dichotomy counterposition of Europe and its Other has, in the course of the intellectual debates on the subject, not only been expanded to include multiple Others, but, more importantly, it has been reversed. Consequently, Europe has been shown to be composed of and by many contributions from "others", and the old debate (partially still ongoing) on the primacy of Christian roots in European identity has largely given way (apart from political instrumentalizations) to the recognition of many other roots, which are often discordant among themselves. Finally, and even more pertinently, Europe herself has been shown to have been and to be "another" or the Other for many in the world (Strath 2000; Bhambra and Narayan 2016), a perspective requiring a revision and reformulation of the concept of cosmopolitanism inherited from the Enlightenment (Benhabib 2006; Delanty 2010; Passerini 2012b). The critique has gone so far that the end of Europe, one of the themes dominant after World War I, has powerfully resurfaced (Balibar 2016).

At the same time, if a new cosmopolitanism is possible, freed from the limitations imposed by the Enlightenment on the notion of "citizen of the world", and if this latter concept is substituted by the idea of "citizens without frontiers" (Isin 2012), then we can say that everybody is entitled to the legacy of all the cultures of the world. This is no easy claim, and its implementation will require a critical and self-critical attitude to every individual's place of origin, residence, and activities. Moreover, it will entail the fostering of attitudes of respect, humbleness, and curiosity towards cultures other than those that an individual knows and shares.

However, this form of reciprocity has already been practiced for centuries around the world by mobile people, who have been able to experiment with a sense of reciprocity without losing the pride and affection that they feel for their original cultures. A prerequisite of the right to inherit the legacy of many cultures is the rejection of exclusivism and superiority, not of uniqueness, which is the prerogative of individuals and can also apply to some aspects of every culture. For Europeans specifically—whether native or not—this type of right to inheritance would mean avoiding any assumption of fixed and solid heritages and instead fully accepting the mixture of continuity and discontinuity in the history of Europe. No birthright, no blood privilege. The term "dissonance" can be taken as encompassing all of these allusions.

The deconstructive process of European identity has encompassed the three connected notions of our cluster: heritage, dissonance, and memory. However, not all of the implications of disrupting the idea of European identity in a decolonial and postcolonial context have been teased out. First of all, while the deconstruction of "identity" can reach the point of dissolving the concept, "heritage" is not always intangible, rather, it is often material and corporeal, visible and touchable in spite of being elusive, and therefore more difficult to erode. Secondly, the terminological and conceptual discussion of the term heritage has not sufficiently explored the connotations in terms of gender and property that this term has in many European languages. Its etymology has repercussions that make it outdated and embarrassing because of the privileges it alludes to: in French (*patrimoine*) and Italian (*patrimonio*), it refers to the property of the father. In Portuguese (*herença*), Spanish (*herencia*), and Greek (*kleronomia*), it was originally connected with terms indicating the passage of property.

These connotations are still present in the notion of heritage, the use of which is often unfounded when its conceptual antecedents remain unexamined. However, the combination of "heritage" and "dissonance" operated by various scholars since the second half of the 1990s has deepened and enriched the problematic aspects of the term (among others, Graham et al. 2000). Indeed, heritage has been subjected to a critique that has aimed to eliminate its implications of exclusivity and has offered the useful concept of an inclusive heritage discourse (Kisić 2017). With our title, as well as in this book, we intend to reflect on the multiplicity of heritages and their internal contradictions, not only using the plural but also bringing together many different approaches.

"Dissonant heritages" (we would like to insist on the plural) are oxymoronic, and we have done our best to accept the challenge that this implies. We have used the metaphor of dissonance not only in the spirit of following other scholars and building on existing scholarship. We also had in mind the history of this term, which has become increasingly popular in recent decades, during which paired concepts such as dissonant subjectivities (Voli 2015), dissonant beauty (Braidotti 2011), and dissonant whispers have been introduced (Dissonant_Whispers).

The history of music reflects the history of the European continent; dissonance has always been a feature of classical music, to a limited extent, existing as a passage to be "resolved" in the following sequence of the musical piece. It was only in the twentieth century, and especially from the period around the time of World War I, that some composers started to place a heavy emphasis on dissonance within their scores, drawing inspiration from popular and world music, and incorporating new musical grammars into the old canon. With time, it became clear—also thanks to improved communications and new technology for reproducing sound—that what sounds dissonant to the ears of people in certain parts of the world, in other epochs and regions does not. We cannot help notice the affinities of musical history with the history of the terms identity and memory on European soil. All of these processes entail an increased acceptance of Europe's internal contradictions and dissonances, while implying a renewed recognition of its connections with other parts and peoples of the world.

While many appropriations and instrumentalizations of the term "heritage" are often disquieting, there have also been notable efforts to confer new meanings to it in fundamental contexts like education, and museums and exhibitions have sought out new practices. In the former field, it is of absolute importance to understand the multiplicity of discourses on heritage from the citizen's perspective (Carretero et al. 2017) and to grasp why "heritage has become the agora of history" within education (Asensio and Pol 2017, 774). In the second context, we find interesting practices of documentation, dissemination, and exhibition, conducted in a non-Eurocentric way, some of which are also analyzed in the present book. A significant example is the experimental initiative to create a "House of European History" in Brussels, one that maintains a balance between institutional aspects—such as displaying European integration, and cultural, social, and artistic products illustrating European history—while simultaneously questioning what Europe is and what the roles of multimedia and material memory in this are on this continent (Mork and Christodoulou 2018).

Concerning the third element of our cluster, it is now widely acknowledged that there has been a deluge of memory in the last fifty years. Writing about this memorial invasion, Philippe Joutard (2015, 9, 14) observes: "aujourd'hui, tout est mémoire" (today, everything is memory). At the same time, the notion of memory has become even more puzzling and vague (Samuel 1994). It has been conceptualized as a technology, for instance, understood as a component of economic globalization (Plate and Smelik 2009). Considering the variety of memories, memory studies has emerged as a central point of contemporary epistemologies and a crucial part of the self-reflection within this domain of knowledge (Kattago 2015). However, in this situation, the mix of concepts can be confused. This is the case with the so-called memory complex, an ensemble that has proved appealing for many, including some of the authors whose contributions feature in this book. Pulling together memory, identity, and heritage (MacDonald 2013) may be helpful for highlighting the diversity and fluidity within European memories, but it does not give sufficient attention to conflict, inequality, and questions of power and resistance. Given our positionality as European scholars (here in the double sense of being based in European institutions and receiving funds for research from the European Union), what we need is a different methodological practice that can succinctly be expressed as multiplying and decentering memory.

The process thus designated has been ongoing in the socio-historical disciplines, particularly in cultural history, for over half a century. It has taken a double course: on the one hand, the multiplication and decentralization of memory has occurred in Europe and in North America, thanks to the increasing priority accorded to the collection of memories from those subjects who for a long time were relatively invisible within traditional historiography. These subjects are the oppressed of history, discriminated against in terms of class, gender, age, and culture. Oral history has contributed a great deal to documenting their memories, thus destabilizing the existing priorities in collective and individual remembering. On the other hand, a similar process of multiplication and decentralization has unfolded with the increasing presence of memories that have long been emerging outside of the North Atlantic area. In scholarly, artistic, and popular fields, memories from all parts of the world have become increasingly evident and relevant. Here too, oral historians have widely documented such developments. Interestingly, these processes show similarities to those described above for "dissonance".

As noted in the introduction to this volume, the methodological and conceptual meeting place that we from the EUROHERIT and BABE research teams have found and adopted is not aimed at resolving tensions between memory and cultural heritage. Rather, our aim is to build on their multiple dimensions, evidenced by the diverse contributions in this book. The introduction also indicates the links and bridges between groups of chapters, or between individual chapters, so that the whole book emerges as a field of crossroads, however, one where the intersections do not ignore the distances between various points on the multiple itineraries. A specific type of convergence unites the chapters emanating respectively from EUROHERIT and BABE, but at the same time, there are differences within each project as well as reciprocal correspondences that overcome the boundaries of the two projects.

One common ground between EUROHERIT and BABE has been the practice of decentering, as documented in this book. EUROHERIT has contributed to decentering heritage, illustrating and analyzing some of the forms that it has taken in recent times in various European countries (and the same can be said, although from a different perspective, for Rob van der Laarse's contribution). BABE has focused on decentering memory, documenting the individual itineraries of people from all over the world towards and across Europe. It has collected—and contributed to the creation of—oral, visual, and written memories generated by and around mobility (Passerini 2018). It has also given particular attention to what can be considered a special type of memory, the archive, in both its material and cultural senses.

The dialogue between the two conceptual approaches and the connected practices has been far from linear and simple, and we believe that it remains ongoing. We see the present book as an initial outcome of our exchanges, and with it we hope to participate in a wider debate. We trust that this will enable the exchange between the two projects to develop further and take on new dimensions that are both European and global.

Acknowledgements This Epilogue owes much to a research that received funding from the European Research Council under the European Union's Seventh Framework Programme (FP/2007–2013), ERC Grant Agreement number 29585 (BABE).

References

Asensio, M., and E. Pol. 2017. The Neverending Story About Heritage and Museums: Four Discursive Models. In *Palgrave Handbook of Research in Historical Culture and Education*, ed. M. Carretero, S. Berger, and M. Grever, 755–780. London: Palgrave Macmillan.

Balibar, E. 2016. *Europe: crise et fin?* Lormont: Le Bord de l'eau.

Benhabib, S. 2006. *Another Cosmopolitanism*. Oxford: Oxford University Press.

Bhambra, G.K., and J. Narayan. 2016. *European Cosmopolitanism: Colonial Histories and Postcolonial Societies*. London: Routledge.

Braidotti, R. 2011. *La bellezza dissonante*. https://rosibraidotti.com/publications/la-bellezza-dissonante/.

Carretero, M., S. Berger, and M. Grever (eds.). 2017. *Palgrave Handbook of Research in Historical Culture and Education*. London: Palgrave Macmillan.

Delanty, G. 2010. *The Cosmopolitan Imagination: The Renewal of Critical Social Theory*. Cambridge: Cambridge University Press.

Dissonant Whispers. https://dnd5e.fandom.com/wiki/Dissonant_Whispers.

Fraser N., et al. 2014. *Transnationalizing the Public Sphere*. Edited by Kate Nash. Cambridge: Polity Press.

Graham, B., G.J. Ashworth, and J.E. Tunbridge (eds.). 2000. *A Geography of Heritage: Power, Culture and Economy*. London: Routledge.

Isin, E.F. 2012. *Citizens Without Frontiers*. New York: Bloomsbury.

Joutard, P. 2015. *Histoire et mémoires, conflits et alliance*. Paris: La Découverte.

Kaelble, H., and L. Passerini. 2002. European Public Sphere and European Identity in 20th Century History. *Journal of European Integration History* 8 (2): 5–8.

Kattago, S. (ed.). 2015. *The Ashgate Research Companion to Memory Studies*. Farnham: Ashgate.

Kisić, V. 2017. *Governing Heritage Dissonance: Promises and Realities of Selected Cultural Policies*. Amsterdam: European Cultural Foundation.

MacDonald, S. 2013. *Memorylands: Heritage and Identity in Europe Today*. London: Routledge.

Mork, A., and P. Christodoulou. 2018. *Creating the House of European History*. Luxembourg: Publications Office of the European Union.

Pagden, A. (ed.). 2002. *The Idea of Europe: From Antiquity to the European Union*. Cambridge, MA: Cambridge University Press.

Passerini, L. 1999. *Europe in Love, Love in Europe: Imagination and Politics in Britain Between the Wars*. London: Tauris.

Passerini, L. 2012a. *Women and Men in Love: European Identities in the Twentieth Century*. Oxford and New York: Berghahn.

Passerini, L. 2012b. Europe and Its Others: Is There a European Identity? In *The Oxford Handbook of Postwar European History*, ed. D. Stone, 120–139. Oxford: Oxford University Press.

Passerini, L. 2018. *Conversations on Visual Memory*. http://hdl.handle.net/1814/60164.

Plate, L., and H. Smelik. 2009. *Technologies of Memory in the Arts*. London: Palgrave Macmillan.

Samuel, R. 1994. *Theatres of Memory: Past and Present in Contemporary Culture*. London: Verso.

Stone, D. (ed.). 2012. *The Oxford Handbook of Postwar European History*. Oxford: Oxford University Press.

Stråth, B. (ed.). 2000. *Europe and the Other and Europe as the Other*. Brussels: P.I.E.-Peter Lang.

Voli, S. 2015. *Soggettività dissonanti*. Firenze: Firenze University Press.

Open Access This chapter is licensed under the terms of the Creative Commons Attribution 4.0 International License (http://creativecommons.org/licenses/by/4.0/), which permits use, sharing, adaptation, distribution and reproduction in any medium or format, as long as you give appropriate credit to the original author(s) and the source, provide a link to the Creative Commons license and indicate if changes were made.

The images or other third party material in this chapter are included in the chapter's Creative Commons license, unless indicated otherwise in a credit line to the material. If material is not included in the chapter's Creative Commons license and your intended use is not permitted by statutory regulation or exceeds the permitted use, you will need to obtain permission directly from the copyright holder.

Index

A
Abbey of Cluny, 54, 72, 197
Africa
  Horn of, 18, 250, 251, 258, 260, 265
  North-, 227, 259
  West-, 235
Afrika Museum, 238
Airports
  as border site, 146
  complex, 144, 154
  control, 139, 140, 145, 146
  cultural hegemony, 43, 146
  cultural heritage, 16, 140, 145, 146, 153, 154, 167
  as (European) cultural archives, 145
  national symbols, 152
  open, 139, 147, 149, 155
  politics of, 139, 145, 153, 155
  power relations, 138, 143, 145
  site of "mediated power", 145
  "supermodern" site, 152
  zones of transit, 145

Albania, 35, 81
Alhaag, Amal, 240
Alpi, Ilaria, 262
Americas, 200, 235
Amsterdam, 17, 99, 137, 138, 145, 147, 154, 217, 222, 234, 239–241
  museum, 17, 217, 222, 239, 240
Anti-Semitism, 105, 109
Archive of the Crown of Aragon, 195
Argentine, 95
Asia, 90, 92, 93, 98, 108, 223, 249, 254, 259
Asmara, 264
Asylum, 138, 139, 147–150
  seeker, 5, 16, 146–148, 150, 154, 268
Atlantic coast, 200
Auschwitz-Birkenau, 117
Austria, 66, 80, 81, 97, 107, 197
Authorized heritage discourse (AHD), 11, 15–17, 32–34, 42, 54, 55, 69–71, 73, 87, 91, 116,

158–160, 162, 165, 167, 175, 190, 191, 194, 198–208
Azerbaijan, 39

B
Balkan countries, 81, 118
Balkenende, Jan Peter, 216
Balk, Tirza, 226
Baltic countries, 176
Baltic region, 199
Bandera, Stepan, 114
Batavia, 2, 224. *See also* Jakarta
Belgium, 54, 65, 81, 92, 97, 110, 112, 117, 207, 225, 242
Belonging
  European narrative/EU narrative, 17, 31, 32, 158, 160, 190, 261
  politics of, 7, 27, 31, 45, 139, 153, 155
  psychological and political, 27
Belvedere (Dutch heritage landscape program), 101
Bennett, Dyonna, 240
Beretta, 262, 266
Berg en Dal, 238
Berger, Martin, 230, 237, 276
Black Mediterranean, 18, 255, 258–261, 265, 267, 268
Black Pete (*Zwarte Piet*), 110, 111
Blokland, Dorothy, 233
Bodies, 3, 10, 28, 29, 138, 140, 142, 146–148, 150, 151, 154, 230, 265–267. *See also* Space
  controlled movement of, 138, 154
Bolivia, 120
Bologna, 260–262, 264
Borders
  conceptualizing, 10, 67, 145, 221
  control, 94, 143, 144
  cultural, 3, 14, 16, 26, 82, 116
  Eastern, 170, 172
  European, 260
  geographical, 3, 243, 260
  invisible, 144
  management, 204
  marker of a liminal space, 251
  national, 2, 7, 16, 26, 94, 144, 146, 245
  political, 103
  practices, 6, 16, 144, 145, 147, 151, 154, 268
  symbolic, 64, 147, 170, 264
  zones, 7, 138, 144
Bosnia, 81
Bossi, Umberto, 104
Boundaries, 44, 116, 140, 144, 157, 161, 174, 253, 268, 278. *See also* Borders
Brexit, 32, 106, 144
Brooker, Charlie, 249
Brothers Grimm, 115
Brussels, 99, 103, 104, 276
Budapest, 83, 104, 105
Bunch, Lonnie, 229

C
Camp Westerbork, 54, 60, 65, 67–69, 72
Cape Finisterre, 200
  End of the Known World, 200
Carnival, 118, 169
Carnuntum, 197
Central and East Europe (CEE), 160, 164
Cerkno, 54, 68
Charter of Fundamental Rights of the European Union, 193
Charter of Law of Abolition of the Death Penalty (1867), 195, 203
China, 93, 94, 97
Christian, 104, 105, 111, 144, 164, 274
  background, 164
  religion, 164

Citizenship
  European, 33, 38, 98
Colonialism
  colonial history, 11, 142, 153, 215, 217, 219–221, 223, 224, 231, 238
  colonial power, 42, 215, 266
  decolonisation, 111, 220, 233
  decolonizing, 217
  postcolonialism, 83, 189, 219, 223
  postcoloniality, 185
Colorblindness, 141, 154
Communality, 26, 28, 31, 44
Communication, 8, 28, 41, 44–46, 58, 166, 237, 276
Community, 18, 30, 35–37, 40, 41, 44–46, 52, 60, 62, 80, 86–88, 91, 96, 97, 99–101, 105, 107, 113, 116, 166, 168, 170, 197, 202, 234, 241, 258, 260, 266
Conflicts, 2, 8, 13–16, 26, 30, 32, 34, 35, 37, 38, 57, 62, 64, 65, 71–73, 84, 105, 112, 113, 115, 159, 218, 221, 252, 264, 277
Copenhagen, 30
Cosmopolitanism, 44, 57, 71, 83, 105, 116, 142, 148, 274
Council of Europe
  Committee of Ministers, 28
  Congress of Local and Regional Authorities, 28
  Convention on Offences Relating to Cultural Property (2017), 30
  Council of Europe Framework Convention on the Value of Cultural Heritage for Cultural Routes Programme Society, the Faro Convention (2005), 27
  Namur Declaration, 37, 39, 40
  Parliamentary Assembly, 28, 38
  Steering Committee for Culture, Heritage and Landscape, 28
  White Paper on Intercultural Dialogue (2008), 37
Crises, 39, 40, 64, 177
Croatia, 209
Crotone, 262
Cultural archive of Europe, 16, 145, 154, 186, 187, 261, 265
Culture. *See also* Multiculturalism
  cultural dissonances, 46, 87
  cultural diversity, 35, 82, 84, 86, 88–91, 93, 96, 98, 100, 103, 107, 108, 113, 116, 195
  cultural hegemony, 43, 89, 146
  cultural identities, 15, 18, 82, 88, 100, 108, 116, 141, 252, 260, 266
  cultural policy, 12, 26, 30, 31, 88, 98
  cultural values, 3, 101, 104, 116, 119
  folk, 96, 97, 101
  intangible cultural heritage, 15, 16, 83, 84, 87–90, 92, 93, 96–101, 103, 108, 111, 117
  metacultural production, 119
  regional, 103, 104
Cyprus, 39, 97
Czech Republic, 205

D

Debrecen, 112
Declaration on European Identity (1973), 30, 52, 192
Democracy, 4, 34, 38, 64, 66, 72, 82, 104, 106, 107, 109, 195, 196, 198, 205
Dene, Urban, 166, 169
Denmark, 171
de Ruyter, Michiel, 112
Dialogue
  cultural, 31

dialogical space, 46
dialoguees, 37, 38
dialoguers, 37, 38
intercultural, 15, 26, 35, 37, 38, 40, 41, 45, 53, 58, 83, 96, 98, 162
Diaspora, 3, 251, 256, 258, 259, 268
Digital turn, 116
Discrimination, 36, 203, 260
Dissonance, 8–14, 16, 26, 28, 33, 37, 40, 44, 45, 65, 69, 83, 143, 155, 159, 160, 164, 167, 174, 175, 189, 199, 208, 219, 221, 238, 243, 245, 252, 257, 267, 273, 275, 276, 278
  site of, 138, 139, 143, 155
Diversity
  cultural, 35, 82, 84, 86, 88–91, 93, 96, 98, 100, 103, 107, 108, 113, 116, 195
  linguistic, 52, 68, 198
  national, 86, 94, 98
  regional, 103, 104
Domestication, 10, 16, 159, 160, 163, 171
Donbass, 114
Dragon of the North, 173
Dubai, 146
Dublin, 5
Dutch Antilles, 239
Dutch East India Company (VOC), 216, 239
  VOC mentality, 216
Dutch Golden Age, 98
Dutch Indies, 222, 223, 227, 232, 233

E
Eastern block, 176
Eccentric subject, 250
Enlightenment, 43, 85, 86, 109, 192, 195, 197, 274
Eritrea, 18, 251, 258, 260–266

Estonia
  Eastern, 160, 171
  government, 172
  Western, 171
Estonian History Museum, 16, 160, 165, 174, 199
Euregio, 62
Eurocentric, 8, 37, 42, 70, 187, 192, 193, 201–203, 207, 208, 216, 223, 226
Eurocentrism, 12, 97, 188, 192–194, 197, 202, 207, 208, 228
Europa Nostra, 52
Europeana, 52
European Coal and Steel Community, 30, 58, 59
European Commission (EC), 15, 28, 34, 41, 53, 54, 158, 160, 164, 188, 189, 195, 197–201, 206
European Communities
  European Atomic Energy Community, 30
  European Coal and Steel Community, 30, 58, 59
  European Economic Community (EEC), 30, 59, 192, 193, 207
European Court of Human Rights, 63
European District of Strasbourg, 54, 63, 64, 69, 72
European Heritage Days, 31, 52
European Heritage Label (EHL)
  action, 188, 202, 208
  application form, 162
  documents, 17, 53, 54, 65–69, 71, 72, 174, 175, 189, 191, 193, 195
  exhibition, 16, 160, 165
  panel report, 54, 67, 68, 165, 174, 189, 195, 206
  panels, 54, 228
  sites, 10, 11, 15, 52–54, 56, 60, 61, 63, 64, 66, 68–73, 158, 159,

INDEX 285

188, 191, 194–196, 198, 199, 202, 203, 206, 208
website, 53, 54, 64, 69, 71, 72, 165, 189, 194
European integration
European project, 31, 58, 198
peace, 15, 51, 52, 54, 57–60, 63, 64, 67, 72, 207
symbols, 54, 67, 198
Europeanization, 10, 83, 84, 95, 143, 159, 160, 163, 171
cultural, 5, 163, 164
racial, 142, 145, 218
Europeanness, 17, 42, 141, 144, 187, 189, 194, 197, 203, 205, 207, 208
European Panel of Experts, 188, 189, 191, 199
European Parliament (EP), 28, 31, 34, 41, 53, 63, 188, 189, 191, 195, 196, 198, 199
Committee of the Regions, 28
European significance, 53, 67–70, 158, 165, 188, 189, 191, 195–200, 202–204
European Solidarity Center, 195
European Spirit, 202
European Union
accession process, 163, 164, 172
eastern enlargement, 160, 161, 163
prize for cultural heritage, 31
European year of cultural heritage, 31
Evaluation, 11, 94, 188–190

F
Finland, vi
Flanders Fields museum, 117
Folklore, 15, 88, 89, 97–99, 102, 103, 107, 108, 110, 111, 114, 115, 120
Folklorization, 100, 116, 118
Folk songs, 16, 80

Folk tales, 80
Fortuyn, Pim, 109
France, 52, 54, 58, 64, 92, 94, 97, 197, 207, 216, 225, 242, 259
Franja Partisan Hospital, 54, 60, 68, 69, 72, 195
Friesland, 103

G
Geography
canonized Eurocentric, 18, 257, 268
of coloniality, 187, 202, 203, 207
counter-geography, 257
emotional turn, 256
of emotions, 250, 251, 255–258, 261, 264–267
from below, 6, 17
human, 252, 257
imaginative, 250, 251, 253–255
migration, 256, 258, 268
official, 18, 258
power, 17, 253, 254, 265, 266
scales, 157
self-irony, 173
Georgia, 39
Germany, 52, 54, 58, 61, 64, 68, 80, 94, 98, 166, 169, 174, 195
Global South, 223, 226, 228, 260
Goeverneur, Jan, 80
Grandjean, Martin, 92, 93
Great Britain, 106, 225
Great Guild Hall (Tallinn), 16, 160, 165–167, 169, 174–176, 197, 199, 200, 204, 207

H
Haarlem, 222
Habsburgs, 80, 104, 111, 112
Hague, 54, 62, 65, 84, 91, 195
Hainaut, 103

Hamelin, 115
Haydn, Joseph, 80
Herder, Rik, 229, 230
Heritage
  archaeological, 30, 87
  architectural, 30
  as diplomacy, 41, 42
  audiovisual, 30
  authorized heritage discourse (AHD), 11, 15–17, 32–34, 42, 54, 55, 70, 71, 73, 87, 91, 116, 158–160, 162, 167, 175, 190, 191, 198–208
  boom, 83
  building of heritage sites/spaces, 142
  canon, 97, 138, 153, 186, 257, 276
  colonial, 10, 11, 13, 17, 37, 87, 186, 187, 202, 207, 220, 230, 233, 236, 263
  commemoration, 55
  common, 10, 12, 15, 29, 31–37, 40, 42, 43, 46, 53, 108, 158, 163, 164, 176
  communities, 8, 35, 36, 44, 46, 80, 86–90, 94, 96, 100, 101, 108, 116, 158
  conflicts, 8, 14–16, 26, 30, 32, 34, 35, 39, 41, 57, 58, 112, 113, 115, 206, 245
  conservation, 27, 41, 46, 55, 83, 100
  conserve, 34, 158
  consumption, 101, 103, 252
  contested, 6, 16, 57, 60, 70, 71, 82, 99, 110, 113, 140, 143, 145, 146, 153, 154, 190, 217, 218
  critical studies, 2, 11, 12, 15, 37, 38, 45, 46, 60, 86, 118, 158, 162, 190, 200
  cultural, 2, 3, 5, 8–10, 12, 15, 16, 26, 29–46, 52, 53, 55, 57, 60, 65, 69, 71, 73, 81–83, 88–90, 94, 95, 101, 108, 119, 140, 145, 146, 153, 154, 158, 163, 167, 186–188, 192, 201, 202, 207, 215, 220, 221, 230, 252, 278
  cultural practice, 3, 7, 190, 219, 231
  dark, 56, 67, 69, 87, 207
  difficult, 45, 56–58, 65, 67, 69, 95, 110, 194, 206
  diplomacy, 41–43, 45
  discourse, 2, 4, 11, 12, 14–17, 25–27, 29–32, 37, 39, 40, 42–46, 54, 57, 65, 68, 83, 87, 91, 100, 109, 116, 158, 176, 190, 191, 198, 207, 221, 244, 245, 275, 276
  dissonance, 8–10, 12, 14, 18, 26, 28, 37, 41, 46, 57, 58, 65, 69, 72, 73, 118, 138, 143, 159, 163, 252, 275
  dissonant, 8–13, 26, 45, 57, 67, 68, 116, 143, 176, 218, 242, 244, 245, 251, 252, 255, 257, 258, 260, 261, 267, 268, 276
Eastern European, 83, 205, 206
education, 97, 111, 276
European, 2, 3, 8, 10–14, 29, 31, 42, 43, 46, 159, 163, 164, 187, 188, 190, 191, 193–195, 200, 202, 206, 217, 220, 236, 262
European Heritage Label (EHL), 10, 11, 15–17, 31, 40, 52–54, 56, 65, 70, 73, 158, 159, 162, 188, 199
Europeanizing, 10, 16, 84, 95, 159, 163
experts, 100, 120, 159, 190
fixed, 162, 275
heritagization, 14, 16, 84, 100, 162

hidden, 17, 158, 190
identity, 2, 3, 5, 10, 12, 13, 17, 27, 31–33, 36, 39, 40, 43, 52, 55–57, 61, 71, 72, 83, 84, 108, 113, 115, 118, 138, 142, 145, 154, 159, 163, 167, 206, 217, 221, 244, 277
in diplomacy, 41
industry, 87
initiatives and programs, 3, 31, 40
institution, 2–4, 10, 60, 73, 159, 186
intangible, 10, 12, 15, 16, 33, 61, 70, 73, 83–87, 89–102, 107–109, 112, 113, 115, 116, 119, 275
intangible heritage policy, 86
intangible heritage turn, 44, 86
landscape, 10, 101, 102, 190, 252
legislation, 32
local, 4, 6, 7, 17, 25, 35, 43, 54, 69, 72, 113, 117–119, 143, 159, 163, 242
management, 4, 29, 31, 32, 42, 44, 55, 174
marginalized, 5, 10, 36, 190
material, 3, 7, 8, 15, 27, 42, 43, 46, 53, 56, 69, 73, 83, 84, 87, 88, 90, 92, 97, 100, 102, 119, 162, 221, 275
materiality, 7, 43, 87, 118
memory, 1–9, 12–14, 16–18, 31, 34, 46, 53, 56, 61, 70, 83, 87, 138, 142, 145, 153, 154, 217, 220, 221, 236, 244, 257, 262, 275, 278
multiheritage, 176
national, 10, 97, 152, 153
natural, 33, 84, 88
ownness of intangible cultural, 15, 16
physical, 10, 15, 33, 36, 61, 73, 162, 218, 244

policies, 3, 4, 6–8, 14, 26, 31, 44, 46, 83
policy actors, 26, 29
policy discourses, 4, 15, 26, 29, 32, 40, 42–46, 191
policy rhetoric, 28, 40, 41, 46
political, 3, 12, 15, 16, 26, 30, 33, 34, 39–42, 46, 60, 71, 109, 145, 188, 191
politics of, 6, 31
potential, 3, 6, 26, 37–39, 108, 159, 190, 242, 252
preservation, 27, 43, 45, 46, 55, 88, 108, 119, 142
production, 12, 100, 119, 190, 257
realms of, 186
regimes, 2, 6, 15, 17, 34, 56, 83
regional, 7, 25, 35, 43, 69
related to the peace, 62
remembering, 52, 55, 71, 73, 118, 162, 221, 242, 244
shared, 13, 33, 41, 42, 46, 53, 81, 84, 89, 113, 116
silenced, 17, 36
sites, 3, 7, 10–12, 35, 37, 60, 69, 72, 73, 86, 87, 93, 94, 138, 142, 143, 146, 151, 153, 158, 159, 162, 166, 188, 190, 194, 196, 198, 200, 202
social construct, 57, 151, 158, 162, 175, 190
static, 11, 15, 40, 118
strategy, 37, 39, 52
taken for granted, 108, 118, 158, 165
tangible, 6, 34, 43
to safeguard, 15, 29, 84, 87–90, 92, 101, 113, 115, 119
tourism, 82, 83, 87, 100, 102, 117, 252
transmission, 39

values, 3, 8, 11, 31, 33, 34, 37, 41–46, 52, 53, 73, 88, 90, 119, 190, 192, 197, 208
Hlubbina Mine, 204
Hoffmann von Fallersleben, August Heinrich, 80, 81
Holland, 103
Holocaust, 34, 82–84, 87, 102, 113, 142, 203, 206, 220
Holodomor, 113
Hooghalen, 54, 67
House of European History (HEH), 191, 276
Houthakker, Jan, 234
Hrovatin, Miran, 262
Humanism, 85
Human rights, 4, 34, 38, 59, 64, 66, 82, 89–91, 96, 103, 110, 111, 113, 193, 195, 196, 198, 203
  policy, 82
Humor, 173, 174
  sarcastic sense of, 173
Hungary, 54, 66, 105

I
Ice Age, 168
ICOMOS (International Council on Monuments and Sites), 88, 117, 119
  ICOMOS Declaration of San Antonio (1996), 119
  ICOMOS Nara Document on Authenticity (1994), 88, 89
Identities
  boundaries, 44, 144
  building, 16, 17, 52–54, 56, 57, 62, 68, 72, 142, 144, 193
  common, 32, 33, 40, 42, 52, 53, 70
  concepts of, 2, 28, 43, 55, 90, 118, 142, 244
  construction of, 10, 55, 57, 58, 61, 70, 71, 175, 254
  cultural, 15, 16, 18, 82, 88, 100, 108, 116, 141, 252, 260, 266
  European, 3, 13, 16, 27, 30–33, 39, 40, 42, 44, 52, 53, 55, 58, 59, 62, 67, 69–71, 144, 160, 163, 164, 175, 176, 193, 201, 273–275
  founding stories, 52
  histories, 144
  individual category, 139, 140
  linguistic, 9, 44, 55
  making, 55, 175
  memory, 3, 5, 9, 12, 13, 17, 56, 61, 115, 138, 142, 145, 154, 217, 221, 254, 276, 277
  myths, 52, 55, 88
  narratives, 9, 69, 70, 72, 83, 109, 158–160, 163, 164, 175, 197, 244, 254
  national, 10, 11, 84, 98, 99, 139
  performative, 139
  political process, 57
  politics, 11, 31, 85, 94, 98, 105, 108, 113, 116, 160, 201
  process, 9, 17, 27, 57, 62, 65, 68, 158, 159, 163, 273, 275
  production, 118, 145
  racialized cultural, 5, 141, 268
  regional, 69, 80
  social category, 140
  spatial category, 140
  stories, 9, 69
  symbolic markers of, 9
  territorial, 15, 35, 140
  traditions, 43, 55, 59, 88, 107, 108, 120
Immigration, 106, 149, 172
  crisis, 18, 196, 208
  policy, 51
Imperial Palace (Vienna), 197
India, 94, 196, 223
Indonesia, 91, 118, 120, 220, 222–224, 227, 230, 232, 239

Inequalities, 36, 38, 87, 106, 218–221, 223, 226, 232, 234, 236, 237, 241–243, 277
Intersubjectivity, 250, 251, 255, 260
Islam, 104, 109, 197, 231
  islamism, 103, 106
  islamophobia, 250
Israel, 102, 105, 114, 263
Istanbul, 81
Italy
  Black, 259

J
Jakarta, 2, 224. *See also* Batavia
Japan, 90, 92, 93, 231
Jülich, 166

K
Kartini, 224
Kaunas, 205
Kipling, Rudyard, 260, 265
Kodjo, Johannes, 234
Kofi, Richard, 229, 230, 237, 239
Korea, 90, 92

L
Lampedusa, 257, 259, 262, 265
Landveld, Onias, 233
Latin America, 91, 93, 186, 223, 235
Legêne, Susan, 99, 223, 238
Leiden, 80, 81, 238
Lenin, Vladimir, 114
Limburg, 103
Limon, Imare, 240
Lithuania, 66, 118, 205
Ljubljana, 35
Lutheran, 169
Luzna, 54, 68

M
Maastricht Treaty (1992), 30, 198
Macedonia, 81, 118, 119
Marijnissen, Jan, 216
Masterpieces list, 92, 94
Máxima, the Queen of the Netherlands, 95
3 May 1791 Constitution in Warsaw, 54, 66
Medieval
  buildings, 16, 160, 165, 175
  era, 166
  festivals, 160, 166, 169
  history, 160, 165, 199
  pleasures, 160, 165, 166, 169, 170, 173, 175, 176
  times, 166, 199
Mediterranean Sea, 259, 261, 264
  black, 18, 255, 258, 259, 267, 268
Memories
  archive of, 260, 267
  art of, 83, 254
  boom, 83, 87
  chronological, 256
  collective, 2, 7, 8, 83, 164, 254
  colonial, 17, 220, 224, 240, 244, 251, 261, 265, 267
  commemoration, 5, 215
  complex, 2, 56, 61, 70, 73, 82, 142, 217, 218, 220, 221, 233, 236, 238, 240–245, 277
  cosmopolization, 142
  disappearance, 100
  dissonance/dissonant, 8, 11, 13, 14, 18, 57, 164, 221, 243, 245, 251, 260, 267, 273, 275
  Dutch, 80, 142, 218, 221, 233, 236, 241
  European, 1–3, 12, 14, 31, 67, 82, 83, 138, 142, 194, 218, 220, 221, 233, 236, 243, 276, 277

historical, 3, 8, 31
identities, 2, 3, 12, 13, 17, 56, 61, 67, 142, 145, 154, 217, 221, 244, 254, 276, 277
individual, 2, 7, 16, 221, 267, 278
marginalized, 5, 36
memorialization, 16
memorylands, 143, 144
mobility, 2, 3, 256, 265, 278
new temporalities, 256
oral, 7, 138, 250, 255, 261, 277, 278
political, 4, 53, 56, 113
politics, 2, 5, 16, 34, 56
postcolonial, 17, 83, 218, 265, 267
postmemory, 265
practices, 2, 4, 6, 8, 14, 56, 61
preservation, 31, 142
process, 2, 5, 7, 16, 56, 101, 220, 254, 255, 257, 265, 277
public, 8, 115, 251, 255
regimes, 2, 5, 14, 17
repository of, 142, 219, 255
reshaping, 251, 257, 261
shared, 18, 33, 46, 67, 256, 257, 260
spatial, 17, 142, 253, 256
trans-individual, 7
usages of, 8, 251, 257, 259
Mestizia, 250
Middle Ages, 164–166, 170, 172, 173
Middle East, 249, 254, 255, 260
Migration
bordering, 6, 68, 143, 265
crisis, 143, 172
immigration, 172
irregular, 143
ordering, 6, 143
others, 143
Milan, 260
Mindscapes, 118
Minorities, 36, 109, 114, 142
Minor literature, 257, 258

Mobility
depoliticizing, 167
entangled mobility and stability, 160
immobility, 36, 161. *See also* Stability
mobile turn, 161
new mobilities paradigm, 161
oppressive, 171, 173, 174, 177
politics of, 159–161, 163, 164, 167
Modest, Wayne, 226, 230, 237–239
Mons, 54, 65
Multiculturalism, 86, 90, 95, 98, 103, 105, 106, 108, 109. *See also* Culture
Mundaneum, 54, 65, 67, 69, 71, 72
Münster, 54, 61–64
Museum
of migration, 2, 102, 103
-plein, 234
Volkenkunde, 238

N
Nantes, 242
Napoleonic era, 80
Narratives
belonging, 9, 158, 160
colonialist, 37, 185, 187, 190, 207, 208, 261, 268
diverse, 45, 208
dominant, 53, 158, 241, 244
elitist, 37
Eurocentric, 37, 70, 187, 202, 208
of Europe, 10, 17, 59, 63, 85, 141, 174, 185, 188, 189, 191, 194, 197, 202, 208
European, 17, 31, 32, 158, 160, 190, 261
Europeanness, 17, 189, 203, 208
hegemonic, 44, 257
history, 17, 32, 52, 63, 174, 175, 191, 194, 199, 202, 208

identity, 52, 70, 72, 109, 158–160, 163, 164, 175, 254
imperialist, 17, 37, 202
production, 252–254, 257, 260, 267
shared, 9, 62, 164
Nation
discursive dimensions, 139
imagined community, 139
imagined union, 139
state, 2, 6, 7, 10, 12, 80, 83, 84, 151, 162, 185, 220
National
anthem, 80
flag, 103, 226
Museum of African American History and Culture, 229, 237
post-, 44
pre-, 54
trans-, 2–4, 13, 14, 26, 44, 80, 82–84, 92, 94, 96, 150, 161, 172, 185, 220, 221, 251, 260, 274
Nationalism, 31, 51, 80, 82, 83, 95, 158, 254
NATO, 176
Netherlands, 15–17, 54, 61, 62, 67, 80, 91, 92, 95–99, 108, 110–112, 118, 119, 137–139, 141, 143, 146, 147, 149, 195, 203, 215, 216, 219, 220, 224, 228, 233, 234, 240–242, 244
Networks, 2, 33, 58, 137, 240
New Guinea, 225, 230, 231
Nobel Peace Prize, 59, 60, 82
Nordic, 166, 168, 176

O
Orbán, Viktor, 104–107
Oslo Noble Peace Prize, 82
Osnabrück, 54, 61–64
Otepää, 168

Others, 4, 9, 10, 16, 26, 35, 36, 39, 41, 44, 46, 55, 57, 86, 90, 95, 106, 119, 140, 144, 148, 150, 151, 154, 175, 187, 202, 208, 218, 223, 225, 235, 253, 255, 258, 259, 261, 274, 275
Muslim, 144, 154
otherness, 141, 217, 218, 250, 254
Ottomans, 81, 104

P
Padua, 260
Pan-European Picnic Park (Sopron), 54, 66, 67, 69, 72, 73
Pan-German, 80, 81
Past-presencing, 174
Päts, Konstantin, 173
Peace
culture, 64, 65, 67
European peace heritage, 72
pacifist, 58
Palace, 54, 60, 62, 63, 65, 66, 69, 71–73, 195, 203
symbols of, 66, 68, 72, 73
of Westphalia (1648), 61
Peeva, Adele, 81, 114
Petrov, Sergei, 114
Pinas, Marcel, 225
Põhja konn, 173
Poland, 54, 66, 68, 114, 195, 197, 205
Politics
of belonging, 7, 27, 31, 45, 139
cultural, 31, 85, 108, 113, 139
national, 94, 113, 116, 139, 159, 163
of regret, 82, 91, 92
Pontida, 104
Popular culture, 80, 97, 113, 115
Populism, 51, 86, 95, 103, 104, 107–109, 143, 219
movements, 15, 42, 86

parties, 15, 42, 196
Portugal, 195, 200, 203, 216, 225
Prague, 83
Psykou, Elina, 79, 80, 82
Public institutions, 152
  monuments, 152
  museums, 152
Putski, 54, 68

R
Randstad, 149
Reconciliation, 34, 39, 52, 57, 59, 67–69, 72, 82
Reformation
  protestant, 169
Refugees, 6, 10, 16, 25, 51, 67, 68, 106, 109, 138, 144, 147, 148, 154, 172, 250, 257, 262, 268
  crisis, 18, 143, 172, 176
Remembering
  agonistic, 57, 71
  antagonistic, 57
  cosmopolitan, 57, 71
Residencia de Estudiantes, 195
Rijksmuseum, 239
Robert Schuman House, 54, 63, 64, 69, 72
Roman Empire, 197
Russia, 68, 86, 93, 94, 106, 113–115, 172, 174, 177, 199, 205
Russian Empire, 171

S
Sagres Promontory, 200, 201
Sahara, 254, 262
Saint Nicholas (Sinterklaas, Sint-Nicolas), 110–112
San Donato, 262
Sawa, 261

Scales
  European, 159, 160, 163, 164, 167, 171, 174–176
  local, 159, 166
  multiscalar, 69
  national, 110, 158, 163, 164, 175, 176
Schengen principle, 143
Schiphol
  airport, 16, 138–140, 145–150, 152, 154
  library, 153
  occupation and destruction by German forces during WWII, 153
  rebuilding, 153
  website, 153
Scy-Chazelles, 54
Self, 9, 140, 255, 261, 265, 268
Serbia, 81
Siberia, 102, 120, 172
Simbirsk, 114
Skopje, 118
Slovenia, 54, 68, 195
Smeets, Rieks, 91, 92, 97
Social media, 221, 226–230, 243
  hashtags, 221
Somalia, 18, 251, 258, 260, 262
Sopron, 54, 66
Soros, George, 105, 116
South America, 254
South Europe, 215, 259, 260
South Korea, 93
Soviet Union, 163, 171, 205
Space
  belonging, 259
  bodies, 16, 138, 140, 147, 150, 151, 154
  bodily practices, 140
  coded, 147, 148

colorblind, 141, 154
cultural heritage, 37, 45, 71, 140, 154, 167, 202
European, 6, 16, 140–142, 144, 147, 151, 152, 154, 157, 218
mobility, 148, 158, 167, 235, 257
national, 140
open, 3, 8, 72, 138, 139, 147, 155
postcolonial, 140, 187, 241
scale, 7, 69, 138, 157, 167
social, 36, 138, 147, 250
whiteness, 140, 141, 148
Spatiality, 17, 139, 140, 256
question of bodily presence, 140
spatial ordering, 139, 148, 154
Spirit of Survival, 160, 165–168, 170, 171, 173, 175, 176, 199
Srebrenica, 82
Stability
depoliticizing, 167
oppressive, 171, 173, 174, 177
politics of, 159–161, 163, 164, 167
Strasbourg, 54, 63–65
Subject
intersubjectivity, 255
mobility of, 256, 257
subjectivity, 250, 255, 256, 268
Sub-Saharan Africa, 254
Sudan, 261, 262
Suriname, 96, 225, 234, 239
Sweden, 158
Symbols, 54, 61, 66, 68, 72, 73, 152, 198, 219, 224
Syria, 51, 138, 139, 146, 150

T
Tallinn, 16, 160, 165, 166, 169, 171, 175, 197, 199, 207
Tervuren, 242
Transculturation, 40
Treaty of Lisbon (2007), 52, 59
Treaty of Maastricht (1992), 59

Treaty of Paris (1951), 59
Treaty of Rome (1957), 30, 59
Tropenmuseum, 18, 217, 221–223, 226–229, 231, 233, 236–244
colonial museum, 222
Trump, Donald, 106
Tula, 233
Turin, 260
Turkey, 81, 97, 259
Turn
cultural, 60, 85, 116
linguistic, 85
narrative, 87, 206

U
Ukraine, 51, 113–115, 119, 176
Ulyanovsk, 114
UNESCO
UNESCO Convention for the Protection of the World Cultural and Natural Heritage (1972), 88
UNESCO Convention for the Safeguarding of the Intangible Heritage (2003), 15, 84, 90, 92, 96
UNESCO Intangible Cultural Heritage, 93, 98
UNESCO Masterpieces of the Oral and Intangible Heritage of Humanity (2001), 92
UNESCO's Convention on the Means of Prohibiting and Preventing the Illicit Import, Export and Transfer of Ownership of cultural Property (1970), 119
UNESCO's International Memory for the World register, 114, 117
UNESCO's Universal Declaration on Cultural Diversity (2001), 88

UNESCO's world heritage list, 92, 98, 117
Union of Lublin, 197
United Kingdom, 158
United Nation, 59, 83, 110
United States, 235, 259
Upper Silesia, 205

V

Values
  collective, 258
  common, 5, 33, 188, 193, 198
  community, 86, 116
  democratic, 34, 38, 64, 193, 195, 196
  enlightenment, 195
  European, 11, 17, 33, 62, 188, 193, 195, 196, 198, 200, 202, 203
  promotion of, 34, 64, 193, 198
  symbolic, 167, 198, 203
  tangible, 119
van Gogh, Theo, 109
Vienna, 83, 197
Villevoye, Roy, 231, 232
Vitkovice Ironworks, 204

W

Warns, 103
Warsame, Hodan, 224, 226, 227, 229
Warsaw, 54, 66
Weimar Republic, 80
Westerbork, 54, 60, 65, 67–69, 72
Westerkamp, Pim, 223, 229, 230
West Germany, 58
West Indies, 67
Westphalia, 54, 60–63, 66, 69, 71–73, 195, 257
Wilders, Geert, 103
Wilhelmina, the Queen of the Netherlands, 224
World Heritage list, 92, 93, 98, 99, 117
World War II (WWII), 4, 15, 29, 34, 51, 52, 56–58, 67, 68, 87, 95, 114, 142, 153, 167, 172, 204, 220, 231
Worp, Johannes, 80, 81
WWI Eastern Front Cemetery No. 123, 54, 68, 69, 72

X

Xenophobia, 90, 106, 250

Y

Ypres, 117
Yugoslavia, 35, 39, 115, 118
Yugoslav Wars, 102

Z

Zeefuik, Simone, 223, 224, 226, 228, 229, 236, 237

The manufacturer's authorised representative in the EU is Springer Nature Customer Service Centre GmbH, Europaplatz 3, 69115 Heidelberg, Germany. If you have any concerns regarding our products, please contact ProductSafety@springernature.com

Printed and bound by CPI Group (UK) Ltd, Croydon, CR0 4YY

28/03/2026

02080358-0002